Understanding Arguments, An Introduction to Informal Logic, Eighth Edition

Modified for the University of Missouri

Walter Sinnott-Armstrong | Robert J. Fogelin

CENGAGE
Learning™

Australia • Brazil • Japan • Korea • Mexico • Singapore • Spain • United Kingdom • United States

CENGAGE
Learning™

**Understanding Arguments,
An Introduction to Informal
Logic, Eighth Edition:
Modified for the University of
Missouri**

Walter Sinnott-Armstrong I
Robert J. Fogelin

Executive Editor:
 Maureen Staudt
 Michael Stranz

Senoir Project Development Manager:
 Linda de Stefano

Marketing Specialist:
 Sara Mercurio
 Lindsay Shapiro

Production/Manufacturing Manager:
 Donna M. Brown

PreMedia Supervisor:
 Joel Brennecke

Rights & Permissions Specialist:

 Kalina Hintz
 Todd Osborne

Cover Image:
 Getty Images*

For product information and
technology assistance, contact us at **Cengage Learning
Customer & Sales Support, 1-800-354-9706**

For permission to use material from this text or product,
submit all requests online at **cengage.com/permissions**
Further permissions questions can be emailed to
permissionrequest@cengage.com

ISBN-13: 978-1-4240-6884-5

ISBN-10: 1-4240-6884-3

Cengage Learning
5191 Natorp Boulevard
Mason, Ohio 45040
USA

Cengage Learning is a leading provider of customized learning solutions with office locations around the globe, including Singapore, the United Kingdom, Australia, Mexico, Brazil, and Japan. Locate your local office at: **international.cengage.com/region**

Cengage Learning products are represented in Canada by Nelson Education, Ltd.

For your lifelong learning solutions, visit **www.cengage.com/custom**

Visit our corporate website at **www.cengage.com**

Printed in the United States of America

Brief Contents

How to Analyze Arguments

Arguments are all around us. They bombard us constantly in advertisements; in courtrooms; in political, moral, and religious debates; in academic courses on mathematics, science, history, literature, and philosophy; and in our personal lives when we make decisions about our careers, finances, and families. These crucial aspects of our lives cannot be understood fully without understanding arguments. The goal of this book, then, is to help us understand arguments and, thereby, to understand our lives.

We will view arguments as tools. To understand a tool, we need to know the purposes for which it is used, the material out of which it is made, and the forms that it takes. For example, hammers are normally used to drive nails or to pound malleable substances. Hammers are usually made out of a metal head and a handle of wood, plastic, or metal. A typical hammer's handle is long and thin, and its head is perpendicular to its handle. Similarly, in order to understand arguments, we need to investigate their purposes, materials, and forms.

Chapter 1 discusses the main purposes or uses of arguments. The material from which arguments are made is language, so Chapters 2–3 explore language in general and then the language of argument in particular. Chapters 4–5 use the lessons learned by then to analyze concrete examples of arguments in detail. The following chapters turn to the forms of arguments, including deductive forms in Part II (Chapters 6–7) and inductive forms in Part III (Chapters 8–12). Each form of argument comes with its own standards of adequacy. Part IV (Chapters 13–17) will then consider the main ways in which arguments can go astray, including fallacies of clarity, relevance, and vacuity. Finally, Part V (Chapters 18–22) will explore examples of arguments in different fields—law, morality, religion, science, and philosophy—in order to see both how such arguments differ and how they share common features of arguments in general. By the end of this journey, we should understand arguments much better.

USES OF ARGUMENTS

What are arguments? In our view, arguments are tools, so the first step toward understanding arguments is to ask what they are used for—what people are trying to accomplish when they give arguments. This brief chapter will propose a definition of arguments and then explore two main purposes of arguments: justification and explanation. Both justifications and explanations try to provide reasons, but reasons of different kinds. Justifications are supposed to give reasons to believe their conclusions, whereas explanations are supposed to give reasons why their conclusions are true. Each of these purposes is more complicated and fascinating than is usually assumed.

WHAT ARGUMENTS ARE

The word *"argument"* may suggest quarrels or squabbles. That is what a child means when she reports that her parents are having an argument. Arguments of that sort often include abuse, name-calling, and yelling. That is not what this book is about. The goal here is not to teach you to yell louder, to be more abusive, or to beat your opponents into submission.

Our topic is the kind of argument defined by Monty Python in their justly famous "Argument Clinic." In this skit, a client enters a clinic and pays for an argument. In the first room, however, all he gets is abuse, which is not argument. When he finally finds the right room to get an argument, the person who is supposed to give him an argument simply denies whatever the client says, so the client complains that mere denial is different from argument, because "an argument is a connected series of statements to establish a definite proposition." This definition is almost correct. As we will see, the purpose of an argument need not always be to "establish" its conclusion, both because some conclusions were established in advance and because many reasons are inconclusive. Nonetheless, Monty Python's definition needs to be modified only a little in order to arrive at an adequate definition:

> An argument is a connected series of sentences, statements, or propositions (called "premises") that are intended to give reasons of some kind for a sentence, statement, or proposition (called the "conclusion").

This definition does not pretend to be precise, but it does tell us what arguments are made of (sentences, statements, or propositions) and what their purpose is (to give reasons).

Another virtue of this definition is that it is flexible enough to cover the wide variety of arguments that people actually give. Different arguments are intended to give reasons of very different sorts. These reasons might be justificatory reasons to believe or to disbelieve some claim. They might, instead, be explanatory reasons why something happened. They might even be practical reasons to do some act. Because reasons come in so many kinds, arguments are useful in a great variety of situations in daily life. Trying to determine why your computer crashed, why your friend acted the way she did, and whether it will rain tomorrow as well as trying to decide which political candidate to vote for, which play to use at a crucial point in a football game, where to go to college, and whether to support or oppose capital punishment—all involve weighing and evaluating reasons.

It is inaccurate, therefore, to think of arguments as serving only one single simple purpose. People often assume that you always use every argument to make other people believe what you believe and what they did not believe before hearing or reading the argument. Actually, however, some arguments are used for that purpose, but others are not. To fully understand arguments in all their glory, then, we need to distinguish different uses of argument. In particular, we will focus on two exemplary purposes: justification and explanation.

JUSTIFICATIONS

One of the most prominent uses of arguments is to justify a disputed claim. For example, if I claim that September 11, 2001, was a Tuesday, and you deny this or simply express some doubt, then we might look for a calendar. But suppose we don't have a calendar for 2001. Luckily, we do find a calendar for 2002. Now I can justify my claim to you by presenting this argument: The calendar shows that September 11 was on Wednesday in 2002; 2002 was not a leap year, since 2002 is not divisible by four; nonleap years have 365 days, which is 1 more day than 52 weeks; so September 11 must have been on Tuesday in 2001. You should now be convinced.

What have I done? My utterance of this argument has the *effect* of changing your mind by getting you to believe a conclusion that you did not believe before. Of course, I might also be able to change your mind by hypnotizing you. But normally I do not want to use hypnosis. I also do not want to change your mind by manufacturing a fake calendar for 2002 with the wrong dates. Such tricks would not satisfy my goals fully. This shows that changing your mind is not all that I am trying to accomplish. What else do I want? My additional aim is to show you that you *should* change your mind, and why. I want to give you a *good reason* to change your mind. I want my argument not only to make you believe my conclusion but also to make you *justified* in believing my conclusion.

The above example is typical of one kind of justification, but there are other patterns. Suppose that I share your doubts about which day of the week it was on September 11, 2001. Then I might use the same argument to justify my belief as well as yours. Indeed, you don't even need to be present. If I am all alone, and I just want to figure out which day of the week it was on September 11, 2001, then I might think in terms of this same argument. Here the goal is not to convince anybody else, but the argument is still used to find a good reason to believe the conclusion.

In cases like these, we can say that the argument is used for *impersonal normative justification*. The justification is normative because the goal is to find a reason that is a good reason. It is impersonal because what is sought is a reason that is or should be accepted as a good reason by everyone capable of grasping this argument, regardless of who they are. The purpose is to show that there *is* a reason to believe the conclusion, regardless of who *has* a reason to believe it. Other arguments, in contrast, are aimed at specific people, and the goal is to show that those particular people are committed to the conclusion or have a reason to believe the conclusion. Such individualized uses of arguments seek what can be called *personal justification*.

There should be nothing surprising about different people having different reasons. I might climb a mountain to appreciate the view at the top, whereas you climb it to get exercise, and your friend climbs it to be able to talk to you while you climb it. Different people can have different reasons for the same action. Similarly, different people can have different reasons to believe the same conclusion. Suppose that someone is murdered in the ballroom with a revolver. I might have good reason to believe that Miss Peacock did not commit the murder, because I saw her in the library at the time the murder was committed. You might not trust me when I tell you that I saw her, but you still might have good reason to believe that she is innocent, because you believe that Colonel Mustard did it alone. Even if I doubt that Colonel Mustard did it, we still each have our own reasons to agree that Miss Peacock is innocent.

When different people with different beliefs are involved, we need to ask who is supposed to accept the reason that is given in an argument. A speaker might give an argument to show a listener that the speaker has a reason to believe something, even though the speaker knows that the audience does not and need not accept that reason. Suppose that you are an atheist, but I am an evangelical Christian, and you ask me why I believe that Jesus rose from the dead. I might respond that the Bible says that Jesus rose from the dead, and what the Bible says must be true, so Jesus rose from the dead. This argument tells you what *my* reasons are for believing what I believe, even if *you* do not accept those reasons. My argument can be used to show you that I have reasons and what my reasons are, regardless of whether you believe that my reasons are good ones and also regardless of whether my reasons really are good ones.

The reverse can also happen. A speaker might give an argument to show a listener that the listener has a reason to believe something, even though the speaker does not accept that reason. Suppose that you often throw loud parties late into the night close to my bedroom. I want to convince you to stop or at least quiet down. Fortunately, you think that every citizen ought to obey the law. I disagree, for I am an anarchist bent on undermining all governments and laws. Still, I want to get a good night's sleep before the protest tomorrow, so I might argue that it is illegal to make that much noise so late, and you ought to obey the law, so you ought to stop throwing such loud parties. This argument can show you that *you* are committed to its conclusion, even if *I* believe that its premises are false.

Of course, whether I succeed in showing my audience that they have a reason to believe my conclusion depends on who my audience is. My argument won't work against loud neighbors who don't care about the law. Consequently, we need to know who the audience is and what they believe in order to be able to show them what reason they have to believe a conclusion.

In all of these cases, arguments are used to show that someone has a reason to believe the conclusion of the argument. That is why all of these uses can be seen as providing different kinds of justification. The differences become crucial when we try to evaluate such arguments. If my goal is to show you that you have a reason to believe something, then I can be criticized for using a premise that you reject. Your beliefs are no basis for criticism, however, if all I want is to show my own reasons for believing the conclusion. Thus, to evaluate an argument properly, we often need to determine not only whether the argument is being used to justify a belief but also which kind of justification is sought and who the audience is.

EXERCISE I

Write the best brief argument you can to justify each of the following claims to someone who does not believe them.

1. Nine is not a prime number.
2. Seven is a prime number.
3. A molecule of water has three atoms in it.
4. Water is not made up of carbon.
5. The U.S. president lives in Washington.
6. The Earth is not flat.
7. Humans have walked on the moon.
8. Most bicycles have two wheels.

When, if ever, is it legitimate to try to convince someone else to believe something on the basis of a premise that you yourself reject? Consider a variety of cases.

EXPLANATIONS

A different but equally important use of arguments is to provide explanations. Explanations answer questions about how or why something happened. We explain how a mongoose got out of his cage by pointing to a hole he dug under the fence. We explain why Smith was acquitted by saying that he got off on a technicality. The purpose of explanations is not to prove that something happened, but to make sense of things.

An example will bring out the difference between justification and explanation. One person claims that a school's flagpole is thirty-five feet tall, and someone else asks her to justify this claim. In response, she might produce a receipt from the Allegiance Flagpole Company acknowledging payment for a flagpole thirty-five feet in height. Alternatively, she may put a stick straight up into the ground, measure the stick's length and its shadow's length, then measure the length of the flagpole's shadow, and calculate the length of the flagpole. Neither of these justifications, however, will answer a different question: *Why* is the flagpole thirty-five feet tall? This new question could be answered in all sorts of ways, depending on context: The school could not afford a taller one. It struck the committee as about the right height for the location. That was the only size flagpole in stock. There is a state law limiting flagpoles to thirty-five feet. And so on. These answers help us understand why the flagpole is thirty-five feet tall. They explain its height.

Sometimes simply filling in the details of a story provides an explanation. For example, we can explain how a two-year-old girl foiled a bank robbery by saying that the robber tripped over her while fleeing from the bank. Here we have made sense out of an unusual event by putting it in the context of a plausible *narrative*. It is unusual for a two-year-old girl to foil a bank robbery, but there is nothing unusual about a person tripping over a child when running recklessly at full speed in a crowded area.

Although the narrative is probably the most common form of explanation in everyday life, we also often use arguments to give explanations. We can explain a certain event by deriving it from established principles and accepted facts. This argument then has the following form:

(1) General principles or laws
(2) A statement of initial conditions
∴ (3) A statement of the phenomenon to be explained

The symbol "∴" is pronounced "therefore" and indicates that the premises above the line are supposed to give a reason for the conclusion below the line. By "initial conditions" we mean those facts in the context that, together with appropriate general principles and laws, allow us to derive the result that the event to be explained occurs.

This sounds quite abstract, but an example should clarify the basic idea. Suppose we put an ice cube into a glass and then fill the glass with water to the brim. The ice will stick out above the surface of the water. What will happen when the ice cube melts? Will the water overflow? Will it remain at the same level? Will it go down? Here we are asking for a *prediction,* and it will, of course, make sense to ask a person to *justify* whatever prediction he or she makes. Stumped by this question, we let the ice cube melt to see what happens. We observe that the water level remains unchanged. After a few experiments, we convince ourselves that this result always occurs. We now have a new question: *Why* does this occur? Now we want an explanation of this phenomenon. The explanation turns upon the law of buoyancy, which says that an object in water is buoyed up by a force equal to the weight of the water it displaces. This law implies that, if we put an object in water, it will continue to sink until it displaces a volume of water whose weight is equal to its own weight (or else the object hits the bottom of the container). With this in mind, go back to the original problem. An ice cube is itself simply water in a solid state. Thus, when it melts, it will exactly fill in the volume of water it displaced, so the water level will remain unchanged.

We can now see how this explanation conforms to the argumentative pattern mentioned above:

(1) General principles or laws (Primarily the law of buoyancy)
(2) Initial conditions (An ice cube in a glass of water filled to the brim)
∴(3) Phenomenon explained (The level of the water remaining unchanged after the ice cube melts)

This explanation is fairly good. People with only a slight understanding of science can follow it and see why the water level remains unchanged. We should also notice that it is not a *complete* explanation, because certain things are simply taken for granted—for example, that things do not change weight when they pass from a solid to a liquid state. To put the explanation into perfect argumentative form, this assumption and many others would have to be stated explicitly. This is never done in everyday life and is only rarely done in the most exact sciences.

Is this explanation any good? Explanations are satisfactory if they remove bewilderment or surprise by telling us *how* or *why* something happened in a way that is relevant to the concerns of a particular context. Our example does seem to accomplish that much. However, it might seem that even the best explanations are not very useful because they take so much for granted. In explaining why the water level remains the same when the ice cube melts, we cited the law of buoyancy. Now, why should that law be true? What explains *it*? To explain the law of buoyancy, we would have to derive it from other laws that are more general and, perhaps, more intelligible. In fact, this has been done. Archimedes simultaneously proved and explained the law of buoyancy by deriving it from the laws of the lever. How about the laws of the lever? Can they be proved and explained by deriving them from still higher and more comprehensive laws? Perhaps. Yet reasons give out, and sooner or later explanation (like justification) comes to an end. It is the task of science and all rational inquiry to move that boundary further and further back. But even when there is more to explain, that does not show that a partial explanation is totally useless. As we have seen, explanations can be useful even when they are incomplete, and even though they are not used to justify any disputed claim. Explanation is, thus, a separate use of arguments.

EXERCISE II

Houses in Indonesia sometimes have their electrical outlets in the middle of the wall rather than at floor level. Why? A beginning of an explanation is that flooding is a danger in the Netherlands. Citing this fact does not help much, however, unless one remembers that Indonesia was formerly a Dutch colony. We can understand why the Dutch might put their electrical outlets above floor level in the Netherlands. It is safer in a country where flooding is a danger. Is flooding, then, a similar danger in Indonesia? Apparently not; so why did the Dutch continue this practice in Indonesia? The answer is that colonial settlers tend to preserve their home customs, practices, and styles. The Dutch continued to build Dutch-style houses with the electrical outlets where (for them) they are normally placed—that is, in the middle of the wall rather than at floor level. Restate this explanation in the form of an argument (that is, specify its premises and conclusion).

EXERCISE III

Write a brief argument to explain each of the following. Indicate what facts and what general principles are employed in your explanations. (Do not forget those principles that may seem too obvious to mention.)

1. Why a lighter-than-air balloon rises.
2. Why there is an infield fly rule in baseball.
3. Why there is an international date line.
4. Why there are more psychoanalysts in New York City than in any other city or, for that matter, in most countries in the world.
5. Why average temperatures tend to be higher closer to the equator.
6. Why there are usually more college freshmen who plan to go to medical school than there are seniors who still plan to go to medical school.
7. Why almost no textbooks are more than eighteen inches high.
8. Why most cars have four tires (instead of more or fewer).
9. Why paintings by Van Gogh cost so much.
10. Why wages go up when unemployment goes down.

It is sometimes said that science tells us *how* things happen but does not tell us *why* they happen. In what ways is this contention right, and in what ways is it wrong?

COMBINATIONS: AN EXAMPLE

Although justification and explanation are distinct uses of arguments, we often want to know both *what* happened and also *why* it happened. Then we need to combine justifications and explanations. We can see how this works by considering a fictional example.

Imagine that Madison was arrested for murdering her husband, Victor. Now she is on trial, and you are on the jury. Presumably, the police and the prosecuting attorneys would not have arrested and prosecuted her if they did not believe that Madison committed the murder, but are their beliefs justified? Should she be convicted and sent to prison? That's up to you and the other jurors to decide.

You do not want to convict her arbitrarily, of course, so you need arguments to justify you in believing that Madison is guilty. The goal of prosecuting attorneys is to provide such justification. Their means of reaching this goal is to present evidence and arguments during the trial. Although their ultimate conclusion is that you should find Madison guilty of murder, the prosecutors need to justify lots of little claims along the way.

It might seem too obvious to mention, but the prosecution first needs an argument to show that the victim died. After all, if nobody died, nobody was killed. This first argument can be pretty simple: This person was walking and talking before he was shot in the head; now his heart has stopped beating for a long time; so he must be dead. There can be complications, since some gunshot victims can be revived, but let's assume that an argument like this justifies the claim that the victim is dead.

We also want to know who the victim was. The body was identified by several of Victor's friends, we assume, so all the prosecution needs to argue is that identifications like this are usually correct, so it was Victor who died. This second argument also provides a justification, but it differs from the first argument in several ways. The first argument referred directly to the facts about Victor that show he died, whereas this second argument does not say which features of the victim show that it was Victor. Instead, this argument relies on trusting other people—Victor's friends—without knowing what it was about the victim's face that made them think it was Victor. Such appeals to authority will be discussed in more detail in Chapters 3 and 15.

The third issue is the cause of death. Here it is common to appeal to a medical authority. In our case, the coroner or medical examiner makes observations or runs scientific tests that provide premises for another argument that is supposed to justify the conclusion that Victor's death was caused by a bullet to the head. This argument is also an appeal to an authority, but here the authority is a scientific expert rather than a friend.

Yet another argument, possibly based on firing marks on the bullet, can then justify you in believing that the bullet came from a certain gun. More arguments, possibly based on eyewitnesses, then justify the claims that Madison was the person who fired that gun at Victor. And so on.

All of these arguments depend on background assumptions. When you see the marks on the bullet that killed Victor line up with the marks on another bullet that was fired from the alleged murder weapon, you assume that guns leave distinctive marks on bullets and that nobody switched the bullets. A good prosecutor will provide arguments for these assumptions, but nobody can prove everything. Arguments always start from assumptions. This problem will occupy us at several points later, including parts of Chapters 3 and 5. The point for now is just that the prosecution needs to produce several arguments of various kinds in order to justify the claim that Madison killed Victor.

It is also crucial that killing violates the law. If not, then Madison should not be found guilty for killing Victor. So, how can the prosecutor justify the assumption that such killing is illegal? Prosecutors usually just quote a statute or cite a common law principle and apply it to the case, but that argument assumes a lot of background information. In the case of a statute, there must be a duly elected legislature, it must have jurisdiction over the place and time where and when the killing occurred, it must follow required procedures, and the content of the law must be constitutionally permissible. Given such a context, if the legislature says that a certain kind of killing is illegal, then it is illegal. It is fascinating that merely announcing that something is illegal thereby makes it illegal. We will explore such performatives and speech acts in Chapter 2. For now we will simply assume that all of these arguments could be provided if needed.

Even so, Madison might have had some justification for killing Victor, such as self-defense. This justification for her act can be presented in an argument basically like this: I have a reason to protect my own life, and I need to kill Victor first in order to protect my own life, so I have a reason to kill Victor. This justification differs in several ways from the kind of justification that we have been discussing so far. For one thing, this argument provides a reason for a different person—a reason for Madison—whereas the preceding arguments provided a reason for you as a juror. This argument also provides a reason with a different kind of object, since it justifies an action (killing Victor) whereas the previous arguments justified a belief (the belief that Madison did kill Victor). It provides a practical reason instead of an intellectual reason. Despite these differences, however, if her attorneys want to show that Madison has this new kind of justification, they need to give an argument to show that she was justified in doing what she did.

Even if Madison had no justification, she still might have had an excuse. Whereas a justification is supposed to show that the act was the right thing to do, an excuse admits that the act was wrong but tries to show that the agent was not fully responsible for doing it. Madison might, for example, argue that she honestly believed that Victor was going to kill her if she did not kill him first. If she offers this only as an excuse, she can admit that her belief was mistaken, so she had no justification for killing Victor. Her claim is, instead, that she was not fully responsible for his death because she was only trying to defend herself.

Excuses like this are, in effect, explanations. By citing her mistake, Madison explains why she did what she did. If she had killed Victor because she hated him or because she wanted to take his money, then she would have no excuse. Her act is less blameworthy, however, if she was mistaken. Of course, you should be careful before you shoot someone, so Madison could still be guilty of carelessness or negligence. But that is not as bad as killing someone out of hatred or for money. Her mistake might even be reasonable. If Victor was aiming a gun at her, then, even if it turned out not to be loaded, any rational person in her position might have thought that Victor was on the attack. Such reasonable mistakes might reduce or even remove responsibility. Thus, by explaining her act as a mistake, Madison puts her act in a better light than it would appear without that explanation. In general, an excuse is just an explanation of an act that puts that act in a better light by reducing the agent's responsibility.

To offer an excuse, then, Madison's defense attorneys will need to give arguments whose purpose is not justification but explanation. This excuse will then determine what she is guilty of. Whether Madison is guilty of first-degree murder or some lesser charge, such as second-degree murder or manslaughter, or even no crime at all, depends on the explanation for her act of killing Victor.

Several of the earlier arguments also provided explanations. The medical examiner cited the head wound to explain why Victor stopped breathing. The victim's identity explained why his friends said he was Victor. The fact that the bullet came out of a particular gun explained why it had certain markings. The legislature's vote explained why the killing was illegal. And so on.

In this way, what appears appears at first to be a simple case actually depends on a complex chain of arguments that mixes justifications with explanations. All of these justifications and explanations can be understood by presenting them explicitly in the form of arguments.

One final point is crucial. Suppose that Madison has no justification or excuse for killing Victor. It is still not enough for the prosecutor to give any old argument that Madison killed Victor. The prosecution must prove guilt beyond a reasonable doubt. This burden of proof makes the strength of the argument crucial. You as a juror should not convict, even if you think Madison is guilty, unless the prosecution's argument meets this high standard. In this case, as in many others, it is not enough just to be able to identify the argument and to understand its purpose. You also need to determine how strong it is.

For such reasons, we all need to understand arguments and to be able to evaluate them. This need arises not only in law but also in life, such as when we decide which candidate to vote for, what course to take, whether to believe that your spouse is cheating on you, and so on. The goal of this book is to teach the skills needed for understanding and assessing arguments about important issues like these.

DISCUSSION QUESTIONS

The following arguments mix justification with explanation. For each part of the argument, determine whether it is a justification or an explanation. How does each sub-argument work? How strong is it? How would you respond if you disagreed? How would you defend that part against criticisms?

It will, of course, be difficult to answer these questions before studying the rest of this book. However, it is worthwhile to reflect on how much you already understand at the start. It is also useful to have some concrete examples to keep in mind as you study arguments in more depth.

1. Dinosaurs are fascinating, and we cannot help but wonder what killed these magnificent creatures. The following argument tries to show that they were killed when a giant meteor struck the earth, but first the authors need to argue against alternatives to this impact hypothesis.

AN EXTRATERRESTRIAL IMPACT

by Walter Alvarez and Frank Asaro
from *Scientific American* (October 1990), pp. 78–92

About 65 million years ago something killed half of all the life on the earth. This sensational crime wiped out the dinosaurs, until then undisputed masters of the animal kingdom, and left the humble mammals to inherit their estate. Human beings, descended from those survivors, cannot avoid asking who or what committed the mass murder and what permitted our distant ancestors to survive. . . .

Murder suspects typically must have means, motive and opportunity. An impact [of a giant meteor, probably in the Yucatan peninsula] certainly had the means to cause the Cretaceous extinction, and the evidence that an impact occurred at exactly the right time points to opportunity.

The impact hypothesis provides, if not motive, then at least a mechanism behind the crime. How do other suspects in the killing of dinosaurs fare?

Some have an air-tight alibi: they could not have killed all the different organisms that died at the KT boundary. The venerable notion that mammals ate the dinosaurs' eggs, for example, does not explain the simultaneous extinction of marine foraminifera and ammonites.

(continued)

Stefan Gartner of Texas A&M University once suggested that marine life was killed by a sudden huge flood of fresh water from the Arctic Ocean, which apparently was isolated from other oceans during the late Cretaceous and filled with fresh water. Yet this ingenious mechanism cannot account for the extinction of the dinosaurs or the loss of many species of land plants.

Other suspects might have had the ability to kill, but they have alibis based on timing. Some scientific detectives have tried to pin the blame for mass extinction on changes in climate or sea level, for example. Such changes, however, take much longer to occur than did the extinction; moreover, they do not seem to have coincided with the extinction, and they have occurred repeatedly throughout the earth's history without accompanying extinctions.

Others consider volcanism a prime suspect. The strongest evidence implicating volcanoes is the Deccan Traps, an enormous outpouring of basaltic lava in India that occurred approximately 65 million years ago. Recent paleomagnetic work by Vincent E. Courtillot and his colleagues in Paris confirms previous studies. They show that most of the Deccan Traps erupted during a single period of reversed geomagnetic polarity, with slight overlaps into the preceding and succeeding periods of normal polarity. The Paris team has found that the interval in question is probably 29R, during which the KT extinction occurred, although it might be the reversed-polarity interval immediately before or after 29R as well.

Because the outpouring of the Deccan Traps began in one normal interval and ended in the next, the eruptions that gave rise to them must have taken place over at least 0.5 Myr. Most workers interested in mass extinction therefore have not considered volcanism a serious suspect in a killing that evidently took place over 0.001 Myr or less. . . .

Moreover, basaltic spherules in the KT boundary argue against explosive volcanism in any case; spherules might be generated by quieter forms of volcanism, but then they could not be transported worldwide. The apparent global distribution of the iridium anomaly, shocked quartz and basaltic spherules is strong evidence exonerating volcanism and pointing to impact. Eruptions take place at the bottom of the atmosphere; they send material into the high stratosphere at best. Spherules and quartz grains, if they came from an eruption, would quickly be slowed by atmospheric drag and fall to the ground.

Nevertheless, the enormous eruptions that created the Deccan Traps did occur during a period spanning the KT extinction. Further, they represent the greatest outpouring of lava on land in the past quarter of a billion years (although greater volumes flow continually out of mid-ocean ridges). No investigator can afford to ignore that kind of coincidence.

It seems possible that impact triggered the Deccan Traps volcanism. A few minutes after a large body hit the earth the initial crater would be 40 kilometers deep, and the release of pressure might cause the hot rock of the underlying mantle to melt. Authorities on the origin of volcanic provinces, however, find it very difficult to explain in detail how an impact could trigger large-scale basaltic volcanism.

In the past few years the debate between supporters of each scenario has become polarized: impact proponents have tended to ignore the Deccan Traps as irrelevant, while volcano backers have tried to explain away evidence for impact by suggesting that it is also compatible with volcanism.

Our sense is that the argument is a Hegelian one, with an impact thesis and a volcanic antithesis in search of a synthesis whose outlines are as yet unclear. . . .

2. In his famous testimony to the United Nations Security Council on February 5, 2003, which was 42 days before U.S. troops entered Iraq, Secretary of Defense Colin Powell gave several arguments for his main conclusion that Saddam Hussein was at that time still trying to obtain fissile material for a nuclear weapons program.

. . . Let me turn now to nuclear weapons. We have no indication that Saddam Hussein has ever abandoned his nuclear weapons program. On the contrary, we have more than a decade of proof that he remains determined to acquire nuclear weapons.

To fully appreciate the challenge that we face today, remember that in 1991 the inspectors searched Iraq's primary nuclear weapons facilities for the first time, and they found nothing to conclude that Iraq had a nuclear weapons program. But, based on defector information, in May of 1991, Saddam Hussein's lie was exposed. In truth, Saddam Hussein had a massive clandestine nuclear weapons program that covered several different techniques to enrich uranium, including electromagnetic isotope separation, gas centrifuge and gas diffusion.

We estimate that this illicit program cost the Iraqis several billion dollars. Nonetheless, Iraq continued to tell the IAEA that it had no nuclear weapons program. If Saddam had not been stopped, Iraq could have produced a nuclear bomb by 1993, years earlier than most worst case assessments that had been made before the war.

In 1995, as a result of another defector, we find out that, after his invasion of Kuwait, Saddam Hussein had initiated a crash program to build a crude nuclear weapon, in violation of Iraq's UN obligations. Saddam Hussein already possesses two out of the three key components needed to build a nuclear bomb. He has a cadre of nuclear scientists with the expertise, and he has a bomb design.

Since 1998, his efforts to reconstitute his nuclear program have been focused on acquiring the third and last component: sufficient fissile material to produce a nuclear explosion. To make the fissile material, he needs to develop an ability to enrich uranium. Saddam Hussein is determined to get his hands on a nuclear bomb.

He is so determined that he has made repeated covert attempts to acquire high-specification aluminum tubes from 11 different countries, even after inspections resumed. These tubes are controlled by the Nuclear Suppliers Group precisely because they can be used as centrifuges for enriching uranium.

By now, just about everyone has heard of these tubes and we all know that there are differences of opinion. There is controversy about what these tubes are for. Most U.S. experts think they are intended to serve as rotors in centrifuges used to enrich uranium. Other experts, and the Iraqis themselves, argue that they are really to produce the rocket bodies for a conventional weapon, a multiple rocket launcher.

(continued)

Let me tell you what is not controversial about these tubes. First, all the experts who have analyzed the tubes in our possession agree that they can be adapted for centrifuge use.

Second, Iraq had no business buying them for any purpose. They are banned for Iraq.

I am no expert on centrifuge tubes, but this is an old army trooper. I can tell you a couple things.

First, it strikes me as quite odd that these tubes are manufactured to a tolerance that far exceeds U.S. requirements for comparable rockets. Maybe Iraqis just manufacture their conventional weapons to a higher standard than we do, but I don't think so.

Second, we actually have examined tubes from several different batches that were seized clandestinely before they reached Baghdad. What we notice in these different batches is a progression to higher and higher levels of specification, including in the latest batch an anodized coating on extremely smooth inner and outer surfaces.

Why would they continue refining the specifications? Why would they go to all that trouble for something that, if it was a rocket, would soon be blown into shrapnel when it went off?

The high-tolerance aluminum tubes are only part of the story. We also have intelligence from multiple sources that Iraq is attempting to acquire magnets and high-speed balancing machines. Both items can be used in a gas centrifuge program to enrich uranium.

In 1999 and 2000, Iraqi officials negotiated with firms in Romania, India, Russia and Slovenia for the purchase of a magnet production plant. Iraq wanted the plant to produce magnets weighing 20 to 30 grams. That's the same weight as the magnets used in Iraq's gas centrifuge program before the Gulf War.

This incident, linked with the tubes, is another indicator of Iraq's attempt to reconstitute its nuclear weapons program.

Intercepted communications from mid-2000 through last summer showed that Iraqi front companies sought to buy machines that can be used to balance gas centrifuge rotors. One of these companies also had been involved in a failed effort in 2001 to smuggle aluminum tubes into Iraq.

People will continue to debate this issue, but there is no doubt in my mind. These illicit procurement efforts show that Saddam Hussein is very much focused on putting in place the key missing piece from his nuclear weapons program, the ability to produce fissile material. . . .

THE WEB OF LANGUAGE

Arguments are made up of language, so we cannot understand arguments without first understanding language. This chapter will examine some of the basic features of language, stressing three main ideas. First, language is conventional. *Words acquire meaning within a rich system of linguistic conventions and rules. Second, the uses of language are* diverse. *We use language to communicate information, but we also use it to ask questions, issue orders, write poetry, keep score, formulate arguments, and perform an almost endless number of other tasks. Third, meaning is often conveyed* indirectly. *To understand the significance of many utterances, we must go beyond what is literally said to examine what is conversationally implied by saying it.*

LANGUAGE AND CONVENTION

The preceding chapter stressed that arguing is a *practical* activity. More specifically, it is a *linguistic* activity. Arguing is one of the many things that we can do with words. In fact, unlike things that we can accomplish both with words and without words (like making people happy, angry, and so forth), arguing is something we can *only* do with words or other meaningful symbols. That is why nonhuman animals never give arguments. To understand how arguments work, then, it is crucial to understand how language works.

Unfortunately, our understanding of human language is far from complete, and linguistics is a young science in which disagreement exists on many important issues. Still, certain facts about language are beyond dispute, and recognizing them will provide a background for understanding how arguments work.

As anyone who has bothered to think about it knows, language is conventional. There is no reason why we, as English speakers, use the word "dog" to refer to a dog rather than to a cat, a tree, or the number of planets in our solar system. It seems that any word might have been used to stand for anything. Beyond this, there seems to be no reason why we put words together the way we do. In English, we put adjectives before the nouns they modify. We thus speak of a "green salad." In French, adjectives usually follow the noun, and so, instead of saying "verte salade," the French say "salade verte." The conventions of our own language are so much with us that it strikes us as odd when we discover that other languages have different conventions. A French diplomat once praised his own language because, as he said, it followed the natural order of thought. This strikes English speakers as silly, but in seeing why it is silly, we see that the word order in our own language is conventional as well.

Although it is important to realize that language is conventional, it is also important not to misunderstand this fact. From the idea that language is conventional, it is easy to conclude that language is totally arbitrary. If language is totally arbitrary, then it might seem that it really does not matter which words we use or how we put them together. It takes only a little thought to see that this view, however daring it might seem, misrepresents the role of conventions in language. If we wish to communicate with others, we must follow the system of conventions that others use. Grapefruits are more like big lemons than like grapes, so you might want to call them "mega-lemons." Still, if you order a glass of mega-lemon juice in a restaurant, you will get stares and smirks but no grapefruit juice. The same point lies behind this famous passage in *Through the Looking Glass*, by Lewis Carroll:

> "There's glory for you!"
> "I don't know what you mean by 'glory'," Alice said.
> Humpty Dumpty smiled contemptuously.
> "Of course you don't—till I tell you. I meant 'there's a nice knock-down argument for you!'"
> "But 'glory' doesn't mean 'a nice knock-down argument'," Alice objected.
> "When I use a word," Humpty Dumpty said, in a rather scornful tone, "it means just what I choose it to mean—neither more nor less."
> "The question is," said Alice, "whether you can make words mean so many different things."

The point, of course, is that Humpty Dumpty cannot make a word mean whatever he wants it to mean, and he cannot communicate if he uses words in his own peculiar way without regard to what those words themselves mean. Communication can take place only within a shared system of conventions. Conventions do not destroy meaning by making it arbitrary; conventions bring meaning into existence.

A misunderstanding of the conventional nature of language can lead to pointless disputes. Sometimes, in the middle of a discussion, someone will declare that "the whole thing is just a matter of definition" or "what you say is true by your definition, false by mine." There are times when definitions are important and the truth of what is said turns on them, but usually this is not the case. Suppose someone has fallen off a cliff and is heading toward certain death on the rocks below. Of course, it is a matter of convention that we use the word "death" to describe the result of the sudden, sharp stop at the end of the fall. We might have used some other word—perhaps "birth"—instead. But it certainly will not help a person who is falling to his certain death to shout out, "By 'birth' I mean death." It will not help even if *everyone* agrees to use these words in this new way. If we all decided to adopt this new convention, we would then say, "He is falling from the cliff to his certain birth" instead of "He is falling from the cliff to his certain death." But speaking in this way will not change the facts. It will not save him from perishing. It will not make those who care for him feel better.

The upshot of this simple example is that the *truth* of what we say is rarely just a matter of definition. Whether what we have said is true or not will depend, for the most part, on how things stand in the world. Abraham Lincoln, during his days as a trial lawyer, is reported to have cross-examined a witness like this:

> "How many legs does a horse have?"
> "Four," said the witness.
> "Now, if we call a tail a leg, how many legs does a horse have?"
> "Five," answered the witness.
> "Nope," said Abe, "calling a tail a leg don't make it a leg."

In general, then, though the *meaning of* what we say is dependent on convention, the *truth* of what we say is not.

In the preceding sentence we used the qualifying phrase, "in general." To say that a claim holds *in general* indicates that there may be exceptions. This qualification is needed because sometimes the truth of what we say *is* simply a matter of definition. Take a simple example: The claim that a triangle has three sides is true by definition, because a triangle is defined as "a closed figure having three sides." Again, if someone says that sin is wrong, he or she has said something that is true by definition, for a sin is defined as, among other things, "something that is wrong." In unusual cases like these, things are true merely as a matter of convention. Still, in general, the truth of what we say is settled not by appealing to definitions but, instead, by looking at the facts. In this way, language is not arbitrary, even though it is conventional.

LINGUISTIC ACTS

In the previous section we saw that a language is a system of shared conventions that allows us to communicate with one another. If we examine language, we will see that it contains many different kinds of conventions. These conventions govern what we will call linguistic acts, speech acts, and conversational acts. We will discuss linguistic acts first.

We have seen that words have meanings conventionally attached to them. The word "dog" is used conventionally to talk about dogs. Given what our words mean, it would be incorrect to call dogs "airplanes." Proper names are also conventionally assigned, for Harry Jones could have been named Wilbur Jones. Still, given that his name is not Wilbur, it would be improper to call him Wilbur. Rules like these, which govern meaning and reference, can be called *semantic* rules.

Other conventions concern the ways words can be put together to form sentences. These are often called *syntactic* or *grammatical* rules. Using the three words "John," "hit," and "Harry," we can formulate sentences with very different meanings, such as "John hit Harry" and "Harry hit John." We recognize that these sentences have different meanings, because we understand the grammar of our language. This grammatical understanding also allows us to see that the sentence "Hit John Harry" has no determinate meaning, even though the individual words do. (Notice that "Hit John, Harry!" *does* mean something: It is a way of telling Harry to hit John.) Grammatical rules are important, for they play a part in giving a meaning to combinations of words, such as sentences.

Some of our grammatical rules play only a small role in this important task of giving meaning to combinations of words. It is bad grammar to say, "If I was you, I wouldn't do that," but it is still clear what information the person is trying to convey. What might be called stylistic rules of grammar are of relatively little importance for logic, but grammatical rules that affect the meaning or content of what is said are essential to logical analysis. Grammatical rules of this kind can determine whether we have said one thing rather than another, or perhaps failed to say anything at all and have merely spoken nonsense.

It is sometimes hard to tell what is nonsense. Consider "The horse raced past the barn fell." This sentence usually strikes people as nonsense when they hear it for the first time. To show them that it actually makes sense, all we need to do is insert two words: "The horse that was raced past the barn fell." Since English allows us to drop "that was," the original sentence means the same as the slightly expanded version. Sentences like these are called "garden path sentences," because the first few words "lead you down the garden path" by suggesting that some word plays a grammatical role that it really does not play. In this example, "The horse raced . . ." suggests at first that the main verb is "raced." That makes it hard to see that the main verb really is "fell."

Another famous example is "Buffalo buffalo buffalo." Again, this seems like nonsense at first, but then someone points out that "buffalo" can be a verb meaning "to confuse." The sentence "Buffalo buffalo buffalo" then means "North American bison confuse North American bison." Indeed, we can even make sense out of "Buffalo buffalo Buffalo buffalo buffalo buffalo Buffalo buffalo Buffalo buffalo buffalo." This means "North American bison from Buffalo, New York, that North American bison from Buffalo, New York, confuse also confuse North American bison from Buffalo, New York, that North American bison from Buffalo, New York, confuse."

Examples like these show that sentences can have linguistic meaning when they seem meaningless. To be meaningful, sentences need to follow both *semantic* conventions that govern meanings of individual words and also *syntactic* or *grammatical* conventions that lay down rules for combining words into meaningful wholes. When a sentence satisfies essential semantic and syntactic conventions, we will say that the person who uttered that sentence performed a *linguistic act:* The speaker said something meaningful in a language.[1] The ability to perform linguistic acts shows a command of a language. What the speaker says may be false, irrelevant, boring, and so on; but, if in saying it linguistic rules are not seriously violated, then that person can be credited with performing a linguistic act.

Later, in Chapters 13–14, we will look more closely at semantic and syntactic conventions, for they are common sources of fallacies and other confusions. In particular, we shall see how these conventions can generate fallacies of ambiguity and fallacies of vagueness. Before examining the defects of our language, however, we should first appreciate that language is a powerful and subtle tool that allows us to perform a wide variety of jobs important for living in the world.

EXERCISE I

Read each of the following sentences aloud. Did you perform a linguistic act? If so, explain what the sentence means and why it might not seem meaningful.

1. The old man the ship.
2. Colorless green ideas sleep furiously.
3. Time flies like an arrow. Fruit flies like bananas.
4. The cotton clothing is made of grows in Mississippi.
5. The square root of pine is tree.
6. The man who whistles tunes pianos.
7. To force heaven, Mars shall have a new angel. (from Monk)
8. "'Twas brillig, and the slithy toves did gyre and gimble in the wabe." (from Lewis Carroll)

And now some weird examples from Dan Wegner's Hidden Brain Damage Scale. If these make sense to you, it might be a sign of hidden brain damage. If they don't make sense, explain why:

9. People tell me one thing one day and out the other.
10. I feel as much like I did yesterday as I do today.
11. My throat is closer than it seems.
12. Likes and dislikes are among my favorites.
13. I've lost all sensation in my shirt.
14. There's only one thing for me.
15. I don't like any of my loved ones.

1. When an actor on a stage says lines such as "To be or not to be, that is the question," does the actor perform a linguistic act?

2. When someone hums (but does not sing) the "Star-Spangled Banner," does she perform a linguistic act? Why or why not?

3. Can a speaker mispronounce a word in a sentence without performing any linguistic act? Why or why not?

THE FAR SIDE® By GARY LARSON

Understanding only German, Fritz was unaware that the clouds were becoming threatening.

SPEECH ACTS

When we are asked about the function of language, it is natural to reply that we use language to communicate ideas. This is, however, only one of the purposes for which we use language. Other purposes become obvious as soon as we look at the ways in which our language actually works. Adding up a column of figures is a linguistic activity—though it is rarely looked at in this way—but it does not communicate any ideas to others. When I add the figures, I am not even communicating anything to myself: I am trying to figure something out. A look at our everyday conversations produces a host of other examples of language being used for different purposes. Grammarians, for example, have divided sentences into various moods, among which are:

Indicative: Barry Bonds hit a home run.

Imperative: Get in there and hit a home run, Barry!

Interrogative: Did Barry Bonds hit a home run?

Expressive: Hurray for Barry Bonds!

The first sentence states a fact. We can use it to communicate information about something that Barry Bonds did. If we use it in this way, then what we say will be either true or false. Notice that none of the other sentences can be called either true or false even though they are all meaningful.

PERFORMATIVES

The different types of sentences recognized by traditional grammarians indicate that we use language to do more than convey information. But this traditional classification of sentences gives only a small idea of the wide variety of things that we can accomplish using language. Sometimes, for example, in using language we actually *do* things in the sense of bringing something about. In one familiar setting, if one person says, "I do," and another person says, "I do," and finally a third person says, "I now pronounce you husband and wife," the relationship between the first two people changes in a fundamental way: They are thereby married. With luck, they begin a life of wedded bliss, but they also alter their legal relationship. For example, they may now file joint income tax returns and may not legally marry other people without first getting divorced.

In uttering sentences of this kind, the speaker thereby *does* something more than merely *stating* something. The philosopher J. L. Austin labeled such utterances *performatives* in order to contrast performing an action with simply describing something.[2] For example, if an umpire shouts, "You're out!" then the batter is out. The umpire is not merely describing the situation but *declaring* the batter out. By way of contrast, if someone in the stands shouts, "He's out!" the batter is not *thereby* out, although the person who shouts this may be encouraging the umpire to call the batter out or complaining because he didn't.

Performatives come in a wide variety of forms. They are often in the first person (like "I do"), but not always. "You're all invited to my house after the game" is in the second person, but uttering it performs the act of inviting. In some circumstances, one person can speak for another person, a group, or an institution. At political conventions, heads of delegations say things like this: "The delegates from Kentucky, the Bluegrass State and the home of the Kentucky Derby, cast their votes for the next President of the United States, Joe W. Blodgett." In saying this, the speaker performs the act of casting Kentucky's votes in favor of Blodgett. Even silence can amount to a performative act in special situations. When the chairperson of a meeting asks if there are any objections to a ruling and none is voiced, then the voters, through their silence, have accepted the ruling.

Because of this diversity of forms that performatives can take, it is not easy to formulate a definition that covers them all. To avoid this difficulty, we will not even try to define performatives here. Instead, we will concentrate on one particularly clear subclass of performatives, what J. L. Austin called *explicit performatives*. All explicit performatives are utterances in the first-person singular indicative noncontinuous[3] present. But not all utterances of that form are explicit performatives. There is one more requirement:

> An utterance of that form is an explicit performative if and only if it yields a true statement when plugged into the following pattern:
> In saying "I _____" in appropriate circumstances, I thereby _____.

For example, "I congratulate you" expresses an explicit performative, because, in saying "I congratulate you," I thereby congratulate you. Here a quoted expression occurs on the left side of the word "thereby" but not on the right side. This reflects the fact that the formula takes us from the words (which are quoted) to the world (the actual act that is performed). The *saying*, which is referred to on the left side of the pattern, amounts to the *doing* referred to on the right side of the word "thereby." We will call this the *thereby test* for explicit performatives. It provides a convenient way of identifying explicit performatives.

The thereby test includes an important qualification: *The context of the utterance must be appropriate.* You have not congratulated anyone if you say, "I congratulate you," when no one is around, unless you are congratulating yourself. Congratulations said by an actor in a play are not real congratulations, and so on. Later in this chapter, we will try to clarify what makes a context appropriate.

Assuming an appropriate context, all of the following sentences meet the thereby test:

> I promise to meet you tomorrow.
>
> I bid sixty-six dollars. (said at an auction)
>
> I bid one club. (said in a bridge game)
>
> I resign from this club.
>
> I apologize for being late.

Notice that it doesn't make sense to *deny* any of these performatives. If someone says, "I bid sixty-six dollars," it is not appropriate for someone to reply "No, you don't" or "That's false." It could, however, be appropriate for someone to reply, "You can't bid sixty-six dollars, because the bidding is already up to seventy dollars." In this case, the person tried to make a bid, but failed to do so.

Several explicit performatives play important roles in constructing arguments. These include sentences of the following kind:

> I *conclude* that this bill should be voted down.
>
> I *base* my conclusion on the assumption that we do not want to hurt the poor.

I *stipulate* that anyone who earns less than $10,000 is poor.

I *assure* you that this bill will hurt the poor.

I *concede* that I am not absolutely certain.

I *admit* that there is much to be said on both sides of this issue.

I *give my support* to the alternative measure.

I *deny* that this alternative will hurt the economy.

I *grant* for the sake of argument that some poor people are lazy.

I *reply* that most poor people contribute to the economy.

I *reserve comment* on other issues raised by this bill.

We will call this kind of performative an *argumentative performative*. Studying such argumentative performatives can help us to understand what is going on in arguments (which is one main reason why we are studying performatives here).

In contrast to the above utterances, which pass the thereby test, none of the following utterances does:

I agree with you. (This describes one's thoughts or beliefs, so, unlike a performative, it can be false.)

I am sorry for being late. (This describes one's feelings and could be false.)

Yesterday I bid sixty dollars. (This is a statement about a past act and might be false.)

I'll meet you tomorrow. (This utterance may only be a prediction that can turn out to be false.)

Questions, imperatives, and exclamations are not explicit performatives, because they cannot sensibly be plugged into the thereby test at all. They do not have the right form, since they are not in the first-person singular indicative noncontinuous present.

EXERCISE II

Using the thereby test as described above, indicate which of the following sentences express explicit performatives (EP) and which do not express explicit performatives (N) in appropriate circumstances:

1. I pledge allegiance to the flag.
2. We pledge allegiance to the flag.
3. I pledged allegiance to the flag.
4. I always pledge allegiance at the start of a game.
5. You pledge allegiance to the flag.

(continued)

6. He pledges allegiance to the flag.
7. He doesn't pledge allegiance to the flag.
8. Pledge allegiance to the flag!
9. Why don't you pledge allegiance to the flag?
10. Pierre is the capital of South Dakota.
11. I state that Pierre is the capital of South Dakota.
12. I order you to leave.
13. Get out of here!
14. I didn't take it.
15. I swear that I didn't take it.
16. I won't talk to you.
17. I refuse to talk to you.
18. I'm out of gas.
19. I feel devastated.
20. Bummer!
21. I claim this land for England.
22. I bring you greetings from home.

KINDS OF SPEECH ACTS

Recognizing explicit performatives helps break the spell of the idea that language functions only to transmit information. It also introduces us to a kind of act distinct from linguistic acts. We will call them *speech acts*.[4] They include such acts as stating, promising, swearing, and refusing. A speech act is the conventional move that a remark makes in a language exchange. It is what is done *in* saying something.

It is difficult to give a precise definition of a speech act, but we can begin by contrasting speech acts with linguistic acts. A linguistic act, we said, is the act of saying something meaningful in a language. It is important to see that the same linguistic act can play different roles as it occurs in different contexts. This is shown by the following brief conversations.

A: Is there any pizza left?
B: Yes.
A: Do you promise to pay me back by Friday?
B: Yes.
A: Do you swear to tell the truth?
B: Yes.
A: Do you refuse to leave?
B: Yes.

Here the same linguistic act, uttering the word "yes," is used to do four different things: to state something, to make a promise, to take an oath, and to refuse to do something.

We can make this idea of a speech act clearer by using the notion of an explicit performative. Explicit performatives provide a systematic way of identifying different kinds of speech acts. The basic idea is that different speech acts are named by the different verbs that occur in explicit performatives. We can thus use the thereby test to search for different kinds of speech acts. For example:

If I say, "I promise," I thereby promise. So "I promise" is a performative, and *promising* is a kind of speech act.

If I say, "I resign," I thereby resign. So "I resign" is a performative, and *resigning* is a kind of speech act.

If I say, "I apologize," I thereby apologize. So "I apologize" is a performative, and *apologizing* is a kind of speech act.

If I say, "I question his honesty," I thereby question his honesty. So "I question his honesty" is a performative, and *questioning* is a kind of speech act.

If I say, "I conclude that she is guilty," I thereby conclude that she is guilty. So "I conclude that she is guilty" is a performative, and *concluding* is a kind of speech act.

The main verbs that appear in such explicit performatives can be called *performative verbs*. Performative verbs name kinds of speech acts.[5]

Still, the same speech act can also be performed without any performative verb. I can deny my opponent's claim by saying either "I deny that" or simply "No way!" Both utterances perform the speech act of denying, even though only the former is a performative. The latter is not a performative and does not contain any performative verb, but it still performs a speech act. Similarly, I can assure you by saying either "I assure you that I am right" or "There's no doubt about it." Both utterances perform the speech act of assuring, even though only the former is a performative.

Thus far, we have emphasized that we do a great deal more with language than make statements, assert facts, and describe things—that is, we do more with language than put forward claims that are either true or false. But we also use language to do these things, so stating, asserting, and describing are themselves kinds of speech acts. This can be shown by using the thereby test:

If I say, "I state that I am a U.S. citizen," I thereby state that I am a U.S. citizen.

If I say, "I assert that the defendant was in Detroit at the time of the crime," I thereby assert that the defendant was in Detroit at that time.

If I say, "I describe him as being dark haired and just over six feet tall," I thereby describe him as being dark haired and just over six feet tall.

We now have a more accurate conception of the way in which language functions than the common conception that the function of language is to convey ideas. Making claims that are either true or false is one important kind of speech act, but we perform a great many other kinds of speech acts that are also important.

EXERCISE III

Which of the following verbs names a speech act?

1. *capture* the suspect
2. *assert* that the suspect is guilty
3. *stare* accusingly at the suspect
4. *find* the defendant guilty
5. *take* the defendant away
6. *punish* the defendant
7. *revoke* the defendant's driver's license
8. *welcome* the prisoner to prison
9. *order* the prisoner to be silent
10. *lock* the cell door

EXERCISE IV

Using a dictionary, find ten verbs that can be used to construct explicit performatives that have not yet been mentioned in this chapter.

SPEECH ACT RULES

The distinctive feature of a performative utterance is that, in a sense we have tried to make clear, the saying constitutes a doing of something. In saying, "I pronounce you husband and wife," a minister is not simply describing a marriage ceremony, she is performing it. Here, however, an objection might arise. Suppose someone who is a supporter of family values goes about the streets pronouncing random couples husband and wife. Unless this person is a member of the clergy, a justice of the peace, a ship's captain, or the like, that person will have no right to make such pronouncements. Furthermore, even if this person is, say, a crazed member of the clergy, the pronouncement will still not come off—that is, the utterance will not succeed in making anyone husband and wife. The parties addressed have to say, "I do," they must have a proper license, and so on. This example shows that a speech act will *fail to come off* or will be *void* unless certain rules or conventions are satisfied. These rules or conventions that must be satisfied for a speech act to come off and not be void will be called *speech act rules*.

The main types of speech act rules can be discovered by considering the following questions:

1. *Must the speaker use any special words or formulas to perform the speech act?*

Sometimes a speech act will come off only if certain words or formulas are used. In baseball the umpire must say, "Strike two," or something very close to this, in order to call a second strike. In a pickup game it might be all right to say instead, "Hey, that's two bad ones on you, baby!" but that way of calling strikes is not permitted in serious play. Similarly, certain legal documents are not valid if they are not properly signed, endorsed, notarized, and so forth.

2. *Is any response or uptake by the audience needed in order to complete the speech act?*

Sometimes a speech act will come off only if there is an uptake by another person. A person can *offer* a bet by saying, "I bet you ten dollars that the Angels will win today," but this person will have *made* a bet only if the other person says, "Done" or "You're on," shakes hands, or in some other way accepts the bet. A marriage ceremony is completely void if one of the parties does not say, "I do," but instead says, "Well, maybe I should think about this for a while."

3. *Must the (a) speaker or (b) audience hold any special position or role in order for the speaker to perform the speech act?*

Sometimes a speech act will come off only if it is performed by someone with an official position. We have already seen that, for someone to make two people husband and wife by pronouncing them husband and wife, that person must hold a certain official position. Similarly, even if a body is plainly dead when it arrives at the hospital, a janitor cannot pronounce it dead on arrival. That is the job of a doctor or a coroner. In the same way, although a shortstop can perform the linguistic act of *shouting*, "You're out," a shortstop cannot perform the speech act of *calling* someone out. Only an umpire can do that. Moreover, even an umpire cannot call out the catcher or a spectator, so sometimes the audience of the speech also needs to have some special position.

4. *Are any other special circumstances required for the speech act?*

Most speech acts also involve assumptions or presuppositions that certain *facts* obtain. A father cannot bequeath an antique car to his son if he does not own such a car. You cannot resign from the American Civil Liberties Union or the Veterans of Foreign Wars if you are not a member. These special circumstances might sometimes include the audience's desires. In promising someone to do something, for example, we usually do so in the belief that the person *wants* us to do it. For example, I will promise to drive someone to the airport only if I believe that person wants to go the airport and would like me to drive her there. Sometimes, however, we do promise to do things a person does not want done. I can promise to throw someone out if he doesn't behave himself. Here, however, I am making a threat, not a promise. Different answers to this question, thus, reveal differences among speech acts.

5. *What feelings, desires, or beliefs is the speaker expected to have?*

If we apologize for something, we are expected to feel sorry for what we have done. If we congratulate someone, we are usually supposed to be pleased with that person's success. If we state something, we are expected to believe what we say. In all these cases—in apologizing, congratulating, and stating—if the speaker lacks the expected feelings, desires, or beliefs, the speaker still does succeed in performing the speech act, but that speaker and speech act are subject to criticism. In this respect, this rule differs from the preceding rules. Those preceding rules reflected conventions that must be satisfied for the speech act to come off (for it not to be void). In contrast, the person who says, "I apologize," has apologized even if he or she does not feel sorry. The speech act does come off and is not void, even though the apology can be criticized as insincere.

6. *What general purpose or purposes are served by this kind of speech act?*

This final question asks why a certain kind of speech act exists at all. Why, for example, is there the speech act of promising? That is a rather complicated question, but the primary reason for the institution of promising is that it helps people coordinate their activities. People who make promises place themselves under an obligation to do something. When promises are contractual, this obligation is a legal obligation. Promise making, then, increases the confidence we can have that someone will do what they said they will do, and, for legal promises at least, provides remedies when they do not. To cite another example of the purpose of a speech act, apologizing expresses regret for harming or insulting someone. One of its purposes is to normalize relations between the speaker and the person harmed or insulted.

Answering the six questions listed above for a particular kind of speech act is called giving a *speech act analysis*. For example, here is a brief speech act analysis of "to appoint," as in, "I appoint you to the judiciary committee":

1. Appointments are usually made by using the word "appoint," but other words can be used as well; for example, "name" and "designate" can also be used to do this job. You cannot, however, say, "I wish you were on the judiciary committee."

2. Sometimes further actions by others are necessary for an appointment to come off. Perhaps ratification is needed. Before ratification, the word "nominate" is often used. In such cases, only after the nomination is ratified has the appointment been made. Usually the appointment does not come off if the person declines the appointment.

3. Normally, someone who appoints a person to something must have the *power* to make such appointments. For example, Queen Elizabeth II does not have the power to appoint the commissioner of baseball.

4. This speech act presupposes a wide variety of facts, for example, that a position exists, that the person appointed to it is eligible for this appointment, and so on.

5. Appointments are often made with the belief that the person appointed will do a good job. This is not always the case, however, as appointments are made for all sorts of different reasons—rewarding an important supporter, for example.

6. An important purpose of an appointment is to explicitly designate someone to play a particular role. For example, it is often important to know who is in charge. It can also be important that the person who gains this role does so through regular, authorized procedures.

EXERCISE V

Give a speech act analysis of the ten verbs below by writing two or three sentences in response to each of the six questions above. Speech act analyses can go on much longer, but your goal here is just to bring out the most interesting features of the speech act named by each verb.

1. to bet
2. to promise
3. to congratulate
4. to state
5. to apologize

6. to deny
7. to vote
8. to give up (in a fight)
9. to thank
10. to invite

DISCUSSION QUESTIONS

1. Imagine that an actor on stage during a modern play screams, "Fire! No, I really mean it. " The audience realizes that he is just acting, so they laugh. Then the actor sees a real fire behind the stage out of view of the audience. The actor again screams, "Fire! No, I really mean it. *Fire!*" Which speech act, if any, does the actor perform in uttering these words the second time? Why? What does this show about speech acts?

2. *Do* the speech acts in which people get married presuppose that the people who are getting married are of different sexes? *Should* these speech acts presuppose this fact? Why or why not?

3. The importance of deciding what kind of speech act has been performed is illustrated by a classic case from the law of contracts, *Hawkins v. McGee.*[6] McGee performed an operation on Hawkins that proved unsuccessful, and Hawkins sued for damages. He did not sue on the basis of malpractice, however, but on the basis of breach of contract. His attorney argued that the doctor initiated a contractual relationship in that he tried to persuade Hawkins to have the operation by saying things such as "I will guarantee to make the hand a hundred percent perfect hand." He made statements of this kind a number of times, and Hawkins finally agreed to undergo the operation on the basis of these remarks. Hawkins's attorney maintained that these exchanges, which took place in the doctor's office on a number of occasions, constituted an offer of a contract that Hawkins explicitly accepted. The attorney for the surgeon replied that these words, even if uttered, would not constitute an offer of a contract, but merely

(continued)

expressed a *strong belief,* and that reasonable people should know that doctors cannot guarantee results.

It is important to remember that contracts do not have to be written and signed to be binding. A proper verbal offer and acceptance are usually sufficient to constitute a contract. The case, then, turned on two questions: (1) Did McGee utter the words attributed to him? In other words, did McGee perform the *linguistic act* attributed to him? The jury decided that he did. (2) The second, more interesting question was whether these words, when uttered in this particular context, amounted to an offer of a contract, as Hawkins's attorney maintained, or merely were an expression of strong belief, as McGee's attorney held. In other words, the fundamental question in this case was what kind of *speech act* McGee performed when trying to convince Hawkins to have the operation.

Explain how you would settle this case. (The court actually ruled in favor of Hawkins, but you are free to disagree.)

CONVERSATIONAL ACTS[7]

In examining linguistic acts (saying something meaningful in a language) and then speech acts (doing something in using words), we have largely ignored some central features of language: It is usually—though not always— a *social* activity that takes place among people. It is also normally a *practical* activity with certain goals. We use language in order to inform people of things, get them to do things, amuse them, calm them down, and so on. We can capture these social and practical aspects of language by introducing the notion of a *conversational exchange,* that is, a situation where various speakers use speech acts in order to bring about some effects in each other. We will call this act of using a speech act to cause a standard effect in another a *conversational act.*

Suppose, for example, Amy says to Bobbi, "Someone is following us." In this case, Amy has performed a linguistic act; that is, she has uttered a meaningful sentence in the English language. Amy has also performed a speech act—specifically, she has *stated* that they are being followed. The point of performing this speech act is to produce in Bobbi a particular belief— namely, that they are being followed. (Amy's utterance might also have other purposes, such as to alert Bobbi to some danger, but it accomplishes those other purposes by means of getting Bobbi to believe they are being followed.) If Amy is successful in this, then Amy has successfully performed the conversational act of producing this belief in Bobbi. Amy, of course, might fail in her attempt to do this. Amy's linguistic act could be successful and her speech act successful as well, yet, for whatever reason, Bobbi might not accept as true what Amy is telling her. Perhaps Bobbi thinks that Amy is paranoid or just trying to frighten her as some kind of joke. In that case, Amy failed to perform her intended conversational act, even though she did perform her intended linguistic and speech acts.

Here are some other examples of the difference between performing a speech act and performing a conversational act:

> We can *warn* people about something in order to *put them on guard* concerning it.
> Here warning is the speech act; putting them on guard is the intended conversational act.

> We can *urge* people to do things in order to *persuade* them to do these things.
> Here urging is the speech act; persuading is the intended conversational act.

> We can *assure* people concerning something in order to *instill confidence in them*.
> Here assuring is the speech act; instilling confidence is the intended conversational act.

> We can *apologize* to people in order to *make them feel better about us.*
> Here apologizing is the speech act; making them feel better about us is the intended conversational act.

In each of these cases, our speech act may not succeed in having its intended conversational effect. Our urging, warning, and assuring may, respectively, fail to persuade, put on guard, or instill confidence. Indeed, speech acts may bring about the opposite of what was intended. People who brag (a speech act) in order to impress others (the intended conversational act) often actually make others think less of them (the actual effect). In many ways like these, we can perform a speech act without performing the intended conversational act.

The relationship between conversational acts and speech acts is confusing, because both of them can be performed at once by the same utterance. Suppose Carl says, "You are invited to my party." By means of this single utterance, he performs a linguistic act of uttering this meaningful sentence, a speech act of inviting you, and perhaps also a conversational act of getting you to come to his party. Indeed, he would not be able to perform this conversational act without also performing such a speech act, assuming that you would not come to his party if you were not invited. He would also not be able to perform this speech act without performing this linguistic act or something like it, since he cannot invite you by means of an inarticulate grunt or by asking, "Are you invited to my party?"

As a result, we cannot sensibly ask whether Carl's utterance of "You are invited to my party" is a linguistic act, a speech act, or a conversational act. That single utterance performs all three acts at once. Nonetheless, we can distinguish those kinds of acts that Carl performs in terms of the verbs that describe the acts. Some verbs describe speech acts; other verbs describe conversational acts. We can tell which verbs describe which kinds of acts by asking whether the verb passes the thereby test (in which case the verb describes a speech act) or whether, instead, it describes a standard effect of the utterance (in which case the verb describes a conversational act).

EXERCISE VI

Indicate whether the verbs in the following sentences name a speech act, a conversational act, or neither. Assume a standard context. Explain your answers.

1. She *thought* that he did it.
2. She *asserted* that he did it.
3. She *convinced* them that he did it.
4. She *condemned* him in front of everyone.
5. She *challenged* his integrity.
6. She *embarrassed* him in front of them.
7. He *denied* doing it.
8. They *believed* her.
9. They *encouraged* him to admit it.
10. She *told* him to get lost.
11. He *praised* her lavishly.
12. His praise *made* her happy.
13. He *threatened* to reveal her secret.
14. He *submitted* his resignation.
15. Her news *frightened* him half to death.
16. He *advised* her to go into another line of work.
17. She *blamed* him for her troubles.
18. His lecture *enlightened* her.
19. His jokes *amused* her.
20. His book *confused* her.

CONVERSATIONAL RULES

Just as there are rules that govern linguistic acts and other rules that govern speech acts, so too there are rules that govern conversational acts. This should not be surprising, because conversations can be complicated interpersonal activities in need of rules to make them effective in attaining their goals. These underlying rules are implicitly understood by users of the language, but the philosopher Paul Grice was the first person to examine them in careful detail.

We can start by examining standard or normal conversational exchanges where conversation is a cooperative venture—that is, where the people involved in the conversation have some common goal they are trying to achieve in talking with one another. (A prisoner being interrogated and a shop owner being robbed are *not* in such cooperative situations.) According to Grice, such exchanges are governed by what he calls the *Cooperative Principle*. This principle states that the parties involved should use language in a way that contributes toward achieving their common goal. It tells them to cooperate.[8]

This general principle gains more content when we consider other forms of cooperation. Carpenters who want to build a house need enough nails and wood, but not too much. They need the right kinds of nails and wood. They also need to put the nails and wood together in the relevant way—that is, according to their plans. And, of course, they also want to perform their tasks quickly and in the right order. Rational people who want to achieve common goals must follow similar general restrictions in other practical activities. Because cooperative conversations are one such practical activity, speakers who want to cooperate with one another must follow rules analogous to those for carpenters.

Grice spells out four such rules. The first he calls the rule of *Quantity*. It tells us to give the right amount of information. More specifically:

1. Make your contribution as informative as is required (for the current purposes of the exchange).

and possibly:

2. Do not make your contribution more informative than is required.

Here is an application of this rule: A person rushes up to you and asks, "Where is a fire extinguisher?" You know that there is a fire extinguisher five floors away in the basement, and you also know that there is a fire extinguisher just down the hall. Suppose you say that there is a fire extinguisher in the basement. Here you have said something true, but you have violated the first part of the rule of Quantity. You have failed to reveal an important piece of information that, under the rule of Quantity, you should have produced. A violation of the second version of the rule would look like this: As smoke billows down the hall, you say where a fire extinguisher is located on each floor, starting with the basement. Eventually you will get around to saying that there is a fire extinguisher just down the hall, but you bury the point in a mass of unnecessary information.

Grice's second rule is called the rule of *Quality*. In general: Try to make your contribution one that is true. More specifically:

1. Do not say what you believe to be false.

2. Do not say that for which you lack adequate evidence.

In a cooperative activity, you are not supposed to tell lies. Beyond this, you are expected not to talk off the top of your head either. When we make a statement, we can be challenged by someone asking, "Do you really believe that?" or "Why do you believe that?" That a person has the right to ask such questions shows that statement making is governed by the rule of Quality.

In a court of law, witnesses promise to tell the whole truth and nothing but the truth. The demand for *nothing but the truth* reflects the rule of Quality. The demand for *the whole truth* roughly reflects the rule of Quantity. Obviously, nobody really tells every truth he or she knows. Here the *whole* truth concerns all the known truths that are relevant in the context.

This brings us to our next rule, the rule of *Relevance*. Simply stated, the rule of Relevance says:

Be relevant!

Though easy to state, the rule is not easy to explain, because relevance itself is a difficult notion. It is, however, easy to illustrate. If someone asks me where he can find a doctor, I might reply that there is a hospital on the next block. Though not a direct answer to the question, it does not violate the rule of Relevance because it provides a piece of useful information. If, however, in response I tell the person that I like his haircut, then I have violated the rule of Relevance. Clear-cut violations of this principle often involve *changing the subject*.

Another rule concerns the manner of our conversation. We are expected to be clear in what we say. Under the general rule of *Manner* come various special rules:

1. Avoid obscurity of expression.
2. Avoid ambiguity.
3. Be brief.
4. Be orderly.

As an example of the fourth part of this rule, when describing a series of events, it is usually important to state them in the order in which they occurred. It would certainly be misleading to say that two people had a child and got married when, in fact, they had a child after they were married.

Many other rules govern our conversations. "Be polite!" is one of them. "Be charitable!" is another. That is, we should put the best interpretation on what others say, and our replies should reflect this. We should avoid quibbling and being picky. For the most part, however, we will not worry about these other rules.

EXERCISE VII

Indicate which, if any, of Grice's conversational rules are violated by the italicized sentence of each of the following conversations. Assume a standard context. More than one rule might be violated.

1. "What did you get on the last test?" *"A grade."*
2. "Did you like her singing?" *"Her costume was beautiful."*
3. *"The governor has the brains of a three-year-old."*
4. *"The Lone Ranger rode into the sunset and jumped on his horse."*
5. *"Without her help, we'd be up a creek without a paddle."*
6. "Where is Palo Alto?" *"On the surface of the Earth."*
7. *"It will rain tomorrow."* "How do you know?" "I just guessed."
8. *"Does the dog need to go out for a W-A-L-K [spelled out]?"*
9. "Why did the chicken cross the road?" *"To get to the other side."*
10. Psychiatrist: "You're crazy." Patient: "I want a second opinion." Psychiatrist: "Okay. *You're ugly, too."*

THE FAR SIDE® By GARY LARSON

When dumb animals attempt murder

CONVERSATIONAL IMPLICATION

In a normal setting where people are cooperating toward reaching a shared goal, they often conform quite closely to Grice's conversational rules. If, on the whole, people did not do this, we could not have the linguistic practices we do. If we thought, for example, that people very often lied (even about the most trivial matters), the business of exchanging information would be badly damaged.

Still, people do not always follow these conversational rules. They withhold information, they elaborate needlessly, they assert what they know to be false, they say the first thing that pops into their heads, they wander off the subject, and they talk vaguely and obscurely. When we observe actual conversations, it is sometimes hard to tell how any information gets communicated at all.

The explanation lies in the same conversational rules. Not only do we usually follow these conventions, we also (1) implicitly realize that we are following them, and (2) expect others to assume that we are following them. This mutual understanding of the commitments involved in a conversational act has the following important consequence: People are able to convey a great deal of information without actually saying it.

A simple example will illustrate this point. Again suppose that a person, with smoke billowing behind him, comes running up to you and asks,

"Where's a fire extinguisher?" You reply, "There's one in the lobby." Through a combination of conversational rules, notably relevance, quantity, and manner, this commits you to the claim that this is the closest, or at least the most accessible, fire extinguisher. Furthermore, the person you are speaking to assumes that you are committed to this. Of course, you have not actually *said* that it is the closest fire extinguisher; but you have, we might say, *implied* this. When we do not actually say something but imply it by virtue of a mutually understood conversational rule, the implication is called a *conversational implication.*

It is important to realize that conversational implication is a pervasive feature of human communication. It is not something we employ only occasionally for special effect. In fact, virtually every conversation relies on these implications, and most conversations would fall apart if people refused to go beyond literal meanings to take into account the implications of saying things. In the following conversation, B is literal-minded in just this way:

A: Do you know what time it is?

B: Not without looking at my watch.

B has answered A's question, but it is hard to imagine that A has received the information she was looking for. Presumably, she wanted to know what time it was, not merely whether B, at that very moment, knew the time. Finding B rather obtuse, A tries again:

A: Can you tell me what time it is?

B: Oh, yes, all I have to do is look at my watch.

Undaunted, A gives it another try:

A: Will you tell me what time it is?

B: I suppose I will as soon as you ask me.

Finally:

A: What time is it?

B: Two o'clock. Why didn't you ask me that in the first place?

Notice that in each of these exchanges B gives a direct and accurate answer to A's question; yet, in all but the last answer, B does not provide A with what A wants. Like a computer in a science-fiction movie, B is taking A's questions too literally. More precisely, B does nothing *more* than take A's remarks literally. In a conversational exchange, we expect others to take our remarks in the light of the obvious purpose we have in making them. We expect them to share our commonsense understanding of why people ask questions. At the very least, we expect people to respond to us in ways that are *relevant* to our purposes. Except at the end, B seems totally oblivious to the point of A's questions. That is what makes B unhelpful and annoying.

Though all the conversational rules we have examined can be the basis of conversational implication, the rule of Relevance is particularly powerful in this respect. Normal conversations are dense with conversational implications that depend on the rule of Relevance. Someone says, "Dinner's ready," and that is immediately taken to be a way of asking people to come to the table. Why? Because dinner's being ready is a transparent *reason* to come to the table to eat. This is an ordinary context that most people are familiar with. Change the context, however, and the conversational implications can be entirely different. Suppose the same words, "Dinner's ready," are uttered when guests have failed to arrive on time. In this context, the conversational implication, which will probably be reflected in an annoyed tone of voice, will be quite different.

To cite another example of context dependence, if someone says, "I broke a finger," people will naturally assume that it is the speaker's own finger that was broken. Why? Because when people break fingers, it is almost always their own fingers that they break. That is the standard context in which this remark is made. If, however, we shift the context, that conversational implication can be lost and another can take its place. Suppose the speaker is a mobster in an extortion racket, that is, someone who physically harms people who do not pay protection money. Among his fellow extortionists, the conversational implication of "I broke a finger" is likely to be that it was someone who refused to pay up who had his finger broken. (We can imagine the extortionist canceling this implication by saying, "No, no, it was *my* finger that got broken when I slugged the guy.")

EXERCISE VIII

Assuming a natural conversational setting, what might a person intend to conversationally imply by making the following remarks? Briefly explain why each of these conversational implications holds; that is, explain the relationship between what the speaker *literally* says and what the speaker intends to convey through conversational implication. Finally, for each example, find a context where the standard conversational implication would fail and another arise in its place.

1. It's getting a little chilly in here. (Said by a visitor in your home)
2. Do you mind if I borrow your pen? (Said to a friend while studying)
3. We are out of soda. (Said by a child to her parents)
4. I got here before he did. (Said in a ticket line)
5. Don't blame me if you get in trouble. (Said by someone who advised you not to do it)
6. Has this seat been taken? (Said in a theater before a show)
7. These sweet potatoes are very filling. (Said when the cook asks if you want more)
8. Don't ask me. (Said in response to a question)
9. Does your dog bite? (Said to a man standing next to a dog)
10. I will be out of town that day. (Said in response to a party invitation)

VIOLATING CONVERSATIONAL RULES

If we look at basic conversational rules, we notice that these rules sometimes clash, or at least push us in different directions. The rule of Quantity encourages us to give as much information as possible, but this is constrained by the rule of Quality, which restricts our claims to things we believe to be true and can back up with good reasons. The demands of the rule of Quantity can also conflict with the demand for brevity. In order to be brief, we must sometimes simplify and even falsify, and this can come into conflict with the rule of Quality, which demands that we say only what we believe to be true. Sometimes it is not important to get things exactly right; sometimes it is. An ongoing conversation can be a constant series of adjustments to this background system of rules.

Because conversational rules can come into conflict with one another, speakers can sometimes *seem* to be violating the Cooperative Principle by violating one of its maxims. This can happen when one conversational rule is overridden by another. Grasping the resolution of such a conflict can generate interesting conversational implications. This may sound complicated, but an example from Grice should make it clear. Suppose *A* tells *B*, "I'm planning to visit *C*; where does he live?" *B* replies, "Somewhere in the south of France." If *A* is interested in visiting *C*, then *B*'s reply really does not give her the information she needs and thus seems to violate the first part of the rule of Quantity. We can explain this departure on the assumption that *B* does not know *exactly* where *C* lives and would thus violate the rule of Quality if he said anything more specific. In this case, *B*'s reply conversationally implies that he does not know exactly where *C* lives.

In a more extreme case, a person may even *flout* one of these conventions, that is, may openly violate a conversational rule without, as in the previous example, there being any other conversational rule that overrides it. Here is an adaptation of one of Grice's examples and his explanation of it:

> *A* is writing a letter of recommendation about one of his students who is applying to law school, and the letter reads as follows: "Dear Sir: Mr. *X*'s command of English is excellent, and his attendance in class has been regular. Yours, etc." (Gloss: *A* cannot be opting out, since if he wished to be uncooperative, why write at all? He cannot be unable, through ignorance, to say more, since the person is his student; moreover, he knows that more information is wanted. He must, therefore, be wishing to impart information he is reluctant to write down. This supposition is only tenable on the assumption that he thinks that Mr. *X* is not a good student. This, then, is what he is implicating.)

This is a case of *damning with faint praise*. Faint praise can be damning because, under the first part of the rule of Quantity, it conversationally implies that no stronger praise is warranted.

We can intentionally violate the rule of Relevance by pointedly changing the subject. Here is variation on another one of Grice's examples:

> Standing outside a classroom, *A* says, "Professor *X* is a moron." There is a moment of shocked silence; then *B* says, "Nice day, isn't it?"

A would have to be fairly dim not to realize that Professor *X*, whom he has just called a moron, may be somewhere nearby. Why else would *B* reply in such an irrelevant manner? So in saying, "Nice day, isn't it?" *B* conversationally implies that Professor *X* is nearby.

Winston Churchill reportedly provided a famous example of intentionally violating the rule of Manner. When criticized for ending a sentence with a preposition, he is said to have replied, "That is the type of criticism up with which I will not put."

EXERCISE IX

These sentences appeared in Exercise VII. For each, explain what the speaker is conversationally implying and how that conversational implication is generated.

1. "What did you get on the last test?" "*A grade.*"
2. "Did you like her singing?" "*Her costume was beautiful.*"
3. "*The governor has the brains of a three-year-old.*"
4. "*Does the dog need to go out for a W-A-L-K* [spelled out]?"

EXERCISE X

For each of the following paired questions and answers, what do the answers conversationally imply in a normal context? Explain why these conversational implications hold. (Try to rely on the content of what is said, rather than on the tone of voice in which it is uttered. In particular, don't think of these remarks being uttered with heavy sarcasm.)

1. Are you going to vote for a Republican? I just might.
2. Are you going to vote for a Republican? You can bet on it.
3. Are you going to vote for a Republican? Not unless hell freezes over.
4. Are you going to vote for a Republican? Don't be silly.
5. Are you going to vote for a Republican? I am voting for an independent.
6. Are you going to vote for a Republican? There is no other choice.
7. Did you vote for a Republican? Maybe yes, maybe no.
8. Did you vote for a Republican? I voted for the winner.

RHETORICAL DEVICES

Many rhetorical devices work by flouting conversational rules in order to generate conversational implications. Consider exaggeration. When someone claims to be hungry enough to eat a horse, it does not dawn on us to treat this as a literal claim about how much she can eat. To do so would be to attribute to the speaker a blatant violation of Grice's first rule of Quality—namely, do not say what you believe to be false. Consequently, her audience will naturally interpret her remark figuratively, rather than literally. They will assume that she is exaggerating the amount she can eat in order to conversationally imply that she is very hungry. This rhetorical device is called *overstatement* or *hyperbole*. It is commonly employed, often in heavy-handed ways.

We sometimes use the opposite ploy and attempt to achieve rhetorical effect by *understating* things. We say that something is pretty good or not too bad when, as all can see, it is terrific. In these cases the speaker is violating something akin to the rule of Quantity. He is not saying just how good something really is. He expects his audience to recognize this and say (inwardly, at least) something like this: "Oh, it is much better than that." Understatement is often used as a way of fishing for compliments.

Sometimes, then, we do not intend to have others take our words at face value. Even beyond this, we sometimes expect our listeners to interpret us as claiming just the *opposite* of what we assert. This occurs, for example, with *irony* and *sarcasm*. Suppose at a crucial point in a game, the second baseman fires the ball ten feet over the first baseman's head, and someone shouts, "Great throw." Literally, it was not a great throw; it was the opposite of a great throw, and this is just what the person who says "Great throw" is indicating. How do the listeners know they are supposed to interpret it in this way? Sometimes this is indicated by tone of voice. A sarcastic tone of voice usually indicates that the person means the opposite of what he or she is saying. Even without the tone of sarcasm, the remark "Great throw" is not likely to be taken literally. The person who shouts this knows that it was not a great throw, as do the people who hear it. Rather than attributing an obviously false belief to the shouter, we assume that the person is blatantly violating the rule of Quality to draw our attention to just how bad the throw really was.

Metaphors and similes are perhaps the most common forms of figurative language. A *simile* is, roughly, an explicit figurative comparison. A word such as "like" or "as" makes the comparison explicit, and the comparison is figurative because it would be inappropriate if taken literally. To say that the home team fought like tigers does not mean that they clawed the opposing team and took large bites out of them. To call someone as dumb as a post is not to claim that they have no brain at all.

With a *metaphor*, we also compare certain items, but without words such as "like" or "as." Metaphorical comparisons are still figurative because the vocabulary, at a literal level, is not appropriate to the subject matter. George Washington was not literally the father of his country. Taken literally, it hardly makes sense to speak of someone fathering a country. But the metaphor is so natural (or so familiar) that it does not cross our minds to treat the remark literally, asking, perhaps, who the mother was.

Taken literally, metaphors are usually obviously false, and then they violate Grice's rule of Quality. Again, as with irony, when someone says something obviously false, we have to decide what to make of that person's utterance. Perhaps the person is very stupid or a very bad liar, but often neither suggestion is plausible. In such a situation, sometimes the best supposition is that the person is speaking metaphorically rather than literally.

Not all metaphors, however, are literally false. In John Donne's Meditation XVII, "No man is an island" is literally true. We treat this remark as a metaphor because, taken literally, it is so obviously and boringly true that we cannot imagine why anyone would want to say it. Taken literally, it would make no greater contribution to the conversation than any other irrelevant, obvious truth—for example, that no man is a socket wrench. Taken literally, this metaphor violates the rule of Relevance and, perhaps, the second part of the rule of Quantity. Taken figuratively, it is an apt, if somewhat overworked, way of indicating that no one is isolated and self-contained.

EXERCISE XI

Here are some more true metaphors. Explain what they mean and how they work.

1. "Blood is thicker than water."
2. "Cream rises to the top."
3. "People who live in glass houses should not throw stones."
4. Robert Frost's poem "The Road Not Taken" begins, "Two roads diverged in a yellow wood."
5. China's Chairman Mao Tse-tung is reported to have said, "A revolution is not the same as inviting people to dinner, or writing an essay, or painting a picture, or doing fancy needle-work."
6. Cuba's Fidel Castro is supposed to have said, "A revolution is not a bed of roses. A revolution is a struggle between the future and the past." (Is this different from item 5?)

EXERCISE XII

Identify each of the following sentences as irony, metaphor, or simile. For each sentence, write another expressing its literal meaning.

1. He missed the ball by a mile.
2. He acted like a bull in a china shop.
3. The exam blew me away.
4. He had to eat his words.
5. It was a real team effort. (Said by a coach after his team loses by forty points.)
6. They are throwing the baby out with the bathwater.
7. The concert was totally awesome.
8. A midair collision can ruin your whole day.
9. This is a case of the tail wagging the dog.
10. "Religion is the opiate of the masses." (Marx)

EXERCISE XIII

Metaphors do not appear only in statements. They also appear in imperatives. For example, "Don't rock the boat" can be employed literally in a context where someone is moving around in a canoe in a way that could tip it. It can also be used metaphorically to tell someone not to do something that will cause a fuss. For each of the following metaphors, find a context where the imperative can be used in its literal way and another context where it is used metaphorically.

1. Keep your eye on the ball.
2. Don't put all your eggs in one basket.
3. Look before you leap.
4. Make hay while the sun shines.
5. Don't count your chickens before they hatch.
6. Don't change horses in midstream.

EXERCISE XIV

Unpack the following political metaphors by giving their literal content.

1. We can't afford a president who needs on-the-job training.
2. It's time for people on the welfare wagon to get off and help pull.
3. If you can't stand the heat, get out of the kitchen.
4. We need to restore a level playing field.
5. The special interests have him in their pockets.
6. The bill was passed through typical horse trading.
7. He's a lame duck.

DISCUSSION QUESTIONS

1. A classic example of rhetoric occurs in Marc Antony's funeral oration in William Shakespeare's play, *Julius Caesar* (act III, scene ii). Brutus and other conspirators had killed Julius Caesar. At Caesar's funeral, Brutus first argued that they needed to kill Caesar to prevent him from becoming too powerful and taking away the freedoms of Roman citizens. Brutus concludes, "As Caesar loved me, I weep for him; as he was fortunate, I rejoice in it; as he was valiant, I honor him. But as he was ambitious, I slew him." On the other side, Marc Antony sees Brutus as a traitor, but Brutus now has power, so Antony does not dare to call Brutus a traitor openly. The central part of Antony's speech is reprinted below. Indicate which lines are ironic, and comment on any other rhetorical devices in this speech. Why was it so effective (and famous) as a speech?

   Come I to speak in Caesar's funeral.

   He was my friend, faithful and just to me.

   But Brutus says he was ambitious,

   And Brutus is an honorable man.

   He hath brought many captives home to Rome,

   Whose ransoms did the general coffers fill.

   Did this in Caesar seem ambition?

   When that the poor have cried, Caesar hath wept—

   Ambition should be made of sterner stuff.

   Yet Brutus says he was ambitious,

   And Brutus is an honorable man.

   You all did see that on the Lupercal

   I thrice presented him a kingly crown,

   Which he did thrice refuse. Was this ambition?

   Yet Brutus says he was ambitious,

   And, sure, he is an honorable man.

   I speak not to disprove what Brutus spoke,

   But here I am to speak what I do know.

   You all did love him once, not without cause.

   What cause withholds you then to mourn for him?

2. At the start of the U.S. war with Iraq in 2003, some described Iraq as another Vietnam, while others described Saddam Hussein (Iraq's president) as another Hitler. Which metaphor was used by supporters of the war? Which was used by opponents? How can you tell? How do these metaphors work?

DECEPTION

In the preceding examples, a speaker openly violates a conversational rule. The listeners recognize that a rule is being intentionally broken, and the speaker knows that the listeners recognize the violation. At other times, however, speakers intentionally break conversational rules because they are trying to mislead their listeners. A speaker may violate the first part of Grice's rule of Quality by uttering something she knows to be false with the intention of producing a false belief in her listeners. That is called *lying*. Notice that lying depends on the general acceptance of the Cooperative Principle. Because audiences generally assume that speakers are telling the truth, speakers can sometimes get away with lying.

Flat-out lying is not the only way (and often not the most effective way) of intentionally misleading people. We can say something literally true that, at the same time, conversationally implies something false. This is sometimes called making a *false suggestion*. If a son tells his parents that he "has had some trouble with the car," that could be true but deeply misleading if, in fact, he had totaled it. It would be misleading because it would violate the rule of Quantity. In saying only that he has had some trouble with the car, he conversationally implies that nothing very serious happened. He conversationally implies this because, in this context, he is expected to come clean and reveal all that actually happened.

A more complex example of false suggestion arose in a lawsuit that reached the United States Supreme Court.

BRONSTON V. UNITED STATES

(409 U.S. 352, 1973)

MR. CHIEF JUSTICE BURGER delivered the opinion of the Court:

Petitioner's perjury conviction was founded on the answers given by him as a witness at that bankruptcy hearing, and in particular on the following colloquy with a lawyer for a creditor of Bronston Productions:

Q. Do you have any bank accounts in Swiss banks, Mr. Bronston?

A. No, sir.

Q. Have you ever?

A. The company had an account there for about six months, in Zurich.

Q. Have you any nominees who have bank accounts in Swiss banks?

A. No, sir.

Q. Have you ever?

A. No, sir.

It is undisputed that for a period of nearly five years, between October 1959 and June 1964, petitioner had a personal bank account at the International Credit Bank in Geneva, Switzerland, into which he made deposits and upon which he drew checks totalling more than $180,000. It is likewise undisputed that petitioner's answers were literally truthful. (i) Petitioner did not at the time of questioning have a Swiss bank account. (ii) Bronston

Productions, Inc., did have the account in Zurich described by petitioner. (iii) Neither at the time of questioning nor before did petitioner have nominees who had Swiss accounts. The government's prosecution for perjury went forward on the theory that in order to mislead his questioner, petitioner answered the second question with literal truthfulness but unresponsively addressed his answer to the company's assets and not to his own—thereby implying that he had no personal Swiss bank account at the relevant time.

It is hard to read the witness's response to the second question in any other way than as a deliberate attempt to mislead the Court, for his response plainly suggests that he did not have a personal account in a Swiss bank, when, in fact, he did. But the issue before the Court was not whether he intentionally misled the Court, but whether in doing so he committed perjury. The relevant statute reads as follows:

> Whoever, having taken an oath before a competent tribunal . . . that he will testify . . . truly, . . . willfully and contrary to such oath states or subscribes to any material matter which he does not believe to be true, is guilty of perjury.
>
> (18 U.S.C. 1621)

The lower courts ruled that Bronston violated this statute and, thus, committed perjury. The Supreme Court reversed this decision, in part for the following reasons:

> It should come as no surprise that a participant in a bankruptcy proceeding may have something to conceal and consciously tries to do so, or that a debtor may be embarrassed at his plight and yield information reluctantly. It is the responsibility of the lawyer to probe; testimonial interrogation, and cross-examination in particular, is a probing, prying, pressing form of inquiry. If a witness evades, it is the lawyer's responsibility to recognize the evasion and to bring the witness back to the mark, to flush out the whole truth with the tools of adversary examination.
>
> (409 U.S. 352 at 358–359 [1973])

In other words, in a courtroom, where the relationship is typically adversarial rather than cooperative, not all the standard conversational rules are in force or fully in force. In particular, it would be unrealistic to assume that the rule of Quantity will be consistently honored in a courtroom clash; therefore, it becomes the task of the cross-examiner to force the witness to produce all the relevant facts.

DISCUSSION QUESTIONS

Refer back to the dialogue quoted in *Bronston v. United States*. Because it is difficult to read the witness's second response as anything but a willful attempt to deceive, why should this case be treated differently from lying? Alternatively, why not even drop the demand that witnesses tell the truth and make it the responsibility of the lawyers to get at the truth itself (rather than just the whole truth) through "probing, prying, pressing" inquiry?

SUMMARY

In this chapter we have developed a rather complex picture of the way our language functions. In the process, we have distinguished three kinds or levels of acts that are performed when we employ language. We have also examined the rules associated with each kind or level of act. The following table summarizes this discussion:

THREE LEVELS OF LANGUAGE

Kinds of Acts	Governing Rules
A LINGUISTIC ACT is an act of saying something meaningful in a language. It is the basic act that is needed to make anything part of language.	Semantic rules (such as definitions) and syntactic rules (as in grammar).
A SPEECH ACT concerns the move a person makes *in* saying something. Different kinds of speech acts are indicated by the various verbs found in explicit performatives.	Speech act rules about special agents, formulas, circumstances, responses, and feelings appropriate to different kinds of speech acts, discovered by speech act analysis.
A CONVERSATIONAL ACT is a speaker's act of causing a standard kind of effect in the listener; it is what I do *by* saying something—for example, I persuade someone to do something.	Conversational rules (the Cooperative Principle; Quantity, Quality, Relevance, and Manner).

EXERCISE XV

1. It is late, and *A* is very hungry. *A* asks *B*, "When will dinner be ready?" Describe the linguistic act, the speech act, and some of the conversational acts this person may be performing in this context.

2. Someone is trying to solve the following puzzle: One of thirteen balls is heavier than the others, which are of equal weight. In no more than three weighings on a balance scale, determine which ball is the heavier one. The person is stumped, so someone says to her: "Begin by putting four balls in each pan of the scale." Describe the linguistic act, the speech act, and the conversational act of the person who makes this suggestion.

NOTES

[1] J. L. Austin used the phrase "locutionary act" to refer to a level of language closely related to what we refer to as a "linguistic act." See J. L. Austin, *How to Do Things with Words*, 2nd ed. (Cambridge, MA: Harvard University Press, 1975), 94–109.

[2] See, for example, J. L. Austin's *How to Do Things with Words*.

[3] An example of the continuous present is "I bet ten dollars every week in the lottery." Since this sentence is not used to make a bet, this sentence and others with the continuous present do not pass the thereby test or express explicit performatives.

[4] Austin calls speech acts "illocutionary acts." See *How to Do Things with Words*, 98–132.

[5] Although performative verbs name kinds of speech acts, not every kind of speech act has a corresponding performative verb. For example, insulting seems to be a kind of speech act, but "insult" is not a performative verb, because you cannot insult someone simply by saying, "I insult you." We might have had a convention that enabled us to insult people just by saying, "I insult you." In English, however, we do not.

[6] Supreme Court of New Hampshire, 1929, 84 N.H. 114, A. 641.

[7] This discussion of conversational rules and implications is based on Paul Grice's important essay, "Logic and Conversation," which appears as the second chapter of his *Studies in the Way of Words* (Cambridge, MA: Harvard University Press, 1989). To avoid British references that an American reader might find perplexing, we have sometimes altered Grice's wording.

[8] Grice states the Cooperative Principle in these words: "Make your conversational contribution such as is required, at the stage at which it occurs, by the accepted purpose or direction of the talk exchange in which you are engaged."

THE LANGUAGE OF ARGUMENT

Using the techniques developed in Chapter 2, this chapter will examine the use of language to formulate arguments and will provide methods to analyze genuine arguments in their richness and complexity. The first stage in analyzing an argument is the discovery of its basic structure. To do this, we will examine the words, phrases, and special constructions that indicate the premises and conclusions of an argument. The second stage is to explore the standards that arguments are supposed to meet. Here we will focus on validity, truth, and soundness. The third stage is the study of techniques used to protect an argument. These include guarding premises so that they are less subject to criticism, offering assurances concerning debatable claims, and discounting possible criticisms in advance.

ARGUMENT MARKERS

In Chapter 2, we saw that language is used for a great many different purposes. One important thing that we do with language is construct arguments. Arguments are constructed out of statements, but arguments are not just lists of statements. Here is a simple list of statements:

Socrates is a man.

All men are mortal.

Socrates is mortal.

This list is not an argument, because none of these statements is presented as a reason for any other statement. It is, however, simple to turn this list into an argument. All we have to do is to add the single word "therefore":

Socrates is a man.

All men are mortal.

Therefore, Socrates is mortal.

Now we have an argument. The word "therefore" converts these sentences into an argument by signaling that the statement following it is a *conclusion,* and the statement or statements that come before it are offered as *reasons* on behalf of this conclusion. The argument we have produced in this way is a good one, because the conclusion follows from the reasons stated on its behalf.

There are other ways of linking these sentences to form an argument. Here is one:

Since Socrates is a man,

and all men are mortal,

Socrates is mortal.

Notice that the word "since" works in roughly the opposite way that "therefore" does. The word "therefore" is a *conclusion marker,* because it indicates that the statement that follows it is a conclusion. In contrast, the word "since" is a *reason marker,* because it indicates that the following statement or statements are reasons. In our example, the conclusion comes at the end, but there is a variation on this. Sometimes the conclusion is given at the start:

Socrates is mortal, since all men are mortal and Socrates is a man.

"Since" flags reasons; the remaining connected statement is then taken to be the conclusion, whether it appears at the beginning or at the end of the sentence.

Many other terms are used to introduce an argumentative structure into language by marking either reasons or conclusions. Here is a partial list:

REASON MARKERS	CONCLUSION MARKERS
since	therefore
because	hence
for	thus
as	then

We shall call such terms "argument markers," because each presents one or more statements as part of an argument or backing for some other statement.

It is important to realize that these words are not always used as argument markers. The words "since" and "then" are often used as indicators of time, as in, "He's been an American citizen since 1973" and "He ate a hot dog, then a hamburger." The word "for" is often used as a preposition, as in "John works for IBM." Because some of these terms have a variety of meanings, it is not possible to identify argument markers in a mechanical way just by looking at words. It is necessary to examine the function of words in the context in which they occur. One test of whether a word is functioning as an argument marker in a particular sentence is whether you can substitute another argument marker without changing the meaning of the sentence. In the last example, it makes no sense to say, "John works since IBM."

Many *phrases* are also available to signal that an argument is being given. Here is just a small sample:

from which it follows that . . .

from which we may conclude that . . .

from which we see that . . .

which goes to show that . . .

which establishes that . . .

We can also indicate conclusions and reasons by using *argumentative performatives,* which we examined briefly in Chapter 2. If someone says, "I conclude that . . . ," the words that follow are given the status of a conclusion. More pretentiously, if someone says, "Here I base my argument on the claim that . . . ," what comes next has the status of a reason.

Examination of actual arguments will show that we have a great many ways of introducing an argumentative structure into our language by using the two forms of argument markers: reason markers and conclusion markers. The first, and in many ways the most important, step in analyzing an argument is to identify the conclusion and the reasons given on its behalf. We do this by paying close attention to these argument markers.

IF . . . , THEN . . .

If-then sentences, which are also called *conditionals,* often occur in arguments, but they do not present arguments by themselves. To see this, consider the following conditional:

> If the Dodgers improve their hitting, then they will win the
> Western Division.

The sentence between the "if" and the "then" is called the *antecedent* of the conditional. The sentence after the "then" is called its *consequent.* In uttering such a conditional, we are not asserting the truth of its antecedent, and we are not asserting the truth of its consequent either. Thus, the person who makes the above remark is not claiming that the Dodgers will win the Western Division. All she is saying is that *if* they improve their hitting, *then* they will win. Furthermore, she is not saying that they will improve their hitting. Because the speaker is not committing herself to either of these claims, she is not presenting an argument. This becomes clear when we contrast this conditional with a statement that does formulate an argument:

> **CONDITIONAL:** *If* the Dodgers improve their hitting, *then* they will win the
> Western Division.

> **ARGUMENT:** *Since* the Dodgers will improve their hitting, they will win the
> Western Division.

The sentence that follows the word "since" is asserted. That is why "since" is an argument marker, whereas the connective "if . . . then . . ." is not an argument marker.

Even though conditionals by themselves do not mark arguments, there is a close relationship between conditionals and arguments: Indicative conditionals provide *patterns* that can be converted into an argument whenever the antecedent is said to be true. (We also get an argument when the consequent is said to be false, but we will focus here on the simpler case of asserting the antecedent.) Thus, we often hear people argue in the following way:

> If inflation continues to grow, there will be an economic crisis. But inflation will certainly continue to grow, so an economic crisis is on the way.

The first sentence is an indicative conditional. It makes no claims one way or the other about whether inflation will grow or whether an economic crisis will occur. The next sentence asserts the antecedent of this conditional and then draws a conclusion signaled by the argument marker "so." We might say that when the antecedent of an indicative conditional is found to be true, the conditional can be *cashed in* for an argument.

Often the antecedent of a conditional is not asserted explicitly but is conversationally implied. When asked which player should be recruited for a team, the coach might just say, "If Deon is as good as our scouts say he is, then we ought to go for Deon." This conditional does not actually assert that Deon is as good as the scouts report. Nonetheless, it would be irrelevant and pointless for the coach to utter this conditional alone if he thought that the scouts were way off the mark. The coach might immediately add that he disagrees with the scouting reports. But unless the coach cancels the conversational implication in some way, it is natural to interpret him as giving an argument that we ought to pick Deon. In such circumstances, then, an indicative conditional can conversationally imply an argument, even though it does not state the argument explicitly.

This makes it easy to see why indicative conditionals are a useful feature of our language. By providing patterns for arguments, they prepare us to draw conclusions when the circumstances are right. Much of our knowledge of the world around us is contained in such conditionals. Here is an example: If your computer does not start, the plug might be loose. This is a useful piece of practical information, for when your computer does not start, you can immediately infer that the plug might be loose, so you know to check it out.

Other words function in similar ways. When your computer fails to start, a friend might say, "Either the plug is loose or you are in deep trouble." Now, if you also assert, "The plug is not loose," you can conclude that you are in deep trouble. "Either . . . or . . ." sentences thus provide patterns for arguments, just as conditionals do. However, neither if-then sentences nor either-or sentences by themselves explicitly assert enough to present a complete argument, so "if . . ., then . . ." and "either . . . or . . ." should not be labeled as argument markers.

Indicate which of the following italicized words or phrases is a reason marker, a conclusion marker, or neither.

1. He apologized, *so* you should forgive him.
2. He apologized. *Accordingly,* you should forgive him.
3. *Since* he apologized, you should forgive him.
4. *Provided that* he apologized, you should forgive him.
5. *In view of the fact that* he apologized, you should forgive him.
6. He apologized. *Ergo,* you should forgive him.
7. *Given that* he apologized, you should forgive him.
8. He apologized, and *because of that* you should forgive him.
9. *After* he apologizes, you should forgive him.
10. He apologized. *As a result,* you should forgive him.
11. *Seeing as* he apologized, you should forgive him.
12. He apologized. *For that reason alone,* you should forgive him.

Indicate whether each of the following sentences is an argument.

1. Charles went bald, and most men go bald.
2. Charles went bald because most men go bald.
3. My roommate likes to ski, so I do, too.
4. My roommate likes to ski, and so do I.
5. I have been busy since Tuesday.
6. I am busy, since my teacher assigned lots of homework.

ARGUMENTS IN STANDARD FORM

Because arguments come in all shapes and forms, it will help to have a standard way of presenting arguments. For centuries, logicians have used a format of the following kind:

(1) All men are mortal.
(2) Socrates is a man.
∴(3) Socrates is mortal. (from 1–2)

The reasons (or premises) are listed and numbered. Then a line is drawn below the premises. Next, the conclusion is numbered and written below the line. The symbol "∴", which is read "therefore," is then added to the left of the conclusion in order to indicate the relation between the premises and the conclusion. Finally, the premises from which the conclusion is supposed to be derived are indicated in parentheses. Arguments presented in this way are said to be in *standard form*.

The notion of a standard form is useful because it helps us see that the same argument can be expressed in different ways. For example, the following three sentences formulate the argument that was given in standard form above.

Socrates is mortal, since all men are mortal, and Socrates is a man.

All men are mortal, so Socrates is mortal, because he is a man.

All men are mortal, and Socrates is a man, which goes to show that Socrates is mortal.

More important, by putting arguments into standard form, we perform the most obvious, and in some ways most important, step in the analysis of an argument: the identification of its premises and conclusion.

EXERCISE III

Identify which of the following sentences expresses an argument. For each that does, (1) circle the argument marker (or markers), (2) indicate whether it is a reason marker or a conclusion marker, and (3) restate the argument in standard form.

1. Since Chicago is north of Boston, and Boston is north of Charleston, Chicago is north of Charleston.
2. Toward evening, clouds formed and the sky grew darker; then the storm broke.
3. Texas has a greater area than Topeka, and Topeka has a greater area than the Bronx Zoo, so Texas has a greater area than the Bronx Zoo.
4. Both houses of Congress may pass a bill, but the president may still veto it.
5. Other airlines will carry more passengers, because United Airlines is on strike.
6. Since Jesse James left town, taking his gang with him, things have been a lot quieter.
7. Things are a lot quieter, because Jesse James left town, taking his gang with him.
8. Witches float because witches are made of wood, and wood floats.
9. The hour is up, so you must hand in your exams.
10. Joe quit, because his boss was giving him so much grief.

SOME STANDARDS FOR EVALUATING ARGUMENTS

Not all arguments are good arguments; so, having identified an argument, the next task is to evaluate the argument. Evaluating arguments is a complex business. In fact, this entire book is aimed primarily at developing procedures for doing so. There are, however, certain basic terms used in evaluating arguments that should be introduced from the start. They are validity, truth, and soundness. Here they will be introduced informally. Later (in Chapters 6–7) they will be examined with more rigor.

VALIDITY

In some good arguments, the conclusion is said to follow from the premises. However, this commonsense notion of *following from* is hard to pin down precisely. The conclusion follows from the premises only when the content of the conclusion is related appropriately to the content of the premises, but which relations count as appropriate?

To avoid this difficult question, most logicians instead discuss whether an argument is *valid*. Calling something "valid" can mean a variety of things, but in this context validity is a technical notion. Here "valid" does not mean "good," and "invalid" does not mean "bad." This will be our definition of validity:

> An argument is *valid* if and only if it is not possible that all of its premises are true and its conclusion false.

Alternatively, one could say that its conclusion *must* be true if its premises are all true (or, again, that at least one of its premises *must* be false if its conclusion is false). The point is that a certain combination—true premises and a false conclusion—is ruled out as impossible.

The following argument passes this test for validity:

(1) All senators are paid.
(2) Sam is a senator.
∴ (3) Sam is paid. (from 1–2)

Clearly, if the two premises are both true, there is no way for the conclusion to fail to be true. To see this, just try to tell a coherent story in which every single senator is paid and Sam is a senator, but Sam is not paid. You can't do it.

Contrast this example with a different argument:

(1) All senators are paid.
(2) Sam is paid.
∴ (3) Sam is a senator. (from 1–2)

Here the premises and the conclusion are all in fact true, let's assume, but that is still not enough to make the argument valid, because validity concerns what is possible or impossible, not what happens to be true. This conclusion *could* be false even when the premises are true, for Sam *could* leave the Senate but still be paid for some other job, such as lobbyist. That possibility shows that this argument is invalid.

Another very common form of argument is called *modus ponens:*

> (1) If it is snowing, then the roads are slippery.
> (2) It is snowing.
> ∴(3) The roads are slippery. (from 1–2)

This argument is valid, because it is not possible for its premises to be true when its conclusion is false. We can show that by assuming that the conclusion is false and then reasoning backwards. Imagine that the roads are not slippery. Then there are two possibilities. Either it is snowing or it is not snowing. If it is not snowing, then the second premise is false. If it is snowing, then the first premise must be false, since we are supposing that it is snowing and that the roads are not slippery. Thus, at least one premise has to be false when the conclusion is false. Hence, this argument is valid.

This argument might seem similar to another:

> (1) If it is snowing, then the roads are slippery.
> (2) It is not snowing.
> ∴(3) The roads are not slippery. (from 1–2)

This argument is clearly invalid, because there are several ways for its premises to be true when its conclusion is false. It might have just stopped snowing or ice might make the roads slippery. Then the roads are slippery, so the conclusion is false, even if both premises are true.

Yet another form of argument is often called *process of elimination:*

> (1) Either Joe or Jack or Jim or Jerry committed the murder.
> (2) Joe didn't do it.
> (3) Jack didn't do it.
> (4) Jim didn't do it.
> ∴(5) Jerry committed the murder. (from 1–4)

The first premise asserts that at least one of these four suspects is guilty. That couldn't be true if all of the other premises were true and the conclusion were false, because that combination would exclude all four of these suspects. So this argument is valid.

Now compare this argument:

> (1) Either Joe or Jack or Jim or Jerry committed the murder.
> (2) Joe did it.
> ∴(3) Jerry did not commit the murder. (from 1–2)

To show that this argument is invalid, all we have to do is explain how the premises could be true and the conclusion false. Here's how: Joe and Jerry did it together. In that case, Jerry did it, so the conclusion is false; Joe also did it, so the second premise is true; and the first premise is true, because it says that at least one of these four suspects did it, and that is true when more than one of the suspects did it. That possibility of complicity, thus, makes this argument invalid.

We will explore many more forms of argument in Chapters 6–7. The goal for now is just to get a feel for how to determine validity. In all of these examples, an argument is said to be *valid* if and only if there is no possible situation in which its premises are true and its conclusion is false. You need to figure out whether there could be any situation like this in order to determine whether an argument is valid. If so, the argument is invalid. If not, it is valid.

This definition shows why validity is a valuable feature for an argument to possess: There can be no valid argument that leads one from true premises to a false conclusion. This should square with your commonsense ideas about reasoning. If you reason well, you should not be led from truth into error.

What are known as *deductive* arguments are put forward as meeting this standard of validity, so validity is one criterion for a good deductive argument. Other arguments—so-called *inductive* arguments—are not presented as meeting this standard. Roughly, an inductive argument is presented as providing strong support for its conclusion. The standards for evaluating inductive arguments will be examined in Chapter 8. For now we will concentrate on deductive arguments.

TRUTH

Although a deductive argument must be valid in order to be a good argument, validity is not enough. One reason is that an argument can be valid even when some (or all) of the statements it contains are false. For example:

> (1) No fathers are female.
> (2) Sam is a father.
> ∴(3) Sam is not female. (from 1–2)

Suppose that Sam has no children or that Sam is female, so premise 2 is false. That would be a serious defect in this argument. Nonetheless, this argument satisfies our definition of validity: If the premises were true, then the conclusion could not be false. There is no way that Sam could be female if Sam is a father and no fathers are female. This example makes it obvious that validity is not the same as truth. It also makes it obvious that another requirement of a good argument is that *all of its premises must be true*.

SOUNDNESS

We thus make at least two demands of a deductive argument:

1. The argument must be valid.

2. The premises must be true.

When an argument meets both of these standards, it is said to be *sound*. If it fails to meet either one or the other, then it is *unsound*. Thus, an argument is unsound if it is invalid, and it is also unsound if at least one of its premises is false.

	ALL PREMISES TRUE	AT LEAST ONE FALSE PREMISE
Valid	Sound	Unsound
Invalid	Unsound	Unsound

Soundness has one great benefit: A sound argument must have a true conclusion. We know this because its premises are true and, since it is valid, it is not possible that its premises are true and its conclusion is false. This is why people who seek truth want sound arguments, not merely valid arguments.

A TRICKY CASE

Our definition of validity yields a surprising result. Consider the following argument:

(1) Frogs are green.
(2) Frogs are not green.
∴(3) I am president. (from 1–2)

It is obviously not possible for both premises to be true, so it is also not possible that both premises are true when the conclusion is false. Consequently, this argument fits our definition of validity. So does any other argument whose premises cannot be true. Such arguments cannot ever take us from truths to falsehoods, because they never start with truths.

This weird example illustrates some of the ways in which the technical notion of *validity* differs from the commonsense notion of *following from*. The content of its premises has no relation to the content of the conclusion. Frogs have nothing to do with who is president. Hence, the conclusion does not follow from the premises. But that does not prevent the argument from being valid.

This example also shows the importance of distinguishing validity from soundness. Any argument whose premises cannot all be true is *valid*, no matter how ridiculous its conclusion. However, an argument cannot be *sound* if its premises can't be true, and a valid argument that is unsound cannot show that its conclusion is true. Consequently, this strange case won't cause any trouble.

EXERCISE IV

Indicate whether each of the following arguments is valid and whether it is sound. Explain your answers where necessary.

1. Most professors agree that they are paid too little, so they are.
2. David Letterman is over four feet tall, so he is over two feet tall.
3. Lee can't run a company right, because he can't do anything right.
4. Barack Obama is smart and good-looking, so he is smart.
5. Barack Obama is either a Democrat or a Republican, so he is a Democrat.
6. Since Jimmy Carter was president, he must have won an election.
7. Since Gerald Ford was president, he must have won an election.
8. Pat is either a mother or a father. If Pat is a mother, then she is a parent. If Pat is a father, he is a parent. So, either way, Pat is a parent. (Assume that this conclusion is true.)
9. People who live in the Carolinas live in either North Carolina or South Carolina. Hillary Clinton does not live in North Carolina or South Carolina. Hence, she does not live in the Carolinas.
10. If all of Illinois were in Canada, then Chicago would be in Canada. But Chicago is not in Canada. Therefore, not all of Illinois is in Canada.
11. If George lives in Crawford, then George lives in Texas. If George lives in Texas, then George lives in the United States. Hence, if George lives in Crawford, he lives in the United States.
12. There can't be a largest six-digit number, because six-digit numbers are numbers, and there is no largest number.

EXERCISE V

Assume that the following sentences are either true (T) or false (F) as indicated.

All my children are teenagers. (T)

All teenagers are students. (T)

All teenagers are my children. (F)

All my children are students. (T)

Using these assigned values, label each of the following arguments as (a) either valid or invalid, and (b) either sound or unsound.

1. All my children are teenagers.
   All teenagers are students.
   ───────────────────────
   ∴ All my children are students.

2. All my children are students.
   All teenagers are students.
   ───────────────────────
   ∴ All my children are teenagers.

(continued)

3. All teenagers are my children.
   All my children are students.

∴ All teenagers are students.

4. All teenagers are students.
   All my children are students.

∴ All my children are students.

EXERCISE VI

Indicate whether each of the following sentences is true. For those that are true, explain why they are true. For those that are false, show why they are false by giving a counterexample.

1. Every argument with a false conclusion is invalid.
2. Every argument with a false premise is invalid.
3. Every argument with a false premise and a false conclusion is invalid.
4. Every argument with a false premise and a true conclusion is invalid.
5. Every argument with true premises and a false conclusion is invalid.
6. Every argument with a true conclusion is sound.
7. Every argument with a false conclusion is unsound.

DISCUSSION QUESTION

Compare these arguments:

(1) Al Gore was president. (1*) George W. Bush was president.

∴(2) Frogs are frogs. ∴(2*) Frogs are frogs.

Are these arguments valid? Why or why not? Are they sound? Why or why not? Is anything wrong with the argument on the right side? If so, what?

A PROBLEM AND SOME SOLUTIONS

Although soundness guarantees a true conclusion, we usually expect even more from an argument than soundness. In the first place, an argument can be sound but trivially uninteresting:

(1) Nigeria is in Africa.

∴(2) Nigeria is in Africa. (from 1)

Here the premise is true. The argument is also valid, because the premise cannot be true without the conclusion (which repeats it) being true as well. Yet the argument is completely worthless as a proof that Nigeria is in Africa. The reason is that this argument is *circular*. We will examine circular arguments in detail in Chapter 16, but it should already be clear why such arguments are useless. If *A* is trying to justify something to *B* that *B* has doubts about, then citing the very matter in question will not do any good. Explanations of a phenomenon that cite that very phenomenon itself also fail to increase our understanding. In general, for *A* to argue successfully, *A* must marshal facts that *B* accepts and then show that they justify or explain the conclusion. In circular arguments, the worries about the conclusion immediately turn into worries about the premise as well.

Now, however, *A* seems to run into a problem. *A* cannot cite a proposition as a reason for *itself*, for that would be circular reasoning. If, however, *A* cites some *other* propositions as premises leading to the conclusion, then the question naturally arises why these premises should be accepted. Does *A* not have to present arguments for them as well? Yet if *A* does that, then *A* will introduce further premises that are also in need of proof, and so on indefinitely. It now looks as if every argument, to be successful, will have to be infinitely long.

This potential regress causes deep problems in theoretical philosophy. In everyday life, however, we try to avoid these problems by relying on shared beliefs—beliefs that will not be challenged. Beyond this, we expect people to believe us when we cite information that only we possess. But there are limits to this expectation, for we all know that people sometimes believe things that are false and sometimes lie about what they know to be true. This presents a practical problem: How can we present our reasons in a way that does not produce just another demand for an argument—a demand for more reasons? Here we use three main strategies:

1. *Assuring*: Indicating that there are backup reasons even though we are not giving them fully right now.
2. *Guarding*: Weakening our claims so that they are less subject to attack.
3. *Discounting*: Anticipating criticisms and dismissing them.

In these three ways we build a defensive perimeter around our premises. Each of these defenses is useful, but each can also be abused.

ASSURING

When will we want to give assurances about some statement we have made? If we state something that we know everyone believes, assurances are not necessary. For that matter, if everyone believes something, we may not even state it at all; we let others fill in this step in the argument. We offer assurances when we think that someone might doubt or challenge what we say.

There are many ways to give assurances. Sometimes we cite authorities:

Doctors agree . . .

Recent studies have shown . . .

An unimpeachable source close to the White House says . . .

It has been established that . . .

Here we indicate that authorities have these reasons without specifying what their reasons are. We merely indicate that good reasons exist, even if we ourselves cannot—or choose not to—spell them out. When the authority cited can be trusted, this is often sufficient, but authorities often can and should be questioned. This topic will be discussed more fully in Chapter 15.

Another way to give assurances is to comment on the strength of our own belief:

I'm certain that . . .

I'm sure that . . .

I can assure you that . . .

I'm not kidding. . . .

Over the years, I have become more and more convinced that . . .

Again, when we use these expressions, we do not explicitly present reasons, but we conversationally imply that there are reasons that back our assertions.

A third kind of assurance abuses the audience:

Everyone with any sense agrees that . . .

Of course, no one will deny that . . .

It is just common sense that . . .

There is no question that . . .

Nobody but a fool would deny that . . .

These assurances not only do not give any reason; they also suggest that there is something wrong with you if you ask for a reason. We call this the *trick of abusive assurances*.

Just as we can give assurances that something is true, we can also give assurances that something is false. For example,

It is no longer held that . . .

It is wholly implausible to suppose that . . .

No intelligent person seriously maintains that . . .

You would have to be pretty dumb to think that . . .

The last three examples clearly involve abusive assurances.

Although many assurances are legitimate, we as critics should always view assurances with some suspicion. People tend to give assurances only when they have good reasons to do so. Yet assuring remarks often mark the weakest parts of the argument, not the strongest. If someone says "I hardly need argue that . . . ," it is often useful to ask why she has gone to the trouble of saying this. When we distrust an argument—as we sometimes do—this is precisely the place to look for weakness. If assurances are used, they are used for some reason. Sometimes the reason is a good one. Sometimes, however, it is a bad one. In honest argumentation, assurances save time and simplify discussion. In a dishonest argument, they are used to paper over cracks.

GUARDING

Guarding represents a different strategy for protecting premises from attack. We reduce our claim to something less strong. Thus, instead of saying "all," we say "many." Instead of saying something straight out, we use a qualifying phrase, such as "it is likely that . . ." or "it is very possible that. . . ." Law school professors like the phrase "it is arguable that. . . ." This is wonderfully noncommittal, for it does not indicate how strong the argument is, yet it does get the statement into the discussion.

Broadly speaking, there are three main ways of guarding what we say:

1. Weakening the *extent* of what has been said: retreating from "all" to "most" to "a few" to "some," and so on.

2. Introducing *probability* phrases such as "It is virtually certain that . . . ," "It is likely that . . . ," "It might happen that . . . ," and so on.

3. Reducing our *level of commitment*: moving from "I know that . . ." to "I believe that . . ." to "I suspect that . . . ," and so on.

Such terms guard premises when they are used in place of stronger alternatives. "Madison probably quit the volleyball team" is weaker than "She definitely quit" but stronger than "She could have quit." Thus, if the context makes one expect a strong claim, such as "I know she quit," then it is guarding to say, "She probably quit." In contrast, if the context is one of speculating about who might have quit the team, then it is not guarding to say, "She probably quit." That is a relatively strong claim when others are just guessing. Thus, you need to pay careful attention to the context in order to determine whether a term has the function of guarding. When a term is used for guarding, you should be able to specify a stronger claim that the guarding term replaces and why that stronger term would be expected in the context.

Guarding terms and phrases are often legitimate and useful. If you want to argue that a friend needs fire insurance for her house, you do not need to claim that her house *will* burn down. All you need to claim is that there is a significant *chance* that her house will burn down. Your argument is better if you start with this weaker premise, because it is easier to defend and it is enough to support your conclusion.

If we weaken a claim sufficiently, we can make it completely immune to criticism. What can be said against a remark of the following kind: "There is some small chance that perhaps a few politicians are honest on at least some occasions"? You would have to have a *very* low opinion of politicians to deny this statement. On the other hand, if we weaken a premise too much, we pay a price. The premise no longer gives strong support to the conclusion.

The goal in using guarding terms is to find a middle way: We should weaken our premises sufficiently to avoid criticism, but not weaken them so much that they no longer provide strong enough evidence for the conclusion. Balancing these factors is one of the most important strategies in making and criticizing arguments.

Just as it was useful to zero in on assuring terms, so it is also useful to keep track of guarding terms. One reason is that, like assuring terms, guarding terms are easily corrupted. A common trick is to use guarding terms to *insinuate* things that cannot be stated explicitly in a conversation. Consider the effect of the following remark: "Perhaps the secretary of state has not been candid with the Congress." This does not actually say that the secretary of state has been less than candid with the Congress, but, by the rule of Relevance, clearly suggests it. Furthermore, it suggests it in a way that is hard to combat.

A more subtle device for corrupting guarding terms is to introduce a statement in a guarded form and then go on to speak as if it were not guarded at all.

> Perhaps the secretary of state has not been candid with the Congress. Of course, he has a right to his own views, but this is a democracy where officials are accountable to Congress. It is time for him to level with us.

The force of the guarding term "perhaps" that begins this passage disappears at the end, where it is taken for granted that the secretary of state has not been candid. This can be called *the trick of the disappearing guard*.

What is commonly called *hedging* is a sly device that operates in the opposite direction from our last example. With hedging, one shifts ground from a strong commitment to something weaker. Things, as they say, get "watered down" or "taken back." Strong statements made at one stage of an argument are later weakened without any acknowledgment that the position has thereby been changed in a significant way. A promise to *pass* a piece of legislation is later whittled down to a promise to *bring it to a vote*.

DISCOUNTING

The general pattern of discounting is to cite a possible criticism in order to reject it or counter it. Notice how different the following statements sound:

> The ring is beautiful, but expensive.

> The ring is expensive, but beautiful.

Both statements assert the same facts—that the ring is beautiful and that the ring is expensive. Both statements also suggest that there is some opposition between these facts. Yet these statements operate in different ways. We might use the first as a reason for *not* buying the ring; we can use the second as a reason *for* buying it. The first sentence acknowledges that the ring is beautiful, but overrides this by pointing out that it is expensive. In reverse fashion, the second statement acknowledges that the ring is expensive, but overrides this by pointing out that it is beautiful. Such assertions of the form "*A* but *B*" thus have four components:

1. The assertion of *A*
2. The assertion of *B*
3. The suggestion of some opposition between *A* and *B*
4. The indication that the truth of *B* is more important than the truth of *A*

The word "but" thus discounts the statement that comes before it in favor of the statement that follows it.

"Although" is also a discounting connective, but it operates in reverse fashion from the word "but." We can see this, using the same example:

Although the ring is beautiful, it is expensive.

Although the ring is expensive, it is beautiful.

Here the statement following the word "although" is discounted in favor of the connected statement.

A partial list of terms that typically function as discounting connectives includes the following conjunctions:

although	even if	but	nevertheless
though	while	however	nonetheless
even though	whereas	yet	still

These terms are not always used to discount. The word "still," for example, is used for discounting in (a) "He is sick; still, he is happy" but not in (b) "He is still happy" (or "Sit still"). We can tell whether a term is being used for discounting by asking whether the sentence makes sense when we substitute another discounting term: It makes sense to say, "He is sick, but he is happy." It makes no sense to say, "He is but happy." It is also illuminating to try to specify the objection that is being discounted. If you cannot say which objection is discounted, then the term is probably not being used for discounting.

The clearest cases of discounting occur when we are dealing with facts that point in different directions. We discount the facts that go against the position we wish to take. But discounting is often more subtle than this. We sometimes use discounting to block certain conversational implications of what we have said. This comes out in examples of the following kind:

Jones is an aggressive player, but he is not dirty.

The situation is difficult, but not hopeless.

The Republicans have the upper hand in Congress, but only for the
time being.

A truce has been declared, but who knows for how long?

Take the first example. There is no opposition between Jones being aggressive and his not being dirty. Both would be reasons to pick Jones for our team. However, the assertion that Jones is aggressive might *suggest* that he is dirty. The "but" clause discounts this suggestion without, of course, denying that Jones is aggressive.

The nuances of discounting terms can be subtle, and a correct analysis is not always easy. All the same, the role of discounting terms is often important. It can be effective in an argument to beat your opponents to the punch by anticipating and discounting criticisms before your opponents can raise them. The proper use of discounting can also help you avoid side issues and tangents.

Still, discounting terms, like the other argumentative terms we have examined, can be abused. People often spend time discounting *weak* objections to their views in order to avoid other objections that they know are harder to counter. Another common trick is to discount objections no one would raise. This is called *attacking straw men*. Consider the following remark: "A new building would be great, but it won't be free." This does not actually say that the speaker's opponents think we can build a new building for free, but it does conversationally imply that they think this, because otherwise it would be irrelevant to discount that objection. The speaker is thus trying to make the opponents look bad by putting words in their mouths that they would never say themselves. To counter tricks like this, we need to ask whether a discounted criticism is one that really would be raised, and whether there are stronger criticisms that should be raised.

EXERCISE VII

For each of the numbered words or expressions in the following sentences, indicate whether it is an argument marker, an assuring term, a guarding term, a discounting term, or none of these. For each argument marker, specify what the conclusion and the reasons are, and for each discounting term, specify what criticism is being discounted and what the response to this criticism is.

1. *Although* [1] no mechanism has been discovered, *most* [2] *researchers in the field agree* [3] that smoking *greatly increases the chances* [4] of heart disease.

2. *Since* [5] *historically* [6] public debt leads to inflation, *I maintain* [7] that, *despite* [8] recent trends, inflation will return.

3. *Take it from me* [9], there hasn't been a decent center fielder *since* [10] Joe DiMaggio.

4. *Whatever anyone tells you* [11], there is *little* [12] to the rumor that Queen Elizabeth II will step down *for* [13] her son, Prince Charles.

5. The early deaths of Janis Joplin and Jimi Hendrix *show* [14] that drugs are *really* [15] dangerous.

6. I *think* [16] he is out back somewhere.

7. I *think* [17], *therefore* [18] I am.

8. I *concede* [19] that the evidence is *hopelessly* [20] weak, *but* [21] I still think he is guilty.

9. I *deny* [22] that I had *anything* [23] to do with it.

10. The wind has shifted to the northeast, *which means* [24] that snow is *likely* [25].

EXERCISE VIII

1. Construct three new and interesting examples of statements containing assuring terms.

2. Do the same for guarding terms.

3. Do the same for discounting terms, and indicate which statement is being discounted in favor of the other.

4. Do the same for argument markers, and indicate what is presented as a reason for what.

EVALUATIVE LANGUAGE

Arguments are often filled with evaluation. The clearest cases of evaluative language occur when we say that something is *good* or *bad*, that some course of action is *right* or *wrong*, or that something *should* or *should not* (or *ought to* or *ought not to*) be done. The meaning of such evaluative terms is very controversial, but we can begin to understand evaluative language by asking which acts—linguistic, speech, and conversational—it is used to perform.

Evaluative terms often come into play when one is faced with a choice or decision. If you are deciding which shirt to buy, and a friend tells you, "That one's nice," your friend would normally be taken to be prescribing that you buy it. A passenger who says, "That's the wrong turn," is telling the driver not to turn that way. In such contexts, evaluative statements are action guiding—that is, they are used to direct someone to do or refrain from doing some action. Evaluative terms do not, however, have such direct prescriptive force when applied to things in remote times or places. Saying that it was wrong for James Earl Ray to assassinate Martin Luther King does not tell Ray not to do anything, for it is idle to address imperatives to people in the past. Someone who says that it would be wrong for the president to pursue a particular policy is not telling the president not to pursue it, unless she happens to be speaking or writing to the president. Nevertheless, even in cases where evaluations lack direct prescriptive force, they sometimes have prescriptive force indirectly. Calling Ray's past action bad or wrong might, through analogy, be a way of telling someone not to do future acts like it. Evaluative language is, in these ways, used to perform speech acts of *prescribing action*.

Evaluative language is also often used for other speech acts. When a fan says, "That band is great," this usually expresses admiration for their music and a desire to hear more. After a meal, someone who announces, "That was horrible," is often expressing aversion or even disgust at the food. To say, "That's too bad," is often to express disappointment or sadness. In these ways, evaluative language is used to perform speech acts of *expressing emotion*.

These speech acts do not, however, exhaust the meaning of evaluative language. For one thing, evaluative language is typically also used to bring about certain effects. When a mother tells her son that that he ought to keep his promises, she not only prescribes that her son not lie; she also standardly intends to have an effect on his behavior—she tries to get him to keep his promises. And when war protesters express their disapproval by calling a war immoral, they are normally trying to get anyone listening to feel the same way about the war. Thus, evaluative language is used to perform conversational acts of *changing people's behavior and feelings*.

There is still more to the meaning of evaluative language. Our lives consist of a constant stream of choices of varying kinds and of various levels of importance. Because we often have to make these choices or decisions under time pressure, it is not possible to make all of them on a case-by-case basis. It is for this reason, among others, that we come to rely on *standards* in making evaluations. In most cases, we call something "good" or "right" because we believe that it meets or satisfies relevant standards, and we call something "bad" or "wrong" because we believe that it violates some relevant standard. This is, roughly, the content of the *linguistic* act of uttering evaluative language.

On this account, calling something good or bad by itself can be fairly empty of content. Such remarks gain content—sometimes a very rich content—by virtue of the particular standards they invoke. This explains why the word "good" can be applied to so many different kinds of things. When we say that Hondas are good cars, we are probably applying standards that involve reliability, efficiency, comfort, and so on. We call someone a good firefighter because we think the person is skilled at the tasks of a firefighter, is motivated to do those tasks, works well with other firefighters, and so on. Our standards for calling someone an ethically good person concern honesty, generosity, fairness, and so on. The standards we have for calling something a good car, a good firefighter, and an (ethically) good person have little in common. Even so, the word "good" functions in the same way in all three cases: It invokes the standards that are relevant in a given context and indicates that something adequately satisfies these standards.

Because evaluative statements invoke standards, they stand in contrast to utterances that *merely* express personal feelings. If I say that I like a particular singer, then I am expressing a personal taste. Unless I were being accused of lying or self-deception, it would be very odd for someone to reply, "No, you don't like that singer." On the other hand, if I call someone a good singer (or the best singer in years), then I am going beyond expressing my personal tastes. I am saying something that others may accept or reject. Of course, the standards for judging singers may be imprecise, and they may shift from culture to culture. Still, to call someone a good singer is to evaluate that person as a singer, which goes beyond merely expressing feelings, because it invokes standards and indicates that the person in question meets them.

The words "good" and "bad" are general evaluative terms. Other evaluative terms are more restrictive in their range of application. The word "delicious" is usually used for evaluating the taste of foods; it means "good-tasting." A *sin* is a kind of wrong action, but, more specifically, it is an action that is wrong according to religious standards. A *bargain* has a good price. An *illegal* action is one that is legally wrong. Our language contains a great many specific terms of evaluation like these. Here are a few more examples:

| beautiful | dangerous | wasteful | sneaky | cute |
| murder | prudent | nosy | sloppy | smart |

Each of these words expresses either a positive or a negative evaluation of a quite specific kind.

Positive and negative evaluations can be subtle. Consider a word like "clever." It presents a positive evaluation in terms of quick mental ability. In contrast, "cunning" often presents a negative evaluation of someone for misusing mental abilities. It thus makes a difference which one of these words we choose. It also makes a difference where we apply them. When something is supposed to be profound and serious, it is insulting to call it merely clever. Prayers, for example, should not be clever.

Sometimes seemingly innocuous words can shift evaluative force. The word "too" is the perfect example of this. This word introduces a negative evaluation, sometimes turning a positive quality into a negative one. Compare the following sentences:

John is smart.	John is too smart.
John is honest.	John is too honest.
John is ambitious.	John is too ambitious.
John is nice.	John is too nice.
John is friendly.	John is too friendly.

The word "too" indicates an excess, and thereby contains a criticism. If you look at the items in the second column, you will see that the criticism is sometimes rather brutal—for example, calling someone "too friendly."

The difference between an evaluative term and a descriptive term is not always obvious. To see this, consider the terms "homicide" and "murder." The words are closely related but do not mean the same thing. "Homicide" is a descriptive term meaning "the killing of a human being." "Murder" is an evaluative term meaning, in part at least, "the *wrongful* killing of a human being." It takes more to show that something is a murder than it does to show that something is a homicide.

Just as it is easy to miss evaluative terms because we fail to recognize the evaluative component built into their meanings, it is also possible to interpret neutral words as evaluative because of positive or negative associations that the words might evoke. The word "nuclear," for example, has bad connotations for some people because of its association with bombs and wars, but the word itself is purely descriptive. To call people nuclear scientists is not to say that they are bad in any way. The test for an evaluative term is this: Does the word mean that something is good or bad (right or wrong) in a particular way?

Farcus
by David Waisglass
Gordon Coulthart

**"Let's hope corporate communications
can put a positive spin on this."**

SPIN DOCTORING

Evaluation need not be problematic, but it is often hidden and abused, most notoriously in *spin doctoring*. The expression "spin doctor" seems to combine two metaphors. The first concerns putting the right spin on things—that is, presenting things in ways that make them look good or bad, depending on how one wants them to be perceived. The second concerns doctoring things up to accomplish this. Spin doctoring often involves trying to find the right way of labeling something.

A classic example comes from Shakespeare's play, *Julius Caesar* (act III, scene i). After Brutus and others killed Caesar, Brutus announced, "So are we Caesar's friends that have abridged his time of fearing death." By redescribing his act in terms of a minor benefit to Caesar, Brutus tries to make people see his treacherous act of killing his friend as a generous act of doing his friend a favor!

Spin doctoring is still rampant in politics today. Referring to the Iraq war, those who favored it spoke of the "liberation" of Iraq, whereas those who opposed it called it an "invasion" or an "occupation." Each label involves evaluation, so the disagreement over what to call it was really about how to evaluate it. This verbal dispute is not purely verbal, because the label can affect attitudes and behaviors by associating the Iraq war with good military actions (liberations) or bad military actions (invasions and occupations).

Often spin doctoring involves attributing questionable views or attitudes to opponents. Supporters of President Bush sometimes refer to his detractors as "the blame-America-first crowd" and describe their policies for getting out of Iraq as "cut and run." These negative labels are applied even to policies, such as partial staged redeployment, that are far from cowardly in the way suggested by "cut and run." Similarly, in 2006, conservative commentator David Brooks described opposition to Joe Lieberman's campaign as a "liberal inquisition." Stephen Colbert lampooned this label in a segment of "The Word" where he joked that, if incumbents like Lieberman continued to be attacked so harshly, then they would actually be forced to defend their records. Colbert concluded, "There is only one word for that—inquisition." But the sidebar read "democracy." Sometimes parody is the most effective response to spin doctoring.

Of course, liberal democrats are often just as guilty of spin doctoring. When discussing a measure that would repeal a large number of environmental regulations, President Clinton sarcastically referred to it as the "Polluter's Bill of Rights"—not exactly a generous way of describing a bill based on the belief that environmental regulations had gone too far. And, to quote Stephen Colbert again, "Affirmative action is a prime example of the Leftist campaign to make ideas seem less dangerous than they are, through the strategic use of positive words. Think about it. How can something be bad if it is 'affirmative'? and how can we ignore it if is it 'action'?" [from *I Am America (and So Can You!)*, New York: Grand Central Publishing, 2007, p. 174].

Spin doctoring like this makes it harder to discuss the real benefits and costs of such laws and policies, because nobody wants to argue against liberation or affirmation or in favor of invasion, inquisition, or pollution. The task of critical analysis is to see through such slogans to the important issues that lie behind them, so that we can intelligently address the real values at stake.

EXERCISE IX

Indicate whether the following italicized terms are positively evaluative (E+), negatively evaluative (E–), or simply descriptive (D). Remember, the evaluations need not be moral evaluations.

1. Janet is an *excellent* golfer.
2. The group was playing very *loudly*.
3. The group was playing *too* loudly.
4. William was *rude* to his parents.
5. William *shouted* at his parents.
6. They mistakenly turned *right* at the intersection.
7. *Fascists* ruled Italy for almost twenty years.
8. That's a *no-no*.
9. *Bummer*.
10. Debbie *lied*.
11. Debbie *said something false*.
12. Joe *copped out*.
13. Jake is a *bully*.
14. Mary Lou was a *gold medalist*.
15. She is *sick*.
16. He suffers from a hormonal *imbalance*.

EXERCISE X

For each of the following sentences, construct two others—one that reverses the evaluative force, and one that is as neutral as possible. The symbol "0" stands for neutral, "+" for positive evaluative force, and "–" for negative evaluative force. Try to make as little change as possible in the descriptive content of the sentence.

Example: – Professor Conrad is rude.

+ Professor Conrad is uncompromisingly honest in his criticisms.

0 Professor Conrad often upsets people with his criticisms.

1. – Larry is a lazy lout.
2. + Brenda is brave.
3. – Sally is a snob.
4. + Bartlett is a blast.
5. – George is a goody-goody.
6. – Walter is a weenie.
7. + Carol is caring.
8. – Bill is bossy.
9. – Oprah is opinionated.
10. – This is a Mickey Mouse exercise.

EXERCISE XI

Be a spin doctor yourself by writing upbeat, good-sounding titles or descriptions for the following proposals. Remember that, as a professional spin doctor, you should be able to make things you personally hate sound good.

1. Imposing a $1,000 fee on graduating seniors
2. Requiring all students to participate in a twenty-one-meal-per-week food plan

3. Abolishing coed dormitories

4. Abolishing fraternities

5. Requiring women students to return to their dormitories by midnight (such rules were once quite common)

6. Abolishing failing grades

7. Restoring failing grades

8. Requiring four years of physical education

9. Abolishing intercollegiate football

10. Introducing a core curriculum in Western civilization

11. Abolishing such a curriculum

12. Abolishing faculty tenure

DISCUSSION QUESTIONS

1. What precisely does "That's too bad" mean?

2. In the Democratic presidential candidate debate on September 26, 2007, Representative Dennis Kucinich was asked the following question by MSNBC correspondent Tim Russert. Was Kucinich's answer spin doctoring? Was it legitimate or illegitimate? Why?

    RUSSERT: . . . Congressman Kucinich, when you were mayor of Cleveland, you let Cleveland go into bankruptcy, the first time that happened since the Depression. The voters of Cleveland rewarded you by throwing you out of office and electing a Republican mayor of Cleveland. How can you claim that you have the ability to manage the United States of America, when you let Cleveland go bankrupt?

    REP. KUCINICH: You know, Tim, that was NBC's story. Now I want the people to know what the real story was. I took a stand on behalf of the people of Cleveland to save a municipal electric system. The banks and the utilities in Cleveland, the private utilities, were trying to force me to sell that system. And so on December 15th, 1978, I told the head of the biggest bank, when he told me I had to sell the system in order to get the city's credit renewed, that I wasn't going to do it. . . . I put my job on the line. How many people would be willing to put their job on the line in the face of pressure from banks and utilities? As this story gets told, people will want me to be their next president because they'll see in me not only the ability to take a stand, but the ability to live with integrity.

HOW TO EVALUATE ARGUMENTS: DEDUCTIVE STANDARDS

After isolating, laying out, and filling in an argument, the next step is to determine whether that uncovered argument is any good. This assessment, like other evaluations, requires standards. There are two main standards for evaluating arguments: the deductive standard of validity and the inductive standard of strength. Part II (which includes Chapters 6 and 7) will investigate the deductive standard of validity. Part III (which includes Chapters 8–12) will then explore the inductive standard of strength.

We already saw in Chapter 3 that an argument is valid in our technical sense if and only if it is not possible that its premises are true and its conclusion false. That standard sounds simple, but it is not so easy to say how to determine whether this combination of truth values is or is not possible in a particular case. Sometimes the validity of an argument can be seen simply by looking at the premises and conclusion viewed as whole propositions. That is the approach of propositional (or sentential) logic, which is the topic of Chapter 6. Another possibility is that the validity of an argument can be seen only by looking inside premises and conclusions to their parts, including their subjects and predicates. That is the approach of categorical (or syllogistic) logic, which is the topic of Chapter 7.

These relatively simple examples of formal logic do not, of course, exhaust the possibilities. There are many more kinds of formal logic. Many arguments remain valid, even though their validity is not captured by either propositional or categorical logic. That creates problems that we will face throughout Chapters 6 and 7. Still, by exploring some simple ways in which arguments can be valid by virtue of their form alone, we can gain greater insight into the nature of validity and, thereby, into the standards for assessing arguments.

6

PROPOSITIONAL LOGIC

This chapter begins our investigation of evaluating arguments by means of formal deductive logic. The first part of the chapter will show how the crucial standard of validity, which was introduced in Chapter 3, can be developed rigorously in one area—what is called propositional logic. This branch of logic deals with connectives such as "and" and "or," which allow us to build up compound propositions from simpler ones. Throughout most of the chapter, the focus will be theoretical rather than immediately practical. It is intended to provide insight into the concept of validity by examining it in an ideal setting. The chapter will close with a discussion of the relationship between the ideal language of symbolic logic and the language we ordinarily speak.

THE FORMAL ANALYSIS OF ARGUMENTS

When we carry out an informal analysis of an argument, we pay close attention to the key words used to present the argument and then ask ourselves whether these key terms have been used properly. So far, we have no exact techniques for answering the question of whether a word is used correctly. We rely, instead, on linguistic instincts that, on the whole, are fairly good.

In a great many cases, people can tell whether an argument marker, such as "therefore," is used correctly in indicating that one claim follows from another. However, if we go on to ask the average intelligent person *why* one claim follows from the other, he or she will probably have little to say except, perhaps, that it is just obvious. In short, it is often easy to see *that* one claim follows from another, but to explain *why* can be difficult. The purpose of this chapter is to provide such an explanation for some arguments.

This quality of "following from" is elusive, but it is related to the technical notion of validity, which was introduced in Chapter 3. The focus of our attention will be largely on the *concept* of validity. We are not, for the time being at least, interested in whether this or that argument is valid; we want to understand validity itself. To this end, the arguments we will examine are so simple that you will not be able to imagine anyone not understanding them at a glance. Who needs logic to deal with arguments of this kind? There is, however, good reason for dealing with simple—trivially simple—arguments at the start. The analytic approach to a complex issue is first to break it down into subissues, repeating the process until we reach problems simple enough to be solved. After these simpler problems are solved, we can reverse the process and construct solutions to larger and more complex problems. When done correctly, the *result* of such an analytic process may seem dull and obvious—and it often is. The *discovery* of such a process, in contrast, often demands the insight of genius.

The methods of analysis to be discussed here are *formal* in a specific way. In Chapter 3, we gave the following argument as an example of a valid argument: "All Senators are paid, and Sam is a Senator, so Sam is paid." The point could have been made just as well with many similar examples: (a) "All Senators are paid, and Sally is a Senator, so Sally is paid." (b) "All plumbers are paid, and Sally is a plumber, so Sally is paid." (c) "All plumbers are dirty, and Sally is a plumber, so Sally is dirty." These arguments are all valid (though not all are sound). Thus, we can change the person we are talking about, the group that we say the person is in, and the property that we ascribe to the person and to the group, all without affecting the validity of the argument at all. That flexibility shows that the validity of this argument does not depend on the particular content of its premises and conclusion. Instead, the validity of this argument results solely from its form. Formal validity of this kind is what formal logics try to capture.

BASIC PROPOSITIONAL CONNECTIVES

CONJUNCTION

The first system of formal logic that we will examine concerns propositional (or sentential) connectives. *Propositional connectives* are terms that allow us to build new propositions from old ones, usually combining two or more propositions into a single proposition. For example, given the propositions "John is tall" and "Harry is short," we can use the term "and" to *conjoin* them, forming a single compound proposition: "John is tall and Harry is short."

Let us look carefully at the simple word "and" and ask how it functions. "And" is a curious word, for it does not seem to stand for anything, at least in the way in which a proper name ("Churchill") and a common noun ("dog") seem to stand for things. Instead of asking what this word stands for, we can ask a different question: What *truth conditions* govern this connective? That is, under what conditions are propositions containing this connective true? To answer this question, we imagine every possible way in which the component propositions can be true or false. Then, for each combination, we decide what truth value to assign to the entire proposition. This may sound complicated, but an example will make it clear:

John is tall.	Harry is short.	John is tall and Harry is short.
T	T	T
T	F	F
F	T	F
F	F	F

Here the first two columns cover every possibility for the component propositions to be either true or false. The third column states the truth value of the whole proposition for each combination. Clearly, the conjunction of two propositions is true if both of the component propositions are true; otherwise, it is false.

Our reflections have not depended on the particular propositions in our example. We could have been talking about dinosaurs instead of people, and we still would have come to the conclusion that the conjunction of two propositions is true if both propositions are true, but false otherwise. This neglect of the particular content of propositions is what makes our account *formal*.

To reflect the generality of our concerns, we can drop the reference to particular sentences altogether and use variables instead. Just as the lowercase letters "x," "y," and "z" can be replaced by any numbers in mathematics, so we can use the lowercase letters "p," "q," "r," "s," and so on as variables that can be replaced by any propositions in logic. We will also use the symbol "&" (called an *ampersand*) for "and."

Consider the expression "p & q." Is it true or false? There is obviously no answer to this question. This is not because we do not know what "p" and "q" stand for, for in fact "p" and "q" do not stand for any proposition at all. Just as "$x + y$" is not any particular number in mathematics, so "p & q" is not a proposition. Instead, "p & q" is a pattern for a whole series of propositions. To reflect this, we will say that "p & q" is a *propositional form*. It is a pattern, or form, for a whole series of propositions, including "John is tall and Harry is short" as well as many other propositions.

To specify precisely which propositions have the form "p & q," we need a little technical terminology. The central idea is that we can pass from a proposition to a propositional form by replacing propositions with propositional variables.

Proposition	*Propositional Form*
John is tall and Harry is short.	p & q

When we proceed in the opposite direction by uniformly substituting propositions for propositional variables, we get what we will call a *substitution instance* of that propositional form.

Propositional Form	*Substitution Instance*
p & q	Roses are red and violets are blue.

Thus, "John is tall and Harry is short" and "Roses are red and violets are blue" are both substitution instances of the propositional form "*p* & *q*."

To get clear about these ideas, it is important to notice that "*p*" is also a propositional form, with *every* proposition, including "Roses are red and violets are blue," among its substitution instances. There is no rule against substituting compound propositions for propositional variables. Perhaps a bit more surprisingly, our definitions allow "Roses are red and roses are red" to be a substitution instance of "*p* & *q*." This example makes sense if you compare it to variables in mathematics. Using only positive integers, how many solutions are there to the equation "$x + y = 4$"? There are three: $3 + 1$, $1 + 3$, and $2 + 2$. The fact that "$2 + 2$" is a solution to "$x + y = 4$" shows that "2" can be substituted for both "x" and "y" in the same solution. That's just like allowing "Roses are red" to be substituted for both "*p*" and "*q*," so that "Roses are red and roses are red" is a substitution instance of "*p* & *q*" in propositional logic.

In general, then, we get a substitution instance of a propositional form by uniformly replacing the same variable with the same proposition throughout, but different variables do not have to be replaced with different propositions. The rule is this:

Different variables may be replaced with the same proposition, but different propositions may not be replaced with the same variable.

According to this rule:

"Roses are red and violets are blue" is a substitution instance of "*p* & *q*."

"Roses are red and violets are blue" is also a substitution instance of "*p*."

"Roses are red and roses are red" is a substitution instance of "*p* & *q*."

"Roses are red and roses are red" is a substitution instance of "*p* & *p*."

"Roses are red and violets are blue" is *not* a substitution instance of "*p* & *p*."

"Roses are red" is *not* a substitution instance of "*p* & *p*."

We are now in a position to give a perfectly general definition of conjunction with the following truth table, using propositional variables where previously we used specific propositions.

p	*q*	*p* & *q*
T	T	T
T	F	F
F	T	F
F	F	F

There is no limit to the number of propositions we can conjoin to form a new proposition. "Roses are red and violets are blue; sugar is sweet and so are you" is a substitution instance of "*p* & *q* & *r* & *s*." We can also use parentheses to group propositions. This last example could be treated as a substitution instance of "$(p \& q) \& (r \& s)$"—that is, as a conjunction of two conjunctions. Later we will see that, just as in mathematics, parentheses can make an important difference to the meaning of a total proposition.

One cautionary note: The word "and" is not always used to connect two distinct sentences. Sometimes a sentence has to be rewritten for us to see that it is equivalent to a sentence of this form. For example,

Serena and Venus are tennis players.

is simply a short way of saying

Serena is a tennis player, and Venus is a tennis player.

At other times, the word "and" is *not* used to produce a conjunction of propositions. For example,

Serena and Venus are playing each other.

does *not* mean that

Serena is playing each other, and Venus is playing each other.

That does not even make sense, so the original sentence cannot express a conjunction of two propositions. Instead, it expresses a single proposition about two people taken as a group. Consequently, it should not be symbolized as "$p \& q$." Often, unfortunately, it is unclear whether a sentence expresses a conjunction of propositions or a single proposition about a group. The sentence

Serena and Venus are playing tennis.

could be taken either way. Maybe Serena and Venus are playing each other. If that is what it means, then the sentence expresses a single proposition about a group, so it should not be symbolized as "$p \& q$." But maybe Serena is playing one match, while Venus is playing another. If that would make it true, then the sentence expresses a conjunction of propositions, so it may be symbolized as "$p \& q$."

When a sentence containing the word "and" expresses the conjunction of two propositions, we will say that it expresses a *propositional conjunction*. When a sentence containing "and" does not express the conjunction of two propositions, we will say that it expresses a *nonpropositional conjunction*. In this chapter we are concerned only with sentences that express propositional conjunctions. A sentence should be translated into the symbolic form "$p \& q$" only if it expresses a propositional conjunction. There is no mechanical procedure that can be followed to determine whether a certain sentence expresses a conjunction of two propositions. You must think carefully about what the sentence means and about the context in which that sentence is used. This takes practice.

EXERCISE I

The proposition "The night is young, and you're so beautiful" is a substitution instance of which of the following propositional forms?

1. p
2. q
3. $p \,\&\, q$
4. $p \,\&\, r$

5. $p \,\&\, q \,\&\, r$
6. $p \,\&\, p$
7. p or q

EXERCISE II

Which of the following propositions is a substitution instance of "$p \,\&\, q \,\&\, q$"?

1. The night is young, and you're so beautiful, and my flight leaves in thirty minutes.
2. The night is young, and you're so beautiful, and my flight leaves in thirty minutes, and my flight leaves in thirty minutes.
3. You're so beautiful, and you're so beautiful, and you're so beautiful.

EXERCISE III

For each of the following propositions, give three different propositional forms of which that proposition is a substitution instance.

1. The night is young, and you're so beautiful, and my flight leaves in thirty minutes.
2. The night is young, and you're so beautiful, and you're so beautiful.

EXERCISE IV

Indicate whether each of the following sentences expresses a propositional conjunction or a nonpropositional conjunction—that is, whether or not it expresses a conjunction of two propositions. If the sentence could be either, then specify a context in which it would naturally be used to express a propositional conjunction and a different context in which it would naturally be used to express a nonpropositional conjunction.

1. A Catholic priest married John and Mary.
2. Fred had pie and ice cream for dessert.
3. The winning presidential candidate rarely loses both New York and California.

4. Susan got married and had a child.

5. Jane speaks both French and English.

6. Someone who speaks both French and English is bilingual.

7. Ken and Naomi are two of my best friends.

8. Miranda and Nick cooked dinner.

9. I doubt that John is poor and happy.

Now we can look at an argument involving conjunction. Here is one that is ridiculously simple:

Harry is short and John is tall.

∴ Harry is short.

This argument is obviously valid. But why is it valid? Why does the conclusion follow from the premise? The answer in this case seems obvious, but we will spell it out in detail as a guide for more difficult cases. Suppose we replace these particular propositions with propositional forms, using a different variable for each distinct proposition throughout the argument. This yields what we will call an *argument form*. For example:

$p \,\&\, q$

∴ p

This is a pattern for endlessly many arguments, each of which is called a substitution instance of this argument form. Every argument that has this general form will also be valid. It really does not matter which propositions we put into this schema; the resulting argument will be valid—so long as we are careful to substitute the same proposition for the same variable throughout.

Let's pursue this matter further. If an argument has true premises and a false conclusion, then we know at once that it is invalid. But in saying that an argument is *valid*, we are not only saying that it does not have true premises and a false conclusion; we are also saying that the argument *cannot* have a false conclusion when the premises are true. Sometimes this is true because the argument has a structure or form that rules out the very possibility of true premises and a false conclusion. We can appeal to the notion of an argument form to make sense of this idea. A somewhat more complicated truth table will make this clear:

p	q	PREMISE $p \,\&\, q$	CONCLUSION p
T	T	T	T
T	F	F	T
F	T	F	F
F	F	F	F

The first two columns give all the combinations for the truth values of the propositions that we might substitute for "*p*" and "*q*." The third column gives the truth value of the premise for each of these combinations. (This column is the same as the definition for "&" given above.) Finally, the fourth column gives the truth value for the conclusion for each combination. (Here, of course, this merely involves repeating the first column. Later on, things will become more complicated and interesting.) If we look at this truth table, we see that no matter how we make substitutions for the variables, we never have a case in which the premise is true and the conclusion is false. In the first line, the premise is true and the conclusion is also true. In the remaining three lines, the premise is not true, so the possibility of the premise being true and the conclusion false does not arise.

Here it is important to remember that a valid argument can have false premises, for one proposition can follow from another proposition that is false. Of course, an argument that is sound cannot have a false premise, because a sound argument is defined as a valid argument with true premises. But our subject here is validity, not soundness.

Let's summarize this discussion. In the case we have examined, validity depends on the form of an argument and not on its particular content. A first principle, then, is this:

An *argument* is valid if it is an instance of a valid argument form.

Hence, the argument "Harry is short and John is tall; therefore, Harry is short" is valid because it is an instance of the valid argument form "*p* & *q*; ∴ *p*."

Next we must ask what makes an argument form valid. The answer to this is given in this principle:

An argument *form* is valid if and only if it has no substitution instances in which the premises are true and the conclusion is false.

We have just seen that the argument form "*p* & *q*; ∴ *p*" passes this test. The truth table analysis showed that. Incidentally, we can use the same truth table to show that the following argument is valid:

John is tall.	p
Harry is short.	q
∴ John is tall and Harry is short.	∴ p & q

The argument on the left is a substitution instance of the argument form on the right. A glance at the truth table will show that there can be no cases for which all the premises could be true and the conclusion false. This pretty well covers the logical properties of conjunction.

Notice that we have not said that *every* argument that is valid is so in virtue of its form. There may be arguments in which the conclusion follows from the premises but we cannot show how the argument's validity is a matter of logical form. There are, in fact, some obviously valid arguments that have yet to be shown to be valid in terms of their form. Explaining validity by means of logical form has long been an ideal of logical theory, but there are arguments—many of them quite common—where this ideal has yet to be adequately fulfilled. Many arguments in mathematics fall into this category. At present, however, we will only consider arguments in which the strategy we used for analyzing conjunction continues to work.

EXERCISE V

Are the following arguments valid by virtue of their propositional form? Why or why not?

1. Donald owns a tower in New York and a palace in Atlantic City. Therefore, Donald owns a palace in Atlantic City.
2. Tom owns a house. Therefore, Tom owns a house and a piece of land.
3. Ilsa is tall. Therefore, Ilsa is tall, and Ilsa is tall.
4. Bernie has a son and a daughter. Bernie has a father and a mother. Therefore, Bernie has a son and a mother.
5. Mary got married and had a child. Therefore, Mary had a child and got married.
6. Bess and Katie tied for MVP. Therefore, Bess tied for MVP.

EXERCISE VI

For each of the following claims, determine whether it is true or false. Defend your answers.

1. An argument that is a substitution instance of a valid argument form is always valid.
2. An argument that is a substitution instance of an invalid argument form is always invalid.
3. An invalid argument is always a substitution instance of an invalid argument form.

DISCUSSION QUESTION

Is a valid argument always a substitution instance of a valid argument form? Why or why not?

DISJUNCTION

Just as we can form a conjunction of two propositions by using the connective "and," we can form a *disjunction* of two propositions by using the connective "or," as in the following compound sentence:

John will win or Harry will win.

Again, it is easy to see that the truth of this whole compound proposition depends on the truth of the component propositions. If they are both false, then the compound proposition is false. If just one of them is true, then the compound proposition is true. But suppose they are both true. What shall we say then?

Sometimes when we say "either-or," we seem to rule out the possibility of both. When a waiter approaches your table and tells you, "Tonight's dinner will be chicken or steak," this suggests that you cannot have both. In other cases, however, it does not seem that the possibility of both is ruled out—for example, when we say to someone, "If you want to see tall mountains, go to California or Colorado."

One way to deal with this problem is to say that the English word "or" has two meanings: one *exclusive*, which rules out both, and one *inclusive*, which does not rule out both. Another solution is to claim that the English word "or" always has the inclusive sense, but utterances with "or" sometimes conversationally imply the exclusion of both because of special features of certain contexts. It is, for example, our familiarity with common restaurant practices that leads us to infer that we cannot have both when the waiter says, "Tonight's dinner will be chicken or steak." If we may have both, then the waiter's utterance would not be as informative as is required for the purpose of revealing our options, so it would violate Grice's conversational rule of Quantity (as discussed in Chapter 2). That explains why the waiter's utterance seems to exclude both.

Because such explanations are plausible, and because it is simpler as well as traditional to develop propositional logic with the inclusive sense of "or," we will adopt that inclusive sense. Where necessary, we will define the exclusive sense using the inclusive sense as a starting point. Logicians symbolize disjunctions using the connective "$\vee$" (called a *wedge*). The truth table for this connective has the following form:

p	q	$p \vee q$
T	T	T
T	F	T
F	T	T
F	F	F

We will look at some arguments involving this connective in a moment.

NEGATION

With conjunction and disjunction, we begin with two propositions and construct a new proposition from them. There is another way in which we can construct a new proposition from just one proposition—by *negating* it.

Given the proposition "John is clever," we can get a new proposition, "John is not clever," simply by inserting the word "not" in the correct place in the sentence.

What, exactly, does the word "not" mean? This can be a difficult question to answer. Does it mean "nothing" or, maybe, "nothingness"? Although some respectable philosophers have sometimes spoken in this way, it is important to see that the word "not" does not stand for anything at all. It has an altogether different function in the language. To see this, think about how conjunction and disjunction work. Given two propositions, the word "and" allows us to construct another proposition that is true only when both original propositions are true, and false otherwise. With disjunction, given two propositions, the word "or" allows us to construct another proposition that is false only when both of the original propositions are false, and true otherwise. (Our truth table definitions reflect these facts.) Using these definitions as models, how should we define negation? A parallel answer is that the negation of a proposition is true just in the cases in which the original proposition is false, and it is false just in the cases in which original proposition is true. Using the symbol "~" (called a *tilde*) to stand for negation, this gives us the following truth table definition:

p	$\sim p$
T	F
F	T

Negation might seem as simple as can be, but people quite often get confused by negations. If Diana says, "I could not breathe for a whole minute," she might mean that there was a minute when something made her unable to breathe (maybe she was choking) or she might mean that she was able to hold her breath for a whole minute (say, to win a bet). If "A" symbolizes "Diana could breathe sometime during this minute," then "$\sim A$" symbolizes the former claim (that Diana was unable to breathe for this minute). Consequently, the latter claim (that Diana could hold her breath for this minute) should not also be symbolized by "$\sim A$." Indeed, this interpretation of the original sentence is not a negation, even though the original sentence did include the word "not." Moreover, some sentences are negations even though they do not include the word "not." For example, "Nobody owns Mars" is the negation of "Somebody owns Mars." If the latter is symbolized as "A," the former can be symbolized as "$\sim A$," even though the former does not include the word "not."

The complexities of negation can be illustrated by noticing that the simple sentence "Everyone loves running" can include negation at four distinct places: "Not everyone loves running," "Everyone does not love running," "Everyone loves not running," and the colloquial "Everyone loves running—not!" Some of these sentences can be symbolized in propositional logic as negations of "Everyone loves running," but others cannot.

To determine whether a sentence can be symbolized as a negation in propositional logic, it is often useful to reformulate the sentence so that it starts with "It is not the case that . . . ." For example, "I did none of the homework" would be reformulated as "It is not the case that I did any of the homework." If the resulting sentence means the same as the original (as it does in this example), then the original sentence can be symbolized as a propositional negation. In contrast, "I promise not to leave you" means something very different from "It is not the case that I promise to leave you," so "I promise not to leave you" should not be symbolized as a propositional negation.

Unfortunately, this test will not always work. There is no complete mechanical procedure for determining whether an English sentence can be symbolized as a negation. All you can do is think carefully about the sentence's meaning and context. The best way to get good at this is to practice.

EXERCISE VII

Explain the differences in meaning among "Not everyone loves running," "Everyone does not love running," "Everyone loves not running," and "Everyone loves running—not!" For each, is it a negation of "Everyone loves running"? Why or why not?

EXERCISE VIII

Negative terms or prefixes can often be interpreted in more than one way. Explain two ways to interpret each of the following sentences. Describe a context in which it would be natural to interpret it in each way.

1. You may not go to the meeting.
2. I cannot recommend him too highly.
3. He never thought he'd go to the Himalayas.
4. Have you not done all of your homework?
5. All of his friends are not students.
6. I will not go to some football games next season.
7. No smoking section available.
8. The lock on his locker was unlockable.

EXERCISE IX

Put each of the following sentences in symbolic form. Be sure to specify exactly which sentence is represented by each capital letter, and pay special attention to the placement of the negation. If the sentence could be interpreted in more than one way, symbolize each interpretation and describe a context in which it would be natural to interpret it in each way.

1. It won't rain tomorrow.
2. It might not rain tomorrow.
3. There is no chance that it will rain tomorrow.
4. I believe that it won't rain tomorrow.
5. Joe is not too smart or else he's very clever.
6. Kristin is not smart or rich.
7. Sometimes you feel like a nut; sometimes you don't. (from an advertisement for Mounds and Almond Joy candies, which are made by the same company and are exactly alike except that only one of them has a nut)

PROCESS OF ELIMINATION

Using only negation and disjunction, we can analyze the form of one common pattern of reasoning, which is called *process of elimination* or, more technically, *disjunctive syllogism*. As an example, consider this argument:

Her phone line is busy, so she must either be talking on the phone or using her modem. She is not using her modem, since I just tried to e-mail her and she did not respond. So she must be talking on the phone.

After trimming off assurances and subarguments that support the premises, the core of this argument can be put in standard form:

(1) She is either using her modem or talking on the phone.
(2) She is not using her modem.
∴(3) She is talking on the phone. (from 1–2)

This core argument is then an instance of this argument form:

1. $p \lor q$
   $\frac{\sim p}{}$
   ∴ q

It does not matter if we change the order of the disjuncts so that the first premise is "She must be either talking on the phone or using her modem." Then the argument takes this form:

2. $p \lor q$
   $\frac{\sim q}{}$
   ∴ p

Both of these argument forms are valid, so the core of the original argument is also valid.

EXERCISE X

Explain why argument forms 1–2 are valid. Use common language that would be understandable to someone who has not read this chapter.

Process of elimination is sometimes confused with a similar but crucially different pattern of reasoning, which can be called *affirming a disjunct*. This pattern includes both of these forms:

3. $p \vee q$
   p
   $\therefore \ \sim q$

4. $p \vee q$
   q
   $\therefore \ \sim p$

These forms of argument are invalid. This can be shown by the following single instance:

> She is either using her modem or talking on the phone.
> She is using her modem.
> $\therefore$ She is not talking on the phone.

This argument might seem valid if one assumes that she cannot talk on the phone while using her modem. The premises, however, do not specify that she has only one phone line. If she talks on one phone line while using her modem on a different phone line, then the premises are true and the conclusion is false. Because this is possible, the argument is invalid, and so is its form, 3. Moreover, this argument would remain invalid if the disjuncts were listed in a different order, so that the argument took the form of 4. Thus, affirming a disjunct is a fallacy.

EXERCISE XI

Give other instances of argument forms 3–4 that are not valid. Explain why these instances are invalid and why they show that the general argument form is invalid.

HOW TRUTH-FUNCTIONAL CONNECTIVES WORK

We have now defined conjunction, disjunction, and negation. That, all by itself, is sufficient to complete the branch of modern logic called propositional logic. The definitions themselves may seem peculiar. They do not look like the definitions we find in a dictionary. But the form of these definitions is important, for it tells us something interesting about the character of such words as "and," "or," and "not." Two things are worth noting: (1) These expressions are used to construct a new proposition from old ones; (2) the newly constructed proposition is always a *truth function* of the original propositions—that is, the truth value of the new proposition is always determined by the truth value of the original propositions. For this reason, these connectives are called *truth-functional connectives*. (Of course, with negation, we start with a *single* proposition, so there are not really two things to connect.) For example, suppose that "*A*" and "*B*" are two true propositions and "*G*" and "*H*" are two false propositions. We can then determine the truth values of more complex propositions built from them using conjunction, disjunction, and negation. Sometimes the correct assignment is obvious at a glance:

A & *B*	True
A & *G*	False
~*A*	False
~*G*	True
A ∨ *H*	True
G ∨ *H*	False
~*A* & *G*	False

As noted earlier, parentheses can be used to distinguish groupings. Sometimes the placement of parentheses can make an important difference, as in the following two expressions:

~*A* & *G*

~(*A* & *G*)

Notice that in one expression the negation symbol applies only to the proposition "*A*," whereas in the other expression it applies to the entire proposition "*A* & *G*." Thus, the first expression above is false, and the second expression is true. Only the second expression can be translated as "Not both *A* and *G*." Both of these expressions are different from "~*A* & ~*G*," which means "Neither *A* nor *G*."

As expressions become more complex, we reach a point where it is no longer obvious how the truth values of the component propositions determine the truth value of the entire proposition. Here a regular procedure is helpful. The easiest method is to fill in the truth values of the basic propositions and then, step-by-step, make assignments progressively wider, going from the inside out. For example:

~((*A* ∨ *G*) & ~(~*H* & *B*))

~((*T* ∨ *F*) & ~(~*F* & *T*))

~((*T* ∨ *F*) & ~(*T* & *T*))

~(*T* & ~(*T*))

~(*T* & *F*)

~(*F*)

T

With a little practice, you can master this technique in dealing with other very complex examples.

> ### EXERCISE XII
>
> Given that "A," "B," and "C" are true propositions and "X," "Y," and "Z" are false propositions, determine the truth values of the following compound propositions:
>
> 1. ~X ∨ Y
> 2. ~(X ∨ Y)
> 3. ~(Z ∨ Z)
> 4. ~(Z ∨ ~Z)
> 5. ~ ~(A ∨ B)
> 6. (A ∨ Z) & B
> 7. (A ∨ X) & (B ∨ Z)
> 8. (A & Z) ∨ (B & Z)
> 9. ~(A ∨ (Z ∨ X))
> 10. ~(A ∨ ~(Z ∨ X))
> 11. ~A ∨ ~(Z ∨ X)
> 12. ~Z ∨ (Z & A)
> 13. ~(Z ∨ (Z & A))
> 14. ~((Z ∨ Z) & A)
> 15. A ∨ ((~B & C) ∨ ~(~B ∨ ~(Z ∨ B)))
> 16. A & ((~B & C) ∨ ~(~B ∨ ~(Z ∨ B)))

TESTING FOR VALIDITY

What is the point of all this? In everyday life, we rarely run into an expression as complicated as the one in our example at the end of the previous section. Our purpose here is to sharpen our sensitivity to how truth-functional connectives work and then to express our insights in clear ways. This is important because the validity of many arguments depends on the logical features of these truth-functional connectives. We can now turn directly to this subject.

Earlier we saw that every argument with the form "p & q; ∴ p" will be valid. This is obvious in itself, but we saw that this claim could be justified by an appeal to truth tables. A truth table analysis shows us that an argument with this form can never have an instance in which the premise is true and the conclusion is false. We can now apply this same technique to arguments that are more complex. In the beginning, we will examine arguments that are still easy to follow without the use of technical help. In the end, we will consider some arguments that most people cannot follow without guidance.

Consider the following argument:

> Valerie is either a doctor or a lawyer.
> Valerie is neither a doctor nor a stockbroker.
> ∴ Valerie is a lawyer.

We can use the following abbreviations:

D = Valerie is a doctor.

L = Valerie is a lawyer.

S = Valerie is a stockbroker.

Using these abbreviations, the argument and its counterpart argument form look like this:

$$D \lor L \qquad\qquad p \lor q$$
$$\underline{\sim(D \lor S)} \qquad\qquad \underline{\sim(p \lor r)}$$
$$\therefore L \qquad\qquad \therefore q$$

The expression on the right gives the argument form of the argument presented on the left. To test the argument for validity, we ask whether the argument form is valid. The procedure is cumbersome, but perfectly mechanical:

			PREMISE		PREMISE	CONCLUSION	
p	q	r	$(p \lor q)$	$(p \lor r)$	$\sim(p \lor r)$	q	
T	T	T	T	T	F	T	
T	T	F	T	T	F	T	
T	F	T	T	T	F	F	
T	F	F	T	T	F	F	
F	T	T	T	T	F	T	
F	T	F	T	F	T	T	OK
F	F	T	F	T	F	F	
F	F	F	F	F	T	F	

Notice that there is only one combination of truth values for which both premises are true, and in that case the conclusion is true as well. So the original argument is valid because it is an instance of a valid argument form—that is, an argument form with no substitution instances for which true premises are combined with a false conclusion.

This last truth table may need some explaining. First, why do we get eight rows in this truth table where before we got only four? The answer to this is that we need to test the argument form for *every possible combination of truth values* for the component propositions. With two variables, there are four possible combinations: (TT), (TF), (FT), and (FF). With three variables, there are eight possible combinations: (TTT), (TTF), (TFT), (TFF), (FTT), (FTF), (FFT), and (FFF). The general rule is this: If an argument form has n variables, the truth table used in its analysis must have 2^n rows. For four variables there will be sixteen rows; for five variables, thirty-two rows; for six variables, sixty-four rows; and so on. You can be sure that you capture all possible combinations of truth values by using the following pattern in constructing the columns of your truth table under each individual variable:

First column	Second column	Third column . . .
First half Ts,	First quarter Ts,	First eighth Ts,
second half Fs.	second quarter Fs,	second eighth Fs,
	and so on.	and so on.

A glance at the earlier examples in this chapter will show that we have been using this pattern, and it is the standard way of listing the possibilities.

Of course, as soon as an argument becomes at all complex, these truth tables become very large indeed. But there is no need to worry about this, because we will not consider arguments with many variables. Those who do so turn to a computer for help.

The style of the truth table above is also significant. The premises are plainly labeled, and so is the conclusion. A line is drawn under every row in which the premises are all true. (In this case, there is only one such row—row 6.) If the conclusion on this line is also true, it is marked "OK." If every line in which the premises are all true is OK, then the argument form is valid. Marking all this may seem rather childish, but it is worth doing. First, it helps guard against mistakes. More importantly, it draws one's attention to the purpose of the procedure being used. Cranking out truth tables without understanding what they are about—or even why they might be helpful—does not enlighten the mind or elevate the spirit.

For the sake of contrast, we can next consider an invalid argument:

(1) Valerie is either a doctor or a lawyer.
(2) Valerie is not both a lawyer and a stockbroker.
∴(3) Therefore, Valerie is a doctor.

Using the same abbreviations as earlier, this becomes:

$D \lor L$ $p \lor q$
$\sim(L \& S)$ $\sim(q \& r)$
∴ D ∴ p

The truth table for this argument form looks like this:

p	q	r	PREMISE $(p \lor q)$	$(q \& r)$	PREMISE $\sim(q \& r)$	CONCLUSION p	
T	T	T	T	T	F	T	
T	T	F	T	F	T	T	OK
T	F	T	T	F	T	T	OK
T	F	F	T	F	T	T	OK
F	T	T	T	T	F	F	
F	T	F	T	F	T	F	Invalid
F	F	T	F	F	T	F	
F	F	F	F	F	T	F	

This time, we find four rows in which all the premises are true. In three cases the conclusion is true as well, but in one of these cases (row 6), the conclusion is false. This line is marked "Invalid." Notice that every line in which all of the premises are true is marked either as "OK" or as "Invalid." If even one row is marked "Invalid," then the argument form as a whole is invalid. The argument form under consideration is thus invalid, because it is possible for it to have a substitution instance in which all the premises are true and the conclusion is false.

The labeling not only shows *that* the argument form is invalid, it also shows *why* it is invalid. Each line that is marked "Invalid" shows a combination of truth values that makes the premises true and the conclusion false. Row 6 presents the combination in which Valerie is not a doctor, is a lawyer, and is not a stockbroker. With these assignments, it will be true that she is either a doctor or a lawyer (premise 1), and also true that she is not both a lawyer and a stockbroker (premise 2), yet false that she is a doctor (the conclusion). It is this possibility that shows why the argument form is not valid.

In sum, we can test a propositional argument form for validity by following these simple steps:

1. Provide a column for each premise and the conclusion.
2. Fill in truth values in each column.
3. Underline each row where all of the premises are true.
4. Mark each row "OK" if the conclusion is true on that row.
5. Mark each row "Invalid" if the conclusion is false on that row.
6. If any row is marked "Invalid," the argument form is invalid.
7. If no row is marked "Invalid," the argument form is valid.

EXERCISE XIII

Using the truth table technique outlined above, show that argument forms 1–2 in the above section on process of elimination are valid and that argument forms 3–4 in the same section are invalid.

EXERCISE XIV

Using the truth table technique outlined above, explain why the "Tricky Case" that was mentioned in Chapter 2 is valid.

EXERCISE XV

Using the truth table technique outlined above, test the following argument forms for validity:

1. $\sim p \vee q$
   $\underline{\quad p \quad\quad\quad}$
   $\therefore \sim q$

2. $\underline{\sim (p \vee q)\quad}$
   $\therefore \sim q$

3. $\sim (p \vee q)$
   $\underline{\quad p \quad\quad\quad}$
   $\therefore q$

4. $\sim (p \vee q)$
   $\underline{\quad p \quad\quad\quad}$
   $\therefore r$

(continued)

5. $\sim (p \ \& \ q)$

   q
_____

∴ $\sim p$

6. $\sim (p \ \& \ q)$

   $\sim q$
_____

∴ p

7. $(p \ \& \ q) \lor (p \ \& \ r)$
_____

∴ $p \ \& \ (q \lor r)$

8. $(p \lor q) \ \& \ (p \lor r)$
_____

∴ $p \ \& \ (q \lor r)$

9. $p \ \& \ q$
_____

∴ $(p \lor r) \ \& \ (q \lor r)$

10. $p \lor q$
_____

∴ $(p \ \& \ r) \lor (q \ \& \ r)$

SOME FURTHER CONNECTIVES

We have developed the logic of propositions using only three basic notions corresponding (perhaps roughly) to the English words "and," "or," and "not." Now let us go back to the question of the two possible senses of the word "or": one exclusive and the other inclusive. Sometimes "or" seems to rule out the possibility that both alternatives are true; at other times "or" seems to allow this possibility. This is the difference between exclusive and inclusive disjunction.

Suppose we use the symbol "$\underline{\lor}$" to stand for exclusive disjunction. This is the same as the symbol for inclusive disjunction except that it is underlined. (After this discussion, we will not use it again.) We could then give two truth table definitions, one for each of these symbols:

		INCLUSIVE	EXCLUSIVE
p	q	$p \lor q$	$p \underline{\lor} q$
T	T	T	F
T	F	T	T
F	T	T	T
F	F	F	F

We could also define this new connective in the following way:

$(p \underline{\lor} q) =$ (by definition) $((p \lor q) \ \& \ \sim(p \ \& \ q))$

It is not hard to see that the expression on the right side of this definition captures the force of exclusive disjunction. Because we can always define exclusive disjunction when we want it, there is no need to introduce it into our system of basic notions.

EXERCISE XVI

Construct a truth table analysis of the expression on the right side of the preceding definition, and compare it with the truth table definition of exclusive disjunction.

Use truth tables to test the following argument forms for validity:

1. p

∴ $p \veebar q$

2. $p \veebar q$

p

∴ $\sim q$

3. $p \& q$

∴ $\sim(p \veebar q)$

4. $\sim(p \& q)$

∴ $p \veebar q$

5. $p \veebar q$

∴ $p \vee q$

6. $p \vee q$

∴ $p \veebar q$

Actually, in analyzing arguments we have been defining new logical connectives without thinking about it much. For example, "not both p and q" was symbolized as "$\sim(p \& q)$." "Neither p nor q" was symbolized as "$\sim(p \vee q)$." Let us look more closely at the example "$\sim(p \vee q)$." Perhaps we should have symbolized it as "$\sim p \& \sim q$." In fact, we could have used this symbolization, because the two expressions amount to the same thing. Again, this may be obvious, but we can prove it by using a truth table in yet another way. Compare the truth table analysis of these two expressions:

p	q	$\sim p$	$\sim q$	$\sim p \& \sim q$	$(p \vee q)$	$\sim(p \vee q)$
T	T	F	F	F	T	F
T	F	F	T	F	T	F
F	T	T	F	F	T	F
F	F	T	T	T	F	T

Under "$\sim p \& \sim q$" we find the column (FFFT), and we find the same sequence under "$\sim(p \vee q)$." This shows that, for every possible substitution we make, these two expressions will yield propositions with the same truth value. We will say that these propositional forms are *truth-functionally equivalent*. The above table also shows that the expressions "$\sim q$" and "$\sim p \& \sim q$" are *not* truth-functionally equivalent, because the columns underneath these two expressions differ in the second row, so some substitutions into these expressions will not yield propositions with the same truth value.

Given the notion of truth-functional equivalence, the problem of more than one translation can often be solved. If two translations of a sentence are truth-functionally equivalent, then it does not matter which one we use in testing for validity. Of course, some translations will seem more natural than others. For example, "$p \vee q$" is truth-functionally equivalent to

$\sim((\sim p \& \sim p) \& (\sim q \vee \sim q))$

Despite this equivalence, the first form of expression is obviously more natural than the second when translating sentences, such as "It is either cloudy or sunny."

Use truth tables to test which of the following propositional forms are truth-functionally equivalent to each other:

1. ~(p ∨ q)
2. ~(~p ∨ ~q)
3. ~p & ~q
4. p & q

Use truth tables to determine whether the expressions in each of the following pairs are truth-functionally equivalent:

1. "p" and "p & p"
2. "p" and "p ∨ p"
3. "p ∨ ~p" and "~(p & ~p)"
4. "p" and "p & (q ∨ ~q)"
5. "p" and "p & (q & ~q)"
6. "p" and "p ∨ (q & ~q)"
7. "p & (q ∨ r)" and "p ∨ (q & r)"
8. "p & (q & r)" and "(p & q) & r"
9. "~(p ∨ q)" and "~p ∨ q"
10. "~(p ∨ q)" and "~p & ~q"
11. "~~(p ∨ q)" and "~~p & ~~q"
12. "~(p & q)" and "~p ∨ q"
13. "~~(p & q)" and "~~p ∨ ~~q"
14. "~~p ∨ ~~q" and "~(~p & ~q)"
15. "~~p & ~~q" and "~(~p ∨ ~q)"
16. "p & ~~q" and "~~p & q"

CONDITIONALS

So far in this chapter we have seen that by using conjunction, disjunction, and negation, it is possible to construct compound propositions out of simple propositions. A distinctive feature of compound propositions constructed in these three ways is that the truth of the compound proposition is always a function of the truth of its component propositions. Thus, these three notions allow us to construct truth-functionally compound propositions. Some arguments depend for their validity simply on these truth-functional connectives. When this is so, it is possible to test for validity in a purely mechanical way. This can be done through the use of truth tables. Thus, in this area at least, we are able to give a clear account of validity and to specify exact procedures for testing for validity.

This truth-functional approach might seem problematic in another area: *conditionals*. We will argue that an important group of conditionals can be handled in much the same way as negation, conjunction, and disjunction. We separate conditionals from the other connectives only because a truth-functional treatment of conditionals is more controversial and faces problems that are instructive.

Conditionals have the form "If _____, then _____." What goes in the first blank of this pattern is called the *antecedent* of the conditional; what goes in the second blank is called its *consequent*. Sometimes conditionals appear in the indicative mood:

If it rains, then the crop will be saved.

Sometimes they occur in the subjunctive mood:

If it had rained, then the crop would have been saved.

There are also conditional imperatives:

If a fire breaks out, then call the fire department first!

And there are conditional promises:

If you get into trouble, then I promise to help you.

Indeed, conditionals get a great deal of use in our language, often in arguments. It is important, therefore, to understand them.

Unfortunately, there is no general agreement among experts concerning the correct way to analyze conditionals. We will simplify matters and avoid some of these controversies by considering only indicative conditionals. We will not examine conditional imperatives, conditional promises, or subjunctive conditionals. Furthermore, at the start, we will examine only what we will call *propositional conditionals*. We get a propositional conditional by substituting indicative sentences that express propositions—something either true or false—into the schema "If _____, then _____." Or, to use technical language already introduced, a propositional conditional is a substitution instance of "If *p*, then *q*" in which "*p*" and "*q*" are propositional variables. Of the four conditional sentences listed above, only the first is clearly a propositional conditional.

Even if we restrict our attention to propositional conditionals, this will not avoid all controversy. Several competing theories claim to provide the correct analysis of propositional conditionals, and no consensus has been reached concerning which is right. It may seem surprising that theorists disagree about such a simple and fundamental notion as the if-then construction, but they do. In what follows, we will first describe the most standard treatment of propositional conditionals, and then consider alternatives to it.

TRUTH TABLES FOR CONDITIONALS

For conjunction, disjunction, and negation, the truth table method provides an approach that is at once plausible and effective. A propositional conditional is also compounded from two simpler propositions, and this suggests that we might be able to offer a truth table definition for these conditionals as well. What should the truth table look like? When we try to answer this question, we get stuck almost at once, for it is unclear how we should fill in the table in three out of four cases.

p	q	If p, then q
T	T	?
T	F	F
F	T	?
F	F	?

It seems obvious that a conditional cannot be true if the antecedent is true and the consequent is false. We record this by putting "F" in the second row. But suppose "p" and "q" are replaced by two arbitrary true propositions— say, "Two plus two equals four" and "Chile is in South America." Consider what we shall say about the conditional:

If two plus two equals four, then Chile is in South America.

This is a *very* strange statement, because the arithmetical remark in the antecedent does not seem to have anything to do with the geographical remark in the consequent. So this conditional is odd—indeed, extremely odd—but is it true or false? At this point, a reasonable response is bafflement.

Consider the following argument, which is intended to solve all these problems by providing reasons for assigning truth values in each row of the truth table. First, it seems obvious that, if "If p, then q" is true, then it is not the case that both "p" is true and "q" is false. That in turn means that "$\sim(p \ \& \sim q)$" must be true. The following, then, seems to be a valid argument form:

If p, then q.
∴ $\sim(p \ \& \sim q)$

Second, we can also reason in the opposite direction. Suppose we know that "$\sim(p \ \& \sim q)$" is true. For this to be true, "$p \ \& \sim q$" must be false. We know this from the truth table definition of negation. Next let us suppose that "p" is true. Then "$\sim q$" must be false. We know this from the truth table definition of conjunction. Finally, if "$\sim q$" is false, then "q" itself must be true. This line of reasoning is supposed to show that the following argument form is valid:

$\sim(p \ \& \sim q)$
∴ If p, then q.

The first step in the argument was intended to show that we can validly derive "$\sim(p \ \& \sim q)$" from "If p, then q." The second step was intended to show that the derivation can be run in the other direction as well. But if each of these expressions is derivable from the other, this suggests that they are equivalent. We use this background argument as a justification for the following definition:

If p, then q = (by definition) not both p and not q.

We can put this into symbolic notation using "⊃" (called a *horseshoe*) to symbolize the conditional connective:

$p \supset q$ = (by definition) $\sim(p \ \& \sim q)$

Given this definition, we can now construct the truth table for propositional conditionals. It is simply the truth table for "~(p & ~q)":

p	q	~(p & ~q)	p ⊃ q	~p ∨ q
T	T	T	T	T
T	F	F	F	F
F	T	T	T	T
F	F	T	T	T

Notice that "~(p & ~q)" is also truth-functionally equivalent to the expression "~p ∨ q." We have cited it here because "~p ∨ q" has traditionally been used to define "p ⊃ q." For reasons that are now obscure, when a conditional is defined in this truth-functional way, it is called a *material conditional*.

Let's suppose, for the moment, that the notion of a material conditional corresponds exactly to our idea of a propositional conditional. What would follow from this? The answer is that we could treat conditionals in the same way in which we have treated conjunction, disjunction, and negation. A propositional conditional would be just one more kind of truth-functionally compound proposition capable of definition by truth tables. Furthermore, the validity of arguments that depend on this notion (together with conjunction, disjunction, and negation) could be settled by appeal to truth table techniques. Let us pause for a moment to examine this.

One of the most common patterns of reasoning is called *modus ponens*. It looks like this:

If p, then q.		p ⊃ q	
p		p	
∴ q		∴ q	

The truth table definition of a material conditional shows at once that this pattern of argument is valid:

PREMISE		PREMISE	CONCLUSION	
p	q	p ⊃ q	q	
T	T	T	T	OK
T	F	F	F	
F	T	T	T	
F	F	T	F	

EXERCISE XX

The argument form called *modus tollens* looks like this:

p ⊃ q
~q
∴ ~p

Use truth tables to show that this argument form is valid.

Farcus

by David Waisglass
Gordon Coulthart

WAISGLASS/COULTHART

© 1997 Farcus Cartoons

Reprinted by permission of LaughingStock Licensing Inc.

**"So, I say if it's not worth doing well,
it's not worth doing at all."**

These same techniques allow us to show that one of the traditional fallacies is, indeed, a fallacy. It is called the fallacy of *denying the antecedent,* and it has this form:

$$p \supset q$$
$$\frac{\sim p}{}$$
$$\therefore \sim q$$

The truth table showing the invalidity of this argument form looks like this:

		PREMISE	PREMISE	CONCLUSION	
p	q	$p \supset q$	$\sim p$	$\sim q$	
T	T	T	F	F	
T	F	F	F	T	
F	T	T	T	F	Invalid
F	F	T	T	T	OK

EXERCISE XXI

A second standard fallacy is called *affirming the consequent*. It looks like this:

$$p \supset q$$
$$\frac{q}{}$$
$$\therefore p$$

Use truth tables to show that this argument form is invalid.

In his radio address to the nation on April 17, 1982, President Ronald Reagan argued that the United States should not accept a treaty with the Soviet Union that would mutually freeze nuclear weapons at current levels, because he believed that the United States had fallen behind. Here is a central part of his argument:

> It would be wonderful if we could restore the balance of power with the Soviet Union without increasing our military power. And, ideally, it would be a long step towards assuring peace if we could have significant and verifiable reductions of arms on both sides. But let's not fool ourselves. The Soviet Union will not come to any conference table bearing gifts. Soviet negotiators will not make unilateral concessions. To achieve parity, we must make it plain that we have the will to achieve parity by our own effort.

Put Reagan's central argument into standard form. Then symbolize it and its form. Does his argument commit any fallacy? If so, identify it.

The relations among these last four argument forms can be seen in this diagram:

	Antecedent	Consequent
Affirming	Affirming the Antecedent = *Modus Ponens* (valid)	Affirming the Consequent (invalid)
Denying	Denying the Antecedent (invalid)	Denying the Consequent = *Modus Tollens* (valid)

Another argument form that has been historically significant is called a *hypothetical syllogism:*

$$p \supset q$$
$$\underline{q \supset r}$$
$$\therefore p \supset r$$

Because we are dealing with an argument form containing three variables, we must perform the boring task of constructing a truth table with eight rows:

p	q	r	PREMISE $p \supset q$	PREMISE $q \supset r$	CONCLUSION $p \supset r$	
T	T	T	T	T	T	OK
T	T	F	T	F	F	
T	F	T	F	T	T	
T	F	F	F	T	F	
F	T	T	T	T	T	OK
F	T	F	T	F	T	
F	F	T	T	T	T	OK
F	F	F	T	T	T	OK

This is fit work for a computer, not for a human being, but it is important to see that it actually works.

Why is it important to see that these techniques work? Most people, after all, could see that hypothetical syllogisms are valid without going through all of this tedious business. We seem only to be piling boredom on top of triviality. This protest deserves an answer. Suppose we ask someone *why* he or she thinks that the conclusion follows from the premises in a hypothetical syllogism. The person might answer that anyone can see that—which, by the way, is false. Beyond this, he or she might say that it all depends on the meanings of the words or that it is all a matter of definition. But if we go on to ask, "which words?" and "what definitions?" then most people will fall silent. We have discovered that the validity of some arguments depends on the meanings of such words as "and," "or," "not," and "if-then." We have then gone on to give explicit definitions of these terms—definitions, by the way, that help us see how these terms function in an argument. Finally, by getting all these *simple* things right, we have produced what is called a *decision procedure* for determining the validity of every argument depending only on conjunctions, disjunctions, negations, and propositional conditionals. Our truth table techniques give us a mechanical procedure for settling questions of validity in this area. In fact, truth table techniques have practical applications, for example, in computer programming. But the important point here is that, through an understanding of how these techniques work, we can gain a deeper insight into the notion of validity.

EXERCISE XXIII

Two more classic, common, and useful argument forms combine conditionals with disjunction. Using truth tables, test them for validity.

Constructive Dilemma	Destructive Dilemma
$p \lor q$	$\sim p \lor \sim q$
$p \supset r$	$r \supset p$
$q \supset r$	$r \supset q$
$\therefore r$	$\therefore \sim r$

EXERCISE XXIV

Using the truth table techniques employed above, test the following argument forms for validity. (For your own entertainment, guess whether the argument form is valid or invalid before working it out.)

1. $p \supset q$
   $\therefore q \supset p$

2. $p \supset q$
   $\therefore \sim q \supset \sim p$

3. $\sim q \supset \sim p$
   $\therefore p \supset q$

4. $p \supset q$
   $q \supset r$
   $\therefore p \supset (q \& r)$

5. $p \supset q$
    $q \supset r$
    $\sim r$
    ―――――
 ∴ $\sim p$

6. $p \supset q$
    $q \supset r$
    ―――――
 ∴ $\sim r \supset \sim p$

7. $p \vee q$
    $p \supset q$
    $q \supset r$
    ―――――
 ∴ r

8. $p \supset (q \vee r)$
    $\sim q$
    $\sim r$
    ―――――
 ∴ $\sim p$

9. $(p \vee q) \supset r$
    ―――――
 ∴ $p \supset r$

10. $(p \,\&\, q) \supset r$
    ―――――
 ∴ $p \supset r$

11. $p \supset (q \supset r)$
    ―――――
 ∴ $(p \,\&\, q) \supset r$

12. $(p \,\&\, q) \supset r$
    ―――――
 ∴ $p \supset (q \supset r)$

13. $p \supset (q \supset r)$
    q
    $\sim r$
    ―――――
 ∴ $\sim p$

14. $p \supset (q \supset r)$
    $p \supset q$
    ―――――
 ∴ r

15. $(p \vee q) \,\&\, (p \vee r)$
    $\sim r$
    ―――――
 ∴ $\sim q$

16. $(p \supset q) \,\&\, (p \supset \sim r)$
    $q \,\&\, r$
    ―――――
 ∴ $\sim p$

17. $(p \vee q) \supset p$
    ―――――
 ∴ $\sim q$

18. $(p \vee q) \supset (p \,\&\, q)$
    ―――――
 ∴ $(p \supset q) \,\&\, (q \supset p)$

19. $(p \,\&\, q) \supset (p \vee q)$
    ―――――
 ∴ $(p \supset q) \vee (q \supset p)$

20. r
    ―――――
 ∴ $(p \supset q) \vee (q \supset p)$

LOGICAL LANGUAGE AND EVERYDAY LANGUAGE

Early in this chapter we started out by talking about such common words as "and" and "or," and then we slipped over to talking about *conjunction* and *disjunction*. The transition was a bit sneaky, but intentional. To understand what is going on here, we can ask how closely these logical notions we have defined match their everyday counterparts. We will start with conjunction, and then come back to the more difficult question of conditionals.

At first sight, the match between conjunction as we have defined it and the everyday use of the word "and" may seem fairly bad. To begin with, in everyday discourse, we do not go about conjoining random bits of information. We do not say, for example, "Two plus two equals four and Chile is in South America." We already know why we do not say such things, for unless the context is quite extraordinary, this is bound to violate the conversational rule of Relevance. But if we are interested in validity, the rule of Relevance—like all other conversational (or pragmatic) rules—is simply beside the point. When dealing with validity, we are interested in only one question: If the premises of an argument are true, must the conclusion be true as well? Conversational rules, as we saw in Chapter 2, do not affect truth.

The truth-functional notion of conjunction is also insensitive to another important feature of our everyday discourse: By reducing all conjunctions to their bare truth-functional content, the truth-functional notion often misses the argumentative point of a conjunction. As we saw in Chapter 3, each of the following remarks has a different force in the context of an argument:

The ring is beautiful, but expensive.

The ring is expensive, but beautiful.

These two remarks point in opposite directions in the context of an actual argument, but from a purely truth-functional point of view, we treat them as equivalent. We translate the first sentence as "B & E" and the second as "E & B." Their truth-functional equivalence is too obvious to need proof. Similar oddities arise for all discounting terms, such as "although," "whereas," and "however."

It might seem that if formal analysis cannot distinguish an "and" from a "but," then it can hardly be of any use at all. This is not true. A formal analysis of an argument will tell us just one thing: whether the argument is valid or not. If we expect the analysis to tell us more than this, we will be sorely disappointed. It is important to remember two things: (1) We expect deductive arguments to be valid, and (2) usually we expect much more than this from an argument. To elaborate on the second point, we usually expect an argument to be sound as well as valid; we expect the premises to be true. Beyond this, we expect the argument to be informative, intelligible, convincing, and so forth. Validity, then, is an important aspect of an argument, and formal analysis helps us evaluate it. But validity is not the only aspect of an argument that concerns us. In many contexts, it is not even our chief concern.

We can now look at our analysis of conditionals, for here we find some striking differences between the logician's analysis and everyday use. The following argument forms are both valid:

1. p
   $\therefore q \supset p$

2. $\sim p$
   $\therefore p \supset q$

Check the validity of the argument forms above using truth tables.

Though valid, both argument forms seem odd—so odd that they have actually been called *paradoxical*. The first argument form seems to say this: If a proposition is true, then it is *implied by* any proposition whatsoever. Here is an example of an argument that satisfies this argument form and is therefore valid:

Lincoln was president.

∴ If the moon is made of cheese, Lincoln was president.

This is a peculiar argument to call valid. First, we want to know what the moon has to do with Lincoln's having been president. Beyond this, how can his having been president depend on a blatant falsehood? We can give these questions even more force by noticing that even the following argument is valid:

Lincoln was president.

∴ If Lincoln was not president, then Lincoln was president.

Both arguments are instances of the valid argument form "p; ∴ $q \supset p$."

The other argument form is also paradoxical. It seems to say that a false proposition implies any proposition whatsoever. The following is an instance of this argument form:

Columbus was not president.

∴ If Columbus was president, then the moon is made of cheese.

Here it is hard to see what the falsehood that Columbus was president has to do with the composition of the moon.

At this point, nonphilosophers become impatient, whereas philosophers become worried. We started out with principles that seemed to be both obvious and simple. Now, quite suddenly, we are being overwhelmed with a whole series of peculiar results. What in the world has happened, and what should be done about it? Philosophers remain divided in the answers they give to these questions. The responses fall into two main categories: (1) Simply give up the idea that conditionals can be defined by truth-functional techniques and search for a different and better analysis of conditionals that avoids the difficulties involved in truth-functional analysis; or (2) take the difficult line and argue that there is nothing wrong with calling the aforementioned argument forms valid.

The first approach is highly technical and cannot be pursued in detail in this book, but the general idea is this: Instead of identifying "If p, then q" with "Not both p and not q," identify it with "Not *possibly* both p and not q." This provides a stronger notion of a conditional and avoids some—though not all—of the problems concerning conditionals. This theory is given a systematic development by offering a logical analysis of the notion of possibility. This branch of logic is called *modal* logic, and it has shown remarkable development in recent decades.

The second line has been taken by Paul Grice, whose theories played a prominent part in Chapter 2. He acknowledges—as anyone must—that the two argument forms above are decidedly odd. He denies, however, that this oddness has anything to do with *validity*. Validity concerns one thing and one thing only: a relationship between premises and conclusion. An argument is valid if the premises cannot be true without the conclusion being true as well. The above arguments are valid by this definition of "validity."

Of course, arguments can be defective in all sorts of other ways. Look at the first argument form: (1) p; $\therefore q \supset p$. Because "q" can be replaced by any proposition (true or false), the rule of Relevance will often be violated. It is worth pointing out violations of the rule of Relevance, but, according to Grice, this issue has nothing to do with validity. Beyond this, arguments having this form can also involve violations of the rule of Quantity. A conditional will be true whenever the consequent is true. Given this, it does not matter to the truth of the whole conditional whether the antecedent is true or false. Yet it can be misleading to use a conditional on the basis of this logical feature. For example, it would be misleading for a museum guard to say, "If you give me five dollars, then I will let you into the exhibition," when, in fact, he will admit you in any case. For Grice, this is misleading because it violates the rule of Quantity. Yet strictly speaking, it is not false. Strictly speaking, it is true.

The Grice line is attractive because, among other things, it allows us to accept the truth-functional account of conditionals, with all its simplicity. Yet sometimes it is difficult to swallow. Consider the following remark:

If God exists, then there is evil in the world.

If Grice's analysis is correct, even the most pious person will have to admit that this conditional is true provided only that he or she is willing to admit that there is evil in the world. Yet this conditional plainly suggests that there is some connection between God's existence and the evil in the world—presumably, that is the point of connecting them in a conditional. The pious will wish to deny this suggestion. All the same, this connection is something that is conversationally implied, not asserted. So, once more, this conditional could be misleading—and therefore is in need of criticism and correction—but it is still, strictly speaking, true.

Philosophers and logicians have had various responses to Grice's position. No consensus has emerged on this issue. The authors of this book find it adequate, at least in most normal cases, and therefore have adopted it. This has two advantages: (1) The appeal to conversational rules fits in well with our previous discussions, and (2) it provides a way of keeping the logic simple and within the range of a beginning student. Other philosophers and logicians continue to work toward a definition superior to the truth table definition for indicative conditionals.

OTHER CONDITIONALS IN ORDINARY LANGUAGE

So far we have considered only one form in which propositional conditionals appear in everyday language: the conditional "If p, then q." But propositional conditionals come in a variety of forms, and some of them demand careful treatment.

We can first consider the contrast between constructions using "if" and those using "only if":

1. I'll clean the barn if Hazel will help me.
2. I'll clean the barn only if Hazel will help me.

Adopting the following abbreviations:

B = I'll clean the barn

H = Hazel will help me

the first sentence is symbolized as follows:

$H \supset B$

Notice that in the prose version of item 1, the antecedent and consequent appear in reverse order; "q if p" means the same thing as "If p, then q."

How shall we translate the second sentence? Here we should move slowly and first notice what seems incontestable: If Hazel does not help me, then I will not clean the barn. This is translated in the following way:

$\sim H \supset \sim B$

And that is equivalent to:

$B \supset H$

If this equivalence is not obvious, it can quickly be established using a truth table.

A more difficult question arises when we ask whether an implication runs the other way. When I say that I will clean the barn only if Hazel will help me, am I committing myself to cleaning the barn if she does help me? There is a strong temptation to answer the question "yes" and then give a fuller translation of item 2 in the following way:

$(B \supset H) \,\&\, (H \supset B)$

Logicians call such two-way implications *biconditionals,* and we will discuss them in a moment. But adding this second conjunct is almost surely a mistake, for we can think of parallel cases where we would not be tempted to include it. A government regulation might read as follows:

A student may receive a New York State Scholarship only if the student attends a New York State school.

From this it does not follow that anyone who attends a New York State school may receive a New York State Scholarship. There may be other requirements as well—for example, being a New York State resident.

Why were we tempted to use a biconditional in translating sentences containing the connective "only if"? Why, that is, are we tempted to think that the statement "I'll clean the barn only if Hazel will help me" implies "If Hazel helps me, then I will clean the barn"? The answer turns on the notion of conversational implication first discussed in Chapter 2. If I am *not* going to clean the barn whether Hazel helps me or not, then it will be misleading—a violation of the rule of Quantity—to say that I will clean the barn only if Hazel helps me. For this reason, in many contexts, the *use* of a sentence of the form "p only if q" will conversationally imply a commitment to "p if and only if q."

To appreciate the complexities of the little word "only," it is useful to notice that it fits at every point in the sentence "I hit him in the eye":

Only I hit him in the eye.

I only hit him in the eye.

I hit only him in the eye.

I hit him only in the eye.

I hit him in only the eye.

I hit him in the only eye.

I hit him in the eye only.

Explain what each of these sentences means.

We can next look at sentences of the form "*p* if and only if *q*"—so-called biconditionals. If I say that I will clean the barn if and only if Hazel will help me, then I am saying that I will clean it if she helps and I will not clean it if she does not. Translated, this becomes:

$(H \supset B) \& (\sim H \supset \sim B)$

This is equivalent to:

$(H \supset B) \& (B \supset H)$

We thus have an implication going both ways—the characteristic form of a biconditional. In fact, constructions containing the expression "if and only if" do not often appear in everyday speech. They appear almost exclusively in technical or legal writing. In ordinary conversation, we capture the force of a biconditional by saying something like this:

I will clean the barn, but only if Hazel helps me.

The decision whether to translate a remark of everyday conversation into a conditional or a biconditional is often subtle and difficult. We have already noticed that the use of sentences of the form "*p* only if *q*" will often conversationally imply a commitment to the biconditional "*p* if and only if *q*." In the same way, the *use* of the conditional "*p* if *q*" will often carry this same implication. If I plan to clean the barn whether Hazel helps me or not, it will certainly be misleading—again, a violation of the rule of Quantity—to say that I will clean the barn *if* Hazel helps me.

We can close this discussion by considering one further, rather difficult case. What is the force of saying "*p* unless *q*"? Is this a biconditional, or just a conditional? If it is just a conditional, which way does the implication go? There is a strong temptation to treat this as a biconditional, but the following example shows this to be wrong:

McCain will lose the election unless he carries the South.

This sentence clearly indicates that McCain will lose the election if he does not carry the South. Using abbreviations, we get the following:

N = McCain will carry the South.

L = McCain will lose the election.

$\sim N \supset L$

The original statement does not imply—even conversationally—that McCain will win the election if he does carry the South. Thus,

p unless $q = \sim q \supset p$

In short, "unless" means "if not." We can also note that "$\sim p$ unless q" means the same thing as "p only if q," and they both are translated thus:

$p \supset q$

Our results can be diagrammed as follows:

	Translates As	Often Conversationally Implies
p if q	$q \supset p$	$(p \supset q)\ \&\ (q \supset p)$
p only if q	$p \supset q$	$(p \supset q)\ \&\ (q \supset p)$
p unless q	$\sim q \supset p$	$(p \supset \sim q)\ \&\ (\sim q \supset p)$

EXERCISE XXVII

Translate each of the following sentences into symbolic notation, using the suggested symbols as abbreviations.

1. The Reds will win only if the Dodgers collapse. (R, D)
2. The Steelers will win if their defense holds up. (S, D)
3. If it rains or snows, the game will be called off. (R, S, O)
4. If she came home with a trophy and a prize, she must have won the tournament. (T, P, W)
5. If you order the dinner special, you get dessert and coffee. (S, D, C)
6. If you order the dinner special, you get dessert; but you can have coffee whether or not you order the dinner special. (S, D, C)
7. If the house comes up for sale, and if I have the money in hand, I will bid on it. (S, M, B)
8. If you come to dinner, I will cook you a lobster, if you want me to. (D, L, W)
9. You can be a success if only you try. (S, T)
10. You can be a success only if you try. (S, T)
11. Only if you try can you be a success. (S, T)
12. You can be a success if you are the only one who tries. (S, O)

(continued)

13. Unless there is a panic, stock prices will continue to rise. (*P, R*)

14. I won't scratch your back unless you scratch mine. (*I, Y*)

15. You will get a good bargain provided you get there early. (*B, E*)

16. You cannot lead a happy life without friends. (Let *H* = You can lead a happy life, and let *F* = You have friends.)

17. The only way that horse will win the race is if every other horse drops dead. (Let *W* = That horse will win the race, and let *D* = Every other horse drops dead.)

18. You should take prescription drugs if, but only if, they are prescribed for you. (*T, P*)

19. The grass will die without rain. (*D, R* = It rains.)

20. Given rain, the grass won't die. (*R, D* = The grass will die.)

21. Unless it doesn't rain, the grass won't die. (*R, D* = The grass will die.)

EXERCISE XXVIII

(a) Translate each of the following arguments into symbolic notation. Then (b) test each argument for truth-functional validity using truth table techniques, and (c) comment on any violations of conversational rules.

Example: Harold is clever; so, if Harold isn't clever, then Anna isn't clever either. (*H, A*)

(a) H _____   *p* _____

∴ $\sim H \supset \sim A$ ∴ $\sim p \supset \sim q$

(b) PREMISE   CONCLUSION

p	*q*	$\sim p$	$\sim q$	$\sim p \supset \sim q$	
T	T	F	F	T	OK
T	F	F	T	T	OK
F	T	T	F	F	
F	F	T	T	T	

(c) The argument violates the rule of Relevance, because Anna's cleverness is irrelevant to Harold's cleverness.

1. Jones is brave, so Jones is brave or Jones is brave. (*J*)

2. The Republicans will carry either New Mexico or Arizona; but, since they will carry Arizona, they will not carry New Mexico. (*A, N*)

3. The Democrats will win the election whether they win Idaho or not. Therefore, they will win the election. (*D, I*)

4. The Democrats will win the election. Therefore, they will win the election whether they win Idaho or not. (*D, I*)

5. The Democrats will win the election. Therefore, they will win the election whether they win a majority or not. (*D, M*)

6. If Bobby moves his queen there, he will lose her. Bobby will not lose his queen. Therefore, Bobby will not move his queen there. (*M, L*)

7. John will play only if the situation is hopeless. But the situation is hopeless. So John will play. (*P, H*)

8. Although Brown will pitch, the Rams will lose. If the Rams lose, their manager will get fired. So their manager will get fired. (*B, L, F*)

9. America will win the Olympics unless China does. China will win the Olympics unless Germany does. So America will win the Olympics unless Germany does. (*A, R, E*)

10. If you dial 0, you will get the operator. So, if you dial 0 and do not get the operator, then there is something wrong with the telephone. (*D, O, W*)

11. The Democrats will run either Jones or Borg. If Borg runs, they will lose the South. If Jones runs, they will lose the North. So the Democrats will lose either the North or the South. (*J, B, S, N*)

12. I am going to order either the fish special or the meat special. Either way, I will get soup. So I'll get soup. (*F, M, S*)

13. The grass will die if it rains too much or it does not rain enough. If it does not rain enough, it won't rain too much. If it rains too much, then it won't not rain enough. So the grass will die. (*D* = The grass will die, *M* = It rains too much, *E* = It rains enough.)

14. If you flip the switch, then the light will go on. But if the light goes on, then the generator is working. So if you flip the switch, then the generator is working. (*F, L, G*) (This example comes from Charles L. Stevenson.)

DISCUSSION QUESTIONS

1. If "~p unless q" is translated as "$p \supset q$," then "p unless q" can be translated as "$p \vee q$." Why?

2. Symbolize the following argument and give its form. Does this example show that *modus ponens* is not always valid? Why or why not?

Opinion polls taken just before the 1980 election showed the Republican Ronald Reagan decisively ahead of the Democrat Jimmy Carter, with the other Republican in the race, John Anderson, a distant third. Those apprised of the poll results believed, with good reason:

1. If a Republican wins the election, then if it's not Reagan who wins it will be Anderson.
2. A Republican will win the election.

Yet they did not have reason to believe:

3. If it's not Reagan who wins, it will be Anderson.[1]

(continued)

3. Symbolize the following argument and give its form. Does this example show that *modus tollens* is not always valid? Why or why not?

> (1) If it rained, it didn't rain hard.
> (2) It rained hard.
>
> ∴ (3) It didn't rain.[2]

4. In order to avoid logical mistakes, it is useful to study our own psychological tendencies. One experiment asked subjects whether the following arguments are valid:

> If the card has an "A" on the left, then it has a "3" on the right. The card has an "A" on the left. Therefore, the card has a "3" on the right. (95–100 percent)
>
> If the card has an "A" on the left, it has a "3" on the right. The card does not have a "3" on the right. Therefore, it does not have an "A" on the left. (70–75 percent)
>
> If the card does not have an "A" on the left, then it has a "3" on the right. The card does not have a "3" on the right. Therefore, it has an "A" on the left. (40–50 percent)

The figures in parentheses give the percentage of people who correctly identified that argument as valid. In another experiment, the indicated percentage of subjects gave the correct answer to these questions:

> If she meets her friend, she will go to a play. She meets her friend. What follows? (96 percent)
>
> If she meets her friend, she will go to a play. If she has enough money, she will go to a play. She meets her friend. What follows? (38 percent)

Again, subjects often deny the validity of arguments with implausible conclusions, like this:

> If her pet is a fish, then it is a phylone. If her pet is a phylone, then it is a whale. So, if her pet is a fish, then it is a whale.

Finally, the Wason Selection Task uses cards with a capital letter on one side and a single-figure number on the other side. Four such cards are placed on a table with, say, "B," "L," "2," and "9" on the top side in this order, then subjects are asked:

> Which cards need to be turned over to check whether the following rule is true or false?
> (1) If a card has a "B" on one side, it has a "2" on other side. (10 percent)
> (2) If a card has a "B" on one side, it does *not* have a "2" on other side. (100 percent)

The figure in parentheses indicates how many subjects on average give the correct answer for each of the rules. What are the correct answers?

How can you explain why so many people make these mistakes? How can you avoid making these mistakes yourself?

NOTES

[1] Vann McGee, "A Counterexample to *Modus Ponens*," *Journal of Philosophy 82*, no. 9 (September 1985): 462. See also Walter Sinnott-Armstrong, James Moor, and Robert Fogelin, "A Defense of *Modus Ponens*," *Journal of Philosophy 83*, no. 5 (May 1986): 296–300.

[2] Ernest Adams, "*Modus Tollens* Revisited," *Analysis 48*, no. 3 (1988): 122–28. See also Walter Sinnott-Armstrong, James Moor, and Robert Fogelin, "A Defense of *Modus Tollens*," *Analysis 50*, no. 1 (1990): 9–16.

7

CATEGORICAL LOGIC

In Chapter 6, we saw how validity can depend on the external connections among propositions. This chapter will demonstrate how validity can depend on the internal structure of propositions. In particular, we will examine two types of categorical arguments—immediate inferences *and* syllogisms—*whose validity or invalidity depends on relations among the subject and predicate terms in their premises and conclusions. Our interest in these kinds of arguments is mostly theoretical. Understanding the theory of the syllogism deepens our understanding of validity, even if this theory is, in some cases, difficult to apply directly to complex arguments in daily life.*

BEYOND PROPOSITIONAL LOGIC

Armed with the techniques developed in Chapter 6, let's look at the following argument:

> All squares are rectangles.
> All rectangles have parallel sides.
> ∴ All squares have parallel sides.

It is obvious at a glance that the conclusion follows from the premises, so this argument is valid. Furthermore, it seems to be valid in virtue of its form. But it is not yet clear what the form of this argument is. To show the form of this argument, we might try something of the following kind:

> $p \supset q$
> $q \supset r$
> ∴ $p \supset r$

But this is a mistake—and a bad mistake. We have been using the letters "*p*," "*q*," and "*r*" as *propositional variables*—they stand for arbitrary propositions. But the proposition "All squares are rectangles" is not itself composed of two propositions. Nor does it contain "if," "then" or any other propositional connective. In fact, if we properly translate the above argument into the language of propositional logic, we get the following result:

> p
> q
> ∴ r

This, of course, is *not* a valid argument form. But if we look back at the original argument, we see that it is obviously valid. This shows that propositional logic—however adequate it is in its own area—is not capable of explaining the validity of all valid arguments. There is more to logic than propositional logic.

CATEGORICAL PROPOSITIONS

To broaden our understanding of the notion of validity, we will examine a modern version of a branch of logic first developed in ancient times—categorical logic. Categorical logic concerns immediate inferences and syllogisms that are composed of categorical propositions, so we need to begin by explaining what a categorical proposition is.

In the argument above, the first premise asserts some kind of relationship between squares and rectangles; the second premise asserts some kind of relationship between rectangles and things with parallel sides; finally, in virtue of these asserted relationships, the conclusion asserts a relationship between squares and things having parallel sides. Our task is to understand these relationships as clearly as possible so that we can discover the *basis* for the validity of this argument. Again, we shall adopt the strategy of starting from simple cases and then use the insights gained there for dealing with more complicated cases.

A natural way to represent the relationships expressed by the propositions in an argument is through diagrams. Suppose we draw one circle standing for all things that are squares and another circle standing for all things that are rectangles. The claim that all squares are rectangles may be represented by placing the circle representing squares completely inside the circle representing rectangles.

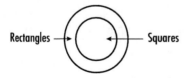

Another way of representing this relationship is to begin with overlapping circles.

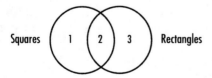

We then shade out the portions of the circles in which nothing exists, according to the proposition we are diagramming. If all squares are rectangles, there is nothing that is a square that is not a rectangle—that is, there is nothing in region 1. So our diagram looks like this:

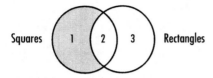

Either method of representation seems plausible. Perhaps the first seems more natural. We shall, however, use the system of overlapping circles, because they will work better when we get to more complex arguments. They are called *Venn diagrams,* after their inventor, John Venn, a nineteenth-century English logician.

Having examined one relationship that can exist between two classes, it is natural to wonder what other relationships might exist. Going to the opposite extreme from our first example, two classes may have *nothing* in common. This relationship could be expressed by saying, "All triangles are not squares," but it is more common and natural to say, "No triangles are squares." We diagram this claim by indicating that there is nothing in the overlapping region of things that are both triangles and squares:

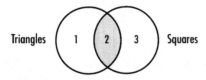

This is one of the relationships that could not be diagrammed by putting one circle inside another. (Just try it!)

In these first two extreme cases, we have indicated that one class is either completely included in another ("All squares are rectangles") or completely excluded from another ("No triangles are squares"). Sometimes, however, we claim only that two classes have at least *some* things in common. We might say, for example, "Some aliens are spies." How shall we indicate this relationship in the following diagram?

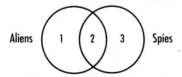

In this case, we do not want to cross out any whole region. We do not want to cross out region 1 because we are not saying that *all* aliens are spies. Plainly, we do not want to cross out region 2, for we are actually saying that some persons *are* both aliens and spies. Finally, we do not want to cross out region 3, for we are not saying that all spies are aliens. Saying that some aliens are spies does not rule out the possibility that some spies are homegrown. So we need some new device to represent claims that two classes have at least *some* members in common. We shall do this in the following way:

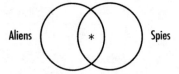

Here the asterisk indicates that there is at least one person who is both an alien and a spy. Notice, by the way, that we are departing a bit from an everyday way of speaking. "Some" is usually taken to mean "more than one"; here we let it mean "at least one." This makes things simpler and will cause no trouble, so long as we remember that this is what we are using "some" to mean.

Given this new method of diagramming class relationships, we can immediately think of other possibilities. The following diagram indicates that there is someone who is an alien but not a spy. In more natural language, it represents the claim that *some aliens are not spies.*

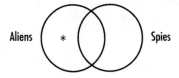

Next we can indicate that there is someone who is a spy but not an alien. More simply, the claim is that *some spies are not aliens,* and it is represented like this:

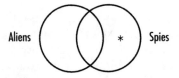

These last three claims are, of course, compatible, because there might be some aliens who are spies, some aliens who are not spies, and some spies who are not aliens.

THE FOUR BASIC CATEGORICAL FORMS

Although two classes can be related in a great many different ways, it is possible to examine many of these relationships in terms of four basic propositional forms:

A: All *S* is *P*.   E: No *S* is *P*.

I: Some *S* is *P*.   O: Some *S* is not *P*.

These forms are called *categorical forms,* and propositions with these forms are called *categorical propositions.*

As with the propositional forms discussed in the previous chapter, the A, E, I, and O forms for categorical propositions are not themselves propositions, so they are neither true nor false. Instead, they are patterns for whole groups of propositions. We get propositions from these forms by uniformly replacing the variables *S* and *P* with terms that refer to classes of things. For example, "Some spies are not aliens" is a substitution instance of the O propositional form. Nonetheless, we will refer to propositions with the A, E, I, or O form simply as A, E, I, or O propositions, except where this might cause confusion.

A and E propositions are said to be *universal* propositions (because they are about *all S*), and I and O propositions are called *particular* propositions (because they are about *some S*). A and I propositions are described as *affirmative* propositions (because they say what *is P*), and E and O propositions are referred to as *negative* propositions (because they say what is *not P*). Thus, these four basic propositional forms can be described this way:

A = Universal Affirmative	E = Universal Negative
I = Particular Affirmative	O = Particular Negative

These four forms fit into the following table:

	Affirmative	Negative
Universal	A: All S is P.	E: No S is P.
Particular	I: Some S is P.	O: Some S is not P.

Here are the Venn diagrams for the four basic categorical forms:

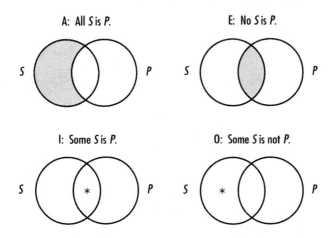

These basic categorical forms, together with their labels, classifications, and diagrams, should be memorized, because they will be referred to often in the rest of this chapter.

Using just the four basic categorical forms, indicate what information is given in each of the following diagrams:

EXAMPLE:

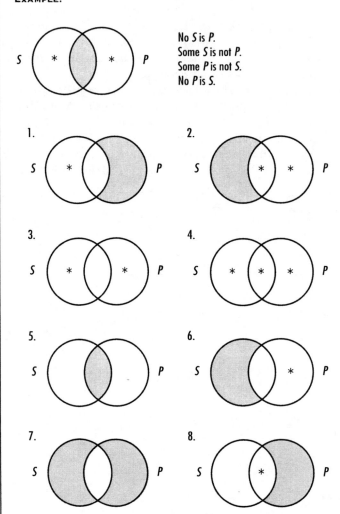

No S is P.
Some S is not P.
Some P is not S.
No P is S.

TRANSLATION INTO THE BASIC CATEGORICAL FORMS

Propositions with the specific A, E, I, and O forms do not appear often in everyday conversations. Normal people rarely say things like "All whales are mammals. All mammals breathe air. Therefore, all whales breathe air." Most people talk more like this: "Whales breathe air, since they're mammals." Thus, if our logical apparatus could be applied only to propositions with the explicit forms of A, E, I, and O, then it would apply to few arguments in everyday life.

Fortunately, however, many common statements that are not explicitly in a categorical form can be translated into a categorical form. For example, when someone says, "Whales are mammals," the speaker presumably means to refer to *all* whales, so this statement can be translated into "All whales are mammals," which is an A proposition. We need to be careful, however. If someone says, "Whales are found in the North Atlantic," the speaker probably does *not* mean to refer to *all* whales, because there are many whales in the Pacific as well. Similarly, if someone says, "A whale is a mammal," this can usually be translated as "All whales are mammals," which is an A proposition, but this translation would be inappropriate for "A whale is stranded on the beach," which seems to mean "One whale is stranded on the beach." Thus, we can be misled badly if we look only at the surface structure of what people say. We also need to pay attention to the context when we translate everyday talk into the basic categorical forms.

Despite these complications, it is possible to give some rough-and-ready guides to help in translating many common forms of expression into propositions with the A, E, I, and O forms. Let's begin with one problem that arises for all these categorical forms: They all require a class of things as a predicate. Thus, "All whales are big" and "No whales live on land" should strictly be reformulated as "All whales are big things" and "No whales are things that live on land" or "No whales are land dwellers." This much is easy.

Things get more complicated when we look at the word "all" in A propositions. We have already seen that the word "all" is sometimes dropped in everyday conversation, as in "Whales are mammals." The word "all" can also be moved away from the start of a sentence. "Democrats are all liberal" usually means "All Democrats are liberal," which is an A proposition. Moreover, other words can be used in place of "all." Each of the following claims can, in standard contexts, be translated into an A proposition with the form "All *S* is *P*":

Every Republican is conservative.

Any investment is risky.

Anyone who is human is mortal.

Each ant is precious to its mother.

To translate such claims, we sometimes need to construct noun phrases out of adjectives and verbs. These transformations are often straightforward, but sometimes they require ingenuity, and even then they can seem somewhat contorted. For example, both "Only a fool would bungee jump" and "Nobody but a fool would bungee jump" can usually be translated into "All people who bungee jump are fools." This translation might not seem as natural as the originals, but, since the translation has the A form, it explicitly shows that this claim has the logical properties shared by other A propositions.

With some stretching, it is also possible to translate statements about individuals into categorical form. The standard method is to translate "Socrates is a man" as the A proposition "All things that are Socrates are men." Similarly,

"The cannon is about to go off" in a typical context must not be translated as the I proposition "Some cannon is about to go off," because the original statement is about a particular cannon. Instead, the original statement should be translated as the A proposition "All things that are that cannon are about to go off." These translations might seem stilted, but they are necessary in order to apply syllogistic logic to everyday forms of expression.

Similar difficulties arise with the other basic propositional forms. If a woman says, "I am looking for a man who is not attached," and a friend responds, "All of the men in my church are not attached," then this response should probably be translated as "No men in my church are attached," which is an E proposition. In contrast, "All ocean dwellers are not fish" should usually be translated not as the E proposition "No ocean dwellers are fish" but rather as "Not all ocean dwellers are fish." This means "Some ocean dwellers are not fish," which is an O proposition. Thus, some statements with the form "All S are not P" should be translated as E propositions, but others should be translated as O propositions. (This ambiguity in the form "All S are not P" explains why it is standard to give E propositions in the less ambiguous form "No S is P.") Other sentences should also be translated as E propositions even though they do not explicitly contain the word "no." "Underground cables are not easy to repair" and "If a cable is underground, it is not easy to repair" and "There aren't any underground cables that are easy to repair" can all be translated as the E proposition "No underground cables are easy to repair."

Similar complications also arise for I and O propositions. We already saw that "Whales are found in the North Atlantic" should be translated as the I proposition "*Some* whales are found in the North Atlantic." In addition, some common forms of expression can be translated as O propositions even though they do not contain either the word "not" or the word "some." For example, "There are desserts without chocolate" can be translated as "Some desserts are not chocolate," which is an O proposition.

Because of such complications, there is no mechanical procedure for translating common English sentences into A, E, I, and O propositions. To find the correct translation, you need to think carefully about the sentence and its context.

EXERCISE II

Translate each of the following sentences into an A, E, I, or O proposition. Be sure that the subjects and predicates in your translations use nouns that refer to classes of things (rather than adjectives or verbs). If the sentence can be translated into different forms in different contexts, give each translation and specify a context in which it seems natural.

1. Real men eat ants.

2. Bats are not birds.

3. The hippo is charging.

4. The hippo is a noble beast.

5. Not all crabs live in water.

6. All crabs do not live in water.

7. Movie stars are all rich.

8. If anybody hits me, I will hate them.

9. If anything is broken, it does not work.

10. Somebody loves you.

11. Somebody does not love you.

12. Nobody loves me but my mother.

13. Anybody who is Mormon believes in God.

14. My friends are the only ones who care.

15. Only seniors may take this course.

16. Our pit bull is a good pet.

17. Everything that is cheap is no good.

18. Some things that are expensive are no good.

19. Some things that are cheap are good.

20. Some things that are not cheap are good.

21. Some things that are cheap are not good.

22. Some things that are not cheap are not good.

23. Not all cars have four wheels.

24. There are couples without children.

25. There are no people who hate chocolate.

26. There are people who hate chocolate.

27. Nothing that is purple is an apple.

28. Nothing that is not white is snow.

29. There aren't any runners who are slow.

30. Flamingos aren't friendly.

CONTRADICTORIES

Once we understand A, E, I, and O propositions by themselves, the next step is to ask how they are related to each other. From their diagrams, some relationships are immediately evident. Consider the Venn diagrams for the E and I propositional forms:

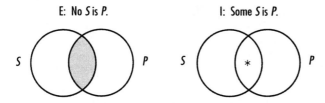

The first diagram has shading in the very same region that contains an asterisk in the second diagram. This makes it obvious that an E proposition and the corresponding I proposition (that is, the I proposition that has the same subject and predicate terms as the E proposition) cannot both be true. For an E proposition to be true, there must be *nothing* in the central region.

But for the corresponding I proposition to be true, there must be *something* in the central region. Thus, they cannot both be true. They also cannot both be false. The only way for an E proposition to be false is for there to be something in the central region, but then the corresponding I proposition is not false but true. The only way for the I proposition to be false is if there is nothing in the central region, and then the E proposition is not false but true. Thus, they cannot both be true, and they cannot both be false. In other words, they always have opposite truth values. This relation is described by saying that these propositions are *contradictories*.

More generally, we can produce a diagram for the denial of a proposition by a simple procedure. The only information given in a Venn diagram is represented either by shading out some region, thereby indicating that nothing exists in it, or by putting an asterisk in a region, thereby indicating that something does exist in it. We are given no information about regions that are unmarked. To represent the denial of a proposition, we simply reverse the information in the diagram. That is, where there is an asterisk, we put in shading; where there is shading, we put in an asterisk. Everything else is left unchanged. Thus, we can see at once that corresponding E and I propositions are denials of one another, so they must always have opposite truth values. This makes them contradictories.

The same relation exists between an A proposition and its corresponding O proposition. Consider their forms:

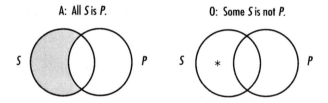

A: All *S* is *P.*   O: Some *S* is not *P.*

The diagram for an A proposition has shading exactly where the corresponding O proposition has an asterisk, and they contain no other information. Consequently, corresponding A and O propositions cannot both be false and cannot both be true, so they are contradictories.

EXERCISE III

1. Is an A proposition a contradictory of its corresponding E proposition? Why or why not?

2. Is an I proposition a contradictory of its corresponding O proposition? Why or why not?

3. If one proposition is the contradictory of another, is the latter always the contradictory of the former? Why or why not?

EXISTENTIAL COMMITMENT

It might also seem that an A proposition (with the form "All *S* is *P*") implies the corresponding I proposition (with the form "Some *S* is *P*"). This, however, raises a difficult problem that logicians have not fully settled. Usually when we make a statement, we are talking about certain specific things. If someone claims that all whales are mammals, that person is talking about whales and mammals and stating a relationship between them. In making this statement, the person seems to be taking the *existence* of whales and mammals for granted. The remark seems to involve what logicians call *existential commitment* to the things referred to in the subject and predicate terms. In the same way, stating an E proposition often seems to commit the speaker to the existence of things in the subject and predicate classes and, thus, to imply an O proposition. For example, someone who says, "No whales are fish" seems committed to "Some whales are not fish."

In other contexts, however, we seem to use universal (A and E) propositions without committing ourselves to the existence of the things referred to in the subject and predicate terms. For example, if we say, "All trespassers will be fined," we are not committing ourselves to the existence of any trespassers or to any actual fines for trespassing; we are only saying, "*If* there are trespassers, then they will be fined." Similarly, if we tell a sleepy child, "No ghosts are under your bed," we are not committing ourselves to the existence of ghosts or anything under the bed. Finally, when Newton said, "All bodies that are acted on by no forces are at rest," he did not commit himself to the existence of bodies that are acted on by no forces. Given these examples of A and E propositions that carry no commitment to the things referred to, it is easy to think of many others.

The question then arises whether we should include existential commitment in our treatment of universal propositions or not. Once more, we must make a decision. (Remember that we had to make decisions concerning the truth-table definitions of both disjunction and conditionals in Chapter 6.) *Classical* logic was developed on the assumption that universal (A and E) propositions carry existential commitment. *Modern* logic makes the opposite decision, treating the claim "All men are mortal" as equivalent to "If someone is a man, then that person is mortal," and the claim "No men are islands" as equivalent to "If someone is a man, then that person is not an island." This way of speaking carries no commitment to the existence of any men.

Which approach should we adopt? The modern approach is simpler and has proved more powerful in the long run. For these reasons, we will adopt the modern approach and *not* assign existential commitment to universal (A and E) propositions, so these propositions do not imply particular (I and O) propositions. All the same, there is something beautiful about the classical approach, and it does seem appropriate in some contexts to some people, so it is worth exploring in its own right. The Appendix to this chapter will show how to develop the classical theory by adding existential commitment to the modern theory.

EXERCISE IV

Give two new examples of contexts in which:

1. Stating an A proposition does not seem to commit the speaker to the existence of the things to which the subject term refers.

2. Stating an A proposition does not seem to commit the speaker to the existence of the things to which the predicate term refers.

3. Stating an E proposition does not seem to commit the speaker to the existence of the things to which the subject term refers.

4. Stating an E proposition does not seem to commit the speaker to the existence of the things to which the predicate term refers.

VALIDITY FOR CATEGORICAL ARGUMENTS

We have introduced Venn diagrams because they provide an efficient and illuminating way to test the validity of arguments made up of categorical (A, E, I, and O) propositions. The basic idea is simple: An argument made up of categorical propositions is valid if all the information contained in the Venn diagram for the conclusion is already contained in the Venn diagram for the premises. There are only two ways to put information into a Venn diagram: We can either shade out an area or put an asterisk in an area. Hence, to test the validity of an argument made up of categorical propositions, we need only examine the diagram of the conclusion for its information (its shading or asterisks) and then check to see if the diagram for the premises contains this information (the same shading or asterisks).

The following simple example will give a general idea of how this works:

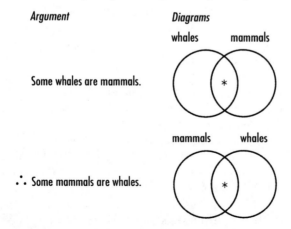

Argument

Diagrams

Some whales are mammals.

∴ Some mammals are whales.

Notice that the only information contained in the diagram for the conclusion is the asterisk in the overlap between the two circles, and that information is already included in the diagram for the premise. Thus, the argument is valid.

The same method can be used to test argument *forms* for validity. The form of the previous argument and the corresponding diagrams look like this:

Argument Form

Diagrams

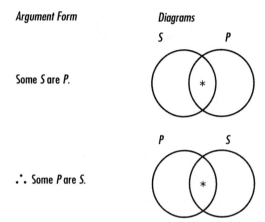

Some S are P.

∴ Some P are S.

This argument form is valid, because all the information contained in the Venn diagram for the conclusion is contained in the Venn diagram for the premise. And any argument that is a substitution instance of a valid argument form is valid.

Notice that we did not say that an argument is *invalid* if it fails these tests—that is, if some of the information in the Venn diagram for the conclusion (or its form) is not contained in the Venn diagram for the premises (or their forms). As with truth tables in propositional logic (see Chapter 6), Venn diagrams test whether arguments are valid by virtue of a certain form, but some arguments will be valid on a different basis, even though they are not valid by virtue of their categorical form. Here is one example:

Argument

Diagrams

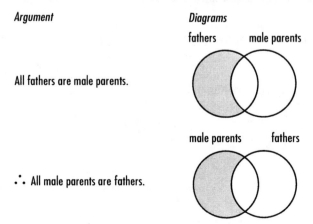

All fathers are male parents.

∴ All male parents are fathers.

The Venn diagram for the conclusion includes shading in the circle for male parents, whereas the Venn diagram for the premise includes shading in the circle for fathers, so the premise does not contain the information for the conclusion. Thus, this *form* of argument is *not* valid, and some arguments of this form are not valid. Nonetheless, this particular argument *is* clearly valid, since it is not possible for the premise to be true when the conclusion is false, for the simple reason that the conclusion cannot be false. Because of such cases, Venn diagrams can show us that an argument is valid, but they cannot prove that an argument is invalid.

Despite this limitation, the method of Venn diagrams can be used to test many different kinds of arguments and argument forms for validity. We will show how this method works for two main kinds of argument: immediate inferences and syllogisms.

CATEGORICAL IMMEDIATE INFERENCES

A categorical *immediate inference* is an argument with the following features:

1. It has a single premise. (That is why the inference is called *immediate*.)
2. It is constructed from A, E, I, and O propositions. (That is why the inference is called *categorical*.)

These arguments deserve attention because they occur quite often in everyday reasoning.

We will focus on the simplest kind of immediate inference, which is *conversion*. We *convert* a proposition (and produce its *converse*) simply by reversing the subject term and the predicate term. By the *subject term,* we mean the term that occurs as the grammatical subject; by the *predicate term,* we mean the term that occurs as the grammatical predicate. In the A proposition "All spies are aliens," "spies" is the subject term and "aliens" is the predicate term; the converse is "All aliens are spies."

In this case, identifying the predicate term is straightforward because the grammatical predicate is a noun—a predicate nominative. Often, however, we have to change the grammatical predicate from an adjective to a noun phrase in order to get a noun that refers to a class of things. "All spies are dangerous" becomes "All spies are dangerous things." Here "spies" is the subject term and "dangerous things" is the predicate term. Although this change is a bit artificial, it is necessary because, when we convert a proposition (that is, reverse its subject and predicate terms), we need a noun phrase to take the place of the grammatical subject. In English we cannot say, "All dangerous are spies," but we can say, "All dangerous things are spies."

Having explained what conversion is, we now want to know when this operation yields a *valid* immediate inference. To answer this question, we use Venn diagrams to examine the relationship between each of the four basic categorical propositional forms and its converse. The immediate inference is valid if the information contained in the conclusion is also contained in the premise—that is, if any region that is shaded in the conclusion is shaded in the premise, and if any region that contains an asterisk in the conclusion contains an asterisk in the premise.

Two cases are obvious: Both I and E propositions validly convert. From an I proposition with the form "Some *S* is *P*," we may validly infer its converse, which has the form "Some *P* is *S*."

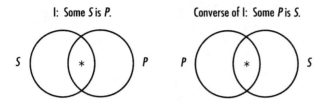

From an E proposition with the form "No *S* is *P*," we may validly infer its converse, which has the form "No *P* is *S*."

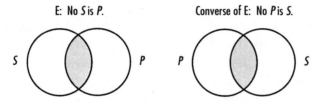

Notice that in both these cases, the information (the asterisk or shading) is in the center of the original diagram, and the diagram for the converse flips the original diagram. Thus, the two diagrams contain the same information, since the diagram for the converse has exactly the same markings in the same areas as does the diagram for the original propositional form. This shows that E and I propositions not only logically *imply* their converses but are also logically *implied by* them. Because the implication runs both ways, these propositions are said to be *logically equivalent* to their converses, and they always have the same truth values as their converses.

The use of a Venn diagram also shows that an O proposition cannot always be converted validly. From a proposition with the form "Some *S* is not *P*," we may not always infer its converse, which has the form "Some *P* is not *S*."

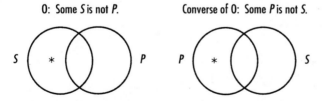

Notice that in this case the information is not in the center but is instead off to one side. As a result, the information changes when the diagram is flipped. The asterisk is in a different circle—it is in the circle for *S* in the diagram for an O proposition, but it is in the circle for *P* in the diagram for the converse of the O proposition. That shows that an argument from an O proposition to its converse is not always valid.[1]

Finally, we can see that A propositions also do not always validly convert. From a proposition with the form "All *S* is *P*," we may not always infer its converse, which has the form "All *P* is *S*."

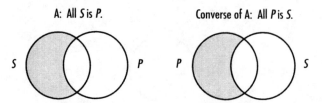

A: All *S* is *P*.   Converse of A: All *P* is *S*.

Since the diagram is not symmetrical, the information changes when the diagram is flipped; the shading ends up in a different circle. That shows why this form of argument is not always valid.

Traditionally, other immediate inferences have also been studied, but we will not run through them all here. The single example of conversion is enough to illustrate how Venn diagrams can be used to test some arguments for validity.

EXERCISE V

Use Venn diagrams to determine whether the following immediate inferences are valid:

1. All dinosaurs are animals. Therefore, all animals are dinosaurs.
2. Some pterodactyls can fly. Therefore, some flying things are pterodactyls.
3. Some eryopses are not meat eaters. Therefore, some things that eat meat are not eryopses.
4. No tyrannosaurus is a king. Therefore, no king is a tyrannosaurus.
5. Some dinosaurs are reptiles. Therefore, all dinosaurs are reptiles.
6. Some dinosaurs are not alive today. Therefore, no dinosaurs are alive today.
7. All dimetrodons eat meat. Therefore, some dimetrodons eat meat.
8. No dinosaurs are warm-blooded. Therefore, some dinosaurs are not warm-blooded.

THE THEORY OF THE SYLLOGISM

In an immediate inference, we draw a conclusion directly from a single A, E, I, or O proposition. Moreover, when two categorical propositions are contradictories, the falsity of one can be validly inferred from the truth of the other, and the truth of one can be validly inferred from the falsity of the other. All these forms of argument contain only one premise. The next step in understanding categorical propositions is to consider arguments with two premises.

An important group of such arguments is called *categorical syllogisms.* The basic idea behind these arguments is commonsensical. Suppose you wish to prove that all squares have four sides. A proof should present some *link* or *connection* between squares and four-sided figures. This link can be provided by some intermediate class, such as rectangles. You can then argue that, because the set of squares is a subset of the set of rectangles and rectangles are a subset of four-sided figures, squares must also be a subset of four-sided figures.

Of course, there are many other ways to link two terms by means of a third term. All such arguments with categorical propositions are called categorical syllogisms. More precisely, a categorical syllogism is any argument such that:

1. The argument has exactly two premises and one conclusion;
2. The argument contains only basic A, E, I, and O propositions;
3. Exactly one premise contains the predicate term;
4. Exactly one premise contains the subject term; and
5. Each premise contains the middle term.

The *predicate term* is simply the term in the predicate of the conclusion. It is also called the *major term,* and the premise that contains the predicate term is called the *major premise.* The *subject term* is the term in the subject of the conclusion. It is called the *minor term,* and the premise that contains the subject term is called the *minor premise.* It is traditional to state the major premise first, the minor premise second.

Our first example of a categorical syllogism then looks like this:

All rectangles are things with four sides.   (Major premise)
All squares are rectangles.   (Minor premise)
∴ All squares are things with four sides.   (Conclusion)

Subject term = "Squares"
Predicate term = "Things with four sides"
Middle term = "Rectangles"

To get the form of this syllogism, we replace the terms with variables:

All M is P.
All S is M.
∴ All S is P.

Of course, many other arguments fit the definition of a categorical syllogism. Here is one with a negative premise:

No ellipses are things with sides.
All circles are ellipses.
∴ No circles are things with sides.

The next categorical syllogism has a particular premise:

All squares are things with equal sides.
Some squares are rectangles.
∴ Some rectangles are things with equal sides.

In each of the last two syllogisms, what is the subject term? The predicate term? The middle term? The major premise? The minor premise? The form of the syllogism (using *S*, *P*, and *M*)? Is the syllogism valid? Why or why not?

Given the restrictions in the definition of a categorical syllogism, there are exactly 256 possible forms of categorical syllogism. Explain why.

VENN DIAGRAMS FOR SYLLOGISMS. In a previous section, we used Venn diagrams to test the validity of immediate inferences. Immediate inferences contain only two terms or classes, so the corresponding Venn diagrams need only two overlapping circles. Categorical syllogisms contain three terms or classes. To reflect this, we will use diagrams with three overlapping circles. If we use a bar over a letter to indicate that things in the area are not in the class (so that $\bar{S}$ indicates what is not in *S*), then our diagram looks like this:

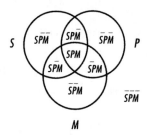

This diagram has eight different areas, which can be listed in an order that resembles a truth table:

S	P	M
S	P	$\bar{M}$
S	$\bar{P}$	M
S	$\bar{P}$	$\bar{M}$
$\bar{S}$	P	M
$\bar{S}$	P	$\bar{M}$
$\bar{S}$	$\bar{P}$	M
$\bar{S}$	$\bar{P}$	$\bar{M}$

Notice that, if something is neither an *S* nor a *P* nor an *M*, then it falls completely outside the system of overlapping circles. In every other case, a thing is assigned to one of the seven compartments within the system of overlapping circles.

TESTING SYLLOGISMS FOR VALIDITY.   To test the validity of a syllogism using a Venn diagram, we first fill in the diagram to indicate the information
contained in the premises. Remember that the only information contained
in a Venn diagram is indicated either by shading out an area or by putting
an asterisk in it. The argument is valid if the information expressed by the
conclusion is already contained in the diagram for the premises.[2] To see
this, consider the diagrams for examples that we have already given:

> All rectangles have four sides.
> All squares are rectangles.
> ∴ All squares have four sides.

Here's the diagram for the premises:

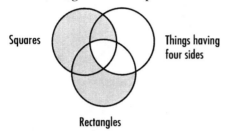

Here's the diagram for the conclusion:

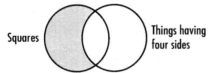

This diagram for the conclusion contains only the information that nothing is
in the circle for squares that is not also in the circle for things having four
sides. In the diagram for the premises, all the things that are squares are cor-
ralled into the region of things that have four sides. Thus, the diagram for the
premises contains all of the information in the diagram for the conclusion.
That shows that this syllogism is valid.

Next, let's try a syllogism with a negative premise:

> No ellipses have sides.
> All circles are ellipses.
> ∴ No circles have sides.

Here's the diagram for the premises:

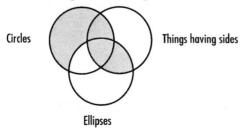

We diagram the conclusion "No circles have sides" as follows:

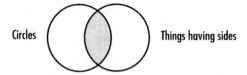

That information is clearly already contained in the Venn diagram for the premises, so this syllogism is also valid.

Let's try a syllogism with a particular premise:

> All squares have equal sides.
> Some squares are rectangles.
> ∴ Some rectangles have equal sides.

It is a good strategy to diagram a universal premise *before* diagramming a particular premise. The diagram for the above argument then looks like this:

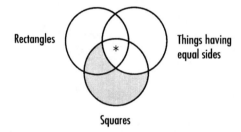

Here's the diagram for the conclusion—that there is something that is a rectangle that has equal sides:

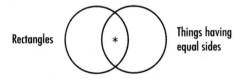

The asterisk in the middle area of this diagram says that something is in both circles, and that information already appears in the diagram for the premises, so this argument is valid.

So far we have looked only at valid syllogisms. Let's see how this method applies to invalid syllogisms. Here is one:

> All pediatricians are doctors.
> All pediatricians like children.
> ∴ All doctors like children.

We can diagram the premises at the left and the conclusion at the right:

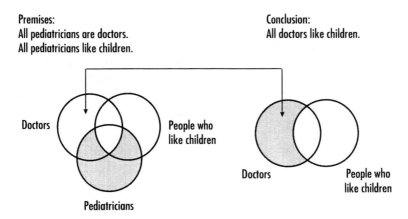

Premises:
All pediatricians are doctors.
All pediatricians like children.

Conclusion:
All doctors like children.

It is evident that the information in the diagram for the conclusion is *not* already contained in the diagram for the premises. The arrow shows differences in informational content. Thus, this form of syllogism is not valid.

Notice that the difference between these diagrams not only tells us *that* this form of syllogism is invalid; it also tells us *why* it is invalid. In the diagram for the premises, there is no shading in the upper left area, which includes people who are doctors but are not pediatricians and do not like children. This shows that the premises do not rule out the possibility that some people are doctors without being pediatricians or liking children. But if anyone is a doctor and not a person who likes children, then it is not true that all doctors like children. Because this is the conclusion of the syllogism, the premises do not rule out all of the ways in which the conclusion might be false. As a result, this conclusion does not follow by virtue of categorical form.[3]

Here is an example of an invalid syllogism with particular premises:

Some doctors are golfers.
Some fathers are doctors.
∴ Some fathers are golfers.

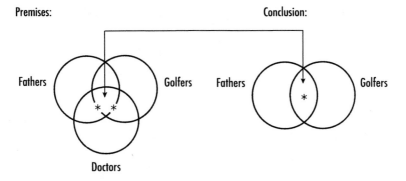

Premises:

Conclusion:

Examine this diagram closely. Notice that in diagramming "Some doctors are golfers," we had to put an asterisk *on the boundary* of the circle for fathers, because we were not given information saying whether anything falls into the category of fathers or not. For the same reason, we had to put an asterisk on the boundary of the circle for golfers when diagramming "Some fathers are doctors." The upshot was that we did not indicate that anything exists in the region of overlap between fathers and golfers. But this is what the conclusion demands, so the form of this syllogism is not valid.

Here is an invalid syllogism with negative premises:

> No babies are golfers.
> No fathers are babies.
> ─────────────────
> ∴ No fathers are golfers.

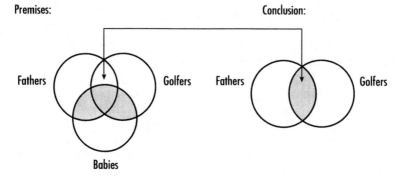

Again, we see that the form of this syllogism is not valid, because the entire area of overlap between the circles is shaded in the diagram for the conclusion, but part of that area is not shaded in the diagram for the premises.

The method of Venn diagrams is adequate for deciding the validity or invalidity of all possible forms of categorical syllogism. To master this method, all you need is a little practice.

EXERCISE VII

Using Venn diagrams, test the following syllogistic forms for validity:

1. All *M* is *P*.
   All *M* is *S*.
   ─────────
   ∴ All *S* is *P*.

2. All *P* is *M*.
   All *M* is *S*.
   ─────────
   ∴ All *S* is *P*.

3. All *M* is *P*.
   Some *M* is *S*.
   ─────────
   ∴ Some *S* is *P*.

4. All *P* is *M*.
   Some *M* is *S*.
   ─────────
   ∴ Some *S* is *P*.

5. All *P* is *M*.
   Some *S* is *M*.
   ─────────
   ∴ Some *S* is *P*.

6. All *P* is *M*.
   Some *S* is not *M*.
   ─────────
   ∴ Some *S* is not *P*.

7. All *M* is *P*.
   Some *S* is not *M*.
   _____
   ∴ Some *S* is not *P*.

8. All *M* is *P*.
   Some *M* is not *S*.
   _____
   ∴ Some *S* is not *P*.

9. No *M* is *P*.
   Some *S* is *M*.
   _____
   ∴ Some *S* is not *P*.

10. No *P* is *M*.
    Some *S* is *M*.
    _____
    ∴ Some *S* is not *P*.

11. No *P* is *M*.
    Some *S* is not *M*.
    _____
    ∴ Some *S* is not *P*.

12. No *M* is *P*.
    Some *S* is not *M*.
    _____
    ∴ Some *S* is not *P*

13. No *P* is *M*.
    Some *M* is not *S*.
    _____
    ∴ Some *S* is not *P*.

14. No *P* is *M*.
    No *M* is *S*.
    _____
    ∴ No *S* is *P*.

15. No *P* is *M*.
    All *M* is *S*.
    _____
    ∴ No *S* is *P*.

16. No *P* is *M*.
    All *S* is *M*.
    _____
    ∴ No *S* is *P*.

17. All *P* is *M*.
    No *S* is *M*.
    _____
    ∴ No *S* is *P*.

18. All *M* is *P*.
    No *S* is *M*.
    _____
    ∴ No *S* is *P*.

19. Some *M* is *P*.
    Some *M* is not *S*.
    _____
    ∴ Some *S* is not *P*.

20. Some *P* is *M*.
    Some *S* is not *M*.
    _____
    ∴ Some *S* is *P*.

EXERCISE VIII

Explain why it is a good strategy to diagram a universal premise before diagramming a particular premise in a syllogism with both.

PROBLEMS IN APPLYING THE THEORY OF THE SYLLOGISM. After mastering the techniques for evaluating syllogisms, students naturally turn to arguments that arise in daily life and attempt to use these newly acquired skills. They are often disappointed with the results. The formal theory of the syllogism seems to bear little relationship to everyday arguments, and there does not seem to be any easy way to bridge the gap.

This gap between formal theory and its application occurs for a number of reasons. First, as we saw in Chapters 2 and 5, our everyday discourse leaves much unstated. Many things are conversationally implied rather than explicitly asserted. We do not feel called on to say many things that are matters of common agreement. Before we can apply the theory of the syllogism to everyday arguments, these things that are simply understood must be made explicit. This is often illuminating, and sometimes boring, but it usually involves a great deal of work. Second, the theory of the syllogism applies to statements only in a highly stylized form. Before we apply the theory of the syllogism to an argument, we must cast its premises and conclusion into the basic A, E, I, and O forms. As we saw earlier in this chapter, the needed translation is not always simple or obvious. It may not always be possible. For these and related reasons, modern logicians have largely abandoned the project of reducing all reasoning to syllogisms.

Why study the theory of the syllogism at all, if it is hard to apply in some circumstances and perhaps impossible to apply in others? The answer to this question was given at the beginning of Chapter 6. The study of formal logic is important because it deepens our insight into a central notion of logic: *validity*. Furthermore, the argument forms we have studied do underlie much of our everyday reasoning, but so much else is going on in a normal conversational setting that this dimension is often hidden. By examining arguments in idealized forms, we can study their validity in isolation from all the other factors at work in a rich conversational setting.

There is a difference, then, between the techniques developed in Chapters 1–5 and the techniques developed in Chapters 6–7. The first five chapters presented methods of informal analysis that may be applied directly to the rich and complex arguments that arise in everyday life. These methods of analysis are not wholly rigorous, but they do provide practical guides for the analysis and evaluation of actual arguments. The chapters concerning formal logic have the opposite tendency. In comparison with the first five chapters, the level of rigor is very high, but the range of application is correspondingly smaller. In general, the more rigor and precision you insist on, the less you can talk about.

DISCUSSION QUESTIONS

1. What are the chief differences between the logical procedures developed in this chapter and those developed in the chapter on propositional logic?

2. If we evaluate arguments as they occur in everyday life by using the exact standards developed in Chapters 6 and 7, we discover that our everyday arguments rarely satisfy these standards, at least explicitly. Does this show that most of our ordinary arguments are illogical? What else might it show?

APPENDIX: THE CLASSICAL THEORY

The difference between classical and modern logic is simply that the classical approach adds one more assumption—namely, that every categorical proposition is about something. More technically, the assumption is that A, E, I, and O propositions all carry commitment to the existence of something in the subject class and something in the predicate class. To draw Venn diagrams for categorical propositions on the classical interpretation, then, all we need to do is add existential commitment to the diagrams for their modern interpretations, which were discussed above.

But how should we add existential commitment to Venn diagrams? The answer might seem easy: Just put an asterisk wherever there is existential commitment. The story cannot be quite so simple, however, for the following reason. The Venn diagram for the E propositional form on the modern interpretation is this:

Modern E: No S is P.

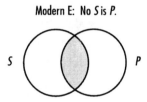

The classical interpretation adds existential commitment in both the subject and the predicate, so if we represent existential commitment with an asterisk, we get this diagram:

Classical E: No S is P. (???)

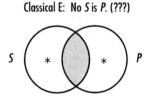

Although this diagram might seem to work, it breaks down when we perform operations on it. We are supposed to be able to diagram the contradictory of a proposition simply by substituting shading for asterisks and asterisks for shading. If we perform this operation on the previous diagram, we get this:

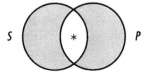

This diagram is very different from the Venn diagram for the I propositional form, which is the same on both classial and modern interpretations:

I: Some S is P.

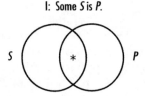

An I proposition, however, is supposed to be the contradictory of the corresponding E proposition even on the classical interpretation. So something has gone wrong. This problem shows that existential commitment cannot be treated exactly like explicit existential assertion, as in I and O propositions. As a result, we cannot use the same asterisk to represent existential commitment in Venn diagrams. Instead, we will use a plus sign: "+." With this new symbol, we can diagram the E propositional form on the classical interpretation this way:

Classical E: No S is P.

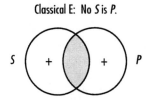

The plus sign indicates that an E proposition carries commitment to the existence of something in each class, even though it does not explicitly assert that something exists in either class.

From this new diagram, we can get the contradictory of a proposition by substituting shading for asterisks and asterisks for shading, as long as we also add plus signs to ensure that no class is empty, and drop plus signs that are no longer needed to indicate this existential commitment. When this procedure is applied to the previous diagram, the shading becomes an asterisk in the central area, and we can then drop the plus signs in the side areas because the central asterisk already assures us that something exists in both circles. Thus, we get the (modern and classical) diagram for the I propositional form. Moreover, when this procedure is applied to the diagram for the I propositional form, it yields the above diagram for the E propositional form on the classical interpretation.

It might not be so clear, however, that E and I propositions are contradictories on their classical interpretations; let us see why this is so. Two propositions are contradictories if and only if they cannot both be true and also cannot both be false. The diagram for an E proposition has shading in the same area in which the diagram for its corresponding I proposition has an asterisk, so they cannot both be true. It is harder to see why these propositions cannot both be false on the classical interpretation, but this can be shown by the following argument. Suppose that an I proposition is false. Then there is nothing in the central area, so that area should be shaded. The classical interpretation insists that the subject and predicate classes are not empty, so if there is nothing in the central area, there must be something in each side area, which is indicated by a plus sign in each side area. That gives us the diagram for the corresponding E proposition, so that proposition is true. Thus, if an I proposition is false, its corresponding E proposition is true. That means that they cannot both be false. We already saw that they cannot both be true. So they are contradictories.

The same procedure yields a classical O proposition when it is applied to a classical A proposition, and a classical A proposition when it is applied to a classical O proposition:

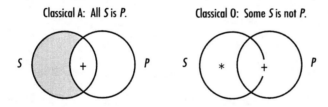

Classical A: All S is P.   Classical O: Some S is not P.

(The plus sign on the line indicates that the commitment is to something in the right-hand circle, but not to anything in either specific part of that circle.) Propositions of these forms on their classical interpretations cannot both be true and cannot both be false, so they are contradictories. Thus, this method of diagramming seems to capture the classical interpretation of the basic propositions.

EXERCISE IX

Explain why an A proposition and its corresponding O proposition are contradictories on their classical interpretations, using the diagrams above.

THE CLASSICAL SQUARE OF OPPOSITION

In addition to the contradictories, there is a more extensive and elegant set of logical relationships among categorical propositions on the classical interpretation. This system of relationships produces what has been called the *square of opposition.*

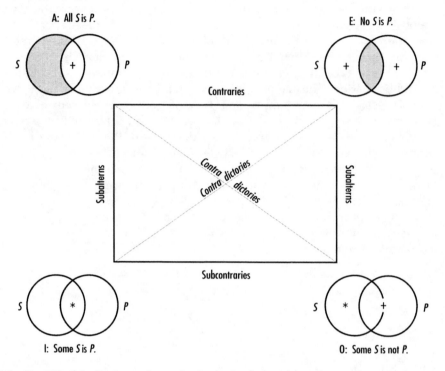

The lines in this diagram show the logical relationships that each proposition has to the other three. These relationships are explained below. Throughout the discussion, it is important to remember that all of the basic propositions are interpreted as carrying existential commitment in both their subjects and their predicates.

CONTRADICTORIES. Two propositions are *contradictories* of each other (and they contradict each other) when they are related in the following way:

1. They cannot both be true, and
2. They cannot both be false.

More simply, contradictory pairs of propositions always have opposite truth values. We have already seen that the E and I propositions are contradictories of one another, as are the A and O propositions. This relationship holds on both the modern interpretation and the classical interpretation.

CONTRARIES. Two propositions are said to be *contraries* of one another if they are related in this way:

1. They cannot both be true, but
2. They can both be false.

On the classical interpretation (but not the modern interpretation), A and E propositions with the same subject and predicate are contraries of one another.

In common life, the relationship between such corresponding A and E propositions is captured by the notion that one claim is the *complete opposite* of another. The complete opposite of "Everyone is here" is "No one is here." Clearly, such complete opposites cannot both be true at once. We see this readily if we look at the diagrams for A and E propositions on the classical interpretation. The middle region of the diagram for an A proposition shows the existence of something that is both *S* and *P*, whereas the middle region of the diagram for the corresponding E proposition is shaded, showing that nothing is both *S* and *P*. It should also be clear that these A and E propositions can both be false. Suppose that there is some *S* that is *P* and also some *S* that is not *P*:

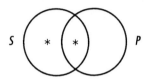

Going from left to right, the first asterisk shows that the A proposition of the form "All *S* is *P*" is false; the second asterisk shows that the corresponding E proposition of the form "No *S* is *P*" is also false. Thus, these propositions can both be false, but they cannot both be true. This makes them contraries.

SUBCONTRARIES.   Propositions are *subcontraries* of one another when

1. They can both be true, and
2. They cannot both be false.

On the classical approach (but not the modern approach), corresponding I and O propositions are subcontraries. To see how this works, compare the diagrams for I and O propositions:

I: Some *S* is *P*.   O: Some *S* is not *P*.

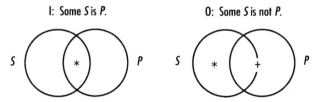

It should be clear that corresponding propositions with these forms can both be true, since there can be some *S* that is *P* and another *S* that is not *P*. But why can't they both be false? Consider the left side of the following diagram:

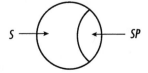

We know that, on the classical approach, there must be something in this circle somewhere. If there is something in the overlapping region *SP*, then the I proposition is true. If there is something in the nonoverlapping region of *S*, then there must be something else in the circle for *P*, because *P* cannot be empty on the classical approach; therefore, the O proposition is true. Thus, either the I proposition or the corresponding O proposition must be true, so they cannot both be false. We already saw that they can both be true. Consequently, corresponding I and O propositions are subcontraries.

SUBALTERNS. *Subalternation* is the relationship that holds down the sides of the classical square of opposition. Quite simply, an A proposition implies the corresponding I proposition, and an E proposition implies the corresponding O proposition. This relationship depends on the existential commitment found on the classical approach and does not hold on the modern approach.

The validity of subalternation is illustrated by the following diagrams:

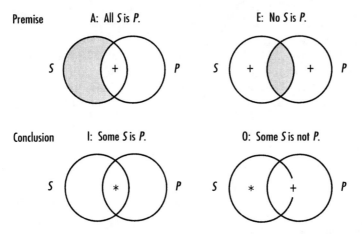

An A proposition includes a plus sign where the corresponding I proposition includes an asterisk, but both symbols indicate that something lies in the middle area. Thus, the information for the I proposition is already included in the diagram for the A proposition, which means that the A proposition implies the I proposition.

The same point applies to the implication on the right-hand side, because the diagram for an E proposition includes a plus sign in the same area as the asterisk in the diagram for the corresponding O proposition. The diagram for the E proposition also has a plus sign in the rightmost area. If something exists in that area, then something exists in either that area or the middle area, which is what is meant by the plus sign on the line in the diagram for the O proposition. Thus, an E proposition implies its corresponding O proposition.

The information given by the classical square of opposition can now be summarized in two charts. We shall ask two questions. First, for each propositional form, if we assume that a proposition with that form is *true*, what consequences follow for the truth or falsity of a corresponding proposition with a different form?

		A	E	I	O
	A	T	F	T	F
Assumed true	E	F	T	F	T
	I	?	F	T	?
	O	F	?	?	T

"T" indicates that the corresponding proposition in that column is true, "F" indicates that it is false, and "?" indicates that it might have either truth value, because neither consequence follows.

Second, for each propositional form, if we assume that a proposition with that form is *false*, what consequences follow for the truth or falsity of a corresponding proposition with a different form?

		A	E	I	O
	A	F	?	?	T
Assumed false	E	?	F	T	?
	I	F	T	F	T
	O	T	F	T	F

THE CLASSICAL THEORY OF IMMEDIATE INFERENCE

The difference between the modern and classical approaches is simply that the classical approach assigns more information—specifically, existential commitment—to the basic propositions than the modern interpretation does. Because of this additional information, certain immediate inferences hold on the classical approach that do not hold on the modern approach. In particular, though conversion of an A proposition fails on both approaches, what is known as *conversion by limitation* holds on the classical approach but not on the modern approach. That is, from a proposition with the form "All *S* is *P*," we may not validly infer the proposition with the form "All *P* is *S*," but on the classical approach, we may validly infer "*Some P* is *S*." The reason is simple: From a proposition with the form "All *S* is *P*" on the classical interpretation, we may infer a proposition with the form "*Some S* is *P*," and then we may convert this to get a proposition with the form "*Some P* is *S*."

EXERCISE X

Using the Venn diagrams for the classical interpretation of the A propositional form given above, show that conversion by limitation is classically valid for an A proposition.

THE CLASSICAL THEORY OF SYLLOGISMS

As in the case of immediate inferences, the premises of syllogisms will contain more information—specifically, existential commitment—on the classical interpretation than they do on the modern interpretation. This will make some syllogisms valid on the classical approach that were not valid on the modern approach.

We begin our study of this matter with an example that has had a curious history:

> All rectangles are four-sided.
> All squares are rectangles.
> ∴ *Some* squares are four-sided.

The argument is peculiar because its conclusion is weaker than it needs to be. We could, after all, conclude that *all* squares are four-sided. The argument thus violates the conversational rule of Quantity. Perhaps for this reason, this syllogism was often not included in traditional lists of valid syllogisms. Yet the argument is valid on the classical interpretation of existential commitment, and our diagram should show this.

Step I: Diagram the first premise

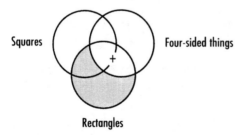

Notice that the plus sign is placed on the outer edge of the circle for squares, because we are not in a position to put it either inside or outside that circle. We now add the information for the second premise:

Step II: Add the second premise

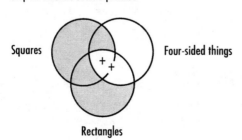

As expected, the conclusion that some squares are four-sided is already diagrammed, so the argument is valid—provided that we take A propositions to have existential commitment.

Because classical logicians tended to ignore the previous argument, their writings did not bring out the importance of existential commitment in evaluating it. There is, however, an argument that did appear on the classical lists that makes clear the demand for existential commitment. These are syllogisms with the following form:

> All *M* is *P*.
> All *M* is *S*.
> ∴ Some *S* is *P*.

This form of syllogism is diagrammed as follows:

Step I: Diagram the first premise

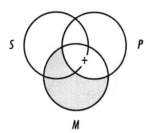

Step II: Add the second premise

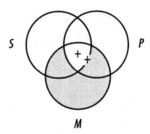

Again, we see that the conclusion follows, but only if we diagram A propositions to indicate existential commitment. This, then, is an argument that was declared valid on the classical approach, but invalid on the modern approach.

EXERCISE XI

Use Venn diagrams to test the following syllogism forms for validity on the classical approach:

1. All *M* is *P*.
   No *M* is *S*.
   ∴ Some *S* is not *P*.

2. No *M* is *P*.
   All *M* is *S*.
   ∴ Some *S* is not *P*.

3. No *M* is *P*.
   All *S* is *M*.
   ∴ Some *S* is not *P*.

4. No *M* is *P*.
   No *M* is *S*.
   ∴ Some *S* is not *P*.

Are the following claims true or false? Explain your answers.

1. Every syllogism that is valid on the modern approach is also valid on the classical approach.
2. Every syllogism that is valid on the classical approach but not on the modern approach has a particular conclusion that starts with "Some."

NOTES

[1] We say "not always" rather than simply "not," because there are some strange cases—logicians call them "degenerate cases"—for which inferences of this pattern are valid. For example, from "Some men are not men," we may validly infer "Some men are not men." Here, by making the subject term and the predicate term the same, we trivialize conversion. Keeping cases of this kind in mind, we must say that the inference from an O proposition to its converse is usually, but not always, invalid. In contrast, the set of valid arguments holds in all cases, including degenerate cases.

[2] We cannot say "only if" here because of degenerate cases of categorical syllogisms that are valid, but not by virtue of their syllogistic form. Here is one example: "All numbers divisible by two are even. No prime number other than two is divisible by two. Therefore, no prime number other than two is even." This syllogism is valid because it is not possible that its premises are true and its conclusion is false, but other syllogisms with this same form are not valid.

[3] We need to add *"by virtue of its categorical form,"* because, as we saw above, it still might be valid on some other basis. In this particular example, however, nothing else makes this argument valid.

HOW TO EVALUATE ARGUMENTS: INDUCTIVE STANDARDS

Previous chapters have been concerned primarily with deductive arguments that aim at validity. Many arguments encountered in daily life, however, are not intended to meet this standard of validity. They are only supposed to provide reasons (perhaps very strong reasons) for their conclusions. Such arguments are called inductive and will be the focus of Part III. This part begins with a discussion of the nature of inductive standards and arguments followed by a survey of five forms of inductive argument: statistical generalizations, statistical applications, causal reasoning, inference to the best explanation, and arguments from analogy. The next topic is probability, because, as we will see, the inductive standard of strength can be understood in terms of probability. Part III will close by discussing how probabilities get deployed in decision making.

8

ARGUMENTS TO AND FROM GENERALIZATIONS

*T*his chapter begins our investigation of inductive arguments by distinguishing the inductive standard of strength from the deductive standard of validity. Inductive arguments are defined as arguments that are intended to be strong rather than valid. Two common examples of inductive arguments are discussed next. In statistical generalizations, *a claim is made about a population on the basis of features of a sample of that population.* In statistical applications, *a claim is made about members of a population on the basis of features of the population. Statistical generalizations take us up from samples to general claims, and statistical applications then take us back down to individual cases.*

INDUCTION *VERSUS* DEDUCTION

The distinction between deductive arguments and inductive arguments can be drawn in a variety of ways, but the fundamental difference concerns the relationship that is claimed to hold between the premises and the conclusion for each type of argument. An argument is *deductive* insofar as it is intended or claimed to be *valid*. As we know from Chapter 3, an argument is valid if and only if it is impossible for the conclusion to be false when its premises are true. The following is a valid deductive argument:

> All ravens are black.
> ∴ If there is a raven on top of Pikes Peak, then it is black.

Because the premise lays down a universal principle governing all ravens, if it's true, then it *must* be true of all ravens (if any) on top of Pikes Peak. This same relationship does not hold for invalid arguments. Nonetheless, arguments that are not valid can still be deductive if they are intended or claimed to be valid.

In contrast, inductive arguments are not intended to be valid, so they should not be criticized for being invalid. The following is an example of an inductive argument:

> All ravens that we have observed so far are black.
> ∴ All ravens are black.

Here we have drawn an inductive inference from the characteristics of *observed* ravens to the characteristics of *all* ravens, most of which we have not observed. Of course, the premise of this argument *could be* true, yet the conclusion turn out to be false. A raven that has not yet been observed might be albino. The obviousness of this possibility suggests that someone who gives this argument does not put it forth as valid, so it is not a deductive argument. Instead, the premise is put forth as a *reason* or *support* for the conclusion. When an argument is not claimed to be valid but is intended only to provide a reason for the conclusion, the argument is *inductive*.

Because inductive arguments are supposed to provide reasons, and reasons vary in strength, inductive arguments can be evaluated as *strong* or *weak*, depending on the strength of the reasons that they provide for their conclusions. If we have seen only ten ravens, and all of them were in our backyard, then the above argument gives at most a very weak reason to believe that all ravens are black. But, if we have traveled around the world and seen over half the ravens that exist, then the above argument gives a strong reason to believe that all ravens are black. Inductive arguments are usually intended to provide strong support for their conclusions, in which case they can be criticized if the support they provide is not strong enough for the purposes at hand.

The most basic distinction, then, is not between two kinds of argument but is instead between two standards for evaluating arguments. The deductive standard is validity. The inductive standard is strength. Arguments themselves are classified as either deductive or inductive in accordance with the standard that they are intended or claimed to meet.

There are several important differences between deductive and inductive standards. One fundamental feature of the deductive standard of validity is that adding premises to a valid argument cannot make it invalid. The definition of validity guarantees this: In a valid argument, it is not possible for the premises to be true without the conclusion being true as well. If any further premises could change this, then it would be possible for this relationship not to hold, so the argument would not be valid after all. Additional information might, of course, lead us to question the truth of one of the premises, but that is another matter.

The situation is strikingly different when we deal with inductive arguments. To cite a famous example, before the time of Captain Cook's voyage to Australia, Europeans had observed a great many swans, and every one of them was white. Thus, up to that time Europeans had very strong inductive evidence to support the claim that all swans are white. Then Captain Cook discovered black swans in Australia. What happens if we add this new piece of information to the premises of the original inductive argument? Provided that we accept Cook's report, we now produce a sound *deductive* argument in behalf of the opposite claim that *not* all swans are white; for, if some swans are black, then not all of them are white. This, then, is a feature of the inductive standard of strength: No matter how strong an inductive argument is, the possibility remains open that further information can undercut, perhaps completely, the strength of the argument and the support that the premises give to the conclusion. Because inductive strength and inductive arguments can always be defeated in this way, they are described as *defeasible*. Valid deductive arguments do not face a similar peril, so they are called *indefeasible*.

A second important difference between inductive and deductive standards is that inductive strength comes in degrees, but deductive validity does not. An argument is either valid or invalid. There is no question of how much validity an argument has. In contrast, inductive arguments can be more or less strong. The more varied ravens or swans we observe, the stronger the inductive arguments above. Some inductive arguments are extremely strong and put their conclusions beyond any reasonable doubt. Other inductive arguments are much weaker, even though they still have some force.

Because of the necessary relationship between the premises and the conclusion of a valid deductive argument, it is often said that the premises of valid deductive arguments (if true) provide *conclusive* support for their conclusions, whereas true premises of strong inductive arguments provide only *partial* support for their conclusions. There is something to this. Because the premises of a valid deductive argument necessitate the truth of the conclusion, if those premises are definitely known to be true, then they do supply conclusive reasons for the conclusion. The same cannot be said for inductive arguments.

It would be altogether misleading, however, to conclude from this that inductive arguments are inherently inferior to deductive arguments in supplying a justification or ground for a conclusion. In the first place, inductive arguments often place matters beyond any reasonable doubt. It is possible that the next pot of water will not boil at any temperature, however high, but this is not something we worry about. We do not take precautions against it, and we shouldn't.

More important, deductive arguments normally enjoy no advantages over their inductive counterparts. We can see this by comparing the two following arguments:

DEDUCTIVE	INDUCTIVE
All ravens are black.	All observed ravens are black.
∴ If there is a raven on top of Pikes Peak, it is black.	∴ If there is a raven on top of Pikes Peak, it is black.

Of course, it is true for the deductive argument (and not true for the inductive argument) that if the premise is true, then the conclusion must be true. This may seem to give an advantage to the deductive argument over the inductive argument. But before we can decide how much support a deductive argument gives its conclusion, we must ask if its premises are, after all, true. That is not something we can just take for granted. If we examine the premises of these two arguments, we see that it is easier to establish the truth of the premise of the inductive argument than it is to establish the truth of the premise of the deductive argument. If we have observed carefully and kept good records, then we might be fully confident that all *observed* ravens have been black. On the other hand, how can we show that *all* ravens (observed and unobserved—past, present, and future) are black? The most obvious way (though there may be other ways) would be to observe ravens to see if they are black or not. This, of course, involves producing an inductive argument (called a statistical generalization) for the premise of the deductive argument. Here our confidence in the truth of the premise of the deductive argument should be no greater than our confidence in the strength of the inference in the statistical generalization. In this case—and it is not unusual—the deductive argument provides no stronger grounds in support of its conclusion than does its inductive counterpart, because any reservations we might have about the *strength* of the inductive inference will be paralleled by doubts concerning the *truth* of the premise of the deductive argument.

We will also avoid the common mistake of saying that deductive arguments always move from the general to the particular, whereas inductive arguments always move from the particular to the general. In fact, both sorts of arguments can move in either direction. There are inductive arguments intended to establish particular matters of fact, and there are deductive arguments that involve generalizations from particulars. For example, when scientists assemble empirical evidence to determine whether the extinction of the dinosaurs was caused by the impact of a meteor, their discussions are models of inductive reasoning. Yet they are not trying to establish a generalization or a scientific law. Instead, they are trying to determine whether a particular event occurred some 65 million years ago. Inductive reasoning concerning particular matters of fact occurs constantly in everyday life as well, for example, when we check to see whether our television reception is being messed up by someone using a hair dryer. Deductive arguments from the particular to the general also exist, though they tend to be trivial, and hence boring. Here's one:

> Benjamin Franklin was the first postmaster general; therefore, anyone who is identical with Benjamin Franklin was the first postmaster general.

Of course, many deductive arguments do move from the general to the particular, and many inductive arguments do move from particular premises to a general conclusion. It is important to remember, however, that this is not the *definitive* difference between these two kinds of arguments. What makes deductive arguments deductive is precisely that they are intended to meet the deductive standard of validity, and what makes inductive arguments inductive is just that they are not intended to be deductively valid but are, instead, intended to be inductively strong.

EXERCISE I

Assuming a standard context, label each of the following arguments as deductive or inductive. Explain what it is about the words or form of argument that indicates whether or not each argument is intended or claimed to be valid. If it is not clear whether the argument is inductive or deductive, say why.

1. The sun is coming out, so the rain will probably stop soon.
2. It's going to rain tomorrow, so it will either rain or be clear tomorrow.
3. No woman has ever been elected president. Therefore, no woman will ever be elected president.
4. Diet cola never keeps me awake at night. I know because I drank it just last night without any problems.
5. The house is a mess, so Jeff must be home from college.
6. If Harold were innocent, he would not go into hiding. Since he is hiding, he must not be innocent.
7. Nobody in Paris seems to understand me, so either my French is rotten or Parisians are unfriendly.
8. Because both of our yards are near rivers in Tennessee, and my yard has lots of mosquitoes, there must also be lots of mosquitoes in your yard.
9. Most likely, her new husband speaks English with an accent, because he comes from Germany, and most Germans speak English with an accent.
10. There is no even number smaller than 2, so 1 is not an even number.

DISCUSSION QUESTIONS

1. The following arguments are not clearly inductive and also not clearly deductive. Explain why.
   a. All humans are mortal, and Socrates is a human, so Socrates is likely to be mortal also.
   b. We checked every continent there is, and every raven in every continent was observed to be black, so every raven is black.
   c. If there's radon in your basement, this monitor will go off. The monitor is going off, so there must be radon in your basement. (Said by an engineer while running the monitor in your basement.)
2. In mathematics, proofs are sometimes employed using the method of *mathematical induction*. If you are familiar with this procedure, determine whether these proofs are deductive or inductive in character. Explain why.

STATISTICAL GENERALIZATIONS

One classic example of an inductive argument is an opinion poll. Suppose a candidate wants to know how popular she is with voters. Because it would be practically impossible to survey all voters, she takes a sample of voting opinion and then infers that the opinions of those sampled indicate the overall opinion of voters. Thus, if 60 percent of the voters sampled say that they will vote for her, she concludes that she will get around 60 percent of the vote in the actual election. As we shall see later, inferences of this kind often go wrong, even when made by experts, but the general pattern of this reasoning is quite clear: Statistical features of a sample are used to make statistical claims about the population as a whole.

Basically the same form of reasoning can be used to reach a universal conclusion. An example is the inductive inference discussed at the start of this chapter: All observed ravens are black, so all ravens are black. Again, we sample part of a population to draw a conclusion about the whole. Arguments of this form, whether the conclusion is universal or partial (as when it cites a particular percentage), are called *statistical generalizations*.

How do we assess such inferences? To begin to answer this question, we can consider a simple example of a statistical generalization. On various occasions, Harold has tried to use Canadian quarters in American payphones and found that they have not worked. From this he draws the conclusion that Canadian quarters do not work in American payphones. Harold's inductive reasoning looks like this:

> In the past, when I tried to use Canadian quarters in American
>   payphones, they did not work.
> ∴ Canadian quarters do not work in American payphones.

The force of the conclusion is that Canadian quarters *never* work in American payphones.

In evaluating this argument, what questions should we ask? We can start with a question that we should ask of any argument.

SHOULD WE ACCEPT THE PREMISES?

Perhaps Harold has a bad memory, has kept bad records, or is a poor observer. For some obscure reason, he may even be lying. It is important to ask this question explicitly, because fairly often the premises, when challenged, will not stand up to scrutiny.

If we decide that the premises are acceptable (that is, true and justified), then we can shift our attention to the relationship between the premises and the conclusion and ask how much support the premises give to the conclusion. One commonsense question is this: "How many times has Harold tried to use Canadian quarters in American payphones?" If the answer is "Once," then our confidence in his argument should drop to almost nothing. So, for statistical generalizations, it is always appropriate to ask about the size of the sample.

IS THE SAMPLE LARGE ENOUGH?

One reason we should be suspicious of small samples is that they can be affected by runs of luck. Suppose Harold flips a Canadian quarter four times and it comes up heads each time. From this, he can hardly conclude that Canadian quarters always come up heads when flipped. He could not even reasonably conclude that *this* Canadian quarter would always come up heads when flipped. The reason for this is obvious enough: If you spend a lot of time flipping coins, runs of four heads in a row are not all that unlikely (the probability is actually one in sixteen), and therefore samples of this size can easily be distorted by chance. On the other hand, if Harold flipped the coin twenty times and it continued to come up heads, he would have strong grounds for saying that this coin, at least, will always come up heads. In fact, he would have strong grounds for thinking that he has a two-headed coin. Because an overly small sample can lead to erroneous conclusions, we need to make sure that our sample includes enough trials.

How many is enough? On the assumption, for the moment, that our sampling has been fair in all other respects, how many samples do we need to provide the basis for a strong inductive argument? This is not always an easy question to answer, and sometimes answering it demands subtle mathematical techniques. Suppose your company is selling 10 million computer chips to the Department of Defense, and you have guaranteed that no more than 0.2 percent of them will be defective. It would be prohibitively expensive to test all the chips, and testing only a dozen would hardly be enough to reasonably guarantee that the total shipment of chips meets the required specifications. Because testing chips is expensive, you want to test as few as possible; but because meeting the specifications is crucial, you want to test enough to guarantee that you have done so. Answering questions of this kind demands sophisticated statistical techniques beyond the scope of this text.

Sometimes, then, it is difficult to decide how many instances are needed to give reasonable support to inductive generalizations; yet many times it is obvious, without going into technical details, that the sample is too small. Drawing an inductive conclusion from a sample that is too small can lead to the fallacy of *hasty generalization.* It is surprising how common this fallacy is. We see a person two or three times and find him cheerful, and we immediately leap to the conclusion that he is a cheerful person. That is, from a few instances of cheerful behavior, we draw a general conclusion about his personality. When we meet him later and find him sad, morose, or grouchy, we then conclude that he has changed—thus swapping one hasty generalization for another.

This tendency toward hasty generalization was discussed over 200 years ago by the philosopher David Hume, who saw that we have a strong tendency to "follow general rules which we rashly form to ourselves, and which are the source of what we properly call prejudice."[1] More recently, this tendency toward hasty generalization has been the subject of extensive psychological investigation. The cognitive psychologists Amos Tversky and Daniel Kahneman put the matter this way:

> We submit that people view a sample randomly drawn from a population as
> highly representative, that is, similar to the population in all essential characteristics.
> Consequently, they expect any two samples drawn from a particular population to
> be more similar to one another and to the population than sampling theory predicts,
> at least for small samples.[2]

To return to a previous example, we make our judgments of someone's personality on the basis of a very small sample of his or her behavior and expect this person to behave in similar ways in the future when we encounter further samples of behavior. We are surprised, and sometimes indignant, when the future behavior does not match our expectations.

By making our samples sufficiently large, we can guard against distortions due to "runs of luck," but even very large samples can give us a poor basis for a statistical generalization. Suppose that Harold has tried hundreds of times to use a Canadian quarter in an American payphone, and it has never worked. This will increase our confidence in his generalization, but size of sample alone is not a sufficient ground for a strong inductive argument. Suppose that Harold has tried the same coin in hundreds of different payphones, or tried a hundred different Canadian coins in the same payphone. In the first case, there might be something wrong with this particular coin; in the second case, there might be something wrong with this particular payphone. In neither case would he have good grounds for making the general claim that *no* Canadian quarters work in *any* American payphones. This leads us to the third question we should ask of any statistical generalization.

IS THE SAMPLE BIASED?

When the sample, however large, is not representative of the population, then it is said to be unfair or biased. Here we can speak of the fallacy of *biased sampling*.

One of the most famous errors of biased sampling was committed by a magazine named the *Literary Digest*. Before the presidential election of 1936, this magazine sent out 10 million questionnaires asking which candidate the recipient would vote for: Franklin Roosevelt or Alf Landon. It received 2.5 million returns, and on the basis of the results, confidently predicted that Landon would win by a landslide: 56 percent for Landon to only 44 percent for Roosevelt. When the election results came in, Roosevelt had won by an even larger landslide in the opposite direction: 62 percent for Roosevelt to a mere 38 percent for Landon.

What went wrong? The sample was certainly large enough; in fact, by contemporary standards it was much larger than needed. It was the way the sample was selected, not its size, that caused the problem: The sample was randomly drawn from names in telephone books and from club membership lists. In 1936 there were only 11 million payphones in the United States, and many of the poor—especially the rural poor—did not have payphones. During the Great Depression there were more than 9 million unemployed in America; they were almost all poor and thus underrepresented on club membership lists. Finally, a large percentage of these underrepresented groups voted for Roosevelt, the Democratic candidate. As a result of these biases in its sampling, along with some others, the *Literary Digest* underestimated Roosevelt's percentage of the vote by a whopping 18 percent.

Looking back, it may be hard to believe that intelligent observers could have done such a ridiculously bad job of sampling opinion, but the story repeats itself, though rarely on the grand scale of the *Literary Digest* fiasco. In 1948, for example, the Gallup poll, which had correctly predicted Roosevelt's victory in 1936, predicted, as did other major polls, a clear victory for Thomas Dewey over Harry Truman. Confidence was so high in this prediction that the *Chicago Tribune* published a banner headline declaring that Dewey had won the election before the votes were actually counted.

What went wrong this time? The answer here is more subtle. The Gallup pollsters (and others) went to great pains to make sure that their sample was representative of the voting population. The interviewers were told to poll a certain number of people from particular social groups—rural poor, suburban middle class, urban middle class, ethnic minorities, and so on—so that the proportions of those interviewed matched, as closely as possible, the proportions of those likely to vote. (The *Literary Digest* went bankrupt after its incorrect prediction, so the pollsters were taking no chances.) Yet somehow bias crept into the sampling; the question was, "How?" One speculation was that a large percentage of those sampled did not tell the truth when they were interviewed; another was that a large number of people changed their minds at the last minute. So perhaps the data collected were not reliable. The explanation generally accepted was more subtle. Although Gallup's workers were told to interview specific numbers of people from particular classes (so many from the suburbs, for example), they were not instructed to choose people randomly from within each group. Without seriously thinking about it, they tended to go to "nicer" neighborhoods and interview "nicer" people. Because of this, they biased the sample in the direction of their own (largely) middle-class preferences and, as a result, under-represented constituencies that would give Truman his unexpected victory.

IS THE RESULT BIASED IN SOME OTHER WAY?

Because professionals using modern techniques can make bad statistical generalizations through biased sampling, it is not surprising that our everyday, informal inductive generalizations are often inaccurate. Sometimes we go astray because of small samples and biased samples. This happens, for example, when we form opinions about what people think or what people are like by asking only our friends. But bias can affect our reasoning in other ways as well.

One of the main sources of bias in everyday life is *prejudice*. Even if we sample a wide enough range of cases, we often reinterpret what we hear or see in light of some preconception. People who are prejudiced will find very little good and a great deal bad in those they despise, no matter how these people actually behave. In fact, most people are a mixture of good and bad qualities. By ignoring the former and dwelling on the latter, it is easy enough for a prejudiced person to confirm negative opinions. Similarly, stereotypes, which can be either positive or negative, often persist in the face of overwhelming counterevidence. Criticizing the beliefs common in Britain in his own day, David Hume remarked:

> An Irishman cannot have wit, and a Frenchman cannot have solidity; for which reason, though the conversation of the former in any instance be very agreeable, and of the latter very judicious, we have entertained such a prejudice against them, that they must be dunces and fops in spite of sense and reason.[3]

Although common stereotypes have changed somewhat since Hume's day, prejudice continues to distort the beliefs of many people in our own time.

Another common source of bias in sampling arises from phrasing questions in ways that encourage certain answers while discouraging others. Even if a fair sample is asked a question, it is well known that the way a question is phrased can exert a significant influence on how people will answer it. Questions like the following are not intended to elicit information, but instead to push people's answers in one direction rather than another.

> Which do you favor: (a) preserving a citizen's constitutional right to bear arms or (b) leaving honest citizens defenseless against armed criminals?

> Which do you favor: (a) restricting the sale of assault weapons or (b) knuckling under to the demands of the well-financed gun lobby?

In both cases, one alternative is made to sound attractive, the other unattractive. When questions of this sort are used, it is not surprising that different pollsters can come up with wildly different results.

Now we can summarize and restate our questions. Confronted with inductive generalizations, there are four questions that we should routinely ask:

1. Are the premises acceptable?
2. Is the sample too small?
3. Is the sample biased?
4. Are the results affected by other sources of bias?

EXERCISE II

By asking the preceding questions, specify what, if anything, is wrong with the following statistical generalizations:

1. This philosophy class is about logic, so most philosophy classes are probably about logic.
2. Most college students like to ski, because I asked a lot of students at several colleges in the Rocky Mountains, and most of them like to ski.
3. K-Mart asked all of their customers throughout the country whether they prefer K-Mart to Walmart, and 90 percent said they did, so 90 percent of all shoppers in the country prefer K-Mart.
4. A Swede stole my bicycle, so most Swedes are thieves.

5. I've never tried it before, but I just put a kiwi fruit in a tub of water. It floated. So most kiwi fruits float in water.

6. I have lots of friends. Most of them think that I would make a great president. So most Americans would probably agree.

7. In exit polls after people had just voted, most people told our candidate that they voted for her, so probably most people did vote for her.

8. Mary told me that all of her older children are geniuses, so her baby will probably be a genius, too.

9. When asked whether they would prefer a tax break or a bloated budget, almost everyone said that they wanted a tax break. So a tax break is overwhelmingly popular with the people.

10. When hundreds of convicted murderers in states without the death penalty were asked whether they would have committed the murder if the state had a death penalty, most of them said that they would not have done it. So most murders can be deterred by the death penalty.

DISCUSSION QUESTION

It is often easy to see that a sample is biased, but how can you tell that a sample is not biased? How can you determine whether a sample is big enough?

STATISTICAL APPLICATIONS

In a statistical generalization, we draw inferences concerning a population from information concerning a sample of that population. If 60 percent of the population sampled said that they would vote for candidate X, we might draw the conclusion that roughly 60 percent of the population will vote for candidate X. With a *statistical application* (sometimes called a *statistical syllogism*), we reason in the reverse direction: From information concerning a population, we draw a conclusion concerning a member or subset of that population. Here is an example:

> Ninety-seven percent of the Republicans in California voted for McCain.
> Marvin is a Republican from California.
> ∴ Marvin voted for McCain.

Such arguments have the following general form:

> X percent of Fs have the feature G.
> a is an F.
> ∴ a has the feature G.[4]

Obviously, when we evaluate the strength of a statistical application, the percentage of *F*s that have the feature *G* will be important. As the figure approaches 100 percent, the argument gains strength. Thus, our original argument concerning Marvin is quite strong. We can also get strong statistical applications when the figure approaches 0 percent. The following is a strong inductive argument:

> Three percent of the socialists from California voted for McCain.
> Maureen is a socialist from California.
> ∴ Maureen did *not* vote for McCain.

Statistical applications of the kind considered here are strong only if the figures are close to 100 percent or 0 percent. When the percentages are in the middle of this range, such statistical applications are weak.

A more interesting problem in evaluating the strength of a statistical application concerns the *relevance* of the premises to the conclusion. In the above schematic representation, *F* stands for what is called the *reference class*. In our first example, being a Republican from California is the reference class; in our second example, being a socialist from California is the reference class. A striking feature of statistical applications is that using different reference classes can yield incompatible results. To see this, consider the following example:

> Three percent of Obama's relatives voted for McCain.
> Marvin is a relative of Obama.
> ∴ Marvin did not vote for McCain.

We now have a statistical application that gives us strong support for the claim that Marvin did not vote for McCain. This is incompatible with our first statistical application, which gave strong support to the claim that he did. To overlook this conflict between arguments based on different reference classes would be a kind of fallacy. Which statistical application, if either, should we trust? This will depend on which of the reference classes we take to be more relevant. Which counts more, political affiliation or family ties? That might be hard to say.

One way of dealing with competing statistical applications is to combine the reference classes. We could ask, for example, what percentage of Republicans from California who are relatives of Obama voted for McCain? The result might come out this way:

> Forty-two percent of Republicans from California who were relatives
> of Obama voted for McCain.
> Marvin is a Republican from California who is a relative of Obama.
> ∴ Marvin voted for McCain.

This statistical application provides very weak support for its conclusion. Indeed, it supplies some weak support for the denial of its conclusion—that is, for the claim that Marvin did *not* vote for McCain.

This situation can be diagrammed with ellipses of varying sizes to represent the percentages of Californians and relatives of Obama who do or do not vote for McCain. First, we draw an ellipse to represent Republicans from California and place a vertical line so that it cuts off roughly (very roughly!) 97 percent of the area of that ellipse to represent the premise that 97 percent of the Republicans from California voted for McCain:

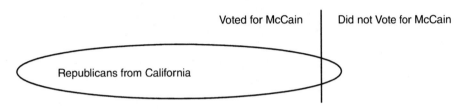

Next, we add a second ellipse to represent Obama's relatives:

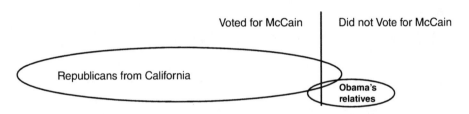

Only about 3 percent of the small ellipse is left of the line to represent the premise that 3 percent of Obama's relatives voted for McCain. The area that lies within both ellipses represents the people who are both Republicans from California and also relatives of Obama. About 42 percent of that area is left of the line to represent the premise that 42 percent of Republicans from California who were relatives of Obama voted for McCain. The whole diagram now shows how all of these premises can be true, even though they lead to conflicting conclusions.

This series of arguments illustrates in a clear way what we earlier called the defeasibility of inductive inferences: A strong inductive argument can be made weak by adding further information to the premises. Given that Marvin is a Republican from California, we seemed to have good reason to think that he voted for McCain. But when we added to this the additional piece of information that he was a relative of Obama, the original argument lost most of its force. And new information could produce another reversal. Suppose we discover that Marvin, though a relative of Obama, actively campaigned for McCain. Just about everyone who actively campaigns for a candidate votes for that candidate, so it seems that we again have good reason for thinking that Marvin voted for McCain.

It is clear, then, that the way we select our reference classes will affect the strength of a statistical application. The general idea is that we should define our reference classes in a way that brings all relevant evidence to bear on the subject. But this raises difficulties. It is not always obvious which factors are relevant and which are not. In our example, party affiliation is relevant to how people voted in the 2008 election; shoe size presumably is not. Whether gender is significant, and, if so, how significant, is a matter for further statistical research.

These difficulties concerning the proper way to fix reference classes reflect a feature of all inductive reasoning: To be successful, such reasoning must take place within a broader framework that helps determine which features are significant and which features are not. Without this framework, there would be no reason not to consider shoe size when trying to decide how someone will vote. This shows how statistical applications, like all of the other inductive arguments that we will study, cannot work properly without appropriate background assumptions.

EXERCISE III

Carry the story of Marvin two steps further, producing two more reversals in the strength of the statistical application with the conclusion that Marvin voted for McCain.

EXERCISE IV

For each of the following statistical applications, identify the reference class, and then evaluate the strength of the argument in terms of the percentages or proportions cited and the relevance of the reference class.

1. Less than 1 percent of the people in the world voted for McCain.
   Michelle is a person in the world.
   ∴ Michelle did not vote for McCain.

2. Very few teams repeat as Super Bowl champions.
   New England was the last Super Bowl champion.
   ∴ New England will not repeat as Super Bowl champion.

3. A very high percentage of people in the Senate are men.
   Hillary Clinton is in the Senate.
   ∴ Hillary Clinton is a man.

4. Three percent of socialists with blue eyes voted for McCain.
   Maureen is a socialist with blue eyes.
   ∴ Maureen did not vote for McCain.

5. Ninety-eight percent of what John says is true.
   John said that his father is also named John.

   ∴ John's father is named John.

6. Ninety-eight percent of what John says is true.
   John said that the Giants are going to win.

   ∴ The Giants are going to win.

7. Half the time he doesn't know what he is doing.
   He is eating lunch.

   ∴ He does not know that he is eating lunch.

8. Most people do not understand quantum mechanics.
   My physics professor is a person.

   ∴ My physics professor probably does not understand quantum mechanics.

9. Almost all birds can fly.
   This penguin is a bird.

   ∴ This penguin can fly.

10. Most people who claim to be psychic are frauds.
    Mary claims to be psychic.

    ∴ Mary is a fraud.

DISCUSSION QUESTION

Although both in science and in daily life, we rely heavily on the methods of inductive reasoning, this kind of reasoning raises a number of perplexing problems. The most famous problem concerning the legitimacy of induction was formulated by the eighteenth-century philosopher David Hume, first in his *Treatise of Human Nature* and then later in his *Enquiry Concerning Human Understanding*. A simplified version of Hume's skeptical argument goes as follows: Our inductive generalizations seem to rest on the assumption that *unobserved* cases will follow the patterns that we discovered in *observed* cases. That is, our inductive generalizations seem to presuppose that nature operates uniformly: The way things are observed to behave here and now are accurate indicators of how things behave anywhere and at any time. But by what right can we assume that nature is uniform? Because this claim itself asserts a contingent matter of fact, it could only be established by inductive reasoning. But because all inductive reasoning presupposes the principle that nature is uniform, any inductive justification of this principle would seem to be circular. It seems, then, that we have no ultimate justification for our inductive reasoning at all. Is this a good argument or a bad one? Why?

NOTES

[1] David Hume, *A Treatise of Human Nature*, 2nd ed. (1739; Oxford: Oxford University Press, 1978), 146.

[2] Amos Tversky and Daniel Kahneman, "Belief in the Law of Small Numbers," *Psychological Bulletin* 76, no. 2 (1971), 105.

[3] Hume, *A Treatise of Human Nature*, 146–47.

[4] We can also have a *probabilistic* version of the statistical syllogism:

> Ninety-seven percent of the Republicans from California voted for McCain.
> Marvin is a Republican from California.
> ∴ There is a 97 percent chance that Marvin voted for McCain.

We will discuss arguments concerning probability in Chapter 11.

9

CAUSAL REASONING

Statistical generalization can tell us that all ravens are black and that most Texans will vote for McCain, but these generalizations alone cannot tell us what makes ravens black or what makes most Texans vote for McCain. To determine what causes such phenomena, we need to engage in a new kind of inductive reasoning—causal reasoning—which is the topic of this chapter. We will show how causal reasoning is often based on negative *and* positive *tests for* necessary *conditions and for* sufficient *conditions. After developing these tests and applying them to a concrete example, we will discuss* concomitant variation *as a method of drawing causal conclusions from imperfect correlations. Our goal throughout this chapter is to improve our ability to identify causes so that we can better understand why certain effects happened and also make better predictions about whether similar events will happen in the future.*

REASONING ABOUT CAUSES

If our car goes dead in the middle of rush-hour traffic just after its 20,000-mile checkup, we assume that there must be some reason why this happened. Cars just don't stop for no reason at all. So we ask, "What caused our car to stop?" The answer might be that it ran out of gas. If we find, in fact, that it did run out of gas, then that will usually be the end of the matter. We will think that we have discovered why this particular car stopped running. This reasoning is about a particular car on a particular occasion, but it rests on certain *generalizations:* We are confident that our *car* stopped running when it ran out of gas, because we believe that all cars stop running when they run out of gas. We probably did not think about this, but our causal reasoning in this particular case appealed to a commonly accepted causal generalization: Lack of fuel causes cars to stop running. Many explanations depend on *causal generalizations.*

Causal generalizations are also used to *predict* the consequences of particular actions or events. A race car driver might wonder, for example, what would happen if he added just a bit of nitroglycerin to his fuel mixture. Would it give him better acceleration, blow him up, do very little, or what?

In fact, the driver may not be in a position to answer this question straight off, but his thinking will be guided by the causal generalization that igniting nitroglycerin can cause a dangerous explosion.

So a similar pattern arises for both causal explanation and causal prediction. These inferences contain two essential elements:

1. The facts in the particular case. (For example, the car stopped and the gas gauge reads empty; or I just put a pint of nitroglycerin in the gas tank of my Maserati, and I am about to turn the ignition key.)

2. Certain causal generalizations. (For example, cars do not run without gas, or nitroglycerin explodes when ignited.)

The basic idea is that causal inferences bring particular facts under causal generalizations.

This shows why causal generalizations are important, but what exactly are they? Although this issue remains controversial, here we will treat them as a kind of *general conditional*. A general conditional has the following form:

For all x, if x has the feature F, then x has the feature G.

We will say that, according to this conditional, x's having the feature F is a *sufficient condition* for its having the feature G; and x's having the feature G is a *necessary condition* for its having the feature F.

Some general conditionals are not *causal*. Neither of these two general conditionals expresses a causal relationship:

If something is a square, then it is a rectangle.

If you are eighteen years old, then you are eligible to vote.

The first conditional tells us that being a square is sufficient for being a rectangle, but this is a mathematical (or *a priori*) relationship, not a causal one. The second conditional tells us that being eighteen years old is a sufficient condition for being eligible to vote. The relationship here is legal, not causal.

Although many general conditionals are not causal, all causal conditionals are general, in our view. Consequently, if we are able to show that a causal conditional is false just by virtue of its being a general conditional, we will have refuted it. This will serve our purposes well, for in what follows we will be largely concerned with finding reasons for *rejecting* causal generalizations.

It is important to weed out false causal generalizations, because they can create lots of trouble. Doctors used to think that bloodletting would cure disease. They killed many people in the process of trying to heal them. Thus, although we need causal generalizations for getting along in the world, we also need to get them right. We will be more likely to succeed if we have proper principles for testing and applying such generalizations.

In the past, very elaborate procedures have been developed for this purpose. The most famous set of such procedures was developed by John Stuart Mill and has come to be known as Mill's methods.[1] Though inspired by Mill's methods, the procedures introduced here involve some fundamental simplifications; whereas Mill introduced five methods, we will introduce only three primary rules.

The first two rules are the sufficient condition test (SCT) and the necessary condition test (NCT). We will introduce these tests first at an abstract level. One advantage of formulating these tests abstractly is so that they can be applied to other kinds of sufficient and necessary conditions, for example, those that arise in legal and moral reasoning, the topics of Chapters 18 and 19. Once it is clear how these tests work in general, we will apply them specifically to causal reasoning.

SUFFICIENT CONDITIONS AND NECESSARY CONDITIONS

To keep our discussion as general as possible, we will adopt the following definitions of sufficient conditions and necessary conditions:

Feature F is a *sufficient* condition for feature G if and only if anything that *has* feature F also *has* feature G.

Feature F is a *necessary* condition for feature G if and only if anything that *lacks* feature F also *lacks* feature G.

These definitions are equivalent to those in the previous section, because, if anything that *lacks* feature F also *lacks* feature G, then anything that *has* feature G must also *have* feature F; and if anything that *has* feature G must also *have* feature F, then anything that *lacks* feature F also *lacks* feature G. It follows that feature F is a sufficient condition for feature G if and only if feature G is a necessary condition for feature F.

When F is sufficient for G, the relation between these features can be diagrammed like this:

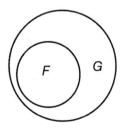

The inside circle represents the sufficient condition, because anything inside that inside circle must also be inside the outside circle. The outside circle represents the necessary condition, for anything outside the outside circle must also be outside the inside circle.

These diagrams, along with the preceding definitions, should make it clear that something can be a sufficient condition for a feature without being a necessary condition for that feature, and vice versa. For example, being the element mercury is a *sufficient* condition for being a metal, but it is not a *necessary* condition for being a metal, since there are other metals. Similarly, being a metal is a *necessary* condition for being mercury, but it is not a *sufficient* condition for being mercury. Of course, some necessary conditions are also sufficient conditions. Being mercury is both necessary and sufficient for being a metallic element that is liquid at twenty degrees Centigrade. Nonetheless, many necessary conditions are not sufficient conditions, and vice versa, so we need to be careful not to confuse the two kinds of conditions.

This distinction becomes complicated when conditions get complex. Our definitions and tests hold for all features, whether positive or negative (such as not having hair) and whether simple or conjunctive (such as having both a beard and a mustache) or disjunctive (such as having either a beard or a mustache). Thus, not having any hair (anywhere) on your head is a sufficient condition of not having a beard, so not having a beard is a necessary condition of not having any hair on your head. But not having any hair on your head is not necessary for not having a beard, because you can have some hair on the top of your head without having a beard. Negation can create confusion, so we need to think carefully about what is being claimed to be necessary or sufficient for what.

Even in simple cases without negation, conjunction, or disjunction, there is a widespread tendency to confuse necessary conditions with sufficient conditions. It is important to keep these concepts straight, for, as we will see, the tests concerning them are fundamentally different.

EXERCISE I

Which of the following claims are true? Which are false?

1. Being a car is a sufficient condition for being a vehicle.
2. Being a car is a necessary condition for being a vehicle.
3. Being a vehicle is a sufficient condition for being a car.
4. Being a vehicle is a necessary condition for being a car.
5. Being an integer is a sufficient condition for being an even number.
6. Being an integer is a necessary condition for being an even number.
7. Being an integer is a sufficient condition for being either an even number or an odd number.
8. Being an integer is a necessary condition for being either an even number or an odd number.
9. Not being an integer is a sufficient condition for not being an odd number.
10. Not being an integer is a sufficient condition for not being an even number.
11. Being both an integer and divisible by 2 without remainder is a sufficient condition for being an even number.

12. Being both an integer and divisible by 2 without remainder is a necessary condition for being an even number.
13. Being an integer divisible by 2 without remainder is a necessary condition for being an even number.
14. Driving seventy-five miles per hour (for fun) is a sufficient condition for violating a legal speed limit of sixty-five miles per hour.
15. Driving seventy-five miles per hour (for fun) is a necessary condition for violating a legal speed limit of sixty-five miles per hour.
16. Cutting off Joe's head is a sufficient condition for killing him.
17. Cutting off Joe's head is a necessary condition for killing him.
18. Cutting off Joe's head and then holding his head under water for ten minutes is a sufficient condition for killing him.

EXERCISE II

Indicate whether the following principles are true or false and why.

1. If having feature F is a *sufficient* condition for having feature G, then having feature G is a *necessary* condition for having feature F.
2. If having feature F is a *sufficient* condition for having feature G, then lacking feature F is a *necessary* condition for lacking feature G.
3. If lacking feature F is a *sufficient* condition for having feature G, then having feature F is a *necessary* condition for lacking feature G.
4. If lacking feature F is a *sufficient* condition for having feature G, then lacking feature F is a *necessary* condition for having feature G.
5. If having either feature F or feature G is a *sufficient* condition for having feature H, then having feature F is a *sufficient* condition for having feature H.
6. If having either feature F or feature G is a *sufficient* condition for having feature H, then having feature G is a *sufficient* condition for having feature H.
7. If having either feature F or feature G is a *sufficient* condition for having feature H, then not having feature F is a *necessary* condition for not having feature H.
8. If having both feature F and feature G is a *necessary* condition for having feature H, then lacking feature F is a *sufficient* condition for lacking feature H.
9. If not having both feature F and feature G is a *sufficient* condition for having feature H, then lacking feature F is a *sufficient* condition for having feature H.
10. If having either feature F or feature G is a *sufficient* condition for having feature H, then having both feature F and feature G is a *sufficient* condition for having feature H.

THE SUFFICIENT CONDITION TEST

We can now formulate tests to determine when something meets our definitions of sufficient conditions and necessary conditions. It will simplify matters if we first state these tests formally using letters. We will also begin with a simple case where we consider only four *candidates*—A, B, C, and D—for sufficient conditions for a *target* feature, G. A will indicate that the feature is present; ~A will indicate that this feature is absent. Using these conventions, suppose that we are trying to decide whether any of the four features—A, B, C, or D—could be a sufficient condition for G. To this end, we collect data of the following kind:

TABLE 1

Case 1:	A	B	C	D	G
Case 2:	~A	B	C	~D	~G
Case 3:	A	~B	~C	~D	~G

We know by definition that, for something to be a sufficient condition of something else, when the former is present, the latter must be present as well. Thus, to test whether a candidate really is a sufficient condition of G, we only have to examine cases in which the target feature, G, is absent, and then check to see whether any of the candidate features are present. The sufficient condition test (SCT) can be stated as follows:

SCT: Any candidate that is present when G is absent is eliminated as a possible sufficient condition of G.

The test applies to Table 1 as follows: Case 1 need not be examined because G is present, so there can be no violation of SCT in Case 1. Case 2 eliminates two of the candidates, B and C, for both are present in a situation in which G is absent. Finally, Case 3 eliminates A for the same reason. We are thus left with D as our only remaining candidate for a sufficient condition for G.

Now let's consider feature D. Having survived the application of the SCT, does it follow that D is a sufficient condition for G? No! On the basis of what we have been told so far, it remains entirely possible that the discovery of a further case will reveal an instance where D is present and G absent, thus showing that D is also not a sufficient condition for G.

Case 4:	~A	B	C	D	~G

In this way, it is always possible for new cases to refute any inference from a limited group of cases to the conclusion that a certain candidate is a sufficient condition. In contrast, no further case can change the fact that A, B, and C are not sufficient conditions, because they fail the SCT.

This observation shows that, when we apply the SCT to rule out a candidate as a sufficient condition, our argument is *deductive*. We simply find a counterexample to the universal claim that a certain feature is sufficient. (See Chapter 17 on counterexamples.) However, when a candidate is not ruled out and we draw the positive conclusion that that candidate *is* a sufficient condition, then our argument is *inductive*. Inductive inferences, however well confirmed, are always defeasible. (Recall Captain Cook's discovery of black swans at the start of Chapter 8.) That is why our inductive inference to the conclusion that D is a sufficient condition could be refuted by the new data in Case 4.

THE NECESSARY CONDITION TEST

The necessary condition test (NCT) is like the SCT, but it works in the reverse fashion. With SCT we eliminated a candidate F from being the sufficient condition for G, if F was ever present when G was absent. With the necessary condition test, we eliminate a candidate F from being a necessary condition for G if we can find a case where G is present, but F is not. This makes sense, because if G can be present when F is not, then F cannot be necessary for the occurrence of G. Thus, in applying the necessary condition test, we only have to examine cases in which the target feature, G, is present, and then check to see whether any of the candidate features are absent.

NCT: Any candidate that is absent when G is present is eliminated as a possible necessary condition of G.

The following table gives an example of an application of this test:

TABLE 2

Case 1:	A	B	C	D	$\sim G$
Case 2:	$\sim A$	B	C	D	G
Case 3:	A	$\sim B$	C	$\sim D$	G

Because Case 1 does not provide an instance where G is present, it cannot eliminate any candidate as a necessary condition of G. Case 2 eliminates A as a necessary condition of G, since it shows that G can be present without A being present. Case 3 then eliminates both B and D, leaving C as the only possible candidate for being a necessary condition for G.

From this, of course, it does not follow that C *is* a necessary condition for G, for, as always, new cases might eliminate it as well. The situation is the same as with the SCT. An argument for a negative conclusion that a candidate is not a necessary condition, because that candidate fails the NCT, is a deductive argument that cannot be overturned by any further cases. In contrast, an argument for a positive conclusion that a candidate is a necessary condition, because that candidate passes the NCT, is an inductive argument that can be overturned by a further case where this candidate fails the NCT. For example, suppose we find:

Case 4:	$\sim A$	$\sim B$	$\sim C$	$\sim D$	G

The information in this new Case 4 is enough to show that C cannot be a necessary condition of the target feature G, regardless of what we found in Cases 1–3.

In applying both the SCT and the NCT, it is crucial to specify the target feature. Case 4 shows that candidate C is not a necessary condition for target feature G. Nonetheless, candidate C still might be necessary for the opposite target feature, ~G. It also might be necessary for features A, B, and D. Nothing in Cases 1–4 rules out these possibilities. Thus, even after Case 4, we cannot say simply that C is not a necessary condition. Case 4 shows that candidate feature C is not a necessary conditions for target feature G, but C still might be necessary for something else. The same point applies to sufficient conditions as well. In Table 1, Case 2 ruled out the possibility that candidate feature B is sufficient for target feature G, but none of the cases in Table 1 show that B is not sufficient for target feature C. To avoid confusion, then, it is always important to specify the target feature when talking about what is or is not a necessary or sufficient condition.

THE JOINT TEST

It is also possible to apply these rules simultaneously in the search for possible conditions that are both sufficient and necessary. Any candidate cannot be both sufficient and necessary if it fails either the SCT or the NCT. In Table 2, C is the only possible necessary condition for G, and it is not also a possible sufficient condition for G, since C fails the SCT in Case 1, where C is present and G is absent. In Table 1, however, D is a possible sufficient condition of G, because D is never present when G is absent; and D might also be a necessary condition for G, since G is never present when D is absent. Thus, none of Cases 1–3 in Table 1 eliminates D as a candidate for a condition that is both sufficient and necessary for G. As before, this possibility still might be refuted by Case 4, so any inference to a positive conclusion that some candidate is a necessary and sufficient condition must be defeasible and, hence, inductive.

EXERCISE III

For each of the following tables determine

a. Which, if any, of the candidates—A, B, C, or D—is not eliminated by the *sufficient* condition test as a sufficient condition for target feature G?

b. Which, if any, of the candidates—A, B, C, or D—is not eliminated by the *necessary* condition test as a necessary condition for target feature G?

c. Which, if any, of the candidates—A, B, C, or D—is not eliminated by *either* test?

EXAMPLE:	Case 1:	A	B	~C	D	~G
	Case 2:	~A	B	C	D	G
	Case 3:	A	~B	C	D	G

a. Only C passes the SCT.

b. Only C and D pass the NCT.

c. Only C passes both tests.

1. Case 1:	*A*	*B*	*C*	*D*	*G*
Case 2:	~*A*	*B*	~*C*	*D*	~*G*
Case 3:	*A*	~*B*	*C*	~*D*	*G*
2. Case 1:	*A*	*B*	*C*	~*D*	*G*
Case 2:	~*A*	*B*	*C*	*D*	*G*
Case 3:	*A*	~*B*	*C*	~*D*	*G*
3. Case 1:	*A*	*B*	*C*	*D*	~*G*
Case 2:	~*A*	*B*	*C*	*D*	*G*
Case 3:	*A*	~*B*	*C*	~*D*	*G*
4. Case 1:	*A*	*B*	~*C*	*D*	*G*
Case 2:	~*A*	~*B*	*C*	*D*	*G*
Case 3:	*A*	*B*	~*C*	~*D*	~*G*
5. Case 1:	*A*	~*B*	*C*	*D*	~*G*
Case 2:	~*A*	*B*	*C*	~*D*	~*G*
Case 3:	*A*	~*B*	~*C*	*D*	*G*
6. Case 1:	*A*	*B*	~*C*	*D*	*G*
Case 2:	~*A*	~*B*	*C*	*D*	~*G*
Case 3:	*A*	~*B*	*C*	~*D*	~*G*
7. Case 1:	*A*	*B*	~*C*	*D*	~*G*
Case 2:	~*A*	*B*	~*C*	*D*	~*G*
Case 3:	*A*	*B*	~*C*	~*D*	~*G*
8. Case 1:	*A*	*B*	*C*	*D*	~*G*
Case 2:	~*A*	~*B*	*C*	*D*	*G*
Case 3:	*A*	~*B*	~*C*	~*D*	~*G*

EXERCISE IV

Imagine that your desktop computer system won't work, and you want to find out why. After checking to make sure that it is plugged in, you experiment with a new central processing unit (CPU), a new monitor (MON), and new system software (SSW) in the combinations on the table below. The candidates for necessary conditions and sufficient conditions of failure are the plug position (in or out), the CPU (old or new), the monitor (old or new), and the software (old or new). For each candidate, say (1) which cases, if any, eliminate it as a sufficient condition of your computer's failure and (2) which cases, if any, eliminate it as a necessary condition of your computer's failure. Which candidates, if any, are not eliminated as a sufficient condition of failure? As a necessary condition of failure? Does it follow that these candidates are necessary conditions or sufficient conditions of failure? Why or why not?

(*continued*)

	Plug	CPU	Monitor	Software	Result
Case 1	In	Old CPU	Old MO	Old SW	Works
Case 2	In	Old CPU	Old MO	New SW	Works
Case 3	In	Old CPU	New MO	Old SW	Fails
Case 4	In	Old CPU	New MO	New SW	Works
Case 5	In	Old CPU	Old MO	Old SW	Works
Case 6	In	Old CPU	Old MO	New SW	Works
Case 7	In	Old CPU	New MO	Old SW	Fails
Case 8	In	Old CPU	New MO	New SW	Works
Case 9	In	New CPU	Old MO	Old SW	Fails
Case 10	In	New CPU	Old MO	New SW	Works
Case 11	In	New CPU	New MO	Old SW	Fails
Case 12	In	New CPU	New MO	New SW	Works

EXERCISE V

After a banquet, several diners get sick and die. You suspect that something they ate or drank caused their deaths. The following table records their meals and fates. The target feature is death. The candidates for necessary conditions and sufficient conditions of death are the soup, entrée, wine, and dessert. For each candidate, say (1) which cases, if any, eliminate it as a sufficient condition of death and (2) which cases, if any, eliminate it as a necessary condition of death. Which candidates, if any, are not eliminated as a sufficient condition of death? Which candidates, if any, are not eliminated as a necessary condition of death? Does it follow that these candidates are necessary conditions or sufficient conditions of death? Why or why not?

Diners	Soup	Entrée	Wine	Dessert	Result
Ann	Tomato	Chicken	White	Pie	Alive
Barney	Tomato	Fish	Red	Cake	Dead
Cathy	Tomato	Beef	Red	Ice Cream	Alive
Doug	Tomato	Beef	Red	Cake	Alive
Emily	Tomato	Fish	Red	Pie	Dead
Fred	Tomato	Fish	Red	Cake	Dead
Gertrude	Leek	Fish	White	Pie	Alive
Harold	Tomato	Beef	White	Cake	Alive
Irma	Leek	Fish	Red	Pie	Dead
Jack	Leek	Beef	Red	Ice Cream	Alive
Ken	Leek	Chicken	Red	Ice Cream	Alive
Leslie	Tomato	Chicken	White	Cake	Alive

RIGOROUS TESTING

Going back to Table 1, it is easy to see that candidates A, B, C, and D are not eliminated by the NCT as necessary conditions of target G, as G is present in only one case (Case 1) and A, B, C, and D are present there as well. So far, so good. But if we wanted to test these features more rigorously, it would be important to find more cases in which target G was present and see whether these candidates are also present and thus continue to survive the NCT.

The following table gives a more extreme example of nonrigorous testing:

TABLE 3

Case 1:	A	$\sim B$	C	D	G
Case 2:	A	$\sim B$	$\sim C$	$\sim D$	$\sim G$
Case 3:	A	$\sim B$	C	$\sim D$	$\sim G$
Case 4:	A	$\sim B$	$\sim C$	D	G

Here candidate feature A is eliminated by SCT (in Cases 2 and 3) but is not eliminated by NCT, so it is a possible necessary condition but not a possible sufficient condition for target feature G. B is not eliminated by SCT but is eliminated by NCT (in Cases 1 and 4), so it is a possible sufficient condition but not a possible necessary condition for target feature G. C is eliminated by both rules (in Cases 3 and 4). Only D is not eliminated by either test, so it is the only candidate for being both a necessary and a sufficient condition for G.

The peculiarity of this example is that candidate A is always present whether target G is present or not, and candidate B is always absent whether target G is absent or not. Now if something is always present, as A is, then it cannot possibly fail the NCT; for there cannot be a case where the target is present and the candidate is absent if the candidate is *always* present. If we want to test candidate A rigorously under the NCT, then we should try to find cases in which A is absent and then check to see whether G is absent as well.

In reverse fashion, but for similar reasons, if we want to test candidate B rigorously under the SCT, then we should try to find cases in which B is present and then check to see if G is present as well. If we restrict our attention to cases where B is always absent, as in Table 3, then B cannot possibly fail the SCT, but passing that test will be trivial for B and so will not even begin to show that B is a sufficient condition for G.

Now consider two more sets of data just like Table 2, except with regard to the target feature, G:

TABLE 4

Case 1:	A	B	C	D	G
Case 2:	$\sim A$	B	C	D	G
Case 3:	A	$\sim B$	C	$\sim D$	G

TABLE 5

Case 1:	A	B	C	D	$\sim G$
Case 2:	$\sim A$	B	C	D	$\sim G$
Case 3:	A	$\sim B$	C	$\sim D$	$\sim G$

Because G is present in all of the cases in Table 4, no candidate can be eliminated by the SCT as a sufficient condition for target feature G. This result is trivial, however. Table 4 does not provide rigorous testing for a sufficient condition of G, because our attention is restricted to a range of cases that is too narrow. Nothing could possibly be eliminated as a sufficient condition of G as long as G is always present.

Similarly, G is absent in all of the cases in Table 5, so no candidate can be eliminated by the NCT as a necessary condition of target feature G. Still, because this data is so limited, its failure to eliminate candidates does not even begin to show that anything is a necessary condition of G.

For both rules, then, rigorous testing involves seeking out cases in which failing the test is a live possibility. For the SCT, this requires looking both at cases in which the candidates are present and also at cases in which the target is absent. For the NCT, rigorous testing requires looking both at cases in which the candidates are absent and also at cases in which the target is present. Without cases like these, passing the tests is rather like a person bragging that he has never struck out when, in fact, he has never come up to bat.

REACHING POSITIVE CONCLUSIONS

Suppose that we performed rigorous testing on candidate C, and it passed the SCT with flying colors. Can we now draw the positive conclusion that C is a sufficient condition for the target G? That depends on which kinds of candidates and cases have been considered. Since rigorous testing was passed, these three conditions are met:

1. We have tested some cases in which the candidate, C, is present.
2. We have tested some cases in which the target, G, is absent.
3. We have not found any case in which the candidate, C, is present and the target, G, is absent.

For it to be reasonable to reach a positive conclusion that C is sufficient for G, this further condition must also be met:

4. We have tested enough cases of the various kinds that are likely to include a case in which C is present and G is absent if there is any such case.

This new condition cannot be applied in the mechanical way that conditions 1–3 could be applied. To determine whether condition 4 is met, we need to rely on *background information* about how many cases are "enough" and about which kinds of cases "are likely to include a case in which C is present and G is absent, if there is any such case." For example, if we are trying to figure out whether our new software is causing our computer to crash, we do not need to try the same kind of computer in different colors. What we need to try are different kinds of CPUs, monitors, software, and so on, because we know that these are the kinds of factors that can affect performance. Background information like this is what tells us when we have tested enough cases of the right kinds.

Of course, our background assumptions might turn out to be wrong. Even if we have tested many variations of every feature that we think might be relevant, we still might be surprised and find a further case in which C and ~G are present. All that shows, however, is that our inference is defeasible, like all inductive arguments. Despite the possibility that future discoveries might undermine it, our inductive inference can still be strong if our background beliefs are justified and if we have looked long and hard without finding any case in which C is present and G is absent.

Similar rules apply in reverse to positive conclusions about necessary conditions. We have good reason to suppose that candidate C is a necessary condition for target G, if the following conditions are met:

1. We have tested some cases in which the candidate, C, is absent.
2. We have tested some cases in which the target, G, is present.
3. We have not found any case in which the candidate, C, is absent and the target, G, is present.
4. We have tested enough cases of the various kinds that are likely to include a case in which C is absent and G is present, if there is any such case.

This argument again depends on background assumptions in determining whether condition 4 is met. This argument is also defeasible, as before. Nonetheless, if our background assumptions are justified, the fact that conditions 1–4 are all met can still provide a strong reason for the positive conclusion that candidate C is a necessary condition for target G.

The SCT and NCT themselves are still negative and deductive; but that does not make them better than the positive tests encapsulated in conditions 1–4. The negative SCT and NCT are of no use when we need to argue that some condition *is* sufficient or *is* necessary. Such positive conclusions can be reached only by applying something like condition 4, which will require background information. These inductive arguments might not be as clear-cut or secure as the negative ones, but they can still be inductively strong under the right circumstances. That is all they claim to be.

APPLYING THESE METHODS TO FIND CAUSES

In stating the SCT and NCT and applying these tests to abstract patterns of conditions to eliminate candidates, our procedure was fairly mechanical. We cannot be so mechanical when we try to reach positive conclusions that certain conditions are necessary, sufficient, or both. Applying these rules to actual concrete situations introduces a number of further complications, especially when using our tests to determine causes.

NORMALITY

First, it is important to keep in mind that, in our ordinary understanding of causal conditions, we usually take it for granted that the setting is normal. It is part of common knowledge that if you strike a match, then it will light.

Thus, we consider striking a match sufficient to make it light. But if someone has filled the room with carbon dioxide, then the match will not light, no matter how it is struck. Here one may be inclined to say that, after all, striking a match is not sufficient to light it. We might try to be more careful and say that if a match is struck *and* the room is not filled with carbon dioxide, then it will light. But this new conditional overlooks other possibilities—for example, that the room has been filled with nitrogen, that the match has been fireproofed, that the wrong end of the match was struck, that the match has already been lit, and so forth. It now seems that the antecedent of our conditional will have to be endlessly long in order to specify a true or genuine sufficient condition. In fact, however, we usually feel quite happy with saying that if you strike a match, then it will light. We simply do not worry about the possibility that the room has been filled with carbon dioxide, the match has been fireproofed, and so on. Normally we think that things are normal, and give up this assumption only when some good reason appears for doing so.

These reflections suggest the following *contextualized* restatement of our original definitions of sufficient conditions and necessary conditions:

> F is a sufficient condition for G if and only if, whenever F is present in a normal context, G is present there as well.

> F is a necessary condition for G if and only if, whenever F is absent from a normal context, G is absent from it as well.

What will count as a normal context will vary with the type and the aim of an investigation, but all investigations into causally sufficient conditions and causally necessary conditions take place against the background of many factors that are taken as fixed.

BACKGROUND ASSUMPTIONS

If we are going to subject a causal hypothesis to rigorous testing with the SCT and the NCT, we have to seek out a wide range of cases that might refute that hypothesis. In general, the wider the range of possible refuters the better. Still, some limit must be put on this activity or else testing will get hopelessly bogged down. If we are testing a drug to see whether it will cure a disease, we should try it on a variety of people of various ages, medical histories, body types, and so on, but we will not check to see whether it works on people named Edmund or check to see whether it works on people who drive Volvos. Such factors, we want to say, are plainly irrelevant. But what makes them irrelevant? How do we distinguish relevant from irrelevant considerations?

The answer to this question is that our reasoning about causes occurs within a framework of beliefs that we take to be established as true. This framework contains a great deal of what is called *common knowledge*—knowledge we expect almost every sane adult to possess. We all know, for example, that human beings cannot breathe underwater, cannot walk through walls, cannot be in two places at once, and so on. The stock of these commonplace beliefs is almost endless. Because they are commonplace beliefs, they tend not to be mentioned; yet they play an important role in distinguishing relevant factors from irrelevant ones.

Specialized knowledge also contains its own principles that are largely taken for granted by experts. Doctors, for example, know a great deal about the detailed structure of the human body, and this background knowledge constantly guides their thought in dealing with specific illnesses. Even if someone claimed to discover that blood does not circulate, no doctor would take the time to refute that claim.

It might seem close-minded to refuse to consider a possibility that someone else suggests. However, giving up our basic beliefs can be very costly. A doctor who took seriously the suggestion that blood does not circulate, for example, would have to abandon our whole way of viewing humans and other animals, along with the rest of biology and science. It is not clear how this doctor could go on practicing medicine. Moreover, there is usually no practical alternative in real life. When faced with time pressure and limited information, we have no way to judge new ideas without taking some background assumptions for granted.

A DETAILED EXAMPLE

To get a clearer idea of the complex interplay between our tests and the reliance on background information, it will be helpful to look in some detail at actual applications of these tests. For this purpose, we will examine an attempt to find the cause of a particular phenomenon, an outbreak of what came to be known as Legionnaires' disease. The example not only shows how causal reasoning relies on background assumptions, it has another interesting feature as well: In the process of discovering the cause of Legionnaires' disease, the investigators were forced to *abandon* what was previously taken to be a well-established causal generalization. In fact, until it was discarded, this false background principle gave them no end of trouble.

The story began at an otherwise boring convention:

> The 58th convention of the American Legion's Pennsylvania Department was held at the Bellevue-Stratford Hotel in Philadelphia from July 21 through 24, 1976. . . . Between July 22 and August 3, 149 of the conventioneers developed what appeared to be the same puzzling illness, characterized by fever, coughing and pneumonia. This, however, was an unusual, explosive outbreak of pneumonia with no apparent cause. . . . Legionnaires' disease, as the illness was quickly named by the press, was to prove a formidable challenge to epidemiologists and laboratory investigators alike.[2]

Notice that at this stage the researchers begin with the assumption that they are dealing with a single illness and not a collection of similar but different illnesses. That assumption could turn out to be wrong; but, if the symptoms of the various patients are sufficiently similar, this is a natural starting assumption. Another reasonable starting assumption is that this illness had a single causative agent. This assumption, too, could turn out to be false, though it did not. The assumption that they were dealing with a single disease with a single cause was at least a good simplifying assumption, one to be held onto until there was good reason to give it up. In any case, we now have a clear specification of our target feature, *G*: the occurrence of a carefully described illness that came to be known as Legionnaires' disease. The situation concerning it was puzzling because people had contracted a disease with symptoms much like those of pneumonia, yet they had not tested positive for any of the known agents that cause such diseases.

The narrative continues as follows:

> The initial step in the investigation of any epidemic is to determine the character of the illness, who has become ill and just where and when. The next step is to find out what was unique about the people who became ill: where they were and what they did that was different from other people who stayed well. Knowing such things may indicate how the disease agent was spread and thereby suggest the identity of the agent and where it came from.

Part of this procedure involves a straightforward application of the NCT: Was there any interesting feature that was always present in the history of people who came down with the illness? Progress was made almost at once on this front:

> We quickly learned that the illness was not confined to Legionnaires. An additional 72 cases were discovered among people who had not been directly associated with the convention. They had one thing in common with the sick conventioneers: for one reason or another they had been in or near the Bellevue-Stratford Hotel.

Strictly speaking, of course, all these people who had contracted the disease had more than one thing in common. They were, for example, all alive at the time they were in Philadelphia, and being alive is, in fact, a necessary condition for getting Legionnaires' disease. But the researchers were not interested in this necessary condition because it is a normal background condition for the contraction of any disease. Furthermore, it did not provide a condition that distinguished those who contracted the disease from those who did not. The overwhelming majority of people who were alive at the time did not contract Legionnaires' disease. Thus, the researchers were not interested in this necessary condition because it would fail so badly when tested by the SCT as a sufficient condition. On the basis of common knowledge and specialized medical knowledge, a great many other conditions were also kept off the candidate list.

One prime candidate on the list was presence at the Bellevue-Stratford Hotel. The application of the NCT to this candidate was straightforward. Everyone who had contracted the disease had spent time in or near that hotel. Thus, presence at the Bellevue-Stratford could not be eliminated as a necessary condition of Legionnaires' disease.

The application of the SCT was more complicated, because not everyone who stayed at the Bellevue-Stratford contracted the disease. Other factors made a difference: "Older conventioneers had been affected at a higher rate than younger ones, men at three times the rate for women." Since some young women (among others) who were present at the Bellevue-Stratford did not get Legionnaires' disease, presence at that hotel could be eliminated as a sufficient condition of Legionnaires' disease. Nonetheless, it is part of medical background knowledge that susceptibility to disease often varies with age and gender. Given these differences, some people who spent time at the Bellevue-Stratford were at higher risk for contracting the disease than others. The investigation so far suggested that, for some people, being at the Bellevue-Stratford was connected with a sufficient condition for contracting Legionnaires' disease. Indeed, the conjunction of spending time at the Bellevue-Stratford and being susceptible to the disease could not be ruled out by the SCT as a sufficient condition of getting the disease.

As soon as spending time at the Bellevue-Stratford became the focus of attention, other hypotheses naturally suggested themselves. Food poisoning was a reasonable suggestion, since it is part of medical knowledge that diseases are sometimes spread by food. It was put on the list of possible candidates, but failed. Investigators checked each local restaurant and each function where food and drink were served. Some of the people who ate in each place did not get Legionnaires' disease, so the food at these locations was eliminated by the SCT as a sufficient condition of Legionnaires' disease. These candidates were also eliminated by the NCT as necessary conditions because some people who did get Legionnaires' disease did not eat at each of these restaurants and functions. Thus, the food and drink could not be the cause.

Further investigation turned up another important clue to the cause of the illness.

> Certain observations suggested that the disease might have been spread through the air. Legionnaires who became ill had spent on the average about 60 percent more time in the lobby of the Bellevue-Stratford than those who remained well; the sick Legionnaires had also spent more time on the sidewalk in front of the hotel than their unaffected fellow conventioneers. . . . It appeared, therefore, that the most likely mode of transmission was airborne.

Merely breathing air in the lobby of the Bellevue-Stratford Hotel still could not be a necessary or sufficient condition, but the investigators reasoned that something in the lobby air probably caused Legionnaires' disease, since the rate of the disease varied up or down in proportion to the time spent in the lobby (or near it on the sidewalk in front). This is an application of the method of concomitant variation, which will be discussed soon.

Now that the focus was on the lobby air, the next step was to pinpoint a specific cause in that air. Again appealing to background medical knowledge, there seemed to be three main candidates for the airborne agents that could have caused the illness: "heavy metals, toxic organic substances, and infectious organisms." Examination of tissues taken from patients who had died from the disease revealed "no unusual levels of metallic or toxic organic substances that might be related to the epidemic," so this left an infectious organism as the remaining candidate. Once more we have an application of NCT. If the disease had been caused by heavy metals or toxic organic substances, then there would have been unusually high levels of these substances in the tissues of those who had contracted the disease. Because this was not always so, these candidates were eliminated as necessary conditions of the disease.

Appealing to background knowledge once more, it seemed that a bacterium would be the most likely source of an airborne disease with the symptoms of Legionnaires' disease. But researchers had already made a routine check for bacteria that cause pneumonia-like diseases, and they had found none. For this reason, attention was directed to the possibility that some previously unknown organism had been responsible but had somehow escaped detection.

It turned out that an undetected and previously unknown bacterium *had* caused the illness, but it took more than four months to find this out. The difficulties encountered in this effort show another important fact about the reliance on a background assumption: Sometimes it turns out to be false. To simplify, the standard way to test for the presence of bacteria is to try to grow them in culture dishes—flat dishes containing nutrients that bacteria can live on. If, after a reasonable number of tries, a colony of a particular kind of bacterium does not appear, then it is concluded that the bacterium is not present. As it turned out, the bacterium that caused Legionnaires' disease would not grow in the cultures commonly used to detect the presence of bacteria. Thus, an important background assumption turned out to be false.

After a great deal of work, a suspicious bacterium was detected using a live-tissue culture rather than the standard synthetic culture. The task, then, was to show that this particular bacterium in fact caused the disease. Again to simplify, when people are infected by a particular organism, they often develop antibodies that are specifically aimed at this organism. In the case of Legionnaires' disease, these antibodies were easier to detect than the bacterium itself. They also remained in the patients' bodies after the infection had run its course. We thus have another chance to apply the NCT: If Legionnaires' disease was caused by this particular bacterium, then whenever the disease was present, this antibody should be present as well. The suspicious bacterium passed this test with flying colors and was named, appropriately enough, *Legionella pneumophila*. Because the investigators had worked so hard to test such a wide variety of candidates, they assumed that the disease must have some cause among the candidates that they checked. So, since only one candidate remained, they felt justified in reaching a positive conclusion that the bacterium was a necessary condition of Legionnaires' disease.

The story of the search for the cause of Legionnaires' disease brings out two important features of the use of inductive methods in the sciences. First, it involves a complicated interplay between what is already established and what is being tested. Confronted with a new problem, established principles can be used to suggest theoretically significant hypotheses to be tested. The tests then eliminate some hypotheses and leave others. If, at the end of the investigation, a survivor remains that fits in well with our previously established principles, then the stock of established principles is increased. The second thing that this example shows is that the inductive method is fallible. Without the background of established principles, the application of inductive principles like the NCT and the SCT would be undirected; yet sometimes these established principles let us down, for they can turn out to be false. The discovery of the false background principle that hindered the search for the cause of Legionnaires' disease led to important revisions in laboratory techniques. The discovery that certain fundamental background principles are false can lead to revolutionary changes in science. (See Chapter 20.)

CALLING THINGS CAUSES

After their research was finally completed, with the bacterium identified, described, and named, it was then said that *Legionella pneumophila* was the *cause* of Legionnaires' disease. What was meant by this? To simplify a bit, suppose *L. pneumophila* (as it is abbreviated) entered the bodies of *all* those who contracted the disease: Whenever the disease was present, *L. pneumophila* was present. Thus, *L. pneumophila* passes the NCT for the disease. We will further suppose, as is common in bacterial infections, that some people's immune systems were successful in combating *L. pneumophila,* and they never actually developed the disease. Thus, the presence of *L. pneumophila* would not pass the SCT for the disease. This suggests that we sometimes call something a cause of an effect if it passes the NCT for that effect, even if it does not pass the SCT for that effect.

But even if we sometimes consider necessary conditions to be causes, we certainly do not consider *all* necessary conditions to be causes. We have already noted that to get Legionnaires' disease, one has to be alive, yet no one thinks that being alive is the cause of Legionnaires' disease. To cite another example, this time one that is not silly, it might be that another necessary condition for developing Legionnaires' disease is that the person be in a run-down condition—healthy people might always be able to resist *L. pneumophila*. Do we then want to say that being in a run-down condition is the cause of Legionnaires' disease? As we have described the situation, almost certainly not, but we might want to say that it is an important *causal factor* or *causally relevant factor.*

Although the matter is far from clear, what we call *the* cause rather than simply *a* causal factor or causally relevant factor seems to depend on a number of considerations. We tend to reserve the expression "the cause" for *changes* that occur prior to the effect, and describe *permanent* or *standing* features of the context as "causal factors" instead. That is how we speak about Legionnaires' disease. Being exposed to *L. pneumophila,* which was a specific event that occurred before the onset of the disease, *caused it.* Being in a run-down condition, which was a feature that patients possessed for some time before they contracted the disease, was not called the cause, but instead called a causal factor.

It is not clear, however, that we always draw the distinction between what we call the cause and what we call a causal factor based on whether something is a prior event or a standing condition. For example, if we are trying to explain why certain people who came in contact with *L. pneumophila* contracted the disease whereas others did not, then we might say that the former group contracted the disease because they were in a rundown condition. Thus, by limiting our investigation only to those who came in contact with *L. pneumophila*, our perspective has changed. We want to know why some within that group contracted the disease and others did not. Citing the run-down condition of those who contracted the disease as the cause now seems entirely natural. These examples suggest that we call something *the* cause when it plays a particularly important role relative to the purposes of our investigation. Usually this will be an event or change taking place against the background of fixed necessary conditions; sometimes it will not.

Sometimes we call *sufficient* conditions causes. We say that short circuits cause fires because in many normal contexts, a short circuit is sufficient to cause a fire. Of course, short circuits are not necessary to cause a fire, because, in the same normal contexts, fires can be caused by a great many other things. With sufficient conditions, as with necessary conditions, we often draw a distinction between what we call the cause as opposed to what we call a causal factor, and we seem to draw it along similar lines. Speaking loosely, we might say that we sometimes call the *key* components of sufficient conditions *causes*. Then, holding background conditions fixed, we can use the SCT to evaluate such causal claims.

In sum, we can use the NCT to eliminate proposed necessary causal conditions. We can use the SCT to eliminate proposed sufficient causal conditions. Those candidates that survive these tests may be called causal conditions or causal factors if they fit in well with our system of other causal generalizations. Finally, some of these causal conditions or causal factors will be called causes if they play a key role in our causal investigations. Typically, though not always, we call something the cause of an event if it is a prior event or change that stands out against the background of fixed conditions.

DISCUSSION QUESTION

Reread the passage on what killed the dinosaurs in the Discussion Question at the end of Chapter 1. Where do the authors use the NCT? Where do they use the SCT? Where do they rely on background assumptions?

CONCOMITANT VARIATION

The use of the sufficient condition test and the necessary condition test depends on certain features of the world being sometimes present and sometimes absent. Some features of the world, however, are always present to

some degree. Because they are always present, the NCT will never eliminate them as possible necessary conditions of any event, and the SCT will
never eliminate anything as a sufficient condition for them. Yet the *extent*
or *degree* to which a feature exists in the world is often a significant phenomenon that demands causal explanation.

An example should make this clear. In recent decades, a controversy has
raged over the impact of acid rain on the environment of the northeastern
United States and Canada. Part of the controversy involves the proper interpretation of the data that have been collected. The controversy has arisen for
the following reason: The atmosphere always contains a certain amount of
acid, much of it from natural sources. It is also known that an excess of acid in
the environment can have severe effects on both plants and animals. Lakes are
particularly vulnerable to the effects of acid rain. Finally, it is also acknowledged that industries, mostly in the Midwest, discharge large quantities of
sulfur dioxide (SO_2) into the air, and this increases the acidity of water in the
atmosphere. The question—and here the controversy begins—is whether the
contribution of acid from these industries is the cause of the environmental
damage downwind of them.

How can we settle such a dispute? The two rules we have introduced provide no immediate help, for, as we have seen, they provide a rigorous test of a
causal hypothesis only when we can find contrasting cases with the presence
or the absence of a given feature. The NCT provides a rigorous test for a necessary condition only if we can find cases in which the feature does not occur
and then check to make sure that the target feature does not occur either. The
SCT provides a rigorous test for a sufficient condition only when we can find
cases in which the target phenomenon is absent and then check whether the
candidate sufficient condition is absent as well. In this case, however, neither
check applies, for there is always a certain amount of acid in the atmosphere,
so it is not possible to check what happens when atmospheric acid is completely absent. Similarly, environmental damage, which is the target phenomenon under investigation, is so widespread in our modern industrial society
that it is also hard to find a case in which it is completely absent.

So, if there is always acid in the atmosphere, and environmental damage
always exists at least to some extent, how can we determine whether the SO_2
released into the atmosphere is *significantly* responsible for the environmental
damage in the affected areas? Here we use what John Stuart Mill called the
Method of Concomitant Variation. We ask whether the amount of environmental
damage varies directly in proportion to the amount of SO_2 released into the
environment. If environmental damage increases with the amount of SO_2
released into the environment and drops when the amount of SO_2 is lowered,
this means that the level of SO_2 in the atmosphere is *positively correlated* with
environmental damage. We would then have good reason to believe that low-
ering SO_2 emissions would lower the level of environmental damage, at least
to some extent.

Arguments relying on the method of concomitant variation are difficult
to evaluate, especially when there is no generally accepted background

theory that makes sense of the concomitant variation. Some such variations are well understood. For example, most people know that the faster you drive, the more gasoline you consume. (Gasoline consumption varies *directly* with speed.) Why? There is a good theory here: It takes more energy to drive at a high speed than at a low speed, and this energy is derived from the gasoline consumed in the car's engine. Other correlations are less well understood. There seems to be a correlation between how much a woman smokes during pregnancy and how happy her children are when they reach age thirty. The correlation here is not nearly as good as the correlation between gasoline consumption and speed, for many people are very happy at age thirty even though their mothers smoked a lot during pregnancy, and many others are very unhappy at age thirty even though their mothers never smoked. Furthermore, no generally accepted background theory has been found to explain the correlation that does exist.

This reference to background theory is important, because two sets of phenomena can be correlated to a very high degree, even with no direct causal relationship between them. A favorite example that appears in many statistics texts is the discovered positive correlation in boys between foot size and quality of handwriting. It is hard to imagine a causal relation holding in either direction. Having big feet should not make you write better and, just as obviously, writing well should not give you big feet. The correct explanation is that both foot size and handwriting ability are positively correlated with age. Here a noncausal correlation between two phenomena (foot size and handwriting ability) is explained by a third common correlation (maturation) that *is* causal.

At times, it is possible to get causal correlations *backward*. For example, a few years ago, sports statisticians discovered a negative correlation between forward passes thrown and winning in football. That is, the more forward passes a team threw, the less chance it had of winning. This suggested that passing is not a good strategy, since the more you do it, the more likely you are to lose. Closer examination showed, however, that the causal relationship, in fact, went in the other direction. Toward the end of a game, losing teams tend to throw a great many passes in an effort to catch up. In other words, teams throw a lot of passes because they are losing, rather than the other way around.

Finally, some correlations seem inexplicable. For example, a strong positive correlation reportedly holds between the birth rate in Holland and the number of storks nesting in chimneys. There is, of course, a background theory that would explain this—storks bring babies—but that theory is not favored by modern science. For the lack of any better background theory, the phenomenon just seems weird.

So, given a strong correlation between phenomena of types A and B, four possibilities exist:

1. *A* is the cause of *B*.
2. *B* is the cause of *A*.

3. Some third thing is the cause of both.

4. The correlation is simply accidental.

Before we accept any one of these possibilities, we must have good reasons for preferring it over the other three.

One way to produce such a reason is to manipulate *A* or *B*. If we vary factor *A* up and down, but *B* does not change at all, this finding provides some reason against possibility 1, since *B* would normally change along with *A* if *A* did cause *B*. Similarly, if we manipulate *B* up and down, but *A* does not vary at all, this result provides some reason against alternative 2 and for the hypothesis that that *B* does not cause *A*. Together these manipulations can reduce the live options to items 3 and 4.

Many scientific experiments work this way. When scientists first discovered the correlation between smoking and lung cancer, some cigarette manufacturers responded that lung cancer might cause the desire to smoke or there might be a third cause of both smoking and lung cancer that explains the correlation. Possibly, it was suggested, smoking relieves discomfort due to early lung cancer or due to a third factor that itself causes lung cancer. To test these hypotheses, scientists manipulated the amount of smoking by lab animals. When all other factors were held as constant as possible, but smoking was increased, lung cancer increased; and when smoking went down, lung cancer went down. These results would not have occurred if some third factor had caused both smoking and lung cancer but remained stable as smoking was manipulated. The findings would also have been different if incipient lung cancer caused smoking, but had remained constant as scientists manipulated smoking levels. Such experiments can, thus, help us rule out at least some of the options 1–4.

Direct manipulation like this is not always possible or ethically permissible. The data would probably be more reliable if the test subjects were human beings rather than lab animals, but that is not an ethical option. Perhaps more complicated statistical methods could produce more reliable results, but they often require large amounts and special kinds of data. Such data is, unfortunately, often unavailable.

EXERCISE VI

In each of the following examples a strong correlation, either negative or positive, holds between two sets of phenomena, *A* and *B*. Try to decide whether *A* is the cause of *B*, *B* is the cause of *A*, both are caused by some third factor, *C*, or the correlation is simply accidental. Explain your choice.

1. For a particular United States president, there is a negative correlation between the number of hairs on his head (*A*) and the population of China (*B*).

(continued)

2. My son's height (A) increases along with the height of the tree outside my front door (B).

3. It has been claimed that there is a strong positive correlation between those students who take sex education courses (A) and those who contract venereal disease (B).

4. At one time there was a strong negative correlation between the number of mules in a state (A) and the salaries paid to professors at the state university (B). In other words, the more mules, the lower professional salaries.[3]

5. There is a high positive correlation between the number of fire engines in a particular borough in New York City (A) and the number of fires that occur there (B).[4]

6. "Washington (UPI)—Rural Americans with locked doors, watchdogs or guns may face as much risk of burglary as neighbors who leave doors unlocked, a federally financed study says. The study, financed in part by a three-year $170,000 grant from the Law Enforcement Assistance Administration, was based on a survey of nearly 900 families in rural Ohio. Sixty percent of the rural residents surveyed regularly locked doors [A], but were burglarized more often than residents who left doors unlocked [B]."[5]

7. The speed of a car (A) is exactly the same as the speed of its shadow (B).

8. The length of a runner's ring finger minus the length of the runner's index finger (A) is correlated with the runner's speed in the one-hundred-yard dash. (B)

DISCUSSION QUESTIONS

1. After it became beyond doubt that smoking is dangerous to people's health, a new debate arose concerning the possible health hazards of secondhand smoke on nonsmokers. Collect statements pro and con on this issue and evaluate the strength of the inductive arguments on each side.

2. The high positive correlation between CO_2 concentrations in the atmosphere and the Earth's mean surface temperatures is often cited as evidence that increases in atmospheric CO_2 cause global warming. This argument is illustrated by the famous "hockey stick" diagram in Al Gore's *An Inconvenient Truth*. Is this argument persuasive? How could skeptics about global warming respond?

3. In *Twilight of the Idols*, Nietzsche claims that the following examples illustrate "the error of mistaking cause for consequence." Do you agree? Why or why not?

Everyone knows the book of the celebrated Cornaro in which he recommends his meager diet as a recipe for a long and happy life—a virtuous one, too. . . . I do not doubt that hardly any book (the Bible rightly excepted) has done so much harm, has shortened so many lives, as this curiosity, which was so well meant.

The reason: mistaking the consequence for the cause. The worthy Italian saw in his diet the *cause* of his long life; while the prerequisite of long life, an extraordinarily slow metabolism, a small consumption, was the cause of his meager diet. He was not free to eat much *or* little as he chose, his frugality was *not* an act of "free will": he became ill when he ate more. But if one is not a bony fellow of this sort one does not merely do well, one positively needs to eat *properly*. A scholar of *our day*, with his rapid consumption of nervous energy, would kill himself with Cornaro's regimen. . . .

Long life, a plentiful posterity is *not* the reward of virtue, virtue itself is rather just that slowing down of the metabolism which also has, among other things, a long life, a plentiful posterity, in short *Cornarism*, as its outcome.—The Church and morality say: "A race, a people perishes through vice and luxury." My *restored* reason says: when a people is perishing, degenerating physiologically, vice and luxury (that is to say the necessity for stronger and stronger and more and more frequent stimulants, such as every exhausted nature is acquainted with) *follow* therefrom. A young man grows prematurely pale and faded. His friends say: this and that illness is to blame. I say: *that* he became ill, *that* he failed to resist the illness, was already the consequence of an impoverished life, an hereditary exhaustion. The newspaper reader says: this party will ruin itself if it makes errors like this. My *higher* politics says: a party which makes errors like this is already finished—it is no longer secure in its instincts. Every error, of whatever kind, is a consequence of degeneration of instinct, degeneration of will: one has thereby virtually defined the *bad*. Everything *good* is instinct—and consequently easy, necessary, free. Effort is an objection, the *god* is typically distinguished from the hero (in my language: *light* feet are the first attribute of divinity).[6]

NOTES

[1] Mill's "methods of experimental inquiry" are found in book 3, chap. 8 of his *A System of Logic* (London: John W. Parker, 1843). Mill's method of difference, method of agreement, and joint method parallel our SCT, NCT, and Joint Test, respectively. Our simplification of Mill's methods derives from Brian Skyrms, *Choice and Chance*, 3rd ed. (Belmont, CA: Wadsworth, 1986), chap. 4.

[2] These excerpts are drawn from David W. Fraser and Joseph E. McDade, "Legionellosis," *Scientific American*, October 1979, 82–99.

[3] From Gregory A. Kimble, *How to Use (and Misuse) Statistics* (Englewood Cliffs, NJ: Prentice-Hall, 1978), 182.

[4] From Kimble, *How to Use (and Misuse) Statistics*, 182.

[5] "Locked Doors No Bar to Crime, Study Says," *Santa Barbara* [California] *Newspress*, Wednesday, February 16, 1977. This title suggests that locking your doors will not increase safety. Is that a reasonable lesson to draw from this study?

[6] Friedrich Nietzsche, *Twilight of the Idols* and *The Anti-Christ*, trans. R. J. Hollingdale (1889; Harmondsworth: Penguin, 1968), 47–48.

10

INFERENCE TO THE BEST
EXPLANATION AND FROM ANALOGY

Once we know the cause of a phenomenon, we can cite this cause in a premise of an argument whose purpose is to explain the phenomenon (as we saw in Chapter 1). Explanation and causation are also related in a different way, for explanations can be used to pick out the cause from among various conditions correlated with the phenomenon (a problem faced at the end of Chapter 9). The general strategy is then to cite the explanatory value of a causal hypothesis as evidence for that hypothesis. This form of argument, which is described as an inference to the best explanation, *is the first topic in this chapter. It requires us to determine which explanation is best, so we will investigate common standards for assessing explanations, including falsifiability, conservativeness, modesty, simplicity, power, and depth. After explaining these standards, this chapter will turn to a related form of argument called an* argument from analogy, *in which the fact that two things have certain features in common is taken as evidence that they have further features in common. The chapter ends by suggesting that many, or maybe even all, arguments from analogy are ultimately based on implicit inferences to the best explanation.*

INFERENCES TO THE BEST EXPLANATION

One of the most common forms of inductive argument is *inference to the best explanation.*[1] The general idea behind such inferences is that a hypothesis gains inductive support if, when added to our stock of previously accepted beliefs, it enables us to explain something that we observe or believe, and no competing explanation works nearly as well.

To see how inferences to the best explanation work, suppose you return to your home and discover that the lock on your front door is broken and some valuables are missing. In all likelihood, you will immediately conclude that you have been burglarized. Of course, other things *could* have produced the mess. Perhaps the police mistakenly busted into your house looking for drugs and took your valuables as evidence. Perhaps your friends are playing a strange joke on you. Perhaps a meteorite struck the door and then vaporized your valuables. In fact, all of these things *could* have happened (even the last), and further investigation could show that one of them did. Why, then, do we so quickly accept the burglary hypothesis without even considering these competing possibilities? The reason is that the hypothesis that your home was robbed is not highly improbable; and this hypothesis, together with other things we believe, provides the best—the strongest and the most natural—explanation of the phenomenon. The possibility that a meteorite struck your door is so wildly remote that it is not worth taking seriously. The possibility that your house was raided by mistake or that your friends are playing a strange practical joke on you is not wildly remote, but neither fits the overall facts very well. If it was a police raid, then you would expect to find a police officer there or at least a note. If it is a joke, then it is hard to see the point of it. By contrast, burglaries are not very unusual, and that hypothesis fits the facts extremely well. Logically, the situation looks like this:

(1) OBSERVATION: Your lock is broken, and your valuables are missing.
(2) EXPLANATION: The hypothesis that your house has been burglarized, combined with previously accepted facts and principles, provides a suitably strong explanation of observation 1.
(3) COMPARISON: No other hypothesis provides an explanation nearly as good as that in 2.
(4) CONCLUSION: Your house was burglarized.

The explanatory power of the conclusion gives us reason to believe it because doing so increases our ability to understand our observations and to make reliable predictions. Explanation is important because it makes sense out of things—makes them more intelligible—and we want to understand the world around us. Prediction is important because it tests our theories with new data and sometimes allows us to anticipate or even control future events. Inference to the best explanation enables us to achieve such goals.

Here it might help to compare inferences to the best explanation with other forms of argument. Prior to any belief about burglars, you were already *justified* in believing *that* your lock was broken and your valuables were missing. You could see that much. What you could not see was *why* your lock was broken. That question is what the explanation answers. Explanations help us understand why things happen, when we are already justified in believing those things did happen. (Recall Chapter 1.)

Explanations often take the form of arguments. In our example, we could argue:

(1) Your house was burglarized.
(2) When houses are burglarized, valuables are missing.
∴(3) Your valuables are missing.

This explanatory argument starts with the hypothesis that was the conclusion of the inference to the best explanation, and it ends with the observation that was the first premise in that inference to the best explanation. The difference is that this new argument *explains* why its conclusion is true—why the valuables are missing—whereas the inference to the best explanation *justified* belief in its conclusion that your house was burglarized.

More generally, in an explanatory use of argument, we try to make sense of something by deriving it (sometimes deductively) from premises that are themselves well established. With an inference to the best explanation, we reason in the opposite direction: Instead of deriving an observation from its explanation, we derive the explanation from the observation. That a hypothesis provides the best explanation of something whose truth is already known provides evidence for the truth of that hypothesis.

Once we grasp the notion of an inference to the best explanation, we can see this pattern of reasoning everywhere. If you see your friend kick the wall, you infer that he must be angry, because there is no other explanation of why he would kick the wall. Then if he turns away when you say, "Hello," you might think that he is angry *at you*, if you cannot imagine any other reason why he would not respond. Similarly, when your car goes dead right after a checkup (as at the start of Chapter 9), you may conclude that it is out of fuel, if that is the best explanation of why your car stopped. Psychologists infer that people care what others think about them, even when they deny it, because that explains why people behave differently in front of others than when they are alone. Linguists argue that the original Indo-European language arose millennia ago in an area that was not next to the sea but did have lakes and rivers, because that is the best explanation of why Indo-European languages have no common word for seas but do share a common root "nav-" that connotes boats or ships. Astronomers believe that our Universe began with a Big Bang, because that hypothesis best explains the background microwave radiation and spreading of galaxies. All of these arguments and many more are basically inferences to the best explanation.

Solutions to murder mysteries almost always have the form of an inference to the best explanation. The facts of the case are laid out and then the clever detective argues that, given these facts, only one person could possibly have committed the crime. In the story "Silver Blaze," Sherlock Holmes concludes that the trainer must have been the dastardly fellow who stole Silver Blaze, the horse favored to win the Wessex Cup, which was to be run the following day. Holmes's reasoning, as usual, was very complex, but the key part of his argument was that the dog kept in the stable did not bark loudly when someone came and took away the horse.

> I had grasped the significance of the silence of the dog, for one true inference invariably suggests others. [I knew that] a dog was kept in the stables, and yet, though someone had been in and fetched out a horse, he had not barked enough to arouse the two lads in the loft. Obviously the midnight visitor was someone whom the dog knew well.[2]

Together with other facts, this was enough to identify the trainer, Straker, as the person who stole Silver Blaze. In this case, it is the fact that something *didn't* occur that provides the basis for an inference to the best explanation.

Of course, Holmes's inference is not absolutely airtight. It is possible that Straker is innocent and Martians with hypnotic powers over dogs committed the crime. But that only goes to show that this inference is neither valid nor deductive in our sense. It does not show anything wrong with Holmes's inference. Since his inference is inductive, it is enough for it to be strong.

Inferences to the best explanation are also defeasible. No matter how strong such an inference might be, it can always be overturned by future experience. Holmes might later find traces of a sedative in the dog's blood or someone else might confess or provide Straker with an alibi. Alternatively, Holmes (or you) might think up some better explanation. Still, unless and until such new evidence or hypothesis comes along, we have adequate reason to believe that Straker stole the horse, because that hypothesis provides the best available explanation of the information that we have now. The fact that future evidence or hypotheses always might defeat inferences to the best explanation does not show that such inferences are all bad. If it did show this, then science and everyday life would be in trouble, because so much of science and our commonsense view of the world depends on inferences to the best explanation.

To assess such inferences, we still need some standards for determining which explanation is the *best*. There is, unfortunately, no simple rule for deciding this, but we can list some factors that go into the evaluation of an explanation.[3]

First, the hypothesis should really *explain the observations*. A good explanation makes sense out of that which it is intended to explain. In our original example, the broken lock can be explained by a burglary but not by the hypothesis that a friend came to see you (unless you have strange friends). Moreover, the hypothesis needs to explain *all* of the relevant observations. The hypothesis of a mistaken police raid might explain the broken lock but not the missing valuables or the lack of any note or police officers when you return home.

The explanation should also be *deep*. An explanation is not deep but shallow when the explanation itself needs to be explained. It does not help to explain something that is obscure by citing something just as obscure. Why did the police raid your house? Because they suspected you. That explanation is shallow if it immediately leads to another question: Why did they suspect you? Because they had the wrong address. If they did not have the wrong address, then we would wonder why they suspected you. Without an explanation of their suspicions, the police raid hypothesis could not adequately explain even the broken lock.

Third, the explanation should be *powerful*. It is a mark of excellence in an explanation that the same kind of explanation can be used successfully over a wide range of cases. Many broken locks can be explained by burglaries. Explanatory range is especially important in science. One of the main reasons why Einstein's theory of relativity replaced Newtonian physics is that Einstein could explain a wider range of phenomena, including very small particles at very high speeds.

Explanations go too far, however, when they could explain any possible event. Consider the hypothesis that each particle of matter has its own individual spirit that makes it do exactly what it does. This hypothesis might seem to explain some phenomena that even Einstein's theory cannot explain. But the spirit hypothesis really explains nothing, because it does not explain why any particle behaves one way as opposed to another. Either behavior is compatible with the hypothesis, so neither is explained. To succeed, therefore, explanations need to be incompatible with some possible outcome. In short, they need to be *falsifiable*. (See Chapter 16 on self-sealers.)

Moreover, explanations should be *modest* in the sense that they should not claim too much—indeed, any more than is needed to explain the observations. When you find your lock broken and valuables gone, you should not jump to the conclusion that there is a conspiracy against you or that gangs have taken over your neighborhood. Without further information, there is no need to specify that there was more than one burglar in order to explain what you see. There is also no need to hypothesize that there was only one burglar. For this reason, the most modest explanation would not specify any number of burglars, so no inference to the best explanation could justify any claim about the number of burglars, at least until more evidence comes along.

Modesty is related to *simplicity*. One kind of simplicity is captured by the celebrated principle known as Occam's razor, which tells us not to multiply entities beyond necessity. Physicists, for example, should not postulate new kinds of subatomic particles or forces unless there is no other way to explain their experimental results. Similar standards apply in everyday life. We should not believe in ghosts unless they really are necessary to explain the noises in our attic or some other phenomenon. Simplicity is not always a matter of new kinds of entities. In comparison with earlier views, the theory that gases are composed of particles too small to see was simpler insofar as the particle theory allowed gas laws to be explained by the standard physical principles governing the motions of larger particles without having to add any new laws. Simplicity is a mark of excellence in an explanation partly because simple explanations are easier to understand and apply, but considerations of plausibility and aesthetics are also at work in judgments of which explanation is simplest.

The tests of modesty and simplicity might seem to be in tension with the test of power. This tension can be resolved only by finding the right balance. The best explanation will not claim any more than is necessary (so it will be modest), but it will claim enough to cover a wide range of phenomena (so it will be powerful). This is tricky, but the best explanations succeed in reconciling and incorporating these conflicting virtues as much as possible.

Finally, an explanation should be *conservative*. Explanations are better when they force us to give up fewer well-established beliefs. We have strong reasons to believe that cats cannot break metal locks. This rules out the hypothesis that your neighbor's cat broke your front-door lock. Explanations should also not contain claims that are themselves too unlikely to be true. A meteorite would be strong enough to break your lock, but it is very unlikely that a meteorite struck your lock. That makes the burglary hypothesis better, at least until we find other evidence (such as meteorite fragments) that cannot be explained except by a meteorite.

In sum, a hypothesis provides the best explanation when it is more explanatory, powerful, falsifiable, modest, simple, and conservative than any competing hypothesis. Each of these standards can be met to varying degrees, and they can conflict. As we saw, the desire for simplicity might have to be sacrificed to gain a more powerful explanation. Conservatism also might have to give way to explain some unexpected observations, and so on. These standards are not always easy to apply, but they can often be used to determine whether a particular explanation is better than its competitors.

Once we determine that one explanation is the best, we still cannot yet infer that it is true. It might turn out that the best explanation out of a group of weak explanations isn't good enough. For centuries people were baffled by the floods that occurred in the Nile River each spring. The Nile, as far as anyone knew, flowed from an endless desert. Where, then, did the flood waters come from? Various wild explanations were suggested—mostly about deities of one kind or another—but none was any good. Looking for the best explanation among these weak explanations would be a waste of time. It was only after it was discovered that central Africa contains a high mountain range covered with snow in the winter that a reasonable explanation became possible. That, in fact, settled the matter. So it must be understood that the best explanation must also be a *good enough* explanation.

Even when an explanation is both good and best, what it explains might be illusory. Many people believe that shark cartilage prevents cancer, because the best explanation of why sharks do not get cancer lies in their cartilage. One serious problem for this inference is that sharks *do* get cancer. They even get cancer in their cartilage. So this inference to the best explanation fails.

When a particular explanation is both good and much better than any competitor, and when the explained observation is accurate, then an inference to the best explanation will provide *strong* inductive support. At other times, no clear winner or even reasonable contender emerges. In such cases, an inference to the best explanation will be correspondingly *weak*.

Whether an inference to the best explanation is strong *enough* depends on the context. As contexts shift, standards of rigor can change. Evidence that is strong enough to justify my belief that my spouse took our car might not be strong enough to convict our neighbor of stealing our car. Good judgment is often required to determine whether a certain degree of strength is adequate for the purposes at hand.

Context can also affect the rankings of various factors. Many explanations, for example, depend on universal premises. In such cases, compatibility with observation is usually the primary test. The universal principle should not be refuted by counterexamples (see Chapter 17). But sometimes explanatory power will take precedence: If a principle has strong explanatory power, we may accept it even in the face of clear disconfirming evidence. We do not give up good explanations lightly—nor should we. To understand why, recall (from Chapter 9) that we do not test single propositions in isolation from other propositions in our system of beliefs. When faced with counterevidence to our beliefs, we often have a choice between what to give up and what to continue to hold on to. A simple example will illustrate this. Suppose that we believe the following things:

(1) Either John or Joan committed the crime.
(2) Whoever committed the crime must have had a motive for doing so.
(3) Joan had no motive to commit the crime.

From these three premises we can validly infer that John committed the crime. Suppose, however, that we discover that John could not have committed the crime. (Three bishops and two judges swear that John was somewhere else at the time.) Now, from the fact that John did not commit the crime, we could not immediately conclude that Joan committed it, for that would lead to an inconsistency. If she committed the crime, then, according to premise 3, she would have committed a motiveless crime, but that conflicts with premise 2, which says that motiveless crimes do not occur. So the discovery that John did not commit the crime entails that at least one of the premises in the argument must be abandoned, but it does not tell us which one or which ones.

This same phenomenon occurs when we are dealing with counterevidence to a complex system of beliefs. Counterevidence shows that there must be something wrong somewhere in the system, but it does not show exactly where the problem lies. One possibility is that the *supposed* counterevidence is itself in error. Imagine that a student carries out an experiment and gets the result that one of the fundamental laws of physics is false. This will not shake the scientific community even a little, for the best explanation of the student's result is that she messed things up. Given well-established principles, she could not have gotten the result she did if she had run the experiment correctly. Of course, if a great many reputable scientists find difficulties with a supposed law, then the situation is different. The hypothesis that all of these scientists, like the student, simply messed up is itself highly unlikely. But it is surprising how much contrary evidence will be tolerated when dealing with a strong explanatory theory. Scientists often continue to employ a theory in the face of counterevidence. Sometimes this perpetuates errors. For years, instruments reported that the levels of ozone above Antarctica were lower than before, but scientists attributed these measurements to bad equipment, until finally they announced an ozone hole there. Still, there is often good reason to hold on to a useful theory despite counterevidence, as long as its defects do not make serious trouble—that is, give bad results in areas that count. Good judgment is required to determine when it is finally time to shift to a different explanation.

EXERCISE I

Imagine that you offer an explanation, and a critic responds in the following way. Which virtue (explanatoriness, depth, power, falsifiability, modesty, simplicity, or conservativeness) is your critic claiming that your explanation lacks?

1. But that won't explain anything other than this particular case.
2. But that conflicts with everything we know about biology.
3. But you don't have to claim all of that in order to explain what we see.
4. But that just raises new questions that you need to answer.
5. But that explains only a small part of the story.
6. But that would apply whatever happened.

EXERCISE II

For each of the following explanations, specify which standard of a good explanation, if any, it violates. The standards require that a good explanation be explanatory, deep, powerful, falsifiable, modest, simple, and conservative. A single explanation might violate more than one standard.

1. Although we usually have class at this time in this room, I don't see anybody in the classroom, because a wicked witch made them all invisible.
2. Although we usually have class at this time in this room, I don't see anybody in the classroom, because they all decided to skip class today.
3. Although we usually have class at this time in this room, I don't see anybody in the classroom, because it's Columbus Day.
4. My house fell down, because it was painted red.
5. My house fell down, because of a powerful earthquake centered on my property that did not affect anything or anybody else.
6. My house fell down, because its boards were struck by a new kind of sub-atomic particle.
7. Although I fished here all day, I didn't catch any fish, because there are no fish in this whole river.
8. Although I fished here all day, I didn't catch any fish, because the river gods don't like me.
9. Although I fished here all day, I didn't catch any fish, because I was unlucky today.
10. That light far up in the night sky is moving quickly, because it is the daily United Airlines flight from Boston to Los Angeles.
11. That light far up in the night sky is moving quickly, because it is an alien space ship.
12. That light far up in the night sky looks like it is moving quickly, because there's something wrong with my eyes right now.

EXERCISE III

Give two competing hypotheses that might be offered to explain each of the following phenomena. Which of these hypotheses is better? Why?

1. You follow a recipe carefully, but the bread never rises.
2. Your house begins to shake so violently that pictures fall off your walls.
3. Your key will not open the door of your house.
4. People start putting television cameras on your lawn, and a man with a big smile comes walking up your driveway.
5. Virtually all of the food in markets has suddenly sold out.
6. You put on a shirt and notice that there is no pocket on the front like there used to be.
7. A cave is found containing the bones of both prehistoric humans and now-extinct predators.
8. A cave is found containing the bones of both prehistoric humans and now-extinct herbivores.
9. After being visited by lobbyists for cigarette producers, your senator votes in favor of tobacco price supports, although he opposed them before.
10. Large, mysterious patterns of flattened wheat appear in the fields of Britain. (Some people attribute these patterns to visitors from another planet.)
11. A palm reader foretells that something wonderful will happen to you soon, and it does.
12. A neighbor sprinkles purple powder on his lawn to keep away tigers, and, sure enough, no tigers show up on his lawn.

DISCUSSION QUESTIONS

1. Put the following inference to the best explanation in standard form, and then evaluate it as carefully as you can, using the tests discussed above.

[During the Archean Era, which extended from about 3.8 to 2.5 million years before the present,] the sun's luminosity was perhaps 25% less than that of today. . . . This faint young sun has led to a paradox. There is no evidence from the scant rock record of the Archean that the planetary surface was frozen. However, if Earth had no atmosphere or an atmosphere of composition like that of today, the amount of radiant energy received by Earth from the sun would not be enough to keep it from freezing. The way out of this dilemma is to have an atmosphere present during the early Archean that was different in composition that that of today. . . . For a variety of reasons, it has been concluded, although still debated, that the most likely gases present in greater abundance in the Archean atmosphere were carbon dioxide, water vapor (the most important greenhouse gas) and perhaps methane. The presence of these greenhouse gases warmed the atmosphere and planetary surface and prevented the early Archean Earth from being frozen.[4]

(continued)

2. Reread the passage on what killed the dinosaurs in the Discussion Questions at the end of Chapter 1. Reconstruct the argument as an inference to the best explanation. How well does that argument meet the standards for assessing explanations?

3. Also in the Discussion Questions at the end of Chapter 1, Colin Powell gives several arguments that in 2003 Saddam Hussein was still trying to obtain fissile material for a nuclear weapons program. Which of his arguments is an inference to the best explanation? How well do these arguments meet the standards for this form of argument?

4. Find three inferences to the best explanation in the readings on scientific reasoning in Chapter 20. This should be easy because scientists use this form of argument often. Put those inferences in standard form, and then evaluate them using the tests discussed above.

5. Sherlock Holmes was lauded for his ability to infer a great deal of information about strangers from simple observations of their clothing and behavior. He displays this ability in the following exchange with his brother, Mycroft, in front of his friend Dr. Watson, who is the first-person narrator. Reconstruct and evaluate the inferences to the best explanation by Holmes and Mycroft in the closing four paragraphs.

"THE GREEK INTERPRETER"

———————■———————

from *The Memoirs of Sherlock Holmes*
by Sir Arthur Conan Doyle

. . . The two sat down together in the bow-window of the club. "To anyone who wishes to study mankind this is the spot," said Mycroft. "Look at the magnificent types! Look at these two men who are coming towards us for example."

"The billiard-marker and the other?"

"Precisely. What do you make of the other?"

The two men had stopped opposite the window. Some chalk marks over the waistcoat pocket were the only signs of billiards which I could see in one of them. The other was a very small, dark fellow, with his hat pushed back and several packages under his arm.

"An old soldier, I perceive," said Sherlock.

"And very recently discharged," remarked the brother.

"Served in India, I see."

"And a non-commissioned officer."

"Royal Artillery, I fancy" said Sherlock.

"And a widower."

"But with a child."

"Children, my dear boy, children."

"Come," said I, laughing, "this is a little too much."

"Surely," answered Holmes, "it is not hard to say that a man with that bearing, expression of authority, and sun-baked skin, is a soldier, is more than a private, and is not long from India."

"That he has not left the service long is shown by his still wearing his am-
munition boots, as they are called," observed Mycroft.

"He had not the cavalry stride, yet he wore his hat on one side, as is shown
by the lighter skin on that side of his brow. His weight is against his being a
sapper [a soldier who builds and repairs fortifications]. He is in the artillery."

"Then, of course, his complete mourning shows that he has lost someone
very dear. The fact that he is doing his own shopping looks as though it were
his wife. He has been buying things for children, you perceive. There is a rat-
tle, which shows that one of them is very young. The wife probably died in
childbed. The fact that he has a picture-book under his arm shows that there is
another child to be thought of."

ARGUMENTS FROM ANALOGY

Another very common kind of inductive argument moves from a premise
that two things are similar in some respects to a conclusion that they must
also be analogous in a further respect. Such arguments from analogy can be
found in many areas of everyday life. When we buy a new car, how can we
tell whether it is going to be reliable? *Consumer Reports* might help if it is an
old model; but if it is a brand-new model with no track record, then all we
can go on is its similarities to earlier models. Our reasoning then seems to be
that the new model is like the old model in various ways, and the old model
was reliable, so the new model is probably reliable, too.

The same form of argument is used in science. Here's an example from
geology:

> Meteorites composed predominantly of iron provide evidence that parts of other
> bodies in the solar system, presumably similar in origin to Earth, were composed
> of metallic iron. The evidence from meteorite compositions and origins lends
> support to the conclusion that Earth's core is metallic iron.[5]

The argument here is that Earth is analogous to certain meteors in their origins, and those meteors have a large percentage of iron, so the Earth as a
whole probably contains about the same percentage of iron. Because a
smaller amount of iron is present in the Earth's crust, the rest must lie in the
Earth's core.

Similarly, archaeologists might argue that a certain knife was used in ritual sacrifices because it resembles other sacrificial knives in its size, shape,
materials, carvings, and so on. The analogy in this case is between the newly
discovered knife and the other knives. This analogy is supposed to support
a conclusion about the function of the newly discovered knife.

Although such arguments from analogy have diverse contents, they share
a common form that can be represented like this:

(1) Object *A* has properties *P, Q, R,* and so on.
(2) Objects *B, C, D,* and so on also have properties *P, Q, R,* and so on.

    (3) Objects *B, C, D*, and so on have property *X*.

∴ (4) Object *A* probably also has property *X*.

In the archaeological example, object *A* is the newly discovered knife, and objects *B, C, D*, and so on are previously discovered knives that are known to have been used in sacrifices. Properties *P, Q, R*, and so on are the size, shape, materials, and carvings that make *A* analogous to *B, C, D*, and so on. *X* is the property of being used as a sacrificial knife. Premise 3 says that the previously discovered artifacts have this property. The conclusion, on line 4, says that the newly discovered artifact probably also has this property.

    Since arguments from analogy are inductive, they normally aren't valid. It is possible that, even though this knife is analogous to other sacrificial knives, this knife was used to shave the king or just to cut bread. These arguments are also defeasible. The argument about knives obviously loses all of its strength if we find "Made in China" printed on the newly discovered knife. Still, none of this shows that arguments from analogy are no good. Despite being invalid and defeasible, some arguments from analogy can still provide reasons—even strong reasons—for their conclusions.

    How can we tell whether an argument from analogy is strong or weak? One obvious requirement is that the premises must be *true*. If the previously discovered knives were not really used in sacrifices, or if they do not really have the same carvings on their handles as the newly discovered knife, then this argument from analogy does not provide much, if any, support for its conclusion.

    In addition, the cited similarities must be *relevant*. Suppose someone argues that his old car was red with a black interior and had four doors and a sunroof, and his new car also has these properties, so his new car is probably going to be as reliable as his old car. This argument is very weak because the cited similarities are obviously irrelevant to reliability. Such assessments of relevance depend on background beliefs, such as that reliability depends on the drive train and the engine rather than on the color or the sunroof.

    The similarities must also be *important*. Similarities are usually more important the more specific they are. Lots of cars with four tires and a motor are reliable, but this is not enough to infer that, because this particular car also has four tires and a motor, it will be reliable, too. The reason is obvious: There are also lots of unreliable cars with four tires and a motor. In general, if many objects have properties *P, Q*, and *R*, and many of those lack property *X*, then arguments from these analogies will be weak. In contrast, if a smaller percentage of objects that have properties *P, Q*, and *R* lack property *X*, then the argument from these analogies will be strong.

    If we are not sure which respects *are* important, we still might have some idea of which respects *might* be important. Then we can try to cite objects that are analogous in as many as possible of those respects. By increasing the number of potentially relevant respects for which the analogy holds, we can increase the likelihood that the important respects will be on our list. That shows why arguments from analogy are usually stronger when they cite *more and closer analogies* between the objects.

Another factor that affects the strength of an argument from analogy is the presence of *relevant disanalogies*. Because arguments from analogy are defeasible, as we saw, a strong argument from analogy can become weak if we add a premise that states an important disanalogy. Suppose my new car is like my old cars in many ways, but there is one difference: The new car has an electric motor, whereas the old cars were powered by gasoline. This one difference is enough to weaken any argument to the conclusion that the new car will be reliable. Of course, other disanalogies, such as a different color, won't matter to reliability; and it will often require background knowledge to determine how important a disanalogy is.

We need to be careful here. Some disanalogies that are relevant do not undermine an argument from analogy. If a new engine design was introduced by top engineers to increase reliability, then this disanalogy might not undermine the argument from analogy. Differences that point to more reliability rather than less might even make the argument from analogy stronger.

Other disanalogies can increase the strength of an argument from analogy in a different way. If the same markings are found on very different kinds of sacrificial knives, then the presence of those markings on the newly discovered knife is even stronger evidence that this knife was also used in sacrifices. Differences among the cases cited only in the premises as analogies (that is, B, C, D, and so on) can strengthen an argument from analogy.

Finally, the strength of an argument from analogy depends on its conclusion. Analogies to other kinds of cars provide stronger evidence for a weak conclusion (such as that the new model will probably be pretty reliable) and weaker evidence for a strong conclusion (such as that the new model will definitely be just as reliable as the old model). As with other forms of argument, an argument from analogy becomes stronger as its conclusion becomes weaker and vice versa.

These standards can be summarized by saying that an argument from analogy is stronger when:

1. It cites more and closer analogies that are more important.

2. There are fewer or less important disanalogies between the object in the conclusion and the other objects.

3. The objects cited only in the premises are more diverse.

4. The conclusion is weaker.

After learning about arguments from analogy, it is natural to wonder how they are related to inferences to the best explanation. Although this is sometimes disputed, it seems to us that arguments from analogy are often—if not always—implicit and incomplete inferences to the best explanation. As we pointed out, analogies don't support any conclusion unless they are relevant, and whether they are relevant depends on how they fit into explanations. The color of a car is irrelevant to its reliability, because color plays no role in explaining its reliability. What explains its reliability is its drive train design, materials, care in manufacturing, and so on. That is why analogies in those respects can support a conclusion about reliability. Similarly, the markings on an artifact are relevant to whether it is a sacrificial knife *if* the best explanation of why it has those markings is that it was used in sacrifices. What makes that explanation best is that it also explains similar markings on other sacrificial knives. Thus, such arguments from analogy can be seen as involving an inference to the best explanation of why objects *B, C, D,* and so on have property *X* followed by an application of that explanation to the newly discovered object *A*.

Sometimes the explanation runs in the other direction. Whereas the conclusion about the knife's use (*X*) is supposed to explain its shared markings (*P, Q, R*), sometimes it is the shared features (*P, Q, R*) that are supposed to explain the feature claimed in the conclusion (*X*). Here is a classic example:

> We may observe a very great [similarity] between this earth which we inhabit, and the other planets, Saturn, Jupiter, Mars, Venus, and Mercury. They all revolve around the sun, as the earth does, although at different distances and in different periods. They borrow all their light from the sun, as the earth does. Several of them are known to revolve around their axis like the earth, and, by that means, must have a like succession of day and night. Some of them have moons that serve to give them light in the absence of the sun, as our moon does to us. They are all, in their motions, subject to the same law of gravitation, as the earth is. From all this similarity it is not unreasonable to think that those planets may, like our earth, be the habitation of various orders of living creatures. There is some probability in this conclusion from analogy.[6]

The argument here seems to be that some other planet probably supports life, because Earth does and other planets are similar to Earth in revolving around the sun and around an axis, getting light from the sun, and so on. What makes certain analogies relevant is not, of course, that the motion of Earth is explained by the presence of life here. Rather, certain features of Earth explain why Earth is habitable. The argument suggests that the best explanation of why there is life on our planet is that certain conditions make life possible. That generalization can then be used to support the conclusion that other planets with the same conditions probably support life as well.

In one way or another, many (or maybe even all) arguments from analogy can be seen as inferences to the best explanation. But they are usually incomplete explanations. The argument for life on other planets did not have to commit itself to any particular theory about the origin of life or about which conditions are needed to support life. Nor did the car argument specify exactly what makes cars reliable. Such arguments from analogy merely list a number of similarities so that the list will be likely to include whatever factors are needed for life or for reliability. In this way, arguments from analogy can avoid depending on any complete theory about what is and what is not relevant.

This incompleteness makes arguments from analogy useful in situations where we do not yet know enough to formulate detailed theories or even to complete an inference to the best explanation. Yet the incompleteness of arguments from analogy also makes them more vulnerable to refutation, since the analogies that they list might fail to include a crucial respect. This does not mean that arguments from analogy are never any good. They can be strong. However, it does suggest that their strength will increase as they approach or approximate more complete inferences to the best explanation.

EXERCISE IV

For each of the following arguments, state whether the indicated changes would make the argument weaker or stronger, and explain why. The strength of the argument might not be affected at all. If so, say why it is not affected.

1. My friend and I have seen many movies together, and we have always agreed on whether they are good or bad. My friend liked the movie trilogy *The Lord of the Rings*. So I probably will like it as well.

Would this argument be weaker or stronger if:

   a. The only movies that my friend and I have watched together are comedies, and *The Lord of the Rings* is not a comedy.

   b. My friend and I have seen very many, very different movies together.

   c. My friend and I always watched movies together on Wednesdays, but my friend watched *The Lord of the Rings* on a weekend.

   d. The conclusion claims that I definitely will like *The Lord of the Rings* a lot.

   e. The conclusion claims that I probably won't totally dislike *The Lord of the Rings*.

2. All the students from Joe's high school with high grades and high board scores did well in college. Joe also had high grades and board scores. So he will probably do well in college.

Would this argument be weaker or stronger if:

   a. The other students worked hard, but Joe's good grades came easily to him, so he never learned to work hard.

   b. Joe is going to a different college than the students with whom he is being compared.

   c. Joe plans to major in some easy subject, but the other students were pre-med.

   d. Joe recently started taking drugs on a regular basis.

   e. Joe needs to work full-time to pay his college expenses, but the others had their expenses paid by their parents.

3. A new drug cures a serious disease in rats. Rats are similar to humans in many respects. Therefore, the drug will probably cure the same disease in humans.

Would this argument be weaker or stronger if:

   a. The disease affects the liver, and rat livers are very similar to human livers.

(continued)

b. The drug does not cure this disease in cats.

c. The drug has to be injected into the rat's tail to be effective (that is, it does not work if it is injected anywhere else in the rat).

d. No drug of this general type has been used on humans before.

e. The effects of the drug are enhanced by eating cooked foods.

EXERCISE V

Using the criteria mentioned above, evaluate each of the following arguments as strong or weak. Explain your answers. Be sure to specify the properties on which the analogy is based, as well as any background beliefs on which your evaluation depends.

1. This landscape by Cézanne is beautiful. He did another painting of a similar scene around the same time. So it is probably beautiful, too.

2. My aunt had a Siamese cat that bit me, so this Siamese cat will probably bite me, too.

3. The students I know who took this course last year got grades of A. I am a lot like them, since I am also smart and hardworking; and the course this year covers very similar material. So I will probably get an A.

4. This politician was caught cheating in his marriage, and he will have to face similarly strong temptations in his public duties, so he will probably cheat in political life as well.

5. A very high minimum wage led to increased unemployment in one country. That country's economy is similar to the economy in a different country. So a very high minimum wage will probably lead to increased unemployment in the other country as well.

6. I feel pain when someone hits me hard on the head with a baseball bat. Your body is a lot like mine. So you would probably feel pain if I hit you hard on the head with a baseball bat. (This is related to the so-called "Problem of Other Minds.")

7. It is immoral for a doctor to lie to a patient about a test result, even if the doctor thinks that lying is in the patient's best interest. We know this because even doctors would agree that it would be morally wrong for a financial adviser to lie to them about a potential investment, even if the financial advisor thinks that this lie is in the doctor's best interests.

8. Chrysler was held legally liable for damages due to defects in the suspension of its Corvair. The defects in the Pinto gas tank caused injuries that were just as serious. Thus, Ford should also be held legally liable for damages due to those defects.

1. As we will see in Chapter 18 of Part V, legal reasoning often uses analogies to legal precedents. In the case of *Plessy v. Ferguson* (1896), Plessy cites similarities to a laundry ordinance in *Yick Wo v. Hopkins* to argue against segregation in public transportation. Later, in *Grutter and Gratz* (excerpted below), critics argue that affirmative action is unconstitutional because of analogies to other forms of racial discrimination that were found unconstitutional in precedents. Reconstruct these arguments from analogy and then evaluate them by applying the criteria discussed above.

2. As we will see in Chapter 19, moral reasoning also often depends on arguments from analogies. One famous example occurs when Judith Jarvis Thomson defends the morality of abortion by means of an analogy to a kidnapped violinist (in the excerpt below). Reconstruct Thomson's argument from analogy and then evaluate it by applying the criteria discussed above.

3. The following excerpt presents evidence that Neanderthals were cannibals. Put the central argument from analogy, which is italicized here, into standard form. Then reconstruct the argument as an inference to the best explanation. Which representation best captures the force of the argument, or are they equally good?

"A GNAWING QUESTION IS ANSWERED"
—■—

from *The Toronto Star*, October 10, 1999
by Michael Downey

Tim White is worried that he may have helped to pin a bad rap on the Neanderthals, the prehistoric Europeans who died out 25,000 years ago. "There is a danger that everyone will think that all Neanderthals were cannibals and that's not necessarily true," he says. White was part of a French-American team of paleoanthropologists who recently found conclusive evidence that at least some Neanderthals ate others about 100,000 years ago. But that doesn't mean they were cannibalistic by nature, he stresses. Most people don't realize that cannibalism is widespread throughout nature, says White, a professor at the University of California at Berkeley and the author of a book on prehistoric cannibalism.

The question of whether the Neanderthals were cannibals had long been a hotly debated topic among anthropologists. No proof had ever been found. That debate ended, however, with the recent analysis by the team of stone tools and bones found in a cave at Moula-Guercy in southern France. The cave is about the size of a living room, perched about 80 metres above the Rhone River. "This one site has all of the evidence right together," says White. "It's as if somebody put a yellow tape around the cave for 100,000 years and kept the scene intact." The bones of deer and other fauna show the clear markings of the nearby stone tools, indicating the deer had been expertly butchered; they were skinned, their body parts cut off and the meat and tendons sliced from the bone. Long bones were bashed open "to get at the fatty marrow inside," says White.

(continued)

So what does all this have to do with cannibalism? *The bones of the six (so far) humans in the same locations have precisely the same markings made by the same tools. That means these fairly modern humans were skinned and eaten in the same manner as the deer.*

And if you are thinking they were eaten after they just happened to die, they do represent all age groups. Two were children about 6 years old, two were teenagers and two were adults.

But maybe they were eaten at a time when food was unusually scarce, right? Not so. There is a large number of animal bones at the same dig, indicating that there were options to eating other Neanderthals.

Human bones with similar cut marks have been found throughout Europe, from Spain to Croatia, providing tantalizing hints of Neanderthal cannibalism activity over tens of thousands of years. But finding such clear evidence of the same preparation techniques being used on deer in the same cave site in France, will "necessitate reassessment of earlier finds," always attributed to ritual burial practices or some other explanation, says White.

It was not clear whether the Neanderthals ate human flesh of their own tribe or exclusively from an enemy tribe, White stresses. Nor was there any indication the purpose of the cannibalism involved nourishment. Eating human flesh could have had another purpose altogether, he says. Surprising to some, cannibalism has been found in 75 mammal species and in 15 primate groups. White says it has often been practiced for reasons not associated with normal hunger. White quotes an archeological maxim: "Actions fossilize, intentions don't." In other words, the reason for the cannibalism remains unknown. He notes that the flesh of other humans has sometimes been eaten to stave off starvation, to show contempt for an enemy or as part of a ritual of affection for the deceased. "Were the victims already dead or killed to be eaten?" he asks, "Were they enemies of the tribe or family members?" Learning these details is the "important and extremely difficult part."

This excavation represents a breakthrough in archeological practice. In a series of papers, White has long advocated the importance of treating a dig site like a crime scene, leaving every piece of evidence in place. In many earlier digs, animal bones were frequently pulled out and thrown away as being irrelevant and human bones were often coated with shellac. The human bones were all tossed into the same bag with no regard to their juxtaposition to each other or precise location. This is one of the first times that modern forensic techniques have been utilized in an archeological excavation, White says, and conclusions drawn have been much more precise than in previous digs that used cruder methods. The project team, which is headed by Alban Defleur of the Universite du Mediterrane at Marseilles, has been digging in the cave since 1991.

4. In the following passage, William Paley argues for the existence of God on the basis of an analogy to a watch. Reconstruct this argument from analogy and then evaluate it by applying the criteria discussed above. Could Paley's argument also be reconstructed as an inference to the best explanation? If so, would that reconstruction better capture the force of the argument?

"THE WATCH AND THE WATCHMAKER"

———————————▪———————————

from *Natural Theology* (New York: Hopkins, 1836)
by William Paley

... In crossing a heath, suppose I pitched my foot against a stone and were asked how the stone came to be there, I might possibly answer that for anything I knew to the contrary it had lain there forever; nor would it, perhaps, be very easy to show the absurdity of this answer. But suppose I had found a watch upon the ground, and it should be inquired how the watch happened to be in that place, I should hardly think of the answer which I had before given, that for anything I knew the watch might have always been there. Yet why should not this answer serve for the watch as well as for the stone? Why is it not as admissible in the second case as in the first? For this reason, and for no other, namely, that when we come to inspect the watch, we perceive—what we could not discover in the stone—that its several parts are framed and put together for a purpose, e.g., that they are so formed and adjusted as to produce motion, and that motion so regulated as to point out the hour of the day; that if the different parts had been differently shaped from what they are, of a different size from what they are, or placed after any other manner or in any other order than that in which they are placed, either no motion at all would have been carried on in the machine, or none which would have answered the use that is now served by it. . . . This mechanism being observed—it requires indeed an examination of the instrument, and perhaps some previous knowledge of the subject, to perceive and understand it; but being once, as we have said, observed and understood—the inference we think is inevitable, that the watch must have had a maker—that there must have existed, at some time and at some place or other, an artificer or artificers who formed it for the purpose which we find it actually to answer, who comprehended its construction and designed its use. . . .

[E]very indication of contrivance, every manifestation of design, which existed in the watch, exists in the works of nature; with the difference, on the side of nature, of being greater and more, and that in a degree which exceeds all computation. I mean that the contrivances of nature surpass the contrivances of art, in the complexity, subtlety, and curiosity of the mechanism; and still more, if possible, do they go beyond them in number and variety; yet in a multitude of cases, are not less evidently mechanical, not less evidently contrivances, not less evidently accommodated to their end, or suited to their office, than are the most perfect productions of human ingenuity.

I know no better method of introducing so large a subject, than that of comparing a single thing with a single thing: an eye, for example, with a telescope. As far as the examination of the instrument goes, there is precisely the same proof that the eye was made for vision, as there is that the telescope was made for assisting it. They are made upon the same principles; both being adjusted to the laws by which the transmission and refraction of rays of light are regulated. I speak not of the origin of the laws themselves; but such laws being fixed, the construction in both cases is adapted to them. . . .

(continued)

To some it may appear a difference sufficient to destroy all similitude between the eye and the telescope, that the one is a perceiving organ, the other an unperceiving instrument. The fact is that they are both instruments. And as to the mechanism, at least as to mechanism being employed, and even as to the kind of it, this circumstance varies not the analogy at all. . . . The end is the same; the means are the same. The purpose in both is alike; the contrivance for accomplishing that purpose is in both alike. The lenses of the telescopes, and the humors of the eye, bear a complete resemblance to one another, in their figure, their position, and in their power over the rays of light, viz. in bringing each pencil to a point at the right distance from the lens; namely, in the eye, at the exact place where the membrane is spread to receive it. How is it possible, under circumstances of such close affinity, and under the operation of equal evidence, to exclude contrivance from the one; yet to acknowledge the proof of contrivance having been employed, as the plainest and clearest of all propositions, in the other? . . .

Were there no example in the world of contrivance except that of the *eye*, it would be alone sufficient to support the conclusion, which we draw from it, as to the necessity of an intelligent Creator. . . . The proof is not a conclusion that lies at the end of a chain of reasoning, of which chain each instance of contrivance is only a link, and of which, if one link fail, the whole fails; but it is an argument separately supplied by every separate example. An error in stating an example affects only that example. The argument is cumulative in the fullest sense of that term. The eye proves it without the ear; the ear without the eye. The proof in each example is complete; for when the design of the part and the conduciveness of its structure to that design is shown, the mind may set itself at rest; no further consideration can detract anything from the force of the example.

NOTES

[1] Gilbert Harman deserves much credit for calling attention to the importance of inferences to the best explanation; see, for example, his *Thought* (Princeton, NJ: Princeton University Press, 1973). A similar form of argument called abduction was analyzed long ago by Charles Sanders Peirce; see, for example, his *Collected Papers of Charles Sanders Peirce* (Cambridge, MA: Harvard University Press, 1931), 5: 189. A wonderful recent discussion is Peter Lipton, *Inference to the Best Explanation* (London: Routledge, 1991).

[2] Sir Arthur Conan Doyle, "Silver Blaze," *The Complete Sherlock Holmes* (Garden City, NY: Doubleday, 1930), 1: 349. The stories describe Holmes as a master of deduction, but his arguments are inductive as we define the terms.

[3] This discussion in many ways parallels and is indebted to the fifth chapter of W. V. Quine and J. S. Ullian, *The Web of Belief*, 2nd ed. (New York: Random House, 1978).

[4] From Fred T. Mackenzie, *Our Changing Planet* (Upper Saddle River, NJ: Prentice-Hall, 1998), 192.

[5] Mackenzie, *Our Changing Planet*, 42.

[6] Thomas Reid, *Essays on the Intellectual Powers of Man* (Cambridge, MA: MIT Press, 1969), essay I, section 4, 48.

11

CHANCES

The kinds of arguments discussed in the preceding three chapters are all inductive, so they need not meet the deductive standard of validity. They are, instead, intended to meet the inductive standard of strength. Whereas deductive validity hinges on what is possible, inductive strength hinges on what is probable. Roughly, an argument is inductively strong to the extent that its premises make its conclusion more likely or probable. Hence, just as we can get a better theoretical understanding of deductive validity by studying formal logic, as we did in Chapters 6–7, so we can get a better theoretical understanding of inductive strength by studying probability, as we will do in this chapter. To complete our survey of inductive arguments, this chapter offers an elementary discussion of probability. It begins by illustrating several common mistakes about probability. To help avoid these fallacies, we need to approach probability more carefully, so formal laws of probability are presented along with Bayes's theorem.

SOME FALLACIES OF PROBABILITY

Probability is pervasive. We all assume or make probability judgments throughout our lives. We do so whenever we form a belief about which we are not certain, as in all of the kinds of inductive arguments studied in Chapters 8–10. Such arguments do not pretend to reach their conclusions with certainty, even if their premises are true. They merely try to show that a conclusion is likely or probable. Judgments about probability are, thus, assumed in assessing such arguments and beliefs. Probability also plays a crucial role in our most important decisions. Mistakes about probability can then lead to disasters. Doctors lose patients' lives, stockbrokers lose clients' money, and coaches lose games because they overestimate or underestimate probabilities. Such mistakes are common and fall into several regular patterns. It is useful to understand these fallacies, so that we can learn to avoid them.

THE GAMBLER'S FALLACY

Casinos thrive partly because so many gamblers misunderstand probability. One mistake is so common that it has been dubbed *the gambler's fallacy*. When people have a run of bad luck, they often increase their bets because they assume that they are due for a run of good luck to even things out. Gambling systems are sometimes based on this fallacious idea. People keep track of the numbers that come up on a roulette wheel, trying to discover a number that has not come up for a long time. They then pile their money on that number on the assumption that it is due. They usually end up losing a bundle.

These gamblers seem to assume, "In the long run, things will even out (or average out)." Interpreted one way, this amounts to what mathematicians call *the law of large numbers,* and it is perfectly correct. When flipping a coin, we expect it to come up heads half the time, so it should come up heads five times in ten flips. If we actually check this out, however, we discover that the number of times it comes up heads in ten flips varies significantly from this predicted value—sometimes coming up heads more than five times, sometimes coming up fewer. What the law of large numbers tells us is that the actual percentage of heads will tend to come closer to the theoretically predicted percentage of heads the more trials we make. If you flipped a coin a million times, it would be very surprising if the percentage of heads were more than 1 percent away from the predicted 50 percent.

This law of large numbers is often misunderstood in a way that leads to the gambler's fallacy. Some people assume that each possible outcome will occur the average number of times in each series of trials. To see that this is a fallacy, we can go back to flipping coins. Toss a coin until it comes up heads three times in a row. (This will take less time than you might imagine.) What is the probability that it will come up heads a fourth time? Put crudely, some people think that the probability of it coming up heads again must be very small, because it is unlikely that a fair coin will come up heads four times in a row, so a tails is needed to even things out. That is wrong. The chances of getting heads on any given toss is the same, regardless of what happened on previous tosses. Previous results cannot affect the probabilities on this new toss.

STRANGE THINGS HAPPEN

Another common mistake is to ignore improbable events. It is very unlikely that a fair coin will come up heads nineteen times in a row, so you might think it could never happen. You would be wrong. Of course, if you sat flipping a single coin, you might spend a very long time before you hit a sequence of nineteen consecutive heads, but there is a way of getting this result (with a little help from your friends) in a single afternoon. You start out with $6,000 worth of pennies and put them in a large truck. (Actually, the truck need not be very large.) Dump the coins out and then pick up all the coins that come up heads. Put them back in the truck and repeat the procedure nineteen times, always returning only those coins that come up heads to the truck. With tolerably good luck, on the nineteenth dump of the coins, you will get at least one coin that comes up heads again. Any such coin will have come up heads nineteen times in a row.

What is the point of this silly exercise? It is intended to show that we often attribute abilities or the lack of abilities to people when, in fact, their performances may be statistically insignificant. When people invest with stockbrokers, they tend to shift to a new broker when they lose money. When they hit on a broker who earns them money, they stay and praise this broker's abilities. In fact, some financial advisers seem to be better than others—they have a long history of sound financial advice—but the financial community is, in many ways, like the truckload of pennies we have just examined. There are many brokers giving all sorts of different advice and, by chance alone, some of them are bound to give good advice. Furthermore, some of them are bound to have runs of success, just as some of the pennies dumped from the truck will have long strings of coming up heads. Thus, in some cases, what appears to be brilliance in predicting stock prices may be nothing more than a run of statistically expected good luck.

The gambling casinos of the world are like the truck full of pennies as well. With roulette wheels spinning in a great many places over a great deal of time, startlingly long runs are bound to occur. For example, in 1918, black came up twenty-six consecutive times on a roulette wheel in Monte Carlo. The odds against this are staggering. But before we can decide what to make of this event, we would have to judge it in the context of the vast number of times that the game of roulette has been played.

HONORS EXERCISE

Students familiar with computer programming should not find it difficult to write a program that will simulate a Monte Carlo roulette wheel and keep track long runs of black and long runs of red. On a Monte Carlo wheel, the odds coming up black are 18/37. The same odds hold for coming up red. Write a program; run it for a day; then report the longest runs.

HEURISTICS

In daily life, we often have to make decisions quickly without full information. To deal with this overload of decisions, we commonly employ what cognitive psychologists call *heuristics*. Technically, a heuristic is a general strategy for solving a problem or coming to a decision. For example, a good heuristic for solving geometry problems is to start with the conclusion you are trying to reach and then work backward.

Recent research in cognitive psychology has shown, first, that human beings rely very heavily on heuristics and, second, that we often have too much confidence in them. The result is that our probability judgments often go very wrong, and sometimes our thinking gets utterly mixed up. In this regard, two heuristics are particularly instructive: the representativeness heuristic and the availability heuristic.

THE REPRESENTATIVENESS HEURISTIC. A simple example illustrates how errors can arise from the representativeness heuristic. Imagine that you are randomly dealt five-card hands from a standard deck. Which of the following two hands is more likely to come up?

HAND #1	HAND #2
Three of clubs	Ace of spades
Seven of diamonds	Ace of hearts
Nine of diamonds	Ace of clubs
Queen of hearts	Ace of diamonds
King of spades	King of spades

A surprisingly large number of people will automatically say that the second hand is much less likely than the first. Actually, if you think about it for a bit, it should be obvious that any two specific hands have exactly the same likelihood of being dealt in a fair game. Here people get confused because the first hand is unimpressive; and, because unimpressive hands come up all the time, it strikes us as a representative hand. In many card games, however, the second hand is very impressive—something worth talking about— and thus looks unrepresentative. Our reliance on representativeness blinds us to a simple and obvious point about probabilities: Any specific hand is as likely to occur as any other.

DISCUSSION QUESTION

Linda is thirty-one years old, single, outspoken, and very bright. As a student, she majored in philosophy, was deeply concerned with issues of discrimination and social justice, and also participated in antinuclear demonstrations. Rank the following statements with respect to the probability that they are also true of Linda, then explain your rankings:

Linda is a teacher in elementary school.
Linda works in a bookstore and takes yoga classes.
Linda is active in the feminist movement.
Linda is a psychiatric social worker.
Linda is a bank teller.
Linda is an insurance salesperson.
Linda is a bank teller and is active in the feminist movement.[1]

THE AVAILABILITY HEURISTIC. Because sampling and taking surveys is costly, we often do it imaginatively, that is, in our heads. If you ask a baseball fan which team has the better batting average, Detroit or San Diego, that person might just remember, might go look it up, or might think about each team and try to decide which has the most good batters. The latter approach, needless to say, would be a risky business, but many baseball fans have remarkable knowledge of the batting averages of top hitters. Even with this knowledge, however, it is easy to go wrong. The players that naturally come to mind are the stars on each team. They are more available to our memory, and we are likely to make our judgment on the basis of them alone. Yet such a sample can easily be biased because all the batters contribute to the team average, not just the stars. The fact that the weak batters on one team are much better than the weak batters on the other can swing the balance.

DISCUSSION QUESTION

In four pages of a novel (about 2,000 words), how many words would you expect to find that have the form _ _ _ _ _n_ (seven-letter words with "n" in the sixth place)? Write down your answer. Now, how many words would you expect to find that have the form _ _ _ _ing (seven-letter words that end with "ing")? Explain your answers.[2]

The point of examining these heuristics and noting the errors that they produce is not to suggest that we should cease relying on them. First, there is a good chance that this would be psychologically impossible, because the use of such heuristics seems to be built into our psychological makeup. Second, over a wide range of standard cases, these heuristics give quick and largely accurate estimates. Difficulties typically arise in using these heuristics when the situation is nonstandard—that is, when the situation is complex or out of the ordinary.

To avoid such mistakes when making important judgments about probabilities, we need to ask, "Is the situation sufficiently standard to allow the use of heuristics?" Because this is a mouthful, we might simply ask, "Is this the sort of thing that people can figure out in their heads?" When the answer to that question is "No," as it often is, then we need to turn to more formal procedures for determining probabilities.

DISCUSSION QUESTION

In a remarkable study,[3] Thomas Gilovich, Robert Vallone, and Amos Tversky found a striking instance of people's tendency to treat things as statistically significant when they are not. In professional basketball, certain players have the reputation of being streak shooters. Streak shooters seem to score points in batches, then go cold and are not able to buy a basket. Stated more precisely, in streak shooting, "the performance of a player during a particular period is significantly better than expected on the basis of the player's overall record." To test whether streak shooting really exists, the authors made detailed study of a year's shooting record for the players on the Philadelphia 76ers. This team

(continued)

included Andrew Toney, noted around the league as being streak shooter. The authors found no evidence for streak shooting, not even for Andrew Toney. How would you go about deciding whether streak shooting exists or not? If, as Gilovich, Vallone, and Tversky have argued, belief phenomenon is a "cognitive illusion," why do so many people, including most professional athletes, believe that it does exist?

THE LANGUAGE OF PROBABILITY

The first step in figuring out probabilities is to adopt a more precise way of talking. Our common language includes various ways of expressing probabilities. Some of the guarding terms discussed in Chapter 3 provide examples of informal ways of expressing probability commitments. Thus, someone might say that it is unlikely that the New England Patriots will win the Super Bowl this year without saying how unlikely it is. We can also specify various degrees of probability. Looking out the window, we might say that there is a fifty-fifty chance of rain. More vividly, someone might have remarked that Ralph Nader does not have a snowball's chance in hell of ever winning a presidential election. In each case, the speaker is indicating the relative strength of the evidence for the occurrence or nonoccurrence of some event. To say that there is a fifty-fifty chance that it will rain indicates that we hold that the evidence is equally strong that it will rain rather than not rain. The metaphor in the third statement indicates that the person who uttered it believed that the probability of Nader winning a presidential election is essentially nonexistent.

We can make our probability claims more precise by using numbers. Sometimes we use percentages. For example, the weather bureau might say that there is a 75 percent chance of snow tomorrow. This can naturally be changed to a fraction: The probability is 3/4 that it will snow tomorrow. Finally, this fraction can be changed to a decimal expression: There is a 0.75 probability that it will snow tomorrow.

The probability scale has two end points: the absolute certainty that the event will occur and the absolute certainty that it will not occur. Because you cannot do better than absolute certainty, a probability can neither rise above 100 percent nor drop below 0 percent (neither above 1, nor below 0). (This should sound fairly obvious, but it is possible to become confused when combining percentages and fractions, as when Yogi Berra was supposed to have said that success is one-third talent and 75 percent hard work.) Of course, what we normally call probability claims usually fall between these two endpoints. For this reason, it sounds somewhat peculiar to say that there is a 100 percent chance of rain and just plain weird to say the chance of rain is 1 out of 1. Even so, these peculiar ways of speaking cause no procedural difficulties and rarely come up in practice.

A PRIORI **PROBABILITY**

When people make probability claims, we have a right to ask why they assign the probability they do. In Chapter 8, we saw how statistical procedures can be used for establishing probability claims. Here we will examine the so-called *a priori* approach to probabilities. A simple example will bring out the differences between these two approaches. We might wonder what the probability is of drawing an ace from a standard deck of fifty-two cards. Using the procedure discussed in Chapter 8, we could make a great many random draws from the deck (replacing the card each time) and then form a statistical generalization concerning the results. We would discover that an ace tends to come up roughly one-thirteenth of the time. From this we could draw the conclusion that the chance of drawing an ace is one in thirteen.

But we do not have to go to all this trouble. We can assume that each of the fifty-two cards has an equal chance of being selected. Given this assumption, an obvious line of reasoning runs as follows: There are four aces in a standard fifty-two-card deck, so the probability of selecting one randomly is four in fifty-two. That reduces to one chance in thirteen. Here the set of favorable outcomes is a subset of the total number of equally likely outcomes, and to compute the probability that the favorable outcome will occur, we merely divide the number of favorable outcomes by the total number of possible outcomes. This fraction gives us the probability that the event will occur on a random draw. Since all outcomes here are equally likely,

$$\text{Probability of drawing an ace} = \frac{\text{number of aces}}{\text{total number of cards}} = \frac{4}{52} = \frac{1}{13}$$

Notice that in coming to our conclusion that there is one chance in thirteen of randomly drawing an ace from a fifty-two-card deck, we used only mathematical reasoning. This illustrates the *a priori* approach to probabilities. It is called the *a priori* approach because we arrive at the result simply by reasoning about the circumstances.

In calculating the probability of drawing an ace from a fifty-two-card deck, we took the ratio of favorable equally likely outcomes to total equally likely outcomes. Generally, then, the probability of a hypothesis h, symbolized "$\Pr(h)$," when all outcomes are equally likely, is expressed as follows:

$$\Pr(h) = \frac{\text{favorable outcomes}}{\text{total outcomes}}$$

We can illustrate this principle with a slightly more complicated example. What is the probability of throwing an eight on the cast of two dice? The following table lists all of the equally likely ways in which two dice can turn up on a single cast. Notice that five of the thirty-six possible outcomes produce an eight. Hence, the probability of throwing an eight is 5/36.

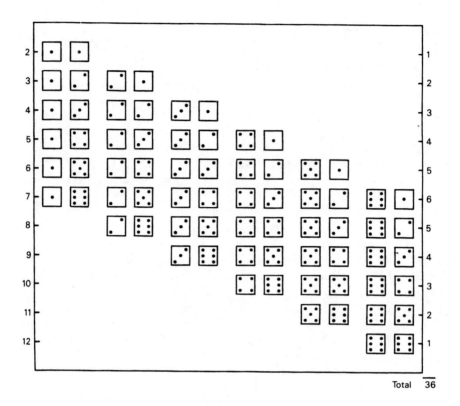

Total 36

Using the above chart, answer the following questions about the total on throw of two dice:

1. What is the probability of throwing a five?
2. Which number has the highest probability of being thrown? What is its probability?
3. What is the probability of throwing an eleven?
4. What is the probability of throwing either a seven or an eleven?
5. Which is more likely: throwing either a five or an eight?
6. Which is more likely: throwing a five or an eight, or throwing a two or a seven?
7. What is the probability of throwing a ten or above?
8. What is the probability of throwing an even number?
9. What is the probability of throwing an odd number?
10. What is the probability of throwing a value from four to six?
11. What is the probability of throwing either a two or a twelve?
12. What is the probability of throwing a value from two to twelve?

SOME RULES OF PROBABILITY

Suppose you have determined the probability that certain simple events will occur; how do you go about applying this information to combinations of events? This is a complex question and one that can be touched on only lightly in this text. There are, however, some simple rules of probability that are worth knowing because they can guide us in making choices when outcomes are uncertain.

By convention, events are assigned probabilities between 0 and 1 (inclusive). An event is going to either occur or not occur; that, at least, is certain (that is, it has a probability of 1). From this it is easy to see how to calculate the probability that the event will *not* occur given the probability that it will occur: We simply subtract the probability that it will occur from 1. This is our first rule:

RULE 1: NEGATION. The probability that an event will *not* occur is 1 minus the probability that it will occur. Symbolically:

$$\Pr(\text{not } h) = 1 - \Pr(h)$$

For example, the probability of drawing an ace from a standard deck is one in thirteen, so the probability of *not* drawing an ace is twelve in thirteen. This makes sense because there are forty-eight out of fifty-two ways of not drawing an ace, and this reduces to twelve chances in thirteen.

RULE 2: CONJUNCTION WITH INDEPENDENCE. Given two independent events, the probability of their *both* occurring is the product of their individual probabilities. Symbolically (where h_1 and h_2 are independent):

$$\Pr(h_1 \text{ \& } h_2) = \Pr(h_1) \times \Pr(h_2)$$

Here the word "independent" needs explanation. Suppose you randomly draw a card from the deck, then put it back, shuffle, and draw again. In this case, the outcome of the first draw provides no information about the outcome of the second draw, so it is *independent* of it. What is the probability of drawing two aces in a row using this system? Using Rule 2, we see that the answer is $1/13 \times 1/13$, or 1 chance in 169.

The situation is different if we do *not* replace the card after the first draw. Rule 2 does not apply to this case because the two events are no longer independent. The chances of getting an ace on the first draw are still one in thirteen, but if an ace is drawn and not returned to the pack, then there is one less ace in the deck, so the chances of drawing an ace on the next draw are reduced to three in fifty-one. Thus, the probability of drawing two consecutive aces without returning the first draw to the deck is $4/52 \times 3/51$, or 1 in 221, which is considerably lower than 1 in 169.

If we want to extend Rule 2 to cover cases in which the events are *not* independent, then we will have to speak of the probability of one event occurring given that another has occurred. The probability that h_2 will occur given that h_1 has occurred is called the *conditional* probability of h_2 on h_1 and is usually symbolized thus: $\Pr(h_2 \mid h_1)$. This probability is calculated by considering only those cases where h_1 is true and then dividing the number of cases within that group where h_2 is also true by the total number of cases in that group. Symbolically:

$$Pr(h_2 \mid h_1) = \frac{\text{favorable outcomes where } h_1}{\text{total outcomes where } h_1} = \frac{\text{outcomes where } h_1 \text{ and } h_2}{\text{total outcomes where } h_1}$$

Using this notion of conditional probability, Rule 2 can be modified as follows to deal with cases in which events need not be independent:

RULE 2G: CONJUNCTION IN GENERAL. Given two events, the probability of their both occurring is the probability of the first occurring times the probability of the second occurring, given that the first has occurred. Symbolically:

$$Pr(h_1 \& h_2) = Pr(h_1) \times Pr(h_2 \mid h_1)$$

Notice that, in the event that h_1 and h_2 are independent, the probability of h_2 is not related to the occurrence of h_1, so the probability of h_2 on h_1 is simply the probability of h_2. Thus, Rule 2 is simply a special case of the more general Rule 2G.

We can extend these rules to cover more than two events. For example, with Rule 2, however many events we might consider, provided that they are independent of each other, the probability of all of them occurring is the product of each one of them occurring. For example, the chances of flipping a coin and having it come up heads is one chance in two. What are the chances of flipping a coin eight times and having it come up heads every time? The answer is:

$$1/2 \times 1/2 \times 1/2 \times 1/2 \times 1/2 \times 1/2 \times 1/2 \times 1/2$$

which equals 1 chance in 256.

Our next rule allows us to answer questions of the following kind: What are the chances of *either* an eight *or* a two coming up on a single throw of the dice? Going back to the chart, we saw that we could answer this question by counting the number of ways in which a two can come up (which is one) and adding this to the number of ways in which an eight can come up (which is five). We could then conclude that the chances of one or the other of them coming up is six chances in thirty-six, or $1/6$. The principle involved in this calculation can be stated as follows:

RULE 3: DISJUNCTION WITH EXCLUSIVITY. The probability that at least one of two mutually exclusive events will occur is the sum of the probabilities that each of them will occur. Symbolically (where h_1 and h_2 are mutually exclusive):

$$Pr(h_1 \text{ or } h_2) = Pr(h_1) + Pr(h_2)$$

To say that events are *mutually exclusive* means that they cannot both occur. You cannot, for example, get both a ten and an eight on the same cast of two dice. You might, however, throw neither one of them.

When events are not mutually exclusive, the rule for calculating disjunctive probabilities becomes more complicated. Suppose, for example, that exactly half the class is female and exactly half the class is over nineteen and the age distribution is the same for females and males. What is the probability that a randomly selected student will be either a female or over nineteen? If we simply add the probabilities $(1/2 + 1/2 = 1)$, we would get the result that we are certain to pick someone who is either female or over nineteen. But that answer is wrong, because a quarter of the class is male and not over nineteen, and one of them might have been randomly selected. The correct answer is that the chances are $3/4$ of randomly selecting someone who is either female or over nineteen.

We can see that this is the correct answer by examining the following table:

	Over Nineteen	Not over Nineteen
Female	25%	25%
Male	25%	25%

It is easy to see that in 75 percent of the cases, a randomly selected student will be either female or over nineteen. The table also shows what went wrong with our initial calculation. The top row shows that 50 percent of the students are female. The left column shows that 50 percent of the students are over nineteen. But we cannot simply add these figures to get the probability of a randomly selected student being either female or over nineteen. Why not? Because that would double-count the females over nineteen. We would count them once in the top row and then again in the left column. To compensate for such double-counting, we need to subtract the students who are both female and over nineteen. The upper left figure shows that this is 25%. So the correct way to calculate the answer is $50\% + 50\% - 25\% = 75\%$.

This pattern is reflected in the general rule governing the calculation of disjunctive probabilities:

RULE 3G: DISJUNCTION IN GENERAL. The probability that at least one of two events will occur is the sum of the probabilities that each of them will occur, minus the probability that they will both occur. Symbolically:

$$\Pr(h_1 \text{ or } h_2) = \Pr(h_1) + \Pr(h_2) - \Pr(h_1 \& h_2)$$

If h_1 and h_2 are mutually exclusive, then $\Pr(h_1 \& h_2) = 0$, and Rule 3G reduces to Rule 3. Thus, as with Rules 2 and 2G, Rule 3 is simply a special case of the more general Rule 3G.

Before stating Rule 4, we can think about a particular example. What is the probability of tossing heads at least once in eight tosses of a coin? Here it is tempting to reason in the following way: There is a 50 percent chance of getting heads on the first toss and a 50 percent chance of getting heads on the second toss, so after two tosses it is already certain that we will toss heads at least once, and thus after eight tosses there should be a 400 percent chance.

In other words, you cannot miss. There are two good reasons for thinking that this argument is fishy. First, probability can never exceed 100 percent. Second, there must be some chance, however small, that we could toss a coin eight times and not have it come up heads.

The best way to look at this question is to restate it so that the first two rules can be used. Instead of asking what the probability is that heads will come up at least once, we can ask what the probability is that heads will *not* come up at least once. To say that heads will not come up even once is equivalent to saying that tails will come up eight times in a row. By Rule 2 we know how to compute that probability: It is 1/2 multiplied by itself eight times, and that, as we saw, is 1/256. Finally, by Rule 1 we know that the probability that this will not happen (that heads will come up at least once) is $1 - (1/256)$. In other words, the probability of tossing heads at least once in eight tosses is 255/256. That comes close to a certainty, but it is not quite a certainty.

We can generalize these results as follows:

RULE 4: SERIES WITH INDEPENDENCE. The probability that an event will occur at least once in a series of independent trials is 1 minus the probability that it will not occur in that number of trials. Symbolically (where n is the number of independent trials):

$$Pr(h \text{ at least once in } n \text{ trials}) = 1 - Pr(\text{not } h)^n$$

Strictly speaking, Rule 4 is unnecessary, since it can be derived from Rules 1 and 2, but it is important to know because it blocks a common misunderstanding about probabilities: People often think that something is a sure thing when it is not.

Another common confusion is between permutations and combinations. A *permutation* is a set of items whose order is specified. A *combination* is a set of items whose order is not specified. Imagine, for example, that three cards—the jack, queen, and king of spades—are facedown in front of you. If you pick two of these cards in turn, there are three possible combinations: jack and queen, jack and king, and queen and king. In contrast, there are six possible permutations: jack then queen, queen then jack, jack then king, king then jack, queen then king, and king then queen.

Rule 2 is used to calculate probabilities of permutations—of conjunctions of events in a particular order. For example, if you flip a fair coin twice, what is the probability of its coming up heads and tails in that order (that is, heads on the first flip and tails on the second flip)? Since the flips are independent, Rule 2 tells us that the answer is $1/2 \times 1/2 = 1/4$. This answer is easily confirmed by counting the possible permutations (heads then heads, heads then tails, tails then heads, tails then tails). Only one of these four permutations (heads then tails) is a favorable outcome.

We need to calculate probabilities of combinations in a different way. For example, if you flip a fair coin twice, what is the probability of its landing heads and tails in *any* order? There are two ways for this to happen. The coin could come up either heads then tails or tails then heads. These alternatives are mutually exclusive, so the probability of this disjunction by Rule 3 is $1/4 + 1/4 = 1/2$. This is confirmed by counting two possibilities (heads then tails, tails then heads) out of four (heads then heads, heads then tails, tails then heads, tails then tails). Another way to calculate this probability is to realize that the first flip doesn't matter. Whatever you get on the first flip (heads or tails), you need the opposite on the second flip. You are certain to get either heads or tails on the first flip, so this probability is 1. Then, regardless of what happens on the first flip, the probability of getting the opposite on the second flip is $1/2$. These results are independent, so the probability of their conjunction by Rule 2 is the product $1 \times 1/2 = 1/2$.

We can also use our rules to calculate probabilities of combinations without independence. Rule 2G tells us that the probability of drawing an ace, not putting this card back in the deck, and then drawing a king is $4/52 \times 4/51 = 16/2,652$. But what is the probability of drawing an ace and a king in any order? It is the probability of drawing either an ace or a king and then drawing the other one given that you drew the first one. That probability by Rule 2G is $8/52 \times 4/51 = 32/2,652$. The difference between this result and the previous one, where the order was specified, shows why we need to determine whether we are dealing with permutations or combinations.

EXERCISE II

Use the rules of probability to calculate these probabilities:

1. What is the probability of rolling a five on one throw of a fair six-sided die?

2. What is the probability of *not* rolling a five on one throw of a fair six-sided die?

3. If you roll a five on your first throw of a fair six-sided die, what is probability of rolling *another* five on a second throw of that die?

4. If you roll two fair six-sided dice one time, what are the chances that *both* of the dice will come up a five?

5. If you roll two fair six-sided dice one time, what are the chances that *one or the other* (or both) of the dice will come up a five?

6. If you roll two fair six-sided dice one time, what are the chances that *one and only one* of the dice will come up a five?

7. If you roll two fair six-sided dice one time, what are the chances that *at least one* of the dice will come up a five?

8. If you roll two fair six-sided dice one time, what are the chances that *at least one* of the dice will *not* come up a five?

9. If you roll six fair six-sided dice one time, what are the chances that *at least one* of the dice will come up a five?

10. If you roll six fair six-sided dice one time, what are the chances that *at least one* of the dice will *not* come up a five?

EXERCISE III

Compute the probability of making the following draws from a standard fifty-two-card deck:

1. Drawing either a seven or a five on a single draw.
2. Drawing neither a seven nor a five on a single draw.
3. Drawing a seven and then, without returning the first card to the deck, drawing a five on the next draw.
4. Same as 3, but the first card is returned to the deck and the deck is shuffled after the first draw.
5. Drawing at least one spade in a series of three consecutive draws, when the card drawn is not returned to the deck.
6. Drawing at least one spade in a series of four consecutive draws, when the card drawn is not returned to the deck.
7. Same as 6, but the card is returned to the deck after each draw and the deck is reshuffled.
8. Drawing a heart and a diamond in that order in two consecutive draws, when the first card is returned to the deck and the deck is reshuffled the first draw.
9. Drawing a heart and a diamond in any order in two consecutive draws, when the first card is returned to the deck and the deck is reshuffled the first draw.
10. Drawing a heart and a diamond in any order in two consecutive draws, when the first card is not returned to the deck after the first draw.

EXERCISE IV

Suppose there are two little lotteries in town, each of which sells exactly 100 tickets.

1. If each lottery has only one winning ticket, and you buy two tickets to the *same* lottery, what is the probability that you will have a winning ticket?
2. If each lottery has only one winning ticket, and you buy one ticket to *each* of the two lotteries, what is the probability that you will have at least one winning ticket?
3. If each lottery has only one winning ticket, and you buy one ticket to each of the two lotteries, what is the probability that you will have *two* winning tickets?
4. If each lottery has two winning tickets, and you buy one ticket to each of the two lotteries, what is the probability that you will have at least one winning ticket?
5. If each lottery has two winning tickets, and you buy two tickets to the same lottery, what is the probability that you will have two winning tickets?
6. If each lottery has two winning tickets, and you buy two tickets to the same lottery, what is the probability that you will have at least one winning ticket?

1. You are presented with two bags, one containing two ham sandwiches and the other containing a ham sandwich and a cheese sandwich. You reach in one bag and draw out a ham sandwich. What is the probability that the other sandwich in the bag is also a ham sandwich?

2. You are presented with three bags: two contain a chicken-fat sandwich and one contains a cheese sandwich. You are asked to guess which bag contains the cheese sandwich. You do so, and the bag you selected is set aside. (You obviously have one chance in three of guessing correctly.) From the two remaining bags, one containing a chicken-fat sandwich is then removed. You are now given the opportunity to switch your selection to the remaining bag. Will such a switch increase, decrease, or leave unaffected your chances of correctly ending up with the bag with the cheese sandwich in it?

In a fair lottery with a million tickets, the probability that ticket #1 will lose is 0.999999, the probability that ticket #2 will lose is also 0.999999, and so on for each ticket. On this basis, you might seem justified in believing each premise in the following argument:

> Ticket #1 will lose.
> Ticket #2 will lose.
> Ticket #3 will lose.
> [and so on, until:]
> Ticket #1,000,000 will lose.
> There are only 1,000,000 tickets.
>
> ∴ Every ticket will lose.

This conclusion must be false, since the lottery is fair. However, the conclusion follows from the premises, and each of the premises seems justified. Does this argument justify us in believing its conclusion? Why or why not?

BAYES'S THEOREM

Although dice and cards provide nice, simple models for learning how to calculate probabilities, real life is usually more complicated. One particularly interesting and important form of problem arises often in medicine. Suppose that Wendy tests positive for colon cancer. The treatment for colon cancer is painful and dangerous, so, before subjecting Wendy to that treatment, her doctor wants to determine how likely it is that Wendy really has colon cancer. After all, no test is perfect. Regarding the test that was used on Wendy, previous studies have revealed the following probabilities:

> The probability that a person in the general population has colon cancer is 0.3 percent (or 0.003).

> If a person has colon cancer, then the probability that the test is positive is 90 percent (or 0.9).

> If a person does not have colon cancer, then the probability that the test is positive is 3 percent (or 0.03).

On these assumptions, what is the probability that Wendy actually has colon cancer, given that she tested positive? Most people guess that this probability is fairly high. Even most trained physicians would say that Wendy probably has colon cancer.[4]

What is the correct answer? To calculate the probability that a person who tests positive actually has colon cancer, we need to divide the number of favorable outcomes by the number of total outcomes. The favorable outcomes include everyone who tests positive and really has colon cancer. This outcome is not "favorable" to Wendy, so we will describe this group as *true positives*. The total outcomes include everyone who tests positive. This includes the true positives plus the *false positives*, which are those who test positive but do not have colon cancer. Given the stipulated probabilities, in a normal population of 100,000 people, there will be 270 true positives (100,000 × 0.003 × 0.9) and 2,991 false positives [(100,000 − 300) × 0.03]. Thus, the probability that Wendy has colon cancer is about 270/(270 + 2,991). That is only about 8.3 percent, when most people estimate above 50 percent!

Why do people, including doctors, overestimate these probabilities so badly? Part of the answer seems to be that they focus on the rate of true positives (90 percent) and forget that, because there are so many people without colon cancer (99.7 percent of the total population), even a small rate of false positives (3 percent) will yield a large number of false positives (2,991) that swamps the much smaller number of true positives (270). (When the question about probability was reformulated in terms of the number of people in each group, most doctors come up with the correct answer.) For whatever reason, people have a strong tendency to make mistakes in cases like these, so we need to be careful, especially when so much is at stake.

One way to calculate probabilities like these uses a famous theorem that was first presented by an English clergyman named Thomas Bayes (1702–1761). A simple proof of this theorem applies the laws of probability from the preceding section. We want to figure out $\Pr(h \,|\, e)$, that is, the probability of the hypothesis h (e.g., Wendy has colon cancer), given the evidence e (e.g., Wendy tested positive for colon cancer). To get there, we start from Rule 2G:

1. $\Pr(e \,\&\, h) = \Pr(e) \times \Pr(h|e)$

Dividing both sides by Pr(*e*) gives us:

2. $\Pr(h|e) = \dfrac{\Pr(e \And h)}{\Pr(e)}$

If two formulas are logically equivalent, they must have the same probability. We can establish by truth tables (as in Chapter 6) that "*e*" is logically equivalent to "(*e*&*h*) ∨ (*e*&~*h*)." Consequently, we may replace "*e*" in the denominator of item 2 with "(*e*&*h*) ∨ (*e*&~*h*)" to get:

3. $\Pr(h|e) = \dfrac{\Pr(e \And h)}{\Pr[(e \And h) \vee (e \And \sim h)]}$

Since "*e*&*h*" and "*e*&~*h*" are mutually exclusive, we can apply Rule 3 to the denominator of item 3 to get:

4. $\Pr(h|e) = \dfrac{\Pr(e \And h)}{\Pr(e \And h) + \Pr(e \And \sim h)}$

Finally, we apply Rule 2G to item 4 and get:

BT: $\Pr(h|e) = \dfrac{\Pr(h) \times \Pr(e|h)}{[\Pr(h) \times \Pr(e|h)] + [\Pr(\sim h) \times \Pr(e|\sim h)]}$

This is a simplified version of Bayes's theorem.

This theorem enables us to calculate the desired probability in our original example:

h = the patient has colon cancer

e = the patient tests positive for colon cancer

$\Pr(h) = 0.003$

$\Pr(\sim h) = 1 - \Pr(h) = 0.997$

$\Pr(e|h) = 0.9$

$\Pr(e|\sim h) = 0.03$

If we substitute these values into Bayes's theorem, we get:

$\Pr(h|e) = \dfrac{0.003 \times 0.9}{[0.003 \times 0.9] + [0.997 \times 0.03]} = \text{about } 0.083$

In this way, we can calculate the conditional probability of the hypothesis given the evidence from its reverse, that is, from the conditional probability of the evidence given the hypothesis. That is what makes Bayes's theorem so useful.

Many people find a different method more intuitive. The first step is to set up a table. The two factors to be related are (1) whether the patient has colon cancer and (2) whether the patient tests positive for colon cancer.

To chart all possible combinations of these two factors, we need a table like this:

	Colon Cancer	Not Colon Cancer	Total
Test Positive			
Do Not Test Positive			
Total			

Next we need to enter a population size in the lower right box. The probabilities will not be affected by the population size, but it is cleaner to pick a population that is large enough to get whole numbers when the population is multiplied by the given probabilities. To determine the right size population, add the number of places to the right of the decimal point in the two most specific probabilities, then pick a population of 10 to the power of that sum. In our example, the most specific probabilities are 0.003 and 0.03, and $3 + 2 = 5$, so we can enter 10^5:

	Colon Cancer	Not Colon Cancer	Total
Test Positive			
Do Not Test Positive			
Total			100,000

This population size represents the total number of people who are tested. We have no information about the ones who are not tested, so they cannot figure into our calculations.

The bottom row can now be filled in by dividing the total population into those who have colon cancer and those who do not have colon cancer. Just multiply the population size by the probability of colon cancer in the general population [$\Pr(h)$] to get a number for the second box on the bottom row. This figure represents the total number of people with colon cancer in this population. Then subtract that product from the population size and put the remainder in the remaining box. This represents the total number of people without colon cancer in this population. Since these two groups exhaust the population, they must add up to the total population size. In our case, we were given that the probability that a person in the general population has colon cancer is 0.003. On this basis, we can fill in the bottom row of the table:

	Colon Cancer	Not Colon Cancer	Total
Test Positive			
Do Not Test Positive			
Total	300	99,700	100,000

Next, fill out the second column by dividing the total number of people with colon cancer into those who test positive and those who do not test positive. These numbers can be calculated with the given conditional probability of testing positive, given colon cancer [Pr($e \mid h$)]. In our example, if a person has colon cancer, the probability that the test is positive is 0.9. Thus, 270 (=0.9 × 300) of the people in the colon cancer column will test positive and the rest (300 − 270 = 30) will not, so we get these figures:

	Colon Cancer	Not Colon Cancer	Total
Test Positive	270		
Do Not Test Positive	30		
Total	300	99,700	100,000

Similarly, we can fill out the third column by dividing the total number of people without colon cancer into those who test positive and those who do not test positive. Here we use the conditional probability of a positive test, given that a person does not have colon cancer [Pr($e \mid {\sim}h$)]. This probability was given as 0.03, and 0.03 × 99,700 = 2,991. This number means that, out of a normal population of 99,700 without colon cancer, 2,991 will test positive. Since the figures in this column must add up to a total of 99,700, the remaining figure is 99,700 − 2,991 = 96,709:

	Colon Cancer	Not Colon Cancer	Total
Test Positive	270	2,991	
Do Not Test Positive	30	96,709	
Total	300	99,700	100,000

Finally, we can fill out the fourth column by calculating total numbers of people who test positive or do not test positive. Simply add across the rows:

	Colon Cancer	Not Colon Cancer	Total
Test Positive	270	2,991	3,261
Do Not Test Positive	30	96,709	96,739
Total	300	99,700	100,000

Check your calculations by adding the right column: 3,261 + 96,739 = 100,000.

Now that our population is divided up, the solution is staring you in the face. This table shows us that, in a normal population of 100,000 tested people distributed according to the given probabilities, a total of 3,261 will test positive. Out of those, 270 will have colon cancer. Thus, the probability that the patient has colon cancer, given that this patient tested positive, is 270/3,261, which is about 0.083 or 8.3 percent, just as before.

You can also read off other conditional probabilities. If you want to know the conditional probability of *not* having colon cancer, given that your test did *not* come out positive, then you need to look at the row for those who do *not* test positive. The figure at the right of this row tells you that a total of 96,739 out of the total population do not test positive. The column under "Not Colon Cancer" then tells you that 96,709 of these do not have colon cancer. Thus, the conditional probability of not having colon cancer given your test did not come out positive is 96,709/96,739 or about 0.9997. That means that, if you test negative, the odds are extremely high that you do not have colon cancer.

Tables like these work by dividing the population into groups. We already learned some names for these groups:

	Hypothesis (*h*)	Not Hypothesis (~*h*)	
Evidence (*e*)	True Positives	False positives	
Not Evidence (~*e*)	False Negatives	True Negatives	
			Population

False positives are sometimes also called *false alarms,* and false negatives are sometimes called *misses.* A little more terminology is also common:

$Pr(h)$ = base rate or prevalence or prior probability

$Pr(h \mid e)$ = solution or posterior probability

$Pr(e \mid h)$ = sensitivity of the test

$Pr(\sim e \mid \sim h)$ = specificity of the test

$1 - Pr(e \mid h) = 1 - $ sensitivity = false negative rate

$1 - Pr(\sim e \mid \sim h) = 1 - $ specificity = false positive rate

You don't need to use these terms in order to calculate the probabilities, but it is useful to learn them so that you will be able to understand people who discuss these issues.

One of the most important lessons of Bayes's theorem is that the base rate has big effects. To see how much it matters, let's recalculate the solution [$Pr(h \mid e)$] in our colon cancer example for different values of the base rate [$Pr(h)$] using the same test with the same sensitivity ($Pr(e \mid h) = 0.9$) and specificity [$Pr(\sim e \mid \sim h) = 0.97$]:

If $Pr(h) = 0.003$, then $Pr(h \mid e) = 0.083$

If $Pr(h) = 0.03$, then $Pr(h \mid e) = 0.48$

If $Pr(h) = 0.3$, then $Pr(h \mid e) = 0.93$

EXERCISE VI

Construct tables to confirm these calculations of Pr($h \mid e$) for base rates of 0.03 and 0.3.

These calculations show that a positive test result for a given test means a lot more when the base rate is high than when it is low. Thus, if doctors use the specified test as a *screening test* in the general population, and if the rate of colon cancer in that general population is only 0.003, then a positive test result by itself does not show that the patient has cancer. In contrast, if doctors instead use the specified test as a *diagnostic test* only for people with certain symptoms, and if the rate of colon cancer among people with those symptoms is 0.3, then a positive test result does show that the patient probably has cancer, though the test still might be mistaken. Bayes's theorem, thus, reveals the right ways and the wrong ways to use and interpret such tests.

Notice also what happens to the probabilities when additional tests are performed. In our original example, one positive test result raises the probability of cancer from the base rate of 0.003 to our solution of 0.083. Now suppose that the doctor orders an additional independent test, and the result is again positive. To apply Bayes's theorem at this point, we can take the probability after the original positive test result (0.083) as the prior probability or base rate in calculating the probability after the second positive test result. This method makes sense because we are now interested not in the general population but only in the subpopulation that already tested positive on the first test. The solution after two tests [Pr($h \mid e$)], where "e" is now two independent positive test results in a row, is 0.731. Next, if the doctor orders a third independent test, and if the result is positive yet again, then Pr($h \mid e$) increases to 0.988. Bayes's theorem, thus, reveals the technical rationale behind the commonsense practice of ordering additional tests. Problems arise only when doctors put too much faith in a single positive test result without doing any additional tests.

EXERCISE VII

Construct tables to confirm the above calculations of probabilities after a second and third positive test result.

EXERCISE VIII

1. What would Wendy's chances of having colon cancer be if the other probabilities remained the same as in the original example, except that the probability that a person in the general population has colon cancer only 0.1 percent (or 0.001)?

(continued)

2. What would Wendy's chances of having colon cancer be if the other probabilities remained the same as in the original example, except that the probability that a person in the general population has colon cancer 1 percent (0.01)?

3. What would Wendy's chances of having colon cancer be if the other probabilities remained the same as in the original example, except that the conditional probability that the test is positive, given that the patient has colon cancer, is only 50 percent (or 0.5)?

4. What would Wendy's chances of having colon cancer be if the other probabilities remained the same as in the original example, except that the conditional probability that the test is positive, given that the patient has colon cancer, is 99 percent (or 0.99)?

5. What would Wendy's chances of having colon cancer be if the other probabilities remained the same as in the original example, except that the conditional probability that the test is positive, given that the patient does not have colon cancer, is 1 percent (or 0.01)?

6. What would Wendy's chances of having colon cancer be if the other probabilities remained the same as in the original example, except that the conditional probability that the test is positive, given that the patient does not have colon cancer, is 10 percent (0.1)?

7. Chris tested positive for cocaine once in a random screening test. This test has a sensitivity and specificity of 95 percent, and 20 percent of the students in Chris's school use cocaine. What is the probability that Chris really did use cocaine?

8. As in problem 7, 20 percent of the students in Chris's school use cocaine, but this time Chris tests positive for cocaine on two independent tests, both of which have a sensitivity and specificity of 95 percent. Now what is the probability that Chris really did use cocaine?

9. In your neighborhood, 20 percent of the houses have high levels of radon gas in their basements, so you ask an expert to test your basement. An inexpensive test comes out positive in 80 percent of the basements that actually have high levels of radon, but it also comes out positive in 10 percent of the basements that do not have high levels of radon. If this inexpensive test comes out positive in your basement, what is the probability that there is a high level of radon gas in your basement?

10. A more expensive test for radon is also more accurate. It comes out positive in 99 percent of the basements that actually have high levels of radon. It also tests positive in 2 percent of the basements that do not high levels of radon. As in problem 7, 20 percent of the houses in your neighborhood have radon in their basement. If the expensive test comes out positive in your basement, what is the probability that there is a high level of radon gas in your basement?

11. Late last night a car ran into your neighbor and drove away. In your town, there are 500 cars, and 2 percent of them are Porsches. The only eyewitness to the hit-and-run says the car that hit your neighbor was a Porsche. Tested

under similar conditions, the eyewitness mistakenly classifies cars of other makes as Porsches 10 percent of the time, and correctly classifies Porsches as such 80 percent of the time. What are the chances that the car that hit your neighbor really was a Porsche?

12. Late last night a dog bit your neighbor. In your town, there are 400 dogs, 95 percent of them are black Labrador retrievers, and the rest are pit bulls. The only eyewitness to the event, a veteran dog breeder, says that the dog who bit your neighbor was a pit bull. Tested under similar low-light conditions, the eyewitness mistakenly classifies black Labs as pit bulls only 2 percent of the time, and correctly classifies pit bulls as pit bulls 90 percent of the time. What are the chances that dog who bit your neighbor really was a pit bull?

13. In a certain school, the probability that a student reads the assigned pages before a lecture is 80 percent (or 0.8). If a student does the assigned reading in advance, then the probability that the student will understand the lecture is 90 percent (or 0.9). If a student does not do the assigned reading in advance, then the probability that the student will understand the lecture is 10 percent (or 0.1). What is the probability that a student did the reading in advance, given that she did understand the lecture? What is the probability that a student did *not* do the reading in advance, given that she did *not* understand the lecture?

14. In a different school, the probability that a student reads the assigned pages before a lecture is 60 percent (or 0.6). If a student does the assigned reading in advance, then the probability that, when asked, the student will tell the professor that he did the reading is 100 percent (or 1.0). If a student does not do the assigned reading in advance, then the probability that, when asked, the student will tell the professor that he did the reading is 70 percent (or 0.7). What is the probability that a student did the reading in advance, given that, when asked, he told the professor that he did the reading? What is the probability that a student did not do the reading in advance, given that, when asked, he told the professor that he did not do the reading?

DISCUSSION QUESTION

Should Sally Clark be found guilty of murder? Why or why not? The following account of her case was extracted from http://pass.maths.org.uk/issue21/features/clark (10/22/04):

Five years ago, a young couple from Cheshire suffered one of the most devastating losses imaginable—their baby Christopher died in his sleep, aged 11 weeks. Doctors, neighbours, all were sympathetic, and the death was certified as natural causes—there was evidence of a respiratory infection, and no sign of any failure of care.

(continued)

But just a year later, in what must have felt like a horribly familiar night-mare, the Clarks' second child Harry died, aged 8 weeks. This time, there was no sympathy from the professionals. Four weeks after Harry's death the cou-ple were arrested, and eventually Sally Clark was charged with murdering both children. She was tried and convicted in 1999 and is now almost three years into a life sentence.

The forensic evidence was slim to nonexistent—certainly neither case would have stood up alone. . . . So how come Sally Clark is serving life in prison? Simply put, because [of] a seemingly authoritative statement by pediatrician Sir Roy Meadow . . . that the chance of two children in the same (affluent non-smoking) family both dying a cot death was 1 in 73 million. . . .

INDEPENDENCE

This statistic of 1 in 73 million came from the Confidential Enquiry for Still-births and Deaths in Infancy (CESDI), an authoritative and detailed study of deaths of babies in five regions of England between 1993 and 1996. There it is estimated that the chances of a randomly chosen baby dying a cot death are 1 in 1,303. If the child is from an affluent, nonsmoking family, with the mother over 26, the odds fall to around 1 in 8,500. The authors go on to say that *if* there is no link between cot deaths of siblings (because we have eliminated the biggest known and possibly shared factors influencing cot death rates) then we would be able to estimate the chances of two children from such a family both suffering a cot death by squaring 1/8,500—giving 1 chance in 73 million.

So far so good. But are cot deaths in the same family really independent? The website for the Foundation for the Study of Infant Death (FSID) says baldly that "second cot deaths in the same family are very rare." This is no help, because so are first-sibling cot deaths—what we need to know is, how comparatively rare? Does having one child die a cot death increase the chances that you will have another do so?

Ray Hill . . . estimates that siblings of children who die of cot death are be-tween 10 and 22 times more likely than average to die the same way. Using the figure of 1 in 1,303 for the chance of a first cot death, we see that the chances of a second cot death in the same family are somewhere between 1 in 60 and 1 in 130. There isn't enough data to be more precise, or to take familial factors into account, but it seems reasonable to use a ballpark figure of 1 in 100. Multiply-ing 1/1,303 by 1/100 gives an estimate for the incidence of double cot death of around 1 in 130,000. . . .

BAYES'S THEOREM

. . . Very possibly, as you're reading this, you are . . . thinking "okay, so the odds aren't as extreme as 1 in 73 million, but they're still astronomi-cally high. There's not that much difference between odds of 1 in 73 million

and 1 in 100,000, so Sally Clark must still be guilty." If so, you're committing the "Prosecutor's Fallacy."

Simply put, this is the incorrect belief that the chance of a rare event hap-
pening is the same as the chance that the defendant is innocent. Even with the
more accurate figure of 1 in 100,000 for the chance that a *randomly chosen* pair
of siblings will both die of cot death, this is not the chance that Sally Clark is
innocent. It is the chance that an *arbitrary* family will lose two children in cot
deaths. . . .

In mathematical language, we need to find the *conditional probabilities* of
the various possible causes of death, *given* the fact that the children died. If H
is some hypothesis (for example, that both of Sally Clark's children died of
natural causes) and D is some data (that both children are dead), we want to
find the probability of the hypothesis given the data, which is written
$P(H|D)$. Let's write A for the alternate hypothesis—that Sally Clark murdered both her children. We will discount all other possibilities, for example
that someone else murdered both children, or that Sally Clark murdered only
one of them.

$$P(H|D) = \frac{P(D|H)P(H)}{P(D|H)P(H) + P(D|A)P(A)}$$

This is not as complicated as it looks. We already have an estimate for $P(H)$
of $1/100{,}000$. . . . Trivially, both $P(D|H)$ and $P(D|A)$ are equal to 1. These
numbers are the probabilities that two of the children are dead, given that
that two of the children have died of natural causes, or been murdered,
respectively.

A completely accurate version of Bayes's Theorem would take into account
all sorts of factors—for example, the fact that social services had not been
involved with the Clark family, their income level, and so on—but there isn't a
sufficient amount of data available to do this. However, if we are only looking
to analyse the case against Sally Clark, it is sufficient . . . to make reasonable
estimates and show that these lead to reasonable doubt.

$P(A)$ is the most difficult figure to estimate. It is the probability that a
randomly chosen pair of siblings will both be murdered. Statistics on such
double murders are pretty much nonexistent, because child murders are
so rare (far, far more rare than cot deaths) and because in most cases,
someone known to have murdered once is not free to murder again. So
we fall back on the Home Office statistic that fewer than 30 children are
known to be murdered by their mother each year in England and Wales.
Since 650,000 are born each year, and murders of pairs of siblings are clearly
rarer than single murders, we should use a figure much smaller than
$30/650{,}000 = 0.000046$. We will put a number ten times as small here—
0.0000046—which is almost certainly overestimating the incidence rate of
double murder.

Now we get a rough and ready estimate of Sally Clark's innocence:

$$P(H|D) = \frac{P(H)}{P(H) + P(A)} = \frac{0.00001}{0.00001 + 0.0000046} > \frac{2}{3}$$

I must warn the reader that this figure isn't intended to be in any way an accurate estimate of the likelihood that Sally Clark is innocent. It is only meant to show that, with some reasonable estimates of the likelihoods of relevant events, the scales come down on the side of her innocence rather than her guilt. The only way to disagree with this analysis is to assume that literally hundreds, or thousands, of mothers murder their children undetected every year. The Campaign to Free Sally Clark say that nearly fifty families have contacted them to say that they have suffered double cot deaths. Are we to believe that the majority of these couples are murderers, confident or mad enough to draw attention to themselves in this way? . . .

Plus readers may be interested to know that Sally Clark's case has been referred to the Appeal Court for a second time. Evidence, not made available to her original defence team, has recently come to light that at the time of Harry's death, he was suffering from a bacterial blood infection known to cause sudden infant death.

NOTES

[1] Amos Tversky and Daniel Kahneman, "Extensional Versus Intuitive Reasoning: The Conjunction Fallacy in Probability Judgment." *Psychological Review* 90 (1983): 297.

[2] Ibid.

[3] Thomas Gilovich, Robert Vallone, and Amos Tversky, "The Hot Hand in Basketball: The Misperception of Random Sequences," *Cognitive Psychology* 17 (1985): 295–314. The quotation is from pages 295–6.

[4] See Gerd Gigerenzer, *Calculated Risk: How to Know When Numbers Deceive You* (New York: Simon & Schuster, 2003).

12

CHOICES

Probabilities are used not only when we determine what to believe but also when we choose what to do. Although we sometimes assume that we know how our actions will turn out, we often have to make decisions in the face of risk, when we do not know what the outcomes of our options will be, but we do know the probabilities of those outcomes. To help us assess reasoning about choices involving risk, this chapter will explain the notions of expected monetary value and expected overall value. Our most difficult choices arise, however, when we do not know even the probabilities of various outcomes. Such decisions under ignorance or uncertainty pose special problems, for which a number of rules have been proposed. Although these rules are useful in many situations, their limitations will also be noted.

EXPECTED MONETARY VALUE

It is obvious that having some sense of probable outcomes is important for running our lives. If we hear that there is a 95 percent chance of rain, this usually provides a good enough reason to call off a picnic. But the exact relationship between probabilities and decisions is complex and often misunderstood.

The best way to illustrate these misunderstandings is to look at lotteries in which the numbers are fixed and clear. A $1 bet in a lottery might make you as much as $10 million. That sounds good. Why not take a shot at $10 million for only a dollar? Of course, there is not much chance of winning the lottery—say, only 1 chance in 20 million—and that sounds bad. Why throw $1 away on nothing? So we are pulled in two directions. What we want to know is just how good the bet is. Is it, for example, better or worse than a wager in some other lottery? To answer questions of this kind, we need to introduce the notion of expected monetary value.

The idea of expected monetary value takes into account three features that determine whether a bet is financially good or bad: the probability of winning, the net amount you gain if you win, and the net amount you lose if you lose. Suppose that on a $1 ticket there is 1 chance in 20 million of winning the New York State Lottery, and you will get $10 million from the state if you do. First, it is worth noticing that, if the state pays you

$10 million, your net gain on your $1 ticket is only $9,999,999. The state, after all, still has your original $1. So the net gain equals the payoff minus the cost of betting. This is not something that those who win huge lotteries worry about, but taking into account the cost of betting becomes important when this cost becomes high relative to the size of the payoff. There is nothing complicated about the net amount that you lose when you lose on a $1 ticket: It is $1.[1]

We can now compute the expected monetary value or financial worth of a bet in the following way:

Expected monetary value =

(the probability of winning times the net gain in money of winning) minus

(the probability of losing times the net loss in money of losing)

In our example, a person who buys a $1 ticket in the lottery has 1 chance in 20 million of a net gain of $9,999,999 and 19,999,999 chances in 20 million of a net loss of a dollar. So the expected monetary value of this wager equals:

$$(1/20,000,000 \times \$9,999,999) - (19,999,999/20,000,000 \times \$1)$$

That comes out to –$0.50.

What does this mean? One way of looking at it is as follows: If you could somehow buy up all the lottery tickets and thus ensure that you would win, your $20 million investment would net you $10 million, or $0.50 on the dollar—certainly a bad investment. Another way of looking at the situation is as follows: If you invested a great deal of money in the lottery over many millions of years, you could expect to win eventually, but, in the long run, you would be losing fifty cents on every ticket you bought. One last way of looking at the situation is this: You go down to your local drugstore and buy a blank lottery ticket for $0.50. Since it is blank, you have no chance of winning, with the result that you lose $0.50 every time you bet. Although almost no one looks at the matter in this way, this is, in effect, what you are doing over the long run when you buy lottery tickets.

We are now in a position to distinguish favorable and unfavorable expected monetary values. The expected monetary value is favorable when it is greater than zero. Changing our example, suppose the chances of hitting a $20 million payoff on a $1 bet are 1 in 10 million. In this case, the state still has the $1 you paid for the ticket, so your gain is actually $19,999,999. The expected monetary value is calculated as follows:

$$(1/10,000,000 \times \$19,999,999) - (9,999,999/10,000,000 \times \$1)$$

That comes to $1. Financially, this is a good bet; for in the long run you will gain $1 for every $1 you bet in such a lottery.

The rule, then, has three parts: (1) If the expected monetary value of the bet is more than zero, then the expected monetary value is favorable. (2) If the expected monetary value of the bet is less than zero, then the expected monetary value is unfavorable. (3) If the expected monetary value of the bet is zero, then the bet is neutral—a waste of time as far as money is concerned.

Compute the probability and the expected monetary value for the following bets. Each time, you lay down $1 to bet that a certain kind of card will appear from a standard fifty-two-card deck. If you win, you collect the amount indicated, so your net gain is $1 less. If you lose, of course, you lose your $1.

Example: Draw a seven of spades. Win: $26.

Probability of winning = 1/52

Expected value: $[1/52 \times \$(26-1)] - (51/52 \times \$1) = -\$0.50$

1. Draw a seven of spades or a seven of clubs. Win: $26.
2. Draw a seven of any suit. Win: $26.
3. Draw a face card (jack, queen, or king). Win: $4.
4. Do *not* draw a face card (jack, queen, or king). Win: $2.
5. On two consecutive draws without returning the first card to the deck, draw a seven of spades and then a seven of clubs. Win: $1,989.
6. Same as in problem 3, but this time the card is returned to the deck and the deck is shuffled before the second draw. Win: $1,989.
7. On two consecutive draws without returning the first card to the deck, do not draw a club. Win: $1.78.
8. Same as in problem 7, but this time the card is returned to the deck and the deck is shuffled before the second draw. Win: $1.78.
9. On four consecutive draws without returning any cards to the deck, a seven of spades, then a seven of clubs, then a seven of hearts, and then seven of diamonds. Win: $1,000,001.
10. On four consecutive draws without returning any cards to the deck, draw four sevens in any order. Win: $1,000,001.

Fogelin's Palace in Border, Nevada, offers the following unusual bet. If you win, you make a 50 percent profit on your bet; if you lose, you take a 40 percent loss. That is, if you bet $1 and win, then you get back $1.50; if you bet $1 and lose, you get back $0.60. The chances of winning are fifty-fifty. This sounds like a marvelous opportunity, but there is one hitch: To play, you must let your bet ride with its winnings, or losses, for four plays. For example, with $100, a four-bet sequence might look like this:

	Win	Win	Lose	Win
Total	$150	$225	$135	$202.50

At the end of this sequence, you can pick up $202.50, and thus make a $102.50 profit. It seems that Fogelin's Palace is a good place to gamble, but consider

(continued)

the following argument on the other side. Because the chances of winning are fifty-fifty, you will, on the average, win half the time. But notice what happens in such a case:

	Win	Lose	Lose	Win
Total	$150	$90	$54	$81

So, even though you have won half the time, you have come out $19 behind.

Surprisingly, it does not matter what order the wins and losses come in; if two are wins and two are losses, you come out behind. (You can check this.) So, because you are only going to win roughly half the time, and when you win half the time you actually lose money, it now seems to be a bad idea to gamble at Fogelin's Palace.

What should you do: gamble at Fogelin's Palace or not? Why?

EXPECTED OVERALL VALUE

Given that lotteries usually have an extremely unfavorable expected monetary value, why do millions of people invest billions of dollars in them each year? Part of the answer is that some people are stupid, superstitious, or both. People will sometimes reason, "Somebody has to win; why not me?" They can also convince themselves that their lucky day has come. But that is not the whole story, for most people who put down money on lottery tickets realize that the bet is a bad bet, but think that it is worth doing anyway. People fantasize about what they will do with the money if they win, and fantasies are fun. Furthermore, if the bet is only $1, and the person making the bet is not desperately poor, losing is not going to hurt much. Even if the expected monetary value on the lottery ticket is the loss of fifty cents, this might strike someone as a reasonable price for the fun of thinking about winning. (After all, you accept a sure loss of $8 every time you pay $8 to see a movie.) So a bet that is bad from a purely monetary point of view might be acceptable when other factors are considered.

The reverse situation can also arise: A bet may be unreasonable, even though it has a positive expected monetary value. Suppose, for example, that you are allowed to participate in a lottery in which a $1 ticket gives you 1 chance in 10 million of getting a payoff of $20 million. Here, as noted above, the expected monetary value of a $1 bet is a profit of $1, so from the point of view of expected monetary value, it is a good bet. This makes it sound reasonable to bet in this lottery, and a small bet probably is reasonable. But under these circumstances, would it be reasonable for you to sell everything you owned to buy lottery tickets? The answer to this is almost certainly no, for, even though the expected monetary value is positive, the odds of winning are still low, and the loss of your total resources would be personally catastrophic.

When we examine the effects that success or failure will have on a particular person relative to his or her own needs, resources, preferences, and so on, we are then examining what we shall call the *expected overall value* or *expected utility* of a choice. Considerations of this kind often force us to make adjustments in weighing the significance of costs and payoffs. In the examples we just examined, the immediate catastrophic consequences of a loss outweigh the long-term gains one can expect from participating in the lottery.

Another factor that typically affects the expected overall value of a bet is the phenomenon known as the *diminishing marginal value* or *diminishing marginal utility* of a payoff as it gets larger. Suppose someone offers to pay a debt by buying you a hamburger. Provided that the debt matches the cost of a hamburger and you feel like having one, you might go along with this. But suppose this person offers to pay off a debt ten times larger by buying you ten hamburgers? The chances are that you will reject the offer, for even though ten hamburgers cost ten times as much as one hamburger, they are not worth ten times as much to you. At some point you will get stuffed and not want any more. After one or two hamburgers, the marginal value of one more hamburger becomes pretty low. The notion of marginal value applies to money as well. If you are starving, $10 will mean a lot to you. You might be willing to work hard to get it. If you are wealthy, $10 more or less makes little difference; losing $10 might only be an annoyance.

Because of this phenomenon of diminishing marginal value, betting on lotteries is an even worse bet than most people suppose. A lottery with a payoff of $20 million sounds attractive, but it does not seem to be twenty times more attractive than a payoff of $1 million. So even if the expected monetary value of your $1 bet in a lottery is the loss of $0.50, the actual value to you is really something less than this, and so the bet is even worse than it seemed at first.

In general, then, when payoffs are large, the expected overall value of the payoff to someone is reduced because of the effects of diminishing marginal value. But not always. It is possible to think of exotic cases in which expected overall value increases with the size of the payoff. Suppose a witch told you that she would turn you into a toad if you did not give her $10 million by tomorrow. You believe her, because you know for a fact that she has turned others into toads when they did not pay up. You have only $1 to your name, but you are given the opportunity to participate in the first lottery described above, where a $1 ticket gives you 1 chance in 20 million of hitting a $10 million payoff. We saw that the expected monetary value of that wager was an unfavorable negative $0.50. But now consider the overall value of $1 to you if you are turned into a toad. Toads have no use for money, so to you, as a toad, the value of the dollar would drop to nothing. Thus, unless some other, more attractive alternatives are available, it would be reasonable to buy a lottery ticket, despite the unfavorable expected monetary value of the wager.

EXERCISE III

1. Though the situation is somewhat far-fetched, suppose you are going to the drugstore to buy medicine for a friend who will die without it. You have only $10—exactly what the medicine costs. Outside the drugstore a young man is playing three-card monte, a simple game in which the dealer shows you three cards, turns them over, shifts them briefly from hand to hand, and then lays them out, face down, on the top of a box. You are supposed to identify a particular card (usually the ace of spades); and, if you do, you are paid even money. You yourself are a magician and know the sleight-of-hand trick that fools most people, and you are sure that you can guess the card correctly nine times out of ten. First, what is the expected monetary value of a bet of $10? In this context, would it be reasonable to make this bet? Why or why not?

2. Provide an example of your own where a bet can be reasonable even though the expected monetary value is unfavorable. Then provide another example where the bet is unreasonable even though the expected monetary value is favorable. Explain what makes these bets reasonable or unreasonable.

DISCUSSION QUESTION

Consider the following game: You flip a coin continuously until you get tails once. If you get no heads (tails on the first flip), then you are paid nothing. If you get one heads (tails on the second flip), then you are paid $2. If you get two heads (tails on the third flip), then you are paid $4. If you get three heads, then you are paid $8. And so on. The general rule is that for any number n, if you get n heads, then you are paid 2^n. What is the expected monetary value of this game? What would you pay to play this game? Why that amount rather than more or less?

DECISIONS UNDER IGNORANCE

So far we have discussed choices where the outcomes of the various options are not certain, but we know their probabilities. Decisions of this kind are called *decisions under risk*. In other cases, however, we do not know the probabilities of various outcomes. Decisions of this kind are called *decisions under ignorance* (or, sometimes, *decisions under uncertainty*). If we do not have any idea where the probabilities of various outcomes lie, the ignorance is complete. If we know that these probabilities lie within some general range, the ignorance is partial.

As an example of partial ignorance, suppose that, just after graduating from college, you are offered three jobs. First, the Exe Company offers you a salary of $20,000. Exe is well-established and secure. The next offer comes from the Wye Company. Here the salary is $30,000, but Wye is a new company, so it is less secure. You think that this new company will probably do well, but you don't know how likely it is to last or for how long. Wye might go bankrupt, and then you will be left without a job. The final offer comes from the Zee Company, which is as stable as Exe and offers you a salary of $40,000 per year. These offers are summarized in the following table:

	Wye does not go bankrupt	Wye goes bankrupt
Take job at Exe	$20,000	$20,000
Take job at Wye	$30,000	$0
Take job at Zee	$40,000	$40,000

Let's assume that other factors (such as benefits, vacations, location, interest, working conditions, bonuses, raises, and promotions) are all equally desirable in the three jobs. Which job should you take?

The answer is clear: Take the job from the Zee Company. This decision is easy because you end up better off regardless of whether or not Wye goes bankrupt, so it doesn't matter how likely Wye's bankruptcy is. Everyone agrees that you should choose any option that is best whatever happens. This is called the *rule of dominance*.

The problem with the rule of dominance is that it can't help you make choices when no option is better regardless of what happens. Suppose you discover that the letter from the Zee Company is a forgery—part of a cruel joke by your roommate. Now your only options are Exe and Wye. The job with Wye will be better if Wye does not go bankrupt, but the job with Exe will be better if Wye does go bankrupt. Neither job is better no matter what happens, so the rule of dominance no longer applies.

To help you choose between Exe and Wye, you might look for a rational way to assign probabilities despite your ignorance of which assignments are correct. One approach of this kind uses the *rule of insufficient reason:* When you have no reason to think that any outcome is more likely than any other, assume that the outcomes are equally probable. This assumption enables us to calculate expected monetary value or utility, as in the preceding sections, and then we can choose the option with the highest expected utility. In our example, this rule of insufficient reason favors the job at Exe, because your expected income in that job is $20,000, whereas your expected income in the job at Wye is only $15,000 (= 0.5 × $30,000), assuming that the Wye company has as much chance of going bankrupt as of staying in business.

The problem with the rule of insufficient reason is that it may seem arbitrary to assume that unknown probabilities are equal. Often we suspect that the probabilities of various outcomes are not equal, even while we do not know what the probabilities are. Moreover, the rule of insufficient reason yields different results when the options are described differently. We can distinguish four possibilities: Wye goes bankrupt, Wye stays the same size, Wye increases in size, and Wye decreases in size but stays in business. If we do not have any reason to see any of these outcomes as more likely than any other, then the rule of insufficient reason tells us to assign them equal probabilities. On that assumption, and if you will keep your job as long as Wye stays in business, then you have only one chance in four of losing your job; so your expected income in the job at Wye is now $22,500 (= ¾ × $30,000). Thus, if we stick with the rule of insufficient reason, the expected value of the job at Wye and whether you should take that job seem to depend on how the options are divided. That seems crazy in this case.

Another approach tries to work without any assumptions about probability in cases of ignorance. Within this approach, several rules might be adopted. One possibility is the *maximax rule,* which tells you to choose the option whose best outcome is better than the best outcome of any other option. If you follow the maximax rule, then you will accept the job with the Wye Company, because the best outcome of that job is a salary of $30,000 when this new company does not go bankrupt, and this is better than any outcome with the Exe Company. Optimists and risk takers will favor this rule.

Other people are more pessimistic and tend to avoid risks. They will favor a rule more like the *maximin rule,* which says to choose the option whose worst outcome is better than the worst outcome of any other option. If you follow the maximin rule, you will accept the job with the Exe Company, because the worst outcome in that job is a steady salary of $20,000, whereas the worst outcome is unemployment if you accept the job with the Wye Company.

Each of these rules works by focusing exclusively on part of your information and disregarding other things that you know. The maximax rule considers only the best outcomes for each option—the best-case scenario. The maximin rule pays attention to only the worst outcome for each option—the worst-case scenario. Because they ignore other outcomes, the maximax rule strikes many people as too risky (since it does not consider how much you could lose by taking a chance), and the maximin rule strikes many people as too conservative (since it does not consider how much you could have gained if you had taken a small risk).

Another problem is that the maximax and maximin rules do not take probabilities into account at all. This makes sense when you know nothing about the probabilities. But when some (even if limited) information about probabilities is available, then it seems better to use as much information as you have. Suppose, for example, that each of two options might lead to disaster, and you do not know how likely a disaster is after either option, but you do know that one option is more likely to lead to disaster than another. In such situations, some decision theorists argue that you should choose the option that minimizes the chance that any disaster will occur. This is called the *disaster avoidance rule.*

To illustrate this rule, consider a different kind of case:

A forty-year-old man is diagnosed as having a rare disease and consults the world's leading expert on the disease. He is informed that the disease is almost certainly not fatal but often causes serious paralysis that leaves its victims bedridden for life. (In other cases it has no lasting effects.) The disease is so rare that the expert can offer only a vague estimate of the probability of paralysis: 20 to 60 percent. There is an experimental drug that, if administered now, would almost certainly cure the disease. However, it kills a significant but not accurately known percentage of those who take it. The expert guesses that the probability of the drug being fatal is less than 20 percent, and the patient thus assumes that he is definitely less likely to die if he takes the drug than he is to be paralyzed if he lets the disease run its course. The patient would regard bedridden life as preferable to death, but he considers both outcomes as totally disastrous compared to continuing his life in good health. Should he take the drug?[2]

Since the worst outcome is death, and this outcome will not occur unless he takes the drug, the maximin rule would tell him not to take the drug. In contrast, the disaster avoidance rule would tell him to take the drug, because both death and paralysis are disasters and taking the drug minimizes his chances that any disaster will occur. Thus, although the disaster avoidance rule opposes risk taking, it does so in a different way than the maximin rule.

We are left, then, with a plethora of rules: dominance, insufficient reason, maximax, maximin, and disaster avoidance. Other rules have been proposed as well. With all of these rules in the offing, it is natural to ask which is correct. Unfortunately, there is no consensus on this issue. Each rule applies and seems plausible in some cases but not in others. Many people conclude that each rule is appropriate to different kinds of situations. It is still not clear, however, which rule should govern decisions in which circumstances. The important problem of decision under ignorance remains unsolved.

DISCUSSION QUESTIONS

1. In the game of ignorance, you draw one card from a deck, but you do not know how many cards or which kinds of cards are in the deck. It might be a normal deck or it might contain only diamonds or only aces of spades or any other combination of cards. It costs nothing to play. If you bet that the card you draw will be a spade, and it is a spade, then you win $100. If you bet that the card you draw will not be a spade, and it is not a spade, then you win $90. You may make only one bet. Which bet would you make if you followed the maximax rule? The maximin rule? The disaster avoidance rule? The rule of insufficient reason? Which rule seems most plausible this case? Which bet should you make? Why?

2. In which circumstances do you think it is appropriate to use the dominance rule? The rule of insufficient reason? The maximax rule? The maximin rule? The disaster avoidance rule? Why?

3. Suppose that you may choose either of two envelopes. You know that one envelope contains twice as much money as the other, but you do not know the amount of money in either envelope. You choose an envelope, open it, and see that it contains $100. Now you know that the other envelope must

(continued)

contain either $50 or $200. At this point, you are given a choice: You may exchange your envelope for the other envelope. Should you switch envelopes, according to the rule of insufficient reason? Is this result plausible? Why or why not?

4. The following article raises a problem in dealing with infinity. How would you answer it?

PLAYING GAMES WITH ETERNITY: THE DEVIL'S OFFER[3]

by Edward J. Gracely

Suppose Ms C dies and goes to hell, or to a place that seems like hell. The devil approaches and offers to play a game of chance. If she wins, she can go to heaven. If she loses, she will stay in hell forever; there is no second chance to play the game. If Ms C plays today, she has a 1/2 chance of winning. Tomorrow the probability will be 2/3. Then 3/4, 4/5, 5/6, etc., with no end to the series. Thus, every passing day increases her chances of winning. At what point should she play the game?

The answer is not obvious: after any given number of days spent waiting, it will still be possible to improve her chances by waiting yet another day. And any increase in the probability of winning a game with infinite stakes has an infinite utility. For example, if she waits a year, her probability of winning the game would be approximately 0.997268; if she waits one more day, the probability would increase to 0.997275, a difference of only 0.000007. Yet even 0.000007 multiplied by infinity is infinite.

On the other hand, it seems reasonable to suppose the cost of delaying for a day to be finite—a day's more suffering in hell. So the infinite expected benefit from a delay will always exceed the cost.

This logic might suggest that Ms C should wait forever, but clearly such a strategy would be self-defeating: why should she stay forever in a place in order to increase her chances of leaving it? So the question remains: what should Ms C do?

5. Pascal is famous for invoking infinite utilities to argue for belief in God. Explain and evaluate his argument in the following passage.

THE WAGER[4]

by Blaise Pascal

. . . Let us weigh the gain and the loss in wagering that God is. Let us estimate these two chances. If you gain, you gain all; if you lose, you lose nothing.

Wager, then, without hesitation that He is.—"That is very fine. Yes, I must wager; but I may perhaps wager too much."—Let us see. Since there is an equal risk of gain and of loss, if you had only to gain two lives, instead of one, you might still wager. But if there were three lives to gain, you would have to play (since you are under the necessity of playing), and you would be imprudent, when you are forced to play, not to chance your life to gain three at a game where there is an equal risk of loss and gain. But there is an eternity of life and happiness. And this being so, if there were an infinity of chances, of which one only would be for you, you would still be right in wagering one to win two, and you would act stupidly, being obliged to play, by refusing to stake one life against three at a game in which out of an infinity of chances there is one for you, if there were an infinity of an infinitely happy life to gain. But there is here an infinity of an infinitely happy life to gain, a chance of gain against a finite number of chances of loss, and what you stake is finite. It is all divided; wherever the infinite is and there is not an infinity of chances of loss against that of gain, there is no time to hesitate, you must give all. And thus, when one is forced to play, he must renounce reason to preserve his life, rather than risk it for infinite gain, as likely to happen as the loss of nothingness. . . .

The end of this discourse.—Now, what harm will befall you in taking this side? You will be faithful, honest, humble, grateful, generous, a sincere friend, truthful. Certainly you will not have those poisonous pleasures, glory and luxury; but will you not have others? I will tell you that you will thereby gain in this life, and that, at each step you take on this road, you will see so great certainty of gain, so much nothingness in what you risk, that you will at last recognize that you have wagered for something certain and infinite, for which you have given nothing.

6. In the following passage, James Cargile responds to Pascal's argument. Explain Cargile's point. How could Pascal best respond? Is this response adequate? Why or why not?

Either (a) there is a god who will send only religious people to heaven or (b) there is not. To be religious is to wager for (a). To fail to be religious is to wager for (b). We can't settle the question whether (a) or (b) is the case, at least not at present. But (a) is clearly vastly better than (b). With (a), infinite bliss is *guaranteed*, while with (b) we are still in the miserable human condition of facing death with no assurance as to what lies beyond. So (a) is clearly the best wager. . . .

This argument just presented is formally similar to the following: Either (a) there is a god who will send you to heaven only if you commit a painful ritual suicide within an hour of first reading this, or (b) there is not. We cannot settle the question whether (a) or (b) is the case or it is at least not settled yet. But (a) is vastly preferable to (b), since in situation (a) infinite bliss is *guaranteed*, while in (b) we are left in the miserable human condition. So we should wager for (a) by performing ritual suicide.

It might be objected that we can be sure that there is not a god who will send us to heaven only if we commit suicide, but we can't be sure that there is not a god who will send us to heaven only if we are religious. However, a sceptic would demand proof of this. . . .[5]

NOTES

[1] If the lottery gave a consolation prize of a shiny new quarter to all losers, their net loss would be only seventy-five cents. Since most lotteries do not give consolation prizes, the net loss equals the cost of playing such lotteries.

[2] Gregory Kavka, "Deterrence, Utility, and Rational Choice," reprinted in *Moral Paradoxes of Nuclear Deterrence* (New York: Cambridge University Press, 1987), 65–66. Kavka uses this medical example to argue for his disaster avoidance rule and, by analogy, to defend the rationality of nuclear deterrence.

[3] From *Analysis* 48 (1988): 113.

[4] From *Pensées and the Provincial Letters,* trans. W. F. Trotter (New York: Modern Library, 1941).

[5] From "Pascal's Wager," *Philosophy* 41 (1966): 254.

FALLACIES

When inferences are defective, they are called fallacious. When defective styles of reasoning are repeated over and over, because people often get fooled by them, then we have an argumentative fallacy that is worth flagging with a name. The number and variety of argumentative fallacies are limited only by the imagination. Consequently, there is little point in trying to construct a complete list of fallacies. What is crucial is to get a feel for the most common and most seductive kinds of fallacy. Once this is done, we should be able to recognize many other kinds as well. The goal of Part IV is to develop that skill.

13

FALLACIES OF VAGUENESS

This chapter examines one of the main ways in which arguments can be defective or fallacious because language is not used clearly enough for the context. This kind of unclarity is vagueness. *Vagueness occurs when, in a given context, a term is used in a way that allows too many cases in which it is unclear whether or not the term applies. Vagueness underlies several common fallacies, including three kinds of* slippery-slope *arguments.*

USES OF UNCLARITY

In a good argument, a person states a conclusion clearly and then, with equal clarity, gives reasons for this conclusion. The arguments of everyday life often fall short of this standard. Usually, unclear language is a sign of unclear thought. There are times, however, when people are intentionally unclear. They might use unclarity for poetic effect or to leave details to be decided later. But often their goal is to confuse others. This is called *obfuscation.*

Before we look at the various ways in which language can be unclear, a word of caution is needed: There is no such thing as absolute clarity. Whether something is clear or not depends on the context in which it occurs. A botanist does not use common vocabulary in describing and classifying plants. At the same time, it would usually be foolish for a person to use botanical terms in describing the appearance of her backyard. Aristotle said that it is the mark of an educated person not to expect more rigor than the subject matter will allow. Because clarity and rigor depend on context, it takes judgment and good sense to pitch an argument at the right level.

Non Sequitur   **by Wiley**

VAGUENESS

Perhaps the most common form of unclarity is *vagueness*. It arises when a concept applies along a continuum or a series of very small changes. The standard example is baldness. A person with a full head of hair is not bald. A person without a hair on his head is bald. In between, however, is a range of cases in which we cannot say definitely whether the person is bald or not. These are called *borderline cases*. Here we say something less definite, such as that this person is "going bald."

Our inability to apply the concept of baldness in a borderline case is not due to ignorance of the number of hairs on the person's head. It will not help to count the number of hairs there. Even if we knew the exact number, we would still not be able to say whether the person was bald or not. The same is true of most adjectives that concern properties admitting of degrees—for example, "rich," "healthy," "tall," "wise," and "ruthless."

For the most part, imprecision—the lack of sharply defined limits—causes little difficulty. In fact, this is a useful feature of our language, for suppose we *did* have to count the number of grains of salt between our fingers to determine whether or not we hold a *pinch* of salt. It would take a long time to follow a simple recipe that calls for a pinch of salt.

Yet difficulties can arise when borderline cases themselves are at issue. Suppose that a state passes a law forbidding all actions that offend a large number of people. There will be many cases that clearly fall under this law and many cases that clearly do not fall under it. There will also be many cases in which it will not be clear whether or not they fall under this law. Laws are sometimes declared unconstitutional for this very reason. Here we shall say that the law is vague. In calling the law vague, we are criticizing it. We are not simply noticing the existence of borderline cases, for there will usually be borderline cases no matter how careful we are. Instead, we are saying that there are *too many* borderline cases for this context. More precisely, we shall say that an expression in a given context is *used vaguely* if it leaves open too wide a range of borderline cases for the successful and legitimate use of that expression in that context.

Vagueness thus depends on context. To further illustrate this context dependence, consider the expression "light football player." There are, of course, borderline cases between those football players who are light and those who are not light. But on these grounds alone, we would not say that the expression is vague. It is usually a perfectly serviceable expression, and we can indicate borderline cases by saying such things as "Jones is a bit light for a football player." Suppose, however, that Ohio State and Cal Tech wish to have a game between their light football players. It is obvious that the previous understanding of what counts as being light is too vague for this new context. At Ohio State, anyone under 210 pounds is considered light. At Cal Tech, anyone over 150 pounds is considered heavy. What is needed, then, is a ruling, such as that anyone under 175 pounds will be considered a lightweight. This example illustrates a common problem and its solution. A term that works perfectly well in one area becomes vague when applied in some other (usually more specialized) area. This vagueness can then be removed by adopting more precise rules in the problematic area. Vagueness is resolved by definition.

EXERCISE I

For each of the following terms, give one case to which the term clearly applies, one case to which the term clearly does not apply, and one borderline case. Then try to explain why the borderline case is a borderline case.

Example: In the northern hemisphere, "summer month" clearly applies to July; clearly does not apply to January; and June is a borderline case, because the summer solstice is June 21, and schools usually continue into June, but June, July, and August are, nonetheless, often described as the summer months.

1. large animal
2. populous state
3. long book
4. old professor
5. popular singer
6. powerful person
7. difficult subject
8. late meeting
9. arriving late to a meeting

EXERCISE II

Each of the following sentences contains words or expressions that are potentially vague. Describe a context in which this vagueness might make a difference, and explain what difference it makes. Then reduce this vagueness by replacing the italicized expression with one that is more precise.

Example: Harold has a *bad* reputation.

Context: If Harold applies for a job as a bank security guard, then some but not all kinds of bad reputation are relevant. A reputation for doing bad construction work is irrelevant, but a reputation for dishonesty is relevant.

Replacement: Harold is a known thief.

1. Ross has a *large* income.
2. Cocaine is a *dangerous* drug.
3. Ruth is a *clever* woman.
4. Andre is a *terrific* tennis player.
5. Mark is not doing *too well* (after his operation).

(continued)

6. Shaq's a *big* fellow.
7. Dan's grades are *low*.
8. Walter can't see *well*.
9. The earthquake was a *disaster*.
10. The news was *wonderful*.

HEAPS

The existence of borderline cases is essential to various styles of reasoning that have been identified and used since ancient times. One such argument was called the *argument from the heap* or the *sorites argument* (from the Greek word "soros," which means "heap"). The classic example was intended to show that it is impossible to produce a heap of sand by adding one grain at a time. As a variation on this, we will show that no one can become rich. The argument can be formulated as a long series like this:

(1) Someone with only one cent is not rich.
(2) If someone with only one cent is not rich, then someone with only two cents is not rich.
∴ (3) Someone with only two cents is not rich.

(4) If someone with only two cents is not rich, then someone with only three cents is not rich.
∴ (5) Someone with only three cents is not rich.

(6) If someone with only three cents is not rich, then someone with only four cents is not rich.
∴ (7) Someone with only four cents is not rich.

[and so on, until:]

∴ (199,999,999,999) Someone with only 100,000,000,000 cents is not rich.

The problem, of course, is that someone with 100,000,000,000 cents *is* rich. If someone denies this, we can keep on going. Or we can just sum up the whole argument like this:

(1*) Someone with only one cent is not rich.
(2*) For any number, n, if someone with only n cents is not rich, then someone with $n + 1$ cents is not rich.
∴ (3*) Someone with any number of cents is not rich.

Premise (2*) is, of course, just a generalization of premises (2), (4), (6), and so on.

Despite its plausibility, everyone should agree that there is something wrong with these arguments. If we hand over enough pennies to Peter, previously poor Peter will become the richest person in the world. Another sign of a problem is that a parallel argument runs in the other direction: Someone with 100 billion cents is rich. For any number, n, if someone with n cents is rich, then someone with $n - 1$ cents is also rich. Therefore, someone with no cents at all is rich. This is absurd (since we are not talking about how rich one's life can be as long as one has friends).

We can see that these arguments turn on borderline cases in the following way: The argument would fail if we removed borderline cases by laying down a ruling (maybe for tax purposes) that anyone with a million dollars or more is rich and anyone with less than this is not rich. A person with $999,999.99 would then pass from not being rich to being rich when given a single penny, so premise (2*) would be false at that point under this ruling. Of course, we do not usually use the word "rich" with this much precision. We see some people as clearly rich and others as clearly not rich, but in between there is a fuzzy area where we are not prepared to say that people either are or are not rich. In this fuzzy area, as well as in the clear areas, a penny one way or the other will make no difference.

That is how the argument works, but exactly where does it go wrong? This question is not easy to answer and remains a subject of vigorous debate. Here is one way to view the problem: Consider a person who is 80 pounds overweight, where we would all agree that that person would pass from being fat to not being fat by losing over 100 pounds. If he or she lost an ounce a day for five years, this would be *equivalent* to losing just over 114 pounds. An argument from the heap denies that this person would ever cease to be fat. (So what is the point of dieting?) Anyone who accepted that conclusion, or (3*), would seem to claim that a series of insignificant changes *cannot* be equivalent to a significant change. Surely, this is wrong. Here we might be met with the reply that every change must occur at some particular time (and place), but there would be no particular day on which this person would pass from being fat to not being fat. The problem with this reply is that, with concepts like this, changes seem to occur gradually over long stretches of time without occurring at any single moment. Anyway, however or whenever it occurs, the change does occur. Some people do cease to be fat if they lose enough weight.

This tells us that conclusions of arguments from the heap, such as (3*), are false, so these arguments cannot be sound. Almost everyone agrees to that much. Moreover, if an appropriate starting point is chosen, then premises like (1) and (1*) will also be accepted as true by almost everyone. So the main debate focuses on premise (2*) and on whether the argument is valid. Some philosophers reject premise (2*) and claim that there is a precise point at which a person becomes rich, even though we don't know where that point is. Others try to avoid any sharp cutoff point by developing some kind of alternative logic. Still others just admit that the premises seem true, and the argument seems valid, but the conclusion seems false, so the argument creates a paradox to which they have no solution. These views become complicated and technical, so we will not discuss them here. Suffice it to say that almost everyone agrees that conclusions like (3*) and (199,999,999,999) are false, so arguments from the heap are unsound for one reason or another. That is why such arguments are labeled *fallacies*.

Where exactly do *you* think arguments from the heap go astray?

SLIPPERY SLOPES

Near cousins to arguments from the heap are *slippery-slope arguments*, but they reach different conclusions. Whereas heap arguments conclude that nothing has a certain property, such as baldness, a slippery-slope argument could be trotted out to try to show that there is no *real* or *defensible* or *significant* or *important* difference between being bald and not being bald. The claim is not that no change occurs because the person who loses all his hair is still not bald, as in an argument from the heap. Instead, the slippery-slope argument claims that we should not classify people as either bald or not bald, because there is no significant difference between these classifications.

Whether a difference is significant depends on a variety of factors. In particular, what is significant for one purpose might not be significant for other purposes. Different concerns then yield different kinds of slippery-slope arguments. We will discuss three kinds, beginning with conceptual slippery-slope arguments.

CONCEPTUAL SLIPPERY-SLOPE ARGUMENTS

Conceptual slippery-slope arguments try to show that things at opposite ends of a continuum do not differ in any way that would be important enough to justify drawing a distinction in one's concepts or theories. As an example, consider the difference between living and nonliving things.

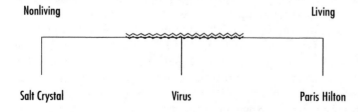

We all agree that a salt crystal is *not* alive. Yet a salt crystal is very similar to other more complex crystals, and these crystals are similar to certain viruses.

Still, a virus is on the borderline between living and nonliving things. A virus does not take nourishment and does not reproduce itself. Instead, a virus invades the reproductive mechanisms of cells, and these cells then produce the virus. As viruses become more complex, the differences between them and "higher" life forms become less obvious. Through a series of such small transitions, we finally reach a creature who is obviously alive: Paris Hilton. So far, we have merely described a series of gradual transitions along a *continuum*. We get a conceptual slippery-slope argument when we draw the following conclusion from these facts: There is no significant difference between living things and nonliving things.

To avoid this conclusion, we need to figure out where the argument goes wrong. Such arguments often seem to depend on the following principles:

1. We should not draw a distinction between things that are not significantly different.

2. If *A* is not significantly different from *B*, and *B* is not significantly different from *C*, then *A* is not significantly different from *C*.

This first principle is interesting, complicated, and at least *generally* true. We shall examine it more closely in a moment. The second principle is obviously false. As already noted, a series of insignificant differences can add up to a significant difference. Senator Everett Dirksen put the point well when he said, "A billion dollars here and a billion dollars there can add up to some real money." To the extent that conceptual slippery-slope arguments depend on this questionable assumption, they provide no more support for their conclusions than do arguments from the heap.

Unlike arguments from the heap, however, conceptual slippery-slope arguments do often lead people to accept their conclusions. Slippery-slope arguments have been used to deny the difference between sanity and insanity (some people are just a little weirder than others) and between amateur and professional athletics (some athletes just get paid a little more or more directly than other athletes). When many small differences make a big difference, such conceptual slippery-slope arguments are fallacious.

This fallacy is seductive, because it is often hard to tell when many small differences *do* make a big difference. Here is a recent controversial example: Some humans have very dark skin. Others have very pale skin. As members of these different groups marry, their children's skin can have any intermediate shade of color. This smooth spectrum leads some people to deny that any differences among races will be important to developed theories in biology. Their argument seems to be that the wealth of intermediate cases will make it difficult or impossible to formulate precise and exceptionless laws that apply to one racial group but not to others, so differences among races will play no important role in sciences that seek such laws. Critics respond that some scientific laws about races still might hold without exception even if skin color and other features do vary in tiny increments.

Whichever side one takes, this controversy shows that, even if there is a smooth spectrum between endpoints, this continuity is not enough *by itself* to show that there are no scientifically significant differences among races. That conclusion would need to be supported by more than just a conceptual slippery-slope argument. To show that certain concepts are useless for the purposes of a certain theory, one would need to add more information, particularly about the purposes of that theory and its laws. That is what determines which differences are important in that particular area. Conceptual slippery-slope arguments might work in conjunction with such additional premises, but they cannot work alone.

EXERCISE III

Whenever we find one thing passing over into its opposite through a gradual series of borderline cases, we can construct (a) an argument from the heap and (b) a conceptual slippery-slope argument by using the following method: Find some increase that will not be large enough to carry us outside the borderline area. Then use the patterns of argument given above. Applying this method, formulate arguments for the following claims. Then explain what is wrong with these arguments.

1. a. There are no heaps.
   b. There is no difference between a heap and a single grain of sand.
2. a. Nobody is tall.
   b. There is no difference between being tall and being short.
3. a. Books do not exist.
   b. There is no difference between a book and a pamphlet.
4. a. Heat is not real.
   b. There is no difference between being hot and being cold.
5. a. Taxes are never high.
   b. There is no difference between high taxes and low taxes.
6. a. Science is an illusion.
   b. There is no difference between science and faith.

DISCUSSION QUESTIONS

1. Do you think that differences among races have any role in developed theories in biology or sociology or any other science? Why or why not?
2. If animals evolve gradually from one species to another, does that show that there is no significant difference in biology between any species (say, horses and dogs)? Why or why not? Does it show that there is no important difference in moral theory between the rights of humans and the rights of animals in other species? Why or why not?

FAIRNESS SLIPPERY-SLOPE ARGUMENTS

When borderline cases form a continuum, if someone classifies a case at one end of the continuum, an opponent often challenges this classification by asking, "Where do you draw the line?" Sometimes this challenge is out of place. If I claim that Babe Ruth was a superstar, I will not be refuted if I cannot draw a sharp dividing line between athletes who are superstars and those who are not. There are some difficult borderline cases, but Babe Ruth is not one of them. Nor will we be impressed if someone tells us that the difference between Babe Ruth and the thousands of players who never made it to the major leagues is "*just* a matter of degree." What is usually wrong with this phrase is the emphasis on the word "just," which suggests that differences of degree do not count. Of course, it is a matter of degree, but the difference in degree is so great that it should be marked by a special word.

There are other occasions when a challenge to drawing a line is appropriate. For example, most schools and universities have grading systems that draw a fundamental distinction between passing grades and failing grades. Of course, a person who barely passes a course does not perform very differently from one who barely fails a course, yet they are treated very differently. Students who barely pass a course get credit for it; those who barely fail it do not. This, in turn, can lead to serious consequences in an academic career and even beyond. It is entirely reasonable to ask for a justification of a procedure that treats cases that are so similar in such strikingly different ways. We are not being tender-hearted; we are raising an issue of *fairness* or *justice*. It seems unfair to treat very similar cases in strikingly different ways.

The point is not that there is no difference between passing and failing. That is why this argument is not a conceptual slippery-slope argument. The claim, instead, is that the differences that do exist (as little as one point out of a hundred on a test) do not make it fair to treat people so differently (credit *versus* no credit for the course). This unfairness does not follow merely from the scores forming a continuum, but the continuum does put pressure on us to show why small differences in scores do justify big differences in treatment.

Questions about the fairness of drawing a line often arise in the law. For example, given reasonable cause, the police generally do not have to obtain a warrant to search a motor vehicle, for the obvious reason that the vehicle might be driven away while the police go to a judge to obtain a warrant. On the other hand, with few exceptions, the police may not search a person's home without a search warrant. In the case of *California v. Carney*,[1] the U.S. Supreme Court had to rule on whether the police needed a warrant to search for marijuana in an "oversized van, fully mobile," parked in a downtown parking lot in San Diego. Because the van was a fully mobile vehicle, it seemed to fall under the first principle; but because it also served as its owner's home, it seemed to fall under the second. The difficulty, as the Court saw, was that there is a gray area between those things that clearly are motor vehicles and not homes (for example, motorcycles) and those things that clearly are homes and not motor vehicles (for example, apartments). Chief Justice

Warren Burger wondered about a mobile home in a trailer park hooked up to utility lines with its wheels removed. Justice Sandra Day O'Connor asked whether a tent, because it is highly mobile, could also be searched without a warrant. As the discussion continued, houseboats (with or without motors or oars), covered wagons, and finally a house being moved from one place to another on a trailer truck came under examination. In the end, our highest court decided that the van in question was a vehicle and could be searched without first obtaining a warrant to do so. The court did not fully explain why it is fair to allow warrantless searches—and to send people to jail as a result—in cases of vans used as homes but not in other very similar cases.

Questions about where to draw a line often have even more important implications than in the case just examined. Consider the death penalty. Most societies have reserved the death penalty for those crimes they consider the most serious. But where should we draw the line between crimes punishable by death and crimes not punishable by death? Should the death penalty be given to murderers of prison guards? To rapists? To drug dealers? To drunk drivers who cause death? Wherever we draw the line, it seems to be an unavoidable consequence of the death penalty that similar cases will be treated in radically different ways. A defender of the death penalty can argue that it is not unfair to draw a line because, once the line is drawn, the public will have fair warning about which crimes are subject to the death penalty and which are not. It will then be up to each person to decide whether to risk his or her life by crossing this line. It remains a matter of debate, however, whether the law can be administered in a predictable way that makes this argument plausible.

The finality of death raises a profoundly difficult problem in another area, too: the legalization of abortion. There are some people who think abortion is never justified and ought to be declared totally illegal. There are others who think abortion does not need any justification at all and should be completely legalized. Between these extremes, there are many people who believe abortion is justified in certain circumstances but not in others (such as when abortion is the only way to save the life of the mother but not when it prevents only lesser harms to the mother). There are also those who think abortion should be allowed for a certain number of months of pregnancy, but not thereafter. People holding these middle positions face the problem of deciding where to draw a line, and this makes them subject to criticisms from holders of either extreme position.

This problem admits of no easy solution. Because every line we draw will seem arbitrary to some extent, a person who holds a middle position needs to argue that it is better to draw *some* line—even a somewhat arbitrary one—than to draw no line at all. The recognition that some line is needed, and why, can often help us locate the real issues. This is the first step toward a reasonable position.

Of course, this still does not tell us *where* to draw the line. A separate argument is needed to show that the line should be drawn at one point, or in one area, rather than another. In the law, such arguments often appeal to value judgments about the effects of drawing the line at one place rather than another.

For example, it is more efficient to draw a line where it is easy to detect, and drawing the line at one place will provide greater protection for some values or some people than will drawing it at another place. Different values often favor drawing different lines, and sometimes such arguments are not available at all. Thus, in the end, it will be difficult to solve many of these profound and important problems.

DISCUSSION QUESTION

Is it unfair for teachers to fail students who get one point out of a hundred less than others students who pass? Why or why not? Would an alternative grading system be fairer?

Farcus

by David Waisglass
Gordon Coulthart

© 1992 Farcus Cartoons

WAISGLASS/COULTHART

Reprinted by permission of LaughingStock Licensing Inc.

What began with a few pencils and paper clips ...

CAUSAL SLIPPERY-SLOPE ARGUMENTS

Another common kind of argument is also often described as a slippery-slope argument. In these arguments, the claim is made that, once a certain kind of event occurs, other similar events will also occur, and this will lead eventually to disaster. The most famous (or infamous) argument of this kind was used by the U.S. government to justify its intervention in Vietnam in the 1960s. It was claimed that, if the communists took over Vietnam, they would then take over Cambodia, the rest of Asia, and other continents, until they ruled the whole world. This was called the domino theory, since the fall of one country would make neighboring countries fall as well. Arguments of this kind are sometimes called *domino arguments*. Such arguments claim that one event, which might not seem bad by itself, would lead to other, more horrible events, so such arguments can also be called *parades of horrors*.

Causal slippery slopes can also slide into good results. After all, someone who wants communists to take over the world might use the above domino argument to show why the United States should *not* intervene in Vietnam. Such optimistic slippery-slope arguments are, however, much less common than parades of horrors, so we will limit our discussion to the pessimistic versions.

These arguments resemble other slippery-slope arguments in that they depend on a series of small changes. The domino argument does not, however, claim that there is no difference between the first step and later steps—between Vietnam going communist and the rest of Asia going communist. Nor is there supposed to be anything unfair about letting Vietnam go communist without letting other countries also go communist. The point of a parade of horrors is that certain events will *cause* horrible effects because of their similarity or proximity to other events. Since the crucial claim is about causes and effects, these arguments will be called *causal slippery-slope arguments*.

We saw another example in Chapter 4. While arguing against an increase in the clerk hire allowance, Kyl says,

> The amount of increase does not appear large. I trust, however, there is no one among us who would suggest that the addition of a clerk would not entail allowances for another desk, another typewriter, more materials, and it is not beyond the realm of possibility that the next step would then be a request for additional office space, and ultimately new buildings.

Although this argument is heavily guarded, the basic claim is that increasing the clerk hire allowance is likely to lead to much larger expenditures that will break the budget. The argument can be represented more formally this way:

(1) If the clerk hire allowance is increased, other expenditures will also probably be increased.
(2) These other increases would be horrible.
∴(3) The clerk hire allowance should not be increased.

Opponents can respond in several ways. One response is to deny that the supposedly horrible effects really are so horrible. One might argue, for example, that additional office space and new buildings would be useful. This response is often foreclosed by describing the effects in especially horrible terms.

A second possible response would be to deny that increasing the clerk hire allowance really would have the horrible effects that are claimed in the first premise. One might argue, for example, that the old offices already have adequate room for additional clerks.

Often the best response is a combination of these. One can admit that certain claimed effects would be horrible, but deny that these horrible effects really are likely. Then one can acknowledge that some more minor problems will ensue, but argue that these costs are outweighed by the benefits of the program.

To determine which, if any, of these responses is adequate, one must look closely at each particular argument and ask the following questions:

Are any of the claimed effects really very bad?

Are any of these effects really very likely?

Do these dangers outweigh all the benefits of what is being criticized?

If the answers to all these questions are "Yes," then the causal slippery-slope argument is strong. But if any of these questions receives a negative answer, then the causal slippery-slope argument is questionable on that basis.

Exercise IV

Classify each of the following arguments as either (H) an argument from the heap, (C) a conceptual slippery-slope argument, (F) a fairness slippery-slope argument, or (S) a causal slippery-slope argument. Explain why you classify each example as you do.

1. We have to take a stand against sex education in junior high schools. If we allow sex education in the eighth grade, then the seventh graders will want it, and then the sixth graders, and pretty soon we will be teaching sex education to our little kindergartners.

2. People are found not guilty by reason of insanity when they cannot avoid breaking the law. But people who are brought up in certain deprived social circumstances are not much more able than the insane to avoid breaking the law. So it would be unjust to find them guilty.

3. People are called mentally ill when they do very strange things, but many so-called eccentrics do things that are just as strange. So there is no real difference between insanity and eccentricity.

4. If you try to smoke one cigarette a day, you will end up smoking two and then three and four and five, and so on, until you smoke two packs every day. So don't try even one.

5. A human egg one minute after fertilization is not very different from what it is one minute later, or one minute after that, and so on. Thus, there is really no difference between just-fertilized eggs and adult humans.

6. Since no moment in the continuum of development between an egg and a baby is especially significant, it is not fair to grant a right to life to a baby unless one grants the same right to every fertilized egg.

7. If we let doctors kill dying patients who are in great pain, then they will kill other patients who are in less pain and patients who are only slightly disabled. Eventually, they will kill anyone who is not wanted by society.

EXERCISE V

Explain the reasons, if any, for drawing a definite line in each of the following cases. Then further explain how this line can be drawn, if at all, in a reasonable way.

1. Minimum (or maximum?) age to drive a car
2. Minimum age to vote
3. Minimum age to enter (or be drafted into) the military
4. Minimum age to drink alcoholic beverages
5. Minimum age for election to the U.S. presidency
6. Maximum age before retirement becomes mandatory

EXERCISE VI

Determine whether each of the following arguments provides adequate support, or any support, for its conclusion. Explain why.

1. I shouldn't get a speeding ticket for going fifty-six miles per hour, because my driving did not all of a sudden get more dangerous when I passed the speed limit of fifty-five.
2. No student should ever be allowed to ask a question during a lecture, because once one student asks a question, then another one wants to ask a question, and pretty soon the teacher doesn't have any time left to lecture.
3. Pornography shouldn't be illegal, because you can't draw a line between pornography and erotic art.
4. Marijuana should be legal, because it is no more dangerous than alcohol or nicotine.
5. Marijuana should be illegal, because people who try marijuana are likely to go on to try hashish, and then snorting cocaine, and then freebasing cocaine or shooting heroin.
6. The government should not put any new restrictions on free trade, because once they place some restrictions, they will place more and more until foreign trade is so limited that our own economy will suffer.
7. Governments should never bargain with any terrorist. Once they do, they will have to bargain with every other terrorist who comes along.
8. If assault weapons are banned, Congress will ban handguns next, and then rifles. Eventually, hunters will not be able to hunt, and law-abiding citizens will have no way to defend themselves against criminals.

1. Explain and evaluate the following argument against restrictions on hate speech:

   To attempt to craft free speech exceptions only for racist speech would create a significant risk of a slide down the proverbial "slippery slope." . . . Censorial consequences could result from many proposed or adopted university policies, including the Stanford code, which sanctions speech intended to "insult or stigmatize" on the basis of race or other prohibited grounds. For example, certain feminists suggest that all heterosexual sex is rape because heterosexual men are aggressors who operate in a cultural climate of pervasive sexism and violence against women. Aren't these feminists insulting or stigmatizing heterosexual men on the basis of their sex and sexual orientation? And how about a Holocaust survivor who blames all ("Aryan") Germans for their collaboration during World War II? Doesn't this insinuation insult and stigmatize on the basis of national and ethnic origin? And surely we can think of numerous other examples that would have to give us pause.[2]

2. Explain and evaluate the following response to critics of college restrictions on hate speech:

   [Defenders of such restrictions] will ask whether an educational institution does not have the power . . . to enact reasonable regulations aimed at assuring equal personhood on campus. If one characterizes the issue this way, . . . a different set of slopes will look slippery. If we do not intervene to protect equality here, what will the next outrage be?[3]

3. When John Stewart interviewed William Bennett (former Secretary of Education under President Ronald Reagan) about gay marriage, both of them used slippery slopes and responded to each other's slippery slopes in the following exchange. What kinds of slippery slopes did they use? Was either argument better than the other? Was either response better than the other? Why or why not?

   BENNETT: The question is: How do you define marriage? Where do you draw the line? What do you say to the polygamist?

   STEWART: You don't say anything to the polygamist. That is a choice, to get three or four wives. That is not a biological condition that "I gots to get laid by different women that I am married to." That's a choice. Being gay is part of the human condition. There's a huge difference.

   BENNETT: Well, some people regard their human condition as having three women. Look, the polygamists are all over this.

   STEWART: Then let's go slippery slope the other way. If government says I can define marriage as between a man and a woman, what says they can't define it between people of different income levels, or they can decide whether or not you are a suitable husband for a particular woman?

   BENNETT: Because gender *matters* in marriage, it has mattered to every human society, it matters in every religion . . .

   STEWART: Race matters in every society as well. Isn't progress understanding?

4. What, if anything, is shown when slippery-slope arguments can be used on both sides of an issue?

NOTES

[1] 1471 U.S. 386 (1984). This case was reported by Linda Greenhouse, "Of Tents with Wheels and Houses with Oars," *New York Times*, May 15, 1985.

[2] Nadine Strossen, "Regulating Racist Speech on Campus: A Modest Proposal?" *Duke Law Journal* (1990): 537–38. When she wrote this, Strossen was on the National Board of Directors of the American Civil Liberties Union.

[3] Richard Delgado, "Campus Antiracism Rules: Constitutional Narratives in Collision," *Northwestern University Law Review* 85 (1991): 346.

14

FALLACIES OF AMBIGUITY

This chapter examines fallacies that arise from a second kind of unclarity: ambiguity. *Ambiguity occurs when it is unclear which meaning of a term is intended in a given context. Ambiguity leads to the fallacy of* equivocation, *which will be defined and illustrated. The chapter closes with a discussion of different kinds of definitions that can be useful in avoiding or responding to fallacies of clarity.*

AMBIGUITY

The idea of vagueness is based on a common feature of words in our language: Many of them leave open a range of borderline cases. The notion of *ambiguity* is also based on a common feature of our language: Words often have a number of different meanings. For example, the *New Merriam-Webster Pocket Dictionary* has the following entry under the word "cardinal":

> **cardinal** adj. 1: of basic importance; chief, main, primary,
> 2: of cardinal red color.
>
> n. 1: an ecclesiastical official of the Roman Catholic Church ranking next below the pope,
> 2: a bright red,
> 3: any of several American finches of which the male is bright red.

In the plural, "the Cardinals" is the name of an athletic team that inhabits St. Louis; "cardinal" also describes the numbers used in simple counting.

It is not likely that people would get confused about these very different meanings of the word "cardinal," but we might imagine a priest, a bird-watcher, and a baseball fan all hearing the remark "The cardinals are in town." The priest would prepare for a solemn occasion, the bird-watcher would get out binoculars, and the baseball fan would head for the stadium. In this context, the remark might be criticized as *ambiguous*. More precisely, we shall say that an expression in a given context is *used ambiguously* if and only if it is misleading or potentially misleading because it is hard to tell which of a number of possible meanings is intended in that context.

Using this definition, the word "bank" is *not* used ambiguously in the following sentence:

Joan deposited $500 in the bank and got a receipt.

Some writers, however, call an expression ambiguous simply if it admits of more than one interpretation, without adding that it is not possible to tell which meaning is intended. With this definition, the above sentence is ambiguous because it could mean that Joan placed $500 in a riverbank, and someone, for whatever reason, gave her a receipt for doing so. On this second definition of ambiguity, virtually every expression is ambiguous, because virtually every expression admits of more than one interpretation. On our first definition, only uses of expressions that are misleading or potentially misleading will be called ambiguous. In what follows, we will use the word "ambiguous" in accordance with the first definition. Ambiguity then depends on the context, because whether something is misleading also depends on context.

In everyday life, context usually settles which of a variety of meanings is appropriate. Yet sometimes genuine misunderstandings do arise. An American and a European discussing "football" may have different games in mind. The European is talking about what Americans call "soccer"; the American is talking about what Europeans call "American football." It is characteristic of the ambiguous use of a term that when it comes to light, we are likely to say something like, "Oh, you mean *that* kind of cardinal!" or "Oh, you were talking about *American* football!" This kind of misunderstanding can cause trouble. When it does, if we want to criticize the expression that creates the problem, we call it ambiguous.

Thus, "ambiguous" is both dependent on context and a term of criticism in much the same ways as "vague." But these kinds of unclarity differ in other ways. In a context where the use of a word is ambiguous, it is not clear which of two meanings to attach to a word. In a context where the use of a word is vague, we cannot attach *any* precise meaning to the use of a word.

Frank and Ernest

© 2000 Thaves. Reprinted with permission. Newspaper dist. by NEA, Inc.

So far we have talked about the ambiguity of individual terms or words. This is called *semantic ambiguity*. But sometimes we do not know which interpretation to give to a phrase or a sentence because its grammar or syntax admits of more than one interpretation. This is called *syntactic ambiguity* or *amphiboly*. Thus, if we talk about *the conquest of the Persians*, we might be referring either to the Persians' conquering someone or to someone's conquering the Persians. Sometimes the grammar of a sentence leaves open a great many possible interpretations. For example, consider the following sentence (from Paul Benacerraf):

Only sons marry only daughters.

One thing this might mean is that a person who is a male only child will marry a person who is a female only child. Again, it might mean that sons are the only persons who marry daughters and do not marry anyone else. Other interpretations are possible as well.

The process of rewriting a sentence so that one of its possible meanings becomes clear is called *disambiguating* the sentence. One way of disambiguating a sentence is to rewrite it as a whole, spelling things out in detail. That is how we disambiguated the sentence "Only sons marry only daughters." Another procedure is to continue the sentence in a way that supplies a context that forces one interpretation over others. Consider the sentence "Mary had a little lamb." Notice how the meaning changes completely under the following continuations:

1. Mary had a little lamb; it followed her to school.
2. Mary had a little lamb and then some broccoli.

Just in passing, it is not altogether obvious how we should describe the ambiguity in the sentence "Mary had a little lamb." The most obvious suggestion is that the word "had" is ambiguous, meaning "owned" on the first reading and "ate" on the second reading. Notice, however, that this also forces alternative readings for the expression "a little lamb." Presumably, it was a small, whole, live lamb that followed Mary to school, whereas it would have been a small amount of cooked lamb that she ate. So if we try to locate the ambiguity in particular words, we must say that not only the word "had" but also the word "lamb" are being used ambiguously. This is a reasonable approach, but another is available. In everyday speech, we often leave things out. Thus, instead of saying "Mary had a little *portion of meat derived from a* lamb *to eat*," we simply say "Mary had a little lamb," dropping out the italicized words on the assumption that they will be understood. In most contexts, such deletions cause no misunderstanding. But sometimes deletions are misunderstood, and this can produce ambiguity.

EXERCISE I

Show that each of the following sentences admits of at least two interpretations by (1) rewriting the sentence as a whole in two different ways and (2) expanding the sentence in two different ways to clarify the context:

Example:	Kenneth let us down.
Rewriting:	Kenneth lowered us.
	Kenneth disappointed us.
Expanding:	Kenneth let us down with a rope.
	Kenneth let us down just when we needed him.

(continued)

1. Barry Bonds (the baseball player) was safe at home.
2. I don't know what state Meredith is in.
3. Where did you get bitten?
4. The president sent her congratulations.
5. Visiting professors can be boring.
6. Wendy ran a marathon.
7. The meaning of the term "altering" is changing.
8. I don't want to get too close to him.
9. I often have my friends for dinner.
10. Slow Children Playing. (on a street sign.)
11. Save Soap and Waste Paper. (on a sign during World War II.)
12. In his will, he left $1,000 to his two sons, Jim and John.
13. There is some explanation for everything.
14. She is an Asian historian.
15. Nobody may be in the lounge this evening.
16. Nobody came to the concert at 8 PM.

EXERCISE II

Follow the same instructions for the following actual newspaper headlines, many of which come from Columbia Journalism Review, editors, *Squad Helps Dog Bite Victim and Other Flubs from the Nation's Press* (Garden City, NY: Doubleday, 1980).

1. Milk Drinkers Turn to Powder
2. Anti-busing Rider Killed by Senate
3. Mrs. Gandhi Stoned in Rally in India
4. College Graduates Blind Senior Citizen
5. Jumping Bean Prices Affect the Poor
6. Tuna Biting off Washington Coast
7. Time for Football and Meatball Stew
8. Police Kill Man with Ax
9. Squad Helps Dog Bite Victim
10. Child Teaching Expert to Speak
11. Prostitutes Appeal to Pope
12. Legalized Outhouses Aired by Legislature
13. Police Can't Stop Gambling
14. Judge Permits Club to Continue Sex Bar
15. Greeks Fine Hookers
16. Survivor of Siamese Twins Joins Parents

17. Caribbean Islands Drift to the Left

18. Teenage Prostitution Problem Is Mounting

19. Miners Refuse to Work After Death

20. Police Begin Campaign to Run Down Jaywalkers

21. Red Tape Holds Up New Bridges

22. Juvenile Court to Try Shooting Defendant

23. Kids Make Nutritious Snacks

24. Study of Obesity Looks for Larger Test Group

25. Hospitals Sued by Seven Foot Doctors

26. Local High School Dropouts Cut in Half

27. Iraqi Head Seeks Arms

28. Drunk Gets Nine Months in Violin Case

29. Teacher Strikes Idle Kids

30. British Left Waffles on Falkland Islands

31. Stolen Painting Found by Tree

32. New Vaccine May Contain Rabies

EXERCISE III

Poetry, songs, and jokes often intentionally exploit multiple meanings for effect. Find examples in poems, songs, and jokes that you like. Are these examples of ambiguity on the above definition? Why or why not?

EQUIVOCATION

Ambiguity can cause a variety of problems for arguments. Often it produces hilarious or embarrassing side effects, and it is hard to get your arguments taken seriously if your listeners are giggling over an unintended double entendre in which one of the double meanings has risqué connotations.

Ambiguity can also generate bad arguments that involve the *fallacy of equivocation*. An argument is said to commit this fallacy when it uses the same expression in different senses in different parts of the argument, and this ruins the argument. Here is a silly example (from Carl Wolf):

Six is an odd number of legs for a horse.
Odd numbers cannot be divided by two.

∴ Six cannot be divided by two.

Clearly, "odd" means "unusual" in the first premise, but it means "not even" in the second premise. Consequently, both premises are true, even though the conclusion is false, so the argument is not valid.

Let's consider another, more serious, example. In *Utilitarianism* (1861), John Stuart Mill claims to "prove" that "happiness is a good" with the following argument:

> The only proof capable of being given that an object is visible is that people actually see it. The only proof that a sound is audible is that people hear it. In like manner the sole evidence it is possible to produce that anything is desirable is that people actually desire it. . . . [E]ach person, so far as he believes it to be attainable, desires his own happiness. This, however, being a fact, we have not only all the proof which the case admits of, but all which it is possible to require, that happiness is a good.

Mill has sometimes been charged with committing a transparent fallacy in this passage. Specifically, the following argument is attributed to him:

(1) If something is desired, then it is desirable.
(2) If it is desirable, then it is good.
∴(3) If something is desired, then it is good.

Mill never presents his argument in this form, and it may be uncharitable to attribute it to him. Still, whether it is Mill's way of arguing or not, it provides a good specimen of a fallacy of equivocation.

The objection to this argument is that the word "desirable" is used in different senses in the two premises. Specifically, in the first premise, it is used to mean "capable of being desired," whereas in the second premise, it is used to mean "worthy of being desired." If so, the argument really amounts to this:

(1*) If something is desired, then it is capable of being desired.
(2*) If something is worthy of being desired, then it is good.
∴(3) If something is desired, then it is good.

This argument is clearly not valid. To make the charge of equivocation stick, however, it has to be shown that the argument is not valid when the meaning of the word "desirable" is used in the same sense in the two premises. This produces two cases to be examined:

(1*) If something is desired, then it is capable of being desired.
(2**) If something is capable of being desired, then it is good.
∴(3) If something is desired, then it is good.

We now have a valid argument, but the second premise is not true, for sometimes people are capable of desiring things that are not good. The second way of restoring validity takes the following form:

(1**) If something is desired, then it is worthy of being desired.
(2*) If something is worthy of being desired, then it is good.
∴(3) If something is desired, then it is good.

Again, we have a valid argument, but this time the first premise is false, since sometimes people do desire things that they should not desire. Thus, in both cases, altering the premises to produce a valid argument produces a false premise, so the argument cannot be sound.

This is a pattern that emerges when dealing with arguments that involve the fallacy of equivocation. When the premises are interpreted in a way that produces a valid argument, then at least one of the premises is false. When the premises are interpreted in a way that makes them true, then the argument is not valid. Here, then, is the strategy for dealing with arguments that may involve a fallacy of equivocation:

1. Distinguish the possible meanings of the potentially ambiguous expressions in the argument.

2. For each possible meaning, restate the argument so that each expression clearly has the same meaning in all of the premises and the conclusion.

3. Evaluate the resulting arguments separately.

If the argument fails whenever each term has a consistent meaning throughout the argument, then the argument is guilty of equivocation.

EXERCISE IV

Each of the following arguments trades on an ambiguity. For each, locate the ambiguity by showing that one or more of the statements can be interpreted in different ways.

1. We shouldn't hire Peter, because our company has a policy against hiring drug users, and I saw Peter take aspirin, which is a drug.

2. Man is the only rational animal, and no woman is a man, so women are not rational.

3. My doctor has been practicing medicine for thirty years, and practice makes perfect, so my doctor must be nearly perfect.

4. Our cereal is all natural, for there is obviously nothing supernatural about it.

5. Ice cream is never all natural, since it never appears in nature without human intervention.

6. I have a right to spend all my money on lottery tickets. Therefore, when I spend all my money on lottery tickets, I am doing the right thing.

7. You passed no one on the road; therefore, you walked faster than no one.

8. Everything must have some cause; therefore, something must be the cause of everything.

9. The apostles were twelve. Matthew was an apostle. Hence, Matthew was twelve. (attributed to Bertrand Russell)

10. If I have only one friend, then I cannot say that I have any number of friends. So one is not any number. (from Timothy Duggan)

(continued)

11. "Our bread does have fiber, because it contains wood pulp." (The Federal Trade Commission actually ordered the Continental Baking Company to indicate in their advertising that this is the kind of fiber in their Fresh Horizons bread.)

12. Anyone who tries to violate a law, even if the attempt fails, should be punished. People who try to fly are trying to violate the law of gravity. So they should be punished. (This argument is reported to have been used in an actual legal case during the nineteenth century, but compare Stephen Colbert, "Physics is the ultimate Big Government interference—universal laws meant to constrain us at every turn. . . . Hey, is it wrong that I sometimes want to act without having to deal with an equal and opposite reaction?"[1])

DISCUSSION QUESTIONS

1. When a newspaper was criticized as a scandalous rumormonger, its editor responded with the following argument (as paraphrased by Deni Elliot). Does the editor's argument commit the fallacy of equivocation?

   It's not wrong for newspapers to pass on rumors about sex scandals. Newspapers have a duty to print stories that are in the public interest, and the public clearly has a great interest in rumors about sex scandals, since, when newspapers print such stories, their circulation increases, and they receive a large number of letters.

2. In the following passage, Tom Hill Jr. claims that a common argument against affirmative action commits a fallacy of equivocation. Do you agree that this argument equivocates? Why or why not?

   Some think that the injustice of all affirmative action programs is obvious or easily demonstrated. [One argument] goes this way: "Affirmative action, by definition, gives preferential treatment to minorities and women. This is discrimination in their favor and against non-minority males. All discrimination by public institutions is unjust, no matter whether it is the old kind or the newer 'reverse discrimination.' So all affirmative action programs in public institutions are unjust."

   This deceptively simple argument, of course, trades on an ambiguity. In one sense, to "discriminate" means to "make a distinction," to pay attention to a difference. In this evaluatively neutral sense, of course, affirmative action programs do discriminate. But public institutions must, and justifiably do, "discriminate" in this sense, for example, between citizens and noncitizens, freshmen and seniors, the talented and the retarded, and those who pay their bills and those who do not. Whether it is unjust to note and make use of a certain distinction in a given context depends upon many factors: the nature of the institution, the relevant rights of the parties involved, the purposes and effects of making that distinction, and so on.

   All this would be obvious except for the fact that the word "discrimination" is also used in a pejorative sense, meaning (roughly) "making use of a distinction in an unjust or illegitimate way." To discriminate in this sense is obviously wrong, but now it remains an open question whether the use of gender and race distinctions in affirmative action programs is really "discrimination" in this sense. The simplistic argument uses the evaluatively neutral sense of "discrimination" to show that affirmative action discriminates; it then shifts to the pejorative sense when it asserts that discrimination is always wrong. Although one may, in the end, *conclude* that all public use of racial and gender distinctions is unjust, to do so requires more of an *argument* than the simple one (just given) that merely exploits an ambiguity of the word "discrimination."[2]

3. Many people argue that homosexuality is immoral because it is unnatural. In the following reading,[3] Burton Leiser criticizes this argument for equivocating on five meanings of the term "natural." Does the argument really equivocate? Why or why not?

HOMOSEXUALITY AND NATURAL LAW
---■---

by Burton Leiser

When theologians and moralists speak of homosexuality, contraception, abortion, and other forms of human behavior as being unnatural and say that for that reason such behavior must be considered to be wrong, in what sense are they using the word *unnatural*? Are they saying that homosexual behavior and the use of contraceptives are [1] *contrary to the scientific laws of nature*, are they saying that they are [2] *artificial* forms of behavior, or are they using the terms *natural* and *unnatural* in some third sense?

They cannot mean that homosexual behavior (to stick to the subject presently under discussion) violates the laws of nature in the first sense [including, for example, Boyle's law that the volume of a gas varies inversely with the pressure that is applied to it], for . . . in *that* sense it is impossible to violate the laws of nature. Those laws, being merely descriptive of what actually does happen, would have to *include* homosexual behavior if such behavior does actually take place. . . .

If those who say that homosexual behavior is unnatural are using the term *unnatural* in the second sense as artificial, it is difficult to understand their objection. That which is artificial is often far better than what is natural. . . . [Moreover,] homosexual behavior can hardly be considered unnatural in this sense. There is nothing artificial about such behavior. On the contrary, it is quite natural, in this sense, to those who engage in it. And, even if it were not, this is not in itself a ground for condemning it.

It would seem, then, that those who condemn homosexuality as an unnatural form of behavior must mean something else by the word *unnatural*, something not covered by either of the preceding definitions. A third possibility is this:

3. *Anything uncommon or abnormal is unnatural.* If this is what is meant by those who condemn homosexuality on the ground that it is unnatural, it is quite obvious that their condemnation cannot be accepted without further argument. The fact that a given form of behavior is uncommon provides no justification for condemning it. . . . Great artists, poets, musicians, and scientists are uncommon in this sense; but clearly the world is better off for having them, and it would be absurd to condemn them or their activities for their failure to be common and normal. If homosexual behavior is wrong, then, it must be for some reason other than its unnaturalness in this sense of the word.

(continued)

4. *Any use of an organ or an instrument that is contrary to its principal purpose or function is unnatural.* Every organ and every instrument—perhaps even every creature—has a function to perform, one for which it is particularly designed. Any use of those instruments and organs that is consonant with their purposes is natural and proper, but any use that is inconsistent with their principal functions is unnatural and improper, and to that extent evil or harmful. Human teeth, for example, are admirably designed for their principal functions—biting and chewing the kinds of food suitable for human consumption. But they are not particularly well suited for prying the caps from beer bottles. If they are used for that purpose, they are likely to crack or break under the strain. . . .

What are the sex organs peculiarly suited to do? . . . Our sexual organs are uniquely adapted for procreation, but that is obviously not the only function for which they are adapted. Human beings may—and do—use those organs for a great many other purposes, and it is difficult to see why any *one* use should be considered to be the only proper one. The sex organs seem to be particularly well adapted to give their owners and others intense sensations of pleasure. Unless one believes that pleasure itself is bad, there seems to be little reason to believe that the use of the sex organs for the production of pleasure in oneself or in others is evil. In view of the peculiar design of these organs, with their great concentration of nerve endings, it would seem that they were designed (if they *were* designed) with that very goal in mind, and that their use for such purposes would be no more unnatural than their use for the purpose of procreation.

Nor should we overlook the fact that human sex organs may be and are used to express, in the deepest and most intimate way open to man, the love of one person for another. Even the most ardent opponents of "unfruitful" intercourse admit that sex does serve this function. They have accordingly conceded that a man and his wife may have intercourse even though she is pregnant, or past the age of child bearing, or in the infertile period of her menstrual cycle. . . .

To sum up, then, the proposition that any use of an organ that is contrary to its principal purpose or function is unnatural assumes that organs *have* a principal purpose or function, but this may be denied on the ground that the purpose or function of a given organ may vary according to the needs or desires of its owner. It may be denied on the ground that a given organ may have more than one principal purpose or function, and any attempt to call one use or another the only natural one seems to be arbitrary, if not question-begging. Also, the proposition suggests that what is unnatural is evil or depraved. This goes beyond the pure description of things, and enters into the problem of the evaluation of human behavior, which leads us to the fifth meaning of *natural*.

5. *That which is natural is good, and whatever is unnatural is bad.* . . . Clearly, [people who say this] cannot have intended merely to reduce the word *natural* to a synonym of *good*, *right*, and *proper*, and *unnatural* to a synonym of *evil*, *wrong*, *improper*, *corrupt*, and *depraved*. If that were all they had intended to do, . . . it would follow inevitably that whatever is good must be natural, and vice versa, by definition. This is certainly not what the opponents of homosexuality have been saying when they claim that homosexuality, being unnatural, is evil. For if it were, their claim would be quite empty. They would be saying merely that homosexuality, being evil, is evil—a redundancy that could as easily be reduced to the simpler assertion that homosexuality is evil. This

assertion, however, is not an argument. . . . "Unnaturalness" and "wrongfulness" are not synonyms, then, but different concepts.

The problem with which we are wrestling is that we are unable to find a meaning for *unnatural* that enables us to arrive at the conclusion that homosexuality is unnatural or that if homosexuality is unnatural, it is therefore wrongful behavior. We have examined [five] common meanings of *natural* and *unnatural*, and have seen that none of them performs the task that it must perform if the advocates of this argument are to prevail. Without some more satisfactory explanation of the connection between the wrongfulness of homosexuality and its alleged unnaturalness, the argument [that homosexuality is wrong because it is unnatural] must be rejected.

DEFINITIONS

It is sometimes suggested that a great many disputes could be avoided if people simply took the precaution of defining their terms. To some extent this is true. People do sometimes seem to disagree just because they are using terms in different ways, even though they agree on the nonverbal issues.

Nonetheless, definitions will not solve all problems, and a mindless insistence on definitions can turn a serious discussion into a semantic quibble. If you insist on defining every term, you will never be satisfied, because every definition will introduce new terms to be defined. Furthermore, definitions themselves can be confusing or obfuscating as, for example, when an economist tells us:

I define "inflation" as too much money chasing too few goods.

Not only is this definition metaphorical and obscure, it also has a theory of the causes of inflation built into it.

To use definitions correctly, we must realize that they come in various forms and serve various purposes. There are at least five kinds of definitions that need to be distinguished:

1. *Lexical* or *dictionary definitions* are the most common kind of definition. We consult a dictionary when we are ignorant about the meaning of a word in a particular language. If you do not happen to know what the words "jejune," "ketone," or "Kreis" mean, then you can look these words up in an English, a scientific, and a German dictionary, respectively.

Except for an occasional diagram, dictionaries explain the meaning of a word by using other words that the reader presumably already understands. These explanations often run in a circle, such as when the *Oxford American Dictionary* defines "car" as "automobile" and "automobile" as "car." Circular definitions can still be useful, because if you know what one of the terms in the circle means, you can use that background knowledge plus the definition to figure out what the other terms mean.

The goal of dictionary definitions is to supply us with factual information about the standard meanings of words in a particular language. As dictionary definitions are, in effect, factual claims about how people in general actually use certain words, dictionary definitions can be either accurate or inaccurate. The *Oxford American Dictionary* defines one meaning of "fan" as "a device waved in the hand or operated mechanically to create a current of air." This is, strictly speaking, incorrect because a bellows also meets these conditions but is not a fan. Dictionary definitions can be criticized or defended on the basis of a speaker's sense of the language or, more formally, by empirical surveys of what speakers accept as appropriate or reject as inappropriate uses of the term.

2. *Disambiguating definitions* specify a sense in which a word or phrase is or might be being used by a particular speaker on a particular occasion. ("When I said that the banks were collapsing, I meant river banks, not financial institutions.") Disambiguating definitions can tell us which dictionary definition actually is intended in a particular context, or they can distinguish several meanings that might be intended. They can also be used to remove syntactic ambiguity or amphiboly. ("When I said that all of my friends are not students, I meant that not all of them are students, not that none of them are students.")

Whether the ambiguity is semantic or syntactic, the goal of a disambiguating definition is to capture what the speaker intended, so such definitions can be justified by asking the speaker what he or she meant. This is a different question than asking what a word means. Whereas dictionary definitions say what words mean or how they are used by most speakers of the language, a disambiguating definition focuses on a particular speaker and specifies which meaning that speaker intended on a particular occasion.

Such disambiguating definitions can be used in response to arguments that seem to commit the fallacy of equivocation. A critic can use disambiguating definitions to distinguish possible meanings and then ask, "Did you mean this or that?" The person who gave the argument can answer by picking one of these alternatives or by providing another disambiguating definition to specify what was meant. Speakers are sometimes not sure which meaning they intended, and then the critic needs to show that the argument cannot work if a single disambiguating definition is followed throughout. Whether one sides with the arguer or the critic, arguments that use terms ambiguously cannot be evaluated thoroughly without the help of disambiguating definitions.

3. *Stipulative definitions* are used to assign a meaning to a new (usually technical) term or to assign a new or special meaning to a familiar term. They have the following general form: "By such and such expression I (or we) will mean so and so." Thus, mathematicians introduced the new term "googol" to stand for the number expressed by 1 followed by 100 zeroes. Physicists use words like "charm," "color," and "strangeness" to stand for certain features of subatomic particles. Stipulative definitions do not report

what a word means; they give a new word a meaning or an old word a new meaning.

Notice that if I say, "I stipulate that . . . " I thereby stipulate that . . . ; so such utterances are explicit performatives, and stipulation is a speech act. (See Chapter 2.) This explains why stipulative definitions cannot be false, since no performatives can be false. Stipulative definitions can, however, be criticized in other ways. They can be vague or ambiguous. They can be useless or confusing. Someone who stipulates a meaning for a term might go on to use the term with a different meaning (just as people sometimes fail to keep their promises). Still, stipulative definitions cannot be false by virtue of failing to correspond to the real meaning of a word, because they give that meaning to that word.

4. *Precising definitions* are used to resolve vagueness. They are used to draw a sharp (or sharper) boundary around the things to which a term refers, when this collection has a fuzzy or indeterminate boundary in ordinary usage. For example, it is not important for most purposes to decide how big a population center must be in order to count as a city rather than as a town. We can deal with the borderline cases by using such phrases as "very small city" or "quite a large town." It will not make much difference which phrase we use on most occasions. Yet it is not hard to imagine a situation in which it might make a difference whether a center of population is a city or not. As a city, it might be eligible for development funds that are not available to towns. Here a precising definition—a definition that draws a sharp boundary where none formerly existed—would be useful.

Precising definitions are, in effect, combinations of stipulative definitions and dictionary definitions. Like stipulative definitions, they involve a choice. One could define a city as any population center with more than 50,000 people, or one could decide to decrease the minimum to 30,000 people. Precising definitions are not completely arbitrary, however, because they usually should conform to the generally accepted meaning of a term. It would be unreasonable to define a city as any population center with more than seventeen people. Dictionary definitions, thus, set limits to precising definitions.

Precising definitions are also not arbitrary in another way: There can be good reasons to prefer one precising definition over another, when adopting the preferred definition will have better effects than the alternative. If development funds are to be distributed only to cities, then to define cities as having more than 50,000 people will deny those funds to smaller population centers with, say, 10,000 people. Consequently, we need some reason to resolve the vagueness of the term "city" in one way rather than another. In this case, the choice might be based on the amount of funds available for development. In a more dramatic example, a precising definition of "death" might be used to resolve controversial issues about euthanasia—about what doctors may or must do to patients who are near death—and then our choices between possible precising definitions might be based on our deepest value commitments. In any case, we need some argument to show that one precising definition is better than other alternatives.

Such arguments often leave some leeway. Even if one can justify defining cities as having a minimum of 50,000 people instead of 10,000, one's reason is not likely to justify a cutoff at 50,000 as opposed to 49,000. A different kind of defense would be needed if someone used a slippery-slope argument to show that it is unfair to provide development funds to one city with 50,000 people but to deny such funds to its neighbor with only 49,000 people. Against this kind of charge, the only way to defend a precising definition might be to show that some precising definition is needed, the cutoff should lie inside a certain general area, one's preferred definition does lie within that area, and no alternative is any better. Such responses might also apply to nearby alternatives, but they are still sometimes enough to support a precising definition. If responses like these are not available, then a precising definition can be criticized as unjustified.

5. *Systematic or theoretical definitions* are introduced to give a systematic order or structure to a subject matter. For example, in geometry, every term must be either a primitive (undefined) term or a term defined by means of these primitive terms. Thus, if we take points and distances as primitives, we can define a straight line as the shortest distance between two points. Then, assuming some more concepts, we can define a triangle as a closed figure with exactly three straight lines as sides. By a series of such definitions, the terms in geometry are placed in systematic relationships with one another.

In a similar way, we might try to represent family relationships using only the primitive notions of parent, male, and female. We could then construct definitions of the following kind:

"A is the brother of B." = "A and B have the same parents and A is male."

"A is B's grandmother." = "A is a parent of a parent of B and A is female."[4]

Things become more complicated when we try to define such notions as "second cousin once removed" or "stepfather." Yet, by extending some basic definitions from simple to more complicated cases, all family relationships can be given a systematic presentation.

Formulating systematic definitions for family relationships is relatively easy, but similar activities in science, mathematics, and other fields can demand genius. It often takes deep insight into a subject to see which concepts are genuinely fundamental and which are secondary and derivative. When Sir Isaac Newton defined force in terms of mass and acceleration, he was not simply stating how he proposed to use certain words; he was introducing a fundamental conceptual relationship that improved our understanding of the physical world.

Such theoretical definitions can be evaluated on the basis of whether they really do help us formulate better theories and understand the world. Evaluating theoretical definitions often requires a great deal of empirical investigation. When water was defined as H_2O,[5] this made it possible to formulate more precise laws about how water interacted with other chemicals. Other alternatives were available. Whereas molecules count as H_2O, and hence as water, even if they contain unusual isotopes of hydrogen and oxygen, chemists could define water so that it would have to contain only the most common isotopes of hydrogen and oxygen. Why don't they? Because they discovered that differences among isotopes generally do not affect how molecules of H_2O react with other chemicals. As a result, the simplest and most useful generalizations about the properties of water can be formulated in terms of H_2O without regard to certain isotopes of hydrogen and oxygen. This illustrates one way in which choosing one theoretical definition over another can lead to a better theory.

Definitions can play important roles in the presentation of arguments, but demands for definitions can also hinder the progress of an argument. In the middle of discussions people often ask for definitions or even state, usually with an air of triumph, that everything depends on the way you define your terms. We saw in Chapter 2 that definitions are not always needed, and most issues do not turn on the way in which words are defined. When asked for a definition, it is appropriate to reply: "What sort of definition do you want, and why do you want it?" Of course, if you are using a word in a way that departs from customary usage, or using it in some special way of your own, or using a word that is too vague for the given context, or using a word in an ambiguous way, then the request for a definition is perfectly in order. In such cases, the demand for a definition represents an important move within the argument rather than a distraction from it.

EXERCISE V

Look up lexical or dictionary definitions for the following words. (For fun, you might try to guess the meanings of these words before you look them up, as in the game "Balderdash.")

1. jejune
2. ketone
3. fluvial
4. xebec
5. plangent

EXERCISE VI

1. Give a stipulative definition for the word "klurg."
2. Stipulate a word to stand for the chunks of ice that form under car fenders in winter.
3. Describe something that does not have a common name, for which it would be useful to stipulate a name. Explain how the name would be useful.

Give precising definitions for the following words. In each case, supply a context that gives your precising definition a point.

1. book
2. alcoholic beverage
3. crime
4. warm
5. fast

Give disambiguating definitions for the following words. In each case, supply a context in which your definition might be needed to avoid confusion.

1. run
2. pen
3. game
4. painting
5. fast

Using the notions of parents, male, and female as basic, give systematic definitions of the following family relationships:

1. *A* and *B* are sisters.
2. *A* and *B* are siblings.
3. *A* is *B*'s half-brother.
4. *A* is *B*'s niece.
5. *A* is *B*'s cousin.

1. The United States federal criminal prohibition against torture (18 U.S.C. §§ 2340-2340A) prohibits conduct "specifically intended to inflict severe physical or mental pain or suffering." On August 1, 2002, the United States attorney general's office issued a statement that "severe" pain under the statute was limited to pain "equivalent in intensity to the pain

accompanying serious physical injury, such as organ failure, impairment of bodily function, or even death." (This interpretation was withdrawn in 2004.) What kind of a definition is this? Is it justified or not? What does this controversy show about the nature and importance of definitions?

2. The definition of "sexual relations" was crucial to the issue of whether President Bill Clinton committed perjury. Find and distinguish the various definitions of "sexual relations" at play in the following selection from President Clinton's testimony before the independent counsel, Kenneth Starr, on August 17, 1998.[6] In your opinion, does either President Clinton or the lawyers who are questioning him use definitions improperly? Why or why not?

Q: (BY MR. BITTMAN): Mr. President, were you physically intimate with Monica Lewinsky? . . .

A: (BY PRESIDENT CLINTON): When I was alone with Ms. Lewinsky on certain occasions in early 1996 and once in early 1997, I engaged in conduct that was wrong. These encounters did not consist of sexual intercourse. They did not constitute sexual relations as I understood that term to be defined at my January 17th, 1998 deposition. . . .

Q: Let us then move to the definition that was provided you during your deposition. We will have that marked as Grand Jury Exhibit WJC-2. . . .

> [Definition of Sexual Relations] For the purposes of this deposition, a person engages in "sexual relations" when the person knowingly engages in or causes—(1) contact with the genitalia, anus, groin, breast, inner thigh, or buttocks of any person with an intent to arouse or gratify the sexual desire of any person; (2) contact between any part of the person's body or an object and the genitals or anus of another person; or (3) contact between the genitals or anus of the person and any part of another person's body. "Contact" means intentional touching, either directly or through clothing.

. . . I'm sure you remember from the deposition that paragraph (1) of the definition remained in effect. Judge Wright ruled that that was to be the guiding definition, and that paragraphs (2) and (3) were stricken. . . . I suppose, since you have now read portions of the transcript again, that you were reminded that you did not ask for any clarification of the terms. Is that correct? Of the definition?

A: No, sir. I thought it was . . . a rather strange definition. But it was the one the Judge decided on and I was bound by it. So, I took it. . . .

Q: And you remember that Ms. Lewinsky's affidavit said that she had had no sexual relationship with you. Do you remember that?

A: I do.

Q: And do you remember in the deposition that Mr. Bennett asked you . . . whether the statement that Ms. Lewinsky made in her affidavit was . . . true. And you indicated that it was absolutely correct.

(continued)

A: I did. . . . I believe at the time that she filled out this affidavit, if she believed that the definition of sexual relationship was two people having intercourse, then this is accurate. And I believe that is the definition that most ordinary Americans would give it. If you said Jane and Harry have a sexual relationship, and you're not talking about people being drawn into a lawsuit and being given definitions, and then a great effort to trick them in some way, but you are just talking about people in ordinary conversations, I'll bet the grand jurors, if they were talking about two people they know, and said they have a sexual relationship, they meant they were sleeping together; they meant they were having intercourse together. So, I'm not at all sure that this affidavit is not true and was not true in Ms. Lewinsky's mind at the time she swore it out. . . .

Q: (BY MR. WISENBERG): Mr. President, I want to, before I go into a new subject area, briefly go over something you were talking about with Mr. Bittman. The statement of your attorney, Mr. Bennett, at the Paula Jones deposition, "Counsel is fully aware . . . that Ms. Lewinsky has filed, has an affidavit which they are in possession of saying that there is absolutely no sex of any kind in any manner, shape or form, with President Clinton." That statement is made by your attorney in front of Judge Susan Webber Wright, correct?

A: That's correct.

Q: That statement is a completely false statement. Whether or not Mr. Bennett knew of your relationship with Ms. Lewinsky, the statement that there was "no sex of any kind in any manner, shape or form, with President Clinton," was an utterly false statement. Is that correct?

A: It depends on what the meaning of the word "is" is. If . . . "is" means is and never has been, . . . that is one thing. If it means there is none, that was a completely true statement. . . .

Q: I just want to make sure I understand, Mr. President. Do you mean today that because you were not engaging in sexual activity with Ms. Lewinsky during the deposition that the statement of Mr. Bennett might be literally true?

A: No, sir. I mean that at the time of the deposition, it had been—that was well beyond any point of improper contact between me and Ms. Lewinsky. So that anyone generally speaking in the present tense, saying there is not an improper relationship, would be telling the truth if that person said there was not, in the present tense; the present tense encompassing many months. That's what I meant by that. . . .

Q: If Monica Lewinsky has stated that her affidavit that she didn't have a sexual relationship with you is, in fact, a lie, I take it you disagree with that?

A: No. I told you before what I thought the issue was there. I think the issue is how do you define sexual relationship. And there was no definition

> imposed on her at the time she executed the affidavit. Therefore, she was
> free to give it any reasonable meaning. . . .
>
> **Q:** Well, the grand jury would like to know, Mr. President, why it is that
> you think that oral sex performed on you does not fall within the defini-
> tion of sexual relations as used in your deposition.
>
> **A:** Because that is—if the deponent is the person who has oral sex per-
> formed on him, then the contact is with—not with anything on that list,
> but with the lips of another person. It seems to be self-evident that that's
> what it is. And I thought it was curious. . . .

NOTES

[1] Stephen Colbert, *I Am America (And So Can You!)* (New York: Grand Central Publishing, 2007), 201.

[2] Thomas E. Hill Jr., "The Message of Affirmative Action," in *Autonomy and Self-Respect*, ed. Thomas E. Hill Jr., 193–94 (New York: Cambridge University Press, 1991).

[3] Burton Leiser, "Homosexuality and Natural Law," in *Liberty, Justice and Morals*, 3rd ed., 52–57 (New York: Macmillan, 1986).

[4] Notice that in these definitions an individual word is not defined in isolation. Instead, a whole sentence containing the word is replaced by another whole sentence in which the defined word does not appear. Definitions of this kind are called "contextual definitions" because a context containing the word is the unit of definition. Dictionary, disambiguating, stipulative, and pre-cising definitions can also be presented in this contextual form.

[5] If you doubt that the identity "Water is H_2O" is used as a definition, just consider how you would react to someone who claims to have discovered some water that is *not* H_2O. We would dismiss this person as linguistically confused, as the discovered stuff cannot properly be called "water" if it is not H_2O.

[6] Reprinted in Kenneth Starr, *Appendices to the Referral . . . by the Office of the Independent Counsel . . .* (House Document 105-311) (Washington, DC: U.S. Government Printing Office, 1998), 393, 460–61, 464, 466, 469–70, 472–74, 509–10, 571–72, 601–2.

15

FALLACIES OF RELEVANCE

This chapter will consider a different kind of defect in arguments. Fallacies of relevance *arise when a premise, true or not, is not adequately related to the conclusion. Such irrelevance comes in endless varieties, but we will focus on two of the most common forms:* arguments ad hominem *and* appeals to authority. *Arguments of these kinds are not always fallacious, so we will discuss various factors that determine when such arguments are defective and when they are not.*

RELEVANCE

In a good argument, we present statements that are true in order to offer support for some conclusion. One way to depart from this ideal is to state things that are true themselves, but have no bearing on the truth of the conclusion.

We might wonder why irrelevant remarks can have any influence at all. The answer is that we generally assume that a person's remarks are relevant, for this is one of the conditions for smooth and successful conversation (as Grice pointed out in his rule of Relevance, discussed in Chapter 2). That it is possible to exploit people by violating this natural assumption is shown in the following passage from *The Catcher in the Rye*.

> The new elevator boy was sort of on the stupid side. I told him, in this very casual voice, to take me up the Dicksteins'. . . .
>
> He had the elevator doors all shut and all, and was all set to take me up, and then he turned around and said, "They ain't in. They're at a party on the fourteenth floor."
>
> "That's all right," I said. "I'm supposed to wait for them. I'm their nephew."
>
> He gave me this sort of stupid, suspicious look. "You better wait in the lobby, fella," he said.
>
> "I'd like to—I really would," I said. "But I have a bad leg. I have to hold it in a certain position. I think I'd better sit down in the chair outside their door."
>
> He didn't know what the hell I was talking about, so all he said was "oh" and took me up. Not bad, boy. It's funny. All you have to do is say something nobody understands and they'll do practically anything you want them to.[1]

It is clear what is going on here. When you offer something as a reason, it is conversationally implied that there is some connection between it and the thing you are arguing for. In most cases, the connection is obvious, and there is no need to spell it out. In other cases, the connection is not obvious, but in the spirit of cooperation others are willing to assume that the connection exists. In the present case, there seems to be no connection between having a bad leg and sitting in one particular chair. Why, then, does the elevator operator not challenge this statement? Part of the reason is that it is not easy to challenge what people say; among other things, it is not polite. But politeness does not seem to hold the elevator operator back; instead, he does not want to appear stupid. The person who offers a reason conversationally implies a connection, and we do not like to admit that we fail to see this connection. This combination of generosity and fear of looking stupid leads us to accept all sorts of irrelevant statements as reasons.

Fallacies of relevance are surprisingly common in everyday life. People often introduce irrelevant details or tangents in order to mislead by diverting attention from the real issue. The irrelevant distraction is sometimes described as a *red herring* (after a man who dragged a red herring across his trail in order to throw pursuing hounds off his scent). The best strategy for dealing with such tricks is simply to cross out all irrelevant claims and then see what is left. Sometimes nothing is left.

On the other hand, we should not be heavy-handed in making charges of irrelevance. Sometimes the occurrence of irrelevance is innocent; good arguments often contain irrelevant asides. More important, relevance is often secured by way of a conversational implication, so we really have to know what is going on in a given context to decide whether a remark is relevant or not. We can illustrate this last point by examining two kinds of arguments that often involve fallacies of irrelevance: *arguments ad hominem* and *appeals to authority*.

AD HOMINEM ARGUMENTS

Literally, an argument ad hominem is an argument directed against a person who is making a claim rather than against that person's claim or argument for it. On the face of it, this move seems to involve irrelevance, for the character or social position or status of a person should have nothing to do with the truth of what that person says or with the soundness or strength of that person's arguments. Even when protesters dress shabbily or fail to bathe, their clothing and hygiene show nothing about the legitimacy of their protest. A speaker's ethnicity, race, sex, or sexual orientation almost never give us any good reason to challenge the truth of what that person says or the soundness of his or her argument. And the fact that a judge was appointed by a Democrat (or Republican) does not show that the judge's legal decisions are incorrect or unfounded. Ad hominem fallacies very often deal in such irrelevant personal characteristics. They are often introduced just to distract us from the real point at issue.

In rare and unusual cases, however, a speaker's character or position *is* a reason to doubt the truth of what he says. Suppose that Lucy is suspected of committing murder, but Louie testifies that he was with her at the time of the murder. Then the prosecution shows that Louie provided a similar alibi for an accused murderer at ten trials in the past year, and every time he was found to have lied in exchange for money. Louie never testifies without being paid, he says whatever he is paid to say, and people do not hire him if they have any better defense. This background about Louie provides some reason to believe that what Louie said was false—that he was not with Lucy at the time of the murder. Lucy still might not have committed the murder, but we can't take Louie's word for it. Ad hominem arguments like this can be called *deniers*, since they deny the truth of what is said or the strength or soundness of an argument. Although most ad hominem deniers are fallacious, the case of Louie shows that a few are not.

A different kind of ad hominem argument questions a person's right to make a claim or present an argument. Imagine that the Senate is debating tax rates. During one session, Tad stands up and argues for a reduction in taxes. Tad can be criticized if he is not a senator, because then he lacks the status that confers the right to speak in this setting. Even outside of any formal institution, if a neighbor tells someone that she ought to take her children to a certain church, the mother might respond, "Mind your own business, you busybody." Responses like this can be called *silencers*, because they revoke the right to speak without necessarily denying the truth of what is said.

A third variety of ad hominem argument is more subtle. Consider the following exchange:

NORM: The cold war is over, and bad relations between Cuba and the United States hurt both countries, so it is time for the United States to develop normal relations with Cuba.

CLIFF: Yeah, so you can make a bundle importing cigars from those commies.

Cliff's reply is an attack on the motives of Norm and not on the truth of what Norm said. Nor is Cliff denying that Norm has a right to speak. Yet the remark is not without some relevance—it is not off the wall. In a conversational exchange, we rely on the integrity of the person who is speaking, and when we have reasons to believe that the person's integrity is questionable, we sometimes say so. This is the significance of Cliff's remark. Cliff points to a fact that gives some reason for us not to trust Norm's integrity in a discussion of the United States' relations with Cuba.

Cliff's attack might or might not be justified. If the only reason why Norm favors normal relations between the United States and Cuba is that this would enable Norm to make more money, then Cliff's ad hominem attack is well founded. But if Norm's real reason for saying what he does is that he honestly believes that normal relations would be beneficial both to the

United States and to Cuba, then Norm's position does not depend on any lack of integrity. In that case, Cliff's attack is not well founded, even if it so happens that Norm would profit from normal relations.

Whether justified or not, ad hominem arguments of this third variety can be called *dismissers*, because they dismiss the speaker as untrustworthy and unreliable. Their point is not to deny the truth of the claim or the speaker's right to say it. Instead, a dismisser is supposed to show why the fact that this speaker supports a claim is not a good reason to believe that claim (or to deny it, for that matter).

These three variations are all ad hominem arguments because they start from premises about the person's character or status. Where they differ is in their conclusions: Deniers conclude that a claim is untrue or that an argument is unsound or weak. Silencers conclude that someone lacks the right to speak in a certain context. Dismissers conclude that someone is untrustworthy or unreliable. Each can be either justified or unjustified, so there are six kinds that can be diagrammed like this:

Ad Hominem Arguments	Justified	Not Justified
Deniers	Louie, the hired perjurer	Shabby protesters
Silencers	Tad if he is not a senator	Tad if he is a senator
Dismissers	Cliff's reply if Norm lacks integrity	Cliff's reply if Norm does not lack integrity

What logicians usually call ad hominem fallacies are unjustified deniers. Even when the premises of such an argument are true, they are irrelevant to the conclusion. That makes them fallacies of relevance. Once you get used to spotting ad hominem fallacies, they seem common and obvious.

When assessing an ad hominem argument, the first step is to determine whether its conclusion is about someone's right to speak, about someone's reliability, or about the truth, soundness, or strength of what is claimed. The second step is to determine whether its premises provide adequate justification for its conclusion. These steps will enable you to place the argument in the above table, but they will often not be easy or obvious. Although perjurers for hire almost always lie, most people exhibit some middling degree of reliability. When people are known for passing on rumors without checking their truth, this might be a reason to doubt what they say when they pass on yet another rumor (even if it is not a reason to believe that what they say is false). In assessing what they say, it would be best to look for additional evidence. If none is available, then we need to ask how often their testimony is true on matters of this kind. Only by careful inspection of individual cases can we determine the strength of such ad hominem arguments.

A related case occurs when someone is accused of inconsistency over time. If your neighbor says that the best time to prune roses is in the autumn, but then the next spring she tells you that the spring is the best time to prune roses, this inconsistency would give you some reason to doubt her expertise as a gardener. Maybe over the winter she got new information that changed her mind, but her reliability is in question until you have some explanation of why she would say different things at different times. If she wavers between contrary positions, no more than half of her views can be correct, so you have reason to ask your neighbor, "Why should I trust you?"

What she is saying now still might be correct. Maybe spring is the right time to prune roses. Moreover, if she gave an argument for her claim (such as that pruned roses grow back more quickly in the spring, and it is better to prune roses when they grow back more quickly), then that argument still might be sound. Her current claim and argument do not depend on what she said last fall. For this reason, it is normally a fallacy to reject people's views on the basis of an inconsistency with their views at other times. Their current positions need to be assessed as they stand now. (Whether we want political leaders whose views blow with the wind is, of course, another issue.)

A different kind of inconsistency occurs in the traditional fallacy called *tu quoque*, a Latin term that means "you are another." When a parent tells a child to quit smoking, the child might respond, "Look who's talking. You've been smoking for years. If it's so bad, why don't you stop?" The force of this charge might be just that the parent is hypocritical or that one has no right to criticize others for doing something that one does oneself. If that is the point, this response is a silencer, and it might or might not be justified. In any case, the parent's smoking does not give any reason at all to conclude that smoking is not bad. To use a *tu quoque* argument to reach *that* conclusion would be an unjustified denier (and an ad hominem fallacy). Even hypocrites can make true claims and give good arguments. Thus, to show that someone's claims and arguments are defective, one normally needs to look at those claims and arguments themselves, not at the behavior of the speaker.

Instead of citing past beliefs or acts of a speaker, some ad hominem arguments aim at the source or origin of the speaker's belief. Stephen Colbert, for example, dismisses scientists by explaining how they got caught up in science: "They're physically awkward and lonely, so they spent their adolescence down by the creek studying the creatures that live there. 'I may be ridiculed at school,' they think, 'but a crawfish would never judge me.'"[2] This parody, of course, is supposed to show how silly it is to reject science because of its origin (even if this origin were plausible). When its origin is irrelevant to the truth of a claim, such arguments commit what is called the *genetic fallacy*. Whole movements are sometimes accused of genetic fallacies. Marxists often reject opposing views because those views arose under capitalism. Freudians sometimes dismiss critics on the basis of how those critics were raised as children. Usually, the same kind of argument is available to their opponents as well. Critics of Freud sometimes cite his childhood and training to explain away his views. The fact that genetic arguments can be used just as well for contrary conclusions suggests that they do not really support either side.

The problem with genetic arguments is that lots of good ideas have questionable origins. Much mathematics originated within Pythagorean cults. Gravity and much of chemical theory were first discussed by alchemists who were trying to turn lead into gold. The structure of the benzene ring is reported to have come to Kekule von Stradonitz in a dream about a snake biting its tail. Early religions were close to magic and were used by rich and powerful leaders to control their subordinates. In all of these cases, the origin of the ideas cannot be used to refute those views or the arguments for them. Learning the genesis of an idea can help improve one's understanding of its content and of the process of discovery. Origins sometimes indicate where to look for evidence or for objections. Still, to evaluate an idea or an argument, one should focus on that idea or argument, not on its origin.

EXERCISE I

For each of the following arguments, indicate whether it involves (1) an ad hominem denier against a speaker's claim or argument, (2) an ad hominem silencer against a person's right to speak, (3) an ad hominem dismisser against someone's trustworthiness, or (4) none of these. Explain your answer. Be sure to focus on what is explicitly said and not on what might be conversationally implied in each example.

Example: Sure, Sara says she saw me cheat in the game, but Sara's stupid, so you shouldn't pay any attention to her.

Answer: This is an ad hominem dismisser, since the point is that Sara is unreliable. The speaker does not deny what Sara says or that she has a right to say it.

1. Sure, Sadie says she saw me cheat, but it was very dark, and her vision is horrible, so she must have seen something else and thought it was me cheating.

2. Sure, Sam says he saw me cheat, but the only reason he says it is that he wants to win the game. He's a real jerk.

3. Sure, Steve says she saw me cheat, but he wasn't even playing the game. It's not his place to accuse those of us who were playing.

4. Sure, Sybill says she saw me cheat, but I didn't even take the exam, so I couldn't have cheated on it.

5. Sure, Sally says she saw me cheat, but she accuses everyone, and she's almost always wrong, so you should know that she is wrong this time, too.

EXERCISE II

Explain the point of each of the following remarks. Indicate whether each remark involves an ad hominem silencer, dismisser, denier, or none of these. Then say whether the argument provides an adequate justification for its conclusion, and why or why not.

1. The American Tobacco Company has argued for years that smoking is not really unhealthy, but what would you expect the company to say? It would take the same position regardless of any evidence, so I can't trust them.

2. The Joint Chiefs of Staff argue that the U.S. government needs to increase its military budget, but an opponent responds, "Well, of course, *they* will want as much money as they can get for their departments. They always ask for more money even though most of the time they don't really need it. So this time, again, they probably don't need it."

3. After Congress passes a military draft during a war, an opponent says, "If members of Congress were eligible for the draft, they would not vote for it. So we must not really need a draft."

4. Of course, the party in power is opposed to term limits. That's just because they want to stay in power.

5. The main opposition to tax reductions comes from people who depend on government programs funded by taxes, so they can hardly be impartial, but only those who are impartial should be allowed to speak on such a crucial issue for our whole country.

6. The main support for tax reductions comes from people who pay taxes, so their views can't be a reliable indicator of what the best policy is.

7. Very few citizens have studied the entire tax code, and nobody understands the effect of taxes on the economy, so we have little reason to believe them when they say that present tax policies will destroy the economy.

8. An economist cites recent trends in sales of raw materials as evidence of an upturn in the economy, and then a critic, who doubts the economist's prediction, responds, "If you're so smart, why ain't you rich?"

9. As a criticism of pro-choice activists, Ronald Reagan said, "I've noticed that everybody who is for abortion has already been born."

10. Attacking male opponents of abortion, a feminist claims, "Most opponents of abortion are men."

11. When a member of a fraternity argued for co-ed houses in place of fraternities, a critic responded, "When he quits his fraternity in protest and joins a co-ed house, then he will earn the right to criticize us."

12. When Fred argues at a fraternity meeting that his house should admit women, another member announces, "Let me remind you all that Fred held exactly the opposite position last year."

13. Let he who is without sin among you cast the first stone. (John 8:7)

DISCUSSION QUESTIONS

1. In a heated discussion, people will sometimes ask an opponent, "Why are you being so defensive?" This is obviously a rhetorical question. What is the point of this question? Does it implicitly involve an ad hominem fallacy?

2. In the biblical story of Job, Job is described as a person who "was blameless and upright, one who feared God and turned away from evil" (Job 1:1). Satan challenges God to allow him to subject Job to the worst

(continued)

calamities to see if Job's faith will remain unchanged. After the most extreme misfortunes, Job finally cries out and asks why he should be made to suffer so (Job 38:1–4):

> Then the Lord answered Job out of the whirlwind:
> Who is this that darkens counsel by words without knowledge?
> Gird up your loins like a man.
> I will question you, and you shall declare to me.
> Where were you when I laid the foundation of the earth?
> Tell me, if you have understanding.

Does God's response to Job involve an ad hominem silencer, dismisser, or denier? Is it justified? Why or why not?

3. Nietzsche is often accused of committing the genetic fallacy when he uses speculation about the origin of Christian moral beliefs as part of his critique of what he called slave morality. In your opinion, does Nietzsche commit a genetic fallacy in the following passage? Why or why not? Can the origin of a moral belief ever show that that moral belief is false or unjustified or indefensible? Why or why not?

> Let us articulate this new demand: we need a critique of moral values, the value of these values themselves must first be called into question—and for that there is needed a knowledge of the conditions and circumstances in which they grew, under which they evolved and changed, . . . a knowledge of a kind that has never yet existed or even been desired. One has taken the value of these "values" as given, as factual, as beyond all question; one has hitherto never doubted or hesitated in the slightest degree in supposing "the good man" to be of greater value than "the evil man," of greater value in the sense of furthering the advancement and prosperity of man in general (the future of man included). But what if the reverse were true? What if a symptom of regression were inherent in the "good," likewise a danger, a seduction, a poison, a narcotic, through which the present was possibly living at the expense of the future? Perhaps more comfortably, less dangerously, but at the same time in a meaner style, more basely?—So that precisely morality would be to blame if the highest power and splendor actually possible to the type man was never in fact attained? So that precisely morality was the danger of dangers?[3]

APPEALS TO AUTHORITY

Often in the midst of an argument, we cite an authority to back up what we say. As we saw in Chapter 3, this is a standard way of offering assurances. In citing an authority, instead of giving reasons for what we say, we indicate that someone (the authority cited) could give them.

Although logicians sometimes speak of the *fallacy* of appealing to authorities, there is often nothing wrong with citing authorities or experts to support what we say. An authority is a person or institution with a privileged position concerning certain information. Through training, a doctor is an expert on certain diseases. A person who works in the Department of Agriculture can be an expert on America's soybean production. Someone who grew up in the swamps might be an expert on trapping muskrats. Because some people stand in a better position to know things than others, there is nothing improper about citing them as authorities. In fact, an appeal to experts and authorities is essential if we are to make up our minds on subjects outside our own range of competence.

At the same time, appeals to authority can be abused, and there are some obvious questions we should ask whenever such an appeal is made. Most obviously, we should always ask whether the person cited is, in fact, an authority at all. Moreover, it is not enough to be an authority in some area or other. We need to ask whether the person cited is an authority in the particular area under discussion. If the answer to this question is "No," then we are dealing with a *fallacy of relevance*. For example, being a movie star does not qualify a person to speak on the merits of a particular brand of toothpaste. Endorsements by athletes of hair creams, deodorants, beer, and automobiles are in the same boat. Of course, we have to be careful in making this charge. It is possible that certain athletes make systematic studies of deodorants before giving one deodorant their endorsement. But it is not likely.

Most people realize that athletes, movie stars, and the like are featured in advertisements primarily to attract attention and not because they are experts concerning the products they are endorsing. It is more surprising how often the wrong authorities are brought in to judge serious matters. To cite one example, Uri Geller had little difficulty convincing a group of distinguished British scientists that he possessed psychic powers. In particular, he was able to convince them that he could bend spoons by mental powers alone. In contrast, James Randi, a professional magician, had little difficulty detecting and duplicating the tricks that bamboozled the scientific observers. The remarkable feature of this case was not that a group of scientists could be fooled by a magician, but rather that these scientists assumed that they had the expertise necessary to decide whether a paranormal phenomenon had taken place or not. After all, the most obvious explanation of Geller's feats was that he had somehow cheated. To test this possibility, what was needed was not a scientist with impeccable scholarly credentials, but a magician who could do the same tricks himself and therefore knew what to look for.[4]

It is, of course, difficult to decide whether someone is an expert in a field when you yourself are not, but certain clues will help you make this decision. If the supposed authority claims to have knowledge of things that he or she could not possibly possess (for example, about private conversations the person could not have heard), then you have little reason to trust other things that person has to say. You know that he or she has no qualms about making things up. Furthermore, it is often possible to spot-check certain claims in order to make sure that they are correct. It may take one expert to determine another, but it often takes little more than good common sense and an unwillingness to be fooled to detect a fraud.

Even when it is clear that the person cited is an expert in the appropriate field, we can still ask whether the question is of the kind that can now be settled by an appeal to experts. One sign that a question cannot yet be settled by experts is that experts in that area do not agree with each other. It does not do much good to cite one authority in support of a claim if another authority with just as much expertise would endorse the opposite claim. Moreover, even the best experts sometimes simply get things wrong. For example, in 1932 Albert Einstein, who was surely an expert in the field, declared, "There is not the slightest indication that [nuclear] energy will ever be obtainable. It would mean that the atom would have to be shattered at will." Just a year later, the atom was, in fact, split. Even so, a leading British physicist, Ernest Lord Rutherford, insisted that the splitting of the atom would not lead to the development of nuclear power, saying, "The energy produced by the atom is a very poor kind of thing. Anyone who expects a source of power from the transformation of these atoms is talking moonshine."[5] Given the knowledge available at the time, both Einstein and Rutherford may have been justified in their claims, but their assertions were, after all, more speculations than scientifically supported statements of fact. The lesson to be learned from this is that the best experts are sometimes fallible, and become more fallible when they go beyond established facts in their discipline to speculate about the future.

Although the next question may seem obvious, we often forget to ask whether the authority has been cited correctly. When a person cites an authority, he or she is making a factual claim that so-and-so holds some particular view. Sometimes the claim is false. If someone told you, "According to medical authorities, the rash from poison ivy is contagious when it is oozing," you would probably believe it. In fact, the citation is incorrect. According to medical authorities, the rash from poison ivy is never contagious. Yet many people hold that it is contagious, and they think that they have medical opinion on their side. It is hard to deal with people who cite authorities incorrectly, for we do not carry an almanac or encyclopedia around with us. Yet, again, it is a good idea to spot-check appeals to authority, for people often twist authorities to support their own opinions.

It is also worth asking whether the authority cited can be trusted to tell the truth. To put this more bluntly, we should ask whether a particular authority has any good reason to lie or misrepresent facts. Presumably, the officials who know most about food production in China will be the heads of the various agricultural bureaus. But it would be utterly naive to take their reports at face value. Inadequate agricultural production has been a standing embarrassment of the Chinese economy. As a consequence, there is pressure at every level to make things look as good as possible. Even if the state officials were inclined to tell the truth, which is a charitable assumption, the information they receive is probably not very accurate.

Experts also lie because it can bring fame and professional advancement. Science, sometimes at the highest level, has been embarrassed by problems of the falsification and misrepresentation of data. Consider the case of Sir Cyril Burt's research on the inheritance of intelligence. Burt wanted to show that there is a significant correlation between the IQs of parents and their children.

The difficulty was to find a way to screen out other influences—for example, that of home environment. To overcome this, Burt undertook a systematic study of identical twins who had been separated at birth and raised in various social settings. His study revealed a very high correlation between the IQs of these twins, and that gave strong reason to believe that IQ, to some significant extent, depends on heredity rather than environment.

Unfortunately, Burt's data, or at least a significantly large portion of them, were cooked—that is, made up. It is interesting that Burt's bogus research could go unchallenged for so long. It is also interesting how he was finally unmasked. First, to many his results seemed too good to be true. He claimed to have found more than fifty identical twins who had been separated at birth and raised in contrasting environments. Given the rarity of such creatures, that is a very large number to have found. Second, the correlations he claimed to find were extremely high—indeed, much higher than those usually found in research in this area. Both of these facts raised suspicions. Stephen Jay Gould describes Burt's final undoing as follows:

> Princeton psychologist Leon Kamin first noted that, while Burt had increased his sample of twins from fewer than twenty to more than fifty in a series of publications, the average correlation between pairs for IQ remained unchanged to the third decimal place—a statistical situation so unlikely that it matches the vernacular definition of impossible. Then, in 1976, Oliver Gillie, medical correspondent of the London *Sunday Times,* elevated the charge from inexcusable carelessness to conscious fakery. Gillie discovered, among many other things, that Burt's two "collaborators" . . . the women who supposedly collected and processed his data, either never existed at all, or at least could not have been in contact with Burt while he wrote the papers bearing their names.[6]

Of course, Burt's claims still might be correct: genes and IQ might be correlated. Nonetheless the point here is just that Burt and his studies should not be trusted as authorities. Outright fraud of this kind by someone so prominent is rare, but even a few cases provides a reason for being suspicious of authorities, at least when their results have not been given independent confirmation.

One last question we can ask is why the appeal to authority is being made at all. To cite an authority is to give assurances. As we noticed in Chapter 3, people usually give assurances to strengthen weak points in their arguments. It is surprising how often we can see what is wrong with an argument just by noticing where it is backed by appeals to authority. Beyond this, we should be suspicious of arguments that rely on too many authorities. (We might call this the fallacy of *excessive footnotes*.) Good arguments tend to stand on their own.

To summarize, reliance on experts and authorities is unavoidable in our complicated and specialized world. Yet we still need to be critical of appeals to authority by asking these questions:

1. Is the cited authority in fact an authority in the appropriate area?
2. Is this the kind of question that can now be settled by expert consensus?

3. Has the authority been cited correctly?

4. Can the cited authority be trusted to tell the truth?

5. Why is an appeal to authority being made at all?

If the answers to questions 1–4 are "Yes," then the appeal to authority is probably justified. Still, even the best authorities make mistakes, so the conclusion of any appeal to authority might turn out to be false. We can reduce errors by appealing to better authorities, but no authority can guarantee the truth.

EXERCISE III

Answer the five questions in the text about each of the following appeals to authority, and then decide whether each appeal to authority is legitimate or fallacious.

1. The surgeon general says that smoking is hazardous to your health, so it is.

2. The surgeon general says that abortion is immoral, so it is.

3. Michael Jordan says that Air Jordan sneakers are springier, so they must be springier.

4. This must be a great movie, because the billboard says that *Time* magazine called it "terrific."

5. My friend Joe says that this new movie is hilarious, so it must be worth watching.

6. Ben and Jerry's ice cream must be the best, because Fat Fred eats more ice cream than anyone else I know, and he says that Ben and Jerry's is the best.

7. There must be life on other planets, because many great scientists are looking for it, so they must think it is there.

8. Lefty Lopez must be the best pitcher of the year, because he won the Cy Young Award (awarded by the Baseball Writers Association to the best pitcher of the year).

9. Vanna must be the most beautiful woman in America, because she won the Miss America contest.

10. There were 250,000 protesters at the rally, because organizers gave that figure.

11. There were 25,000 protesters at the rally, because its opponents said so.

12. True Christians ought to give away all their money, because the Bible says, "Blessed are the poor."

MORE FALLACIES OF RELEVANCE

Questions like those used to evaluate appeals to authority can also be used to assess some other common styles of reasoning that are often accused of being fallacious. Here is one example:

The American people are convinced that, if we get involved in North Korea, we will be stuck there for a long time. So we shouldn't invade in the first place.

This argument, of course, depends on suppressed premises. On one reconstruction, the argument is that, because Americans fear getting stuck in North Korea, they oppose American involvement, and a democratic government should not do what the people oppose, so we should not get involved in North Korea. The argument also seems to suggest another reason why America should not get involved—namely, that if we do, our troops will be stuck in North Korea. The only reason given for believing this is that lots of American people believe it. So the argument seems to be that, because so many Americans believe it, it must be true.

Such an argument is not an appeal to authority, since no person is claimed to be an authority or an expert. Instead, the argument is an *appeal to popular opinion*. When the popular opinion is supposed to have been shared for a long time, the argument can be called an *appeal to tradition*. Such arguments assume that, when many people agree on some issue or agree for a long time, they are likely to be right. This assumption is often incorrect. An opinion might be shared by many people just because they all learned it from a common source, such as television or some prominent politicians. Then the shared opinion is not reliable unless its source is reliable. Of course, the shared opinion *might* be true; America might get stuck in North Korea if it got involved. But the argument for this conclusion is still fallacious, because the mere fact that an opinion is widely held is not enough to show that the opinion is true.

Although such appeals to popular opinion are often fallacious, there are also some areas where popular opinion is evidence of truth. If most people think that a book is entertaining and easy to understand, then it is entertaining and easy to understand. If most people think that the sky looks blue, this is evidence that the sky does look blue. Thus, not all appeals to popular opinion are defective or fallacious.

To determine whether or not a particular appeal to popular opinion is fallacious, we need to ask questions that are much like the questions we asked about appeals to authority. These include:

1. Is this opinion actually widely held?
2. Is this the kind of area where popular opinion is likely to be right?
3. Why is an appeal to popular opinion being made at all?

Even when superficial examination reveals that an appeal to popular opinion is fallacious, such arguments still seem to convince many people. This might be because many people want to agree with others so that they will be popular and will not have to think for themselves.

Other appeals are not to beliefs, but instead to emotions. One common form of appeal to emotion is an *appeal to pity*. Defense lawyers often dwell on the sad circumstances in which a defendant grew up or on how badly the defendant's family will be hurt if the defendant goes to prison. Such an appeal to pity might show that the defendant should not receive the maximum sentence. But when such an appeal to pity is used to argue that the defendant is not guilty or should not be found guilty, then the argument is almost always fallacious.

Appeals to fear are also common, especially since al Qaeda's destruction of the World Trade Center towers in New York on September 11, 2001. After another terrorist attack occurred in London in 2005, television news anchors and talk-show hosts flashed headlines like "Who's at risk?", "Are we next in America?", "How safe are we in America?", "How prepared are we?", "Can we prevent a subway or a bus attack in the US?", and "You have to wonder, will we ever truly feel safe again?" To be fair, televisions stations asked these questions because they knew that their audiences wanted answers to those very questions. A problem arises only when the media stirs up fears and fails to provide a balanced estimation of the real dangers. Such fearmongering is parodied in Stephen Colbert's segment, "The Threat Down," which lists more and more outrageous fears. An even more serious problem arises when politicians use exaggerated fears to gain support for costly policies that could not be justified by the actual threats that people face. Of course, it is controversial how much fear and which policies are justified. Democrats accuse Republicans of distortion when Republicans use fear of terrorism to justify their counterterrorist policies; Republicans accuse Democrats of exaggeration when Democrats paint a scary picture of the effects of global warming. Defenders of any particular policy can reply that it really is needed to ward off peril. Some fears are justified, including some fears of terrorism and of global warming, of course. Appeals to fear are fallacious only when they are overdone or exaggerated in order to lead people away from an accurate assessment of the risks that really exist. But this happens all-too often; so, whenever anyone appeals to fear, we need to ask whether those fears are being amplified and abused.

Outrage is another emotion that many arguments appeal to. On Day 3 of the 2004 Republican National Convention, for example, Democratic Senator Zell Miller proclaimed, "Today's Democratic leaders see America as an occupier, not a liberator; and nothing makes this marine madder than someone calling American troops occupiers rather than liberators!" This line drew thunderous applause, even though Miller did not give any reason either against calling American troops occupiers or for describing them as liberators. Nonetheless, a receptive audience will tend to assume that, if such an impressive speaker is *that* outraged (and if others in the audience share that outrage), then there must be something terribly objectionable about whatever the outrage is directed against. To assess such appeals to outrage, as for other emotions, we need to become aware of these common assumptions so that they can be critically evaluated.

Appeals to emotion can also be positive. Many advertisements work by linking a product to positive feelings. Everyone knows that a car does not become better just because it is displayed in beautiful scenery, but it is amazing how much the scenery in advertisements can affect people's inclinations to buy a certain car. Similarly, advocates of a treaty or government program often paint pictures of how wonderful life will be if the treaty or program works out well. Such appeals to emotion might provide some reason to adopt their plan, but these arguments can be very misleading if it is unlikely that everything will work out so well and if serious dangers will arise when something goes wrong.

Thus, even when emotional reactions are relevant to some extent, one must be careful not to let them cloud the other side of the issue.

EXERCISE IV

For each of the following arguments, indicate whether it is an appeal to popular opinion, an appeal to tradition, or an appeal to emotion. (The argument might fit into more than one of these categories. If so, explain why.) Then determine whether it is fallacious, and why.

1. For centuries throughout Europe, women were burned for being witches, so there must have been lots of witches.

2. There must be life on other planets, because most people think there is. Just read a few tabloids.

3. Most people who live in the United States think that it is the greatest country ever, so it must be.

4. There are more Buddhists than followers of any other religion, so there must be more truth in Buddhism.

5. Incest must be immoral, because people all over the world for many centuries have seen it as immoral.

6. The Golden Rule is accepted in almost every system of ethics both in the past and in the present, so there is probably something to it.

7. Chris must not be guilty, because twelve jurors, who saw all the evidence, agreed on a verdict of not guilty.

8. "Polls show an overwhelming majority of the American people want a lot less immigration or even an immigration moratorium. . . . These are persistent results over time. Most of the people cannot be wrong all of the time!" (from an advertisement placed by Federation for American Immigration Reform, *Atlantic Monthly* [June 1995], 67)

NOTES

[1] J. D. Salinger, *The Catcher in the Rye* (New York: Bantam Books, 1951), 157–58.

[2] Stephen Colbert, *I Am America (and So Can You!)* (New York: Grand Central Publishing, 2007), 193.

[3] Friedrich Nietzsche, *On the Genealogy of Morals*, trans. Walter Kaufmann, in *Basic Writings of Nietzsche* (New York: Random House, 1968), 456. Nietzsche goes on to argue that (slave) morality is the danger of dangers, so the reader is supposed to answer the rhetorical questions at the end of the passage in the affirmative.

[4] For an entertaining and instructive account of this case, see James Randi, *The Magic of Uri Geller* (New York: Ballantine Books, 1975).

[5] Both quotations are from Christopher Cerf and Victor Navasky, *The Experts Speak* (New York: Pantheon Books, 1984), 215. This work contains a marvelous collection of false and sometimes just plain stupid things that have been claimed by experts. One notable example is the remark made by the Union general John B. Sedgwick just before being fatally shot in the head by a Confederate marksman: "They couldn't hit an elephant at this dist—"(135).

[6] Stephen Jay Gould, *The Mismeasure of Man* (New York: Norton, 1981), 235.

16

FALLACIES OF VACUITY

Arguments are vacuous when they don't go anywhere. This happens in two main ways. Sometimes an argument begins by assuming its conclusion or some independent reason for its conclusion, so the argument makes no real progress beyond its own assumptions. In other cases, the argument's conclusion is empty, so the argument has nowhere in particular to go. Both kinds of argument are fallacious and vacuous, so we call them fallacies of vacuity. Circular arguments and arguments that beg the question fall into this category. So do positions that make themselves immune to criticism by being self-sealing.

CIRCULARITY

One purpose of arguments is to establish the truth of a claim to someone who doubts it. In a typical situation, one person, *A*, makes a claim; another person, *B*, raises objections to it; then *A* tries to find arguments that respond to the objections and justify the original statement. Schematically:

A asserts that *p* is true.

B raises objections *x*, *y*, and *z* against it.

A then offers reasons to overcome these objections.

What must *A*'s responses be like to meet *B*'s objections? To start with the simplest case, *A* cannot meet *B*'s challenge simply by repeating the original assertion. If someone is maintaining that terrorists can't be stopped without torture, it will not help to offer as a justification for this the very claim that is in dispute—that terrorists can't be stopped without torture. The argument would look like this:

Terrorists can't be stopped without torture.
∴ Terrorists can't be stopped without torture.

This argument is, of course, *valid*, since the premise cannot be true without the conclusion being true as well. Furthermore, if the premise is true, then the argument is also *sound*. All the same, the argument has no force in this conversational setting because any objection that *B* has to the conclusion is straight off an objection to the premise, since they are identical.

Unfortunately, people usually do not make it so easy to tell when they reason in a circle. Often, circular reasoning is disguised by restating the conclusion in different words. Someone might argue that terrorists can't be stopped without torture, because, if you do not use torture, there is no other way to stop terrorists. This premise means the same as the conclusion, so this reasoning is still circular.

Another way to hide circularity is by suppressing the premise that repeats the conclusion. (See Chapter 5 on suppressed premises.) Suppose someone argues that terrorists cannot be stopped without torture, because they are so callous that their goal is to kill and maim innocent civilians. This argument depends on the suppressed premise that anyone whose goal is to kill and maim innocent civilians cannot be stopped without torture. If terrorists are then defined as people whose goal is to kill and maim innocent civilians, then this suppressed premise reduces to the conclusion that terrorists cannot be stopped without torture. So this argument is also circular.

Yet another trick is to put forward a statement first as a conclusion to be proved, and then only much later—after several subarguments or tangents—use the same statement as a premise on its own behalf. Consider this simple argument:

> The only way to prevent terrorists from committing their horrible crimes is to inflict enough pain on them either to scare them off or to force them to reveal information that enables the police to head off terrorist attacks. Because these are the only methods that work, we cannot reason with them or talk them into giving up. We cannot make friends or sign a treaty with them. We cannot buy them off or satisfy their demands. Therefore, terrorists cannot be stopped without torture.

If the first sentence is supposed to provide a reason for the next three sentences, then those three sentences cannot later be used as a reason for the last sentence without the whole argument becoming circular, because the last sentence, "Terrorists can't be stopped without torture," means pretty much the same as the first sentence, "The only way to prevent terrorists . . . is to inflict enough pain on them. . . ." Although this trick is often harder to detect in a long and complex argument, such reasoning is still indirectly circular if any premise in a chain of arguments repeats or restates the eventual conclusion. Thus, we have *circular reasoning* if and only if one of the premises that is used directly or indirectly to support a conclusion is equivalent to the conclusion itself.

BEGGING THE QUESTION

Reasoning in a circle is normally bad reasoning, but it is not easy to say exactly what is bad about it. The problem with circular reasoning becomes clearer when we notice that the same basic defect is shared by arguments that are not circular. Instead of arguing, "Terrorists can't be stopped without torture, so they can't," we could avoid circularity by adding a few words to get this new argument:

> If terrorists can be stopped without torture, then I'm a monkey's uncle.
> I'm not a monkey's uncle.
> ∴ Terrorists can't be stopped without torture.

This argument is not circular, because neither premise repeats the conclusion. It is also valid, and it might even be sound. Still, it is no good as an argument for the same reason as "Terrorists can't be stopped without torture, so it can't." The problem lies in its first premise. The consequent of the first premise ("I'm a monkey's uncle") is obviously false, so that first premise is false unless its antecedent ("Terrorists can be stopped without torture.") is false. But that means that the conclusion must be true in order for the first premise to be true. Thus, one could not have any reason to believe the first premise if one did not already have the very same reason to believe the conclusion. One's reason to believe the premise depends on one's prior belief in the conclusion or on one's reason to believe the conclusion. In short, one has no independent reason for the premise.

This is a problem if the conclusion is disputed and the argument is being used to get someone who rejects the conclusion to change his or her mind and accept it. Anyone who rejects the conclusion will simply reject the premise. For the argument to show someone that he or she ought to accept the conclusion, the arguer would need an independent reason to believe the premise. But then that independent reason does all of the real work, and the argument as stated does nothing to establish the conclusion. It is, in a word, vacuous.

The point is not just that an opponent would deny the premise. If that were enough to make an argument fail, then arguments would almost never succeed. The point is instead that, when an opponent objects to a premise, the arguer cannot show that the opponent has reason to accept that premise simply by asserting what the opponent denies. Bare assertion and reassertion do nothing to overcome objections. To show that the opponent has reason to accept the premise and, hence, the conclusion, the arguer needs some independent evidence for the premise. Because there needs to be—but cannot be—an independent reason for the premise, "If terrorists can be stopped without torture, then I'm a monkey's uncle," the argument with this premise must beg the question in any normal context.

More generally, we can say that an argument *begs the question* in a context if and only if (1) it depends on a premise that is not supported by any reason that is independent of the conclusion, and (2) there is a need for such an independent reason.

To say that an argument begs the question in this sense is not, of course, to say that it raises the question. That is what a sports announcer means, for example, when she says, "His injury begs the question of whether he will return in time for the playoffs." This common use of the phrase "begs the question" is separate from the fallacy, but they are not completely unrelated. An argument can also be seen as begging the question when its context raises the question of why anyone who denies its conclusion should accept its premises and when that question has no adequate answer.

More precisely, the need for an independent justification arises from the context and the purpose for which the argument is being used. A premise *needs* support from an independent reason, for example, when it is in dispute or subject to objection and the arguer's goal is to give an audience some reason to accept the premise and, on that basis, to accept the conclusion. That such a need for an independent reason exists but is not satisfied explains why the argument can be criticized by saying that it commits the fallacy of *begging the question.*

This fallacy is often very hard to detect, both because it is affected by the context and because there are many ways to hide the fact that a premise depends on the conclusion. Consequently, people often use arguments that beg the question when they have nothing better to say, especially on a controversial issue. It is common, for example, to hear an argument something like the following:

> It's always wrong to murder human beings.
> Capital punishment involves murdering human beings.
> ∴ Capital punishment is wrong.

Here the first premise is true by definition, since calling something murder implies that it is a wrongful killing. The second premise is, however, question begging, for calling capital punishment murder assumes the point at issue—that capital punishment is wrong. As a result, anyone who objects to the conclusion would or should raise exactly the same objections to the second premise, and one could not give any adequate reason for the second premise without first arguing for the conclusion.

More subtly than this, opponents of abortion typically refer to the human fetus as an unborn baby or simply as a baby. It may seem a matter of indifference how the fetus is referred to, but this is not true. One of the central points in the debate over abortion is whether the fetus has the status of a person and thus has the rights that any person has. It is generally acknowledged in our society that babies are persons and therefore have the rights of persons. By referring to the fetus as an unborn baby (or simply as a baby), a point that demands argument is taken for granted without argument. That counts as begging the question. Of course, many opponents of abortion argue for the claim that a human fetus has the moral status of a person and thus do not beg this central question in the debate. Still, if they give no such independent argument, then they do beg the question.

Similarly, if someone argues for the pro-choice position simply on the grounds that a woman has a right to control the destiny of her own body, this also begs an important question, because it takes for granted the claim that the fetus is part of a woman's body, not an independent being with rights of its own. Of course, defenders of the pro-choice position need not beg the question in this way, but they often do. Whether a particular argument or premise is question begging will depend on whether there is a need for an independent reason, which in turn depends on the context in which the argument is given. One way for an argument to beg the question is for it to rely, either explicitly or implicitly, on an unsupported premise that is a matter of dispute in the particular argumentative context. Thus, referring to a human fetus as a baby will be question begging in contexts in which the moral status of the fetus is at issue, but it may not be question begging when this is not an issue.

Because begging the question depends in this way on context, we should be careful before charging opponents with begging the question. Some people charge every opponent with begging the question, almost like a knee-jerk reaction. However, even if an opponent uses a premise that you reject, this does not yet show that the argument begs the question, since your opponent might have plenty of independent evidence for the premise. Before you accuse people of begging the question, you should ask them to give you their reasons for the disputed premise. If they can come up with an independent reason, then they did not beg the question, and you might learn something from them. However, if they do not have any independent reason for the premise, then they did indeed beg the question.

EXERCISE I

For each of the following arguments, does it involve circular reasoning? Does it beg the question in any context? If so, in which contexts? Explain your answers.

1. A student of mine told me that I am her favorite professor, and I know that she is telling the truth, because no student would lie to her favorite professor.

2. Intoxicating beverages should be banned, because they can make people drunk.

3. Capitalism is the only correct economic system, because without it free enterprise would be impossible.

4. Free trade is good for the country, because it brings the country all of the advantages of an unimpeded flow of goods.

5. Gun-control laws are wrong, because they violate the citizen's right to bear arms.

6. When *B* applies for a job from *A*:

   A: How can we know that you are trustworthy?

   B: Mr. Davidson will write me a recommendation.

   A: But why should we trust him?

   B: I assure you that he is honest and accurate.

(continued)

7. The Bible is the inerrant word of God, because God speaks only the truth, and repeatedly in the Bible God tells us that the Bible consists of His words.

8. We have to accept change, because without change there is no progress.

9. Premarital sex is wrong, because premarital sex is fornication, and fornication is a sin.

10. The drinking age should be lowered to eighteen, because eighteen-year-olds are mature enough to drink.

11. We should never give security clearances to homosexuals, because they can be blackmailed into revealing classified information. They are subject to blackmail, because we will revoke their security clearances if we find out they are gay.

12. People with suicidal tendencies are insane, because they want to kill themselves.

13. Jeffrey can't really be insane, because he says he is.

DISCUSSION QUESTIONS (ADVANCED)

1. Explanations are often presented in the form of arguments that sometimes seem circular. Are the following arguments circular? Do they beg the question? Are they defective in some other way? Why or why not? More generally, when, if ever, can circular arguments provide good explanations?

   A. **TOM:** Why are so many people moving out of Claremont this year?

      SUE: Because its economy is going down so fast.

      TOM: But why is its economy going down so fast?

      SUE: Because so many people are moving out of town.

   B. **AMY:** Why is Jarred going down on the seesaw right now?

      JOHN: Because Jeremiah is going up on the other side of the seesaw.

      AMY: But why is Jeremiah going up right now?

      JOHN: Because Jarred is going down.

2. Explain John Stuart Mill's argument in the following passage (from *A System of Logic* [London, 1843], book 2, chapter 3, section 2). Do you agree? Why or why not?

   It must be granted that in every syllogism, considered as an argument to prove the conclusion, there is a *petitio principii* [a begging of the question]. When we say,

   All men are mortal.
   Socrates is a man.
   ∴ Socrates is mortal;

   it is unanswerably urged by the adversaries of the syllogistic theory that the proposition, "Socrates is mortal," is presupposed in the more general assumption, "All men are mortal"; that we cannot be assured of the mortality of all men unless we are already certain of the mortality of every individual man. . . . That, in short, no reasoning from generals to particulars can, as such, prove anything, since from a general principle we cannot infer any particulars but those which the principle itself assumes as known.

3. Suppose Andrea asks, "How many days are there in November?" In response, Cummings says, "Let's see. How does that mnemonic go? Oh yeah: Thirty days has September, April, June, and November. So November has thirty days." Is this argument circular? Does it beg the question? Why or why not?

4. Does the following argument (from Roy Sorensen) beg the question in any contexts? If so, in which contexts? Why?

> Some arguments beg the question.
> ∴ Some arguments beg the question.

5. St. Thomas Aquinas gave the following argument for the existence of God:

> In the world of sense we find there is an order of efficient causes. There is no case known (neither is it, indeed, possible) in which a thing is found to be the efficient cause of itself; for so it would be prior to itself, which is impossible. Now in efficient causes it is not possible to go on to infinity, because in all efficient causes following in order, the first is the cause of the intermediate cause, and the intermediate is the cause of the ultimate cause, whether the intermediate cause be several, or only one. Now to remove the cause is to remove the effect. Therefore, if there be no first cause among efficient causes, there will be no ultimate, nor any intermediate cause. But if in efficient causes it is possible to go on to infinity, there will be no first efficient cause, neither will there be an ultimate effect, nor any intermediate efficient causes; all of which is plainly false. Therefore it is necessary to admit a first efficient cause, to which everyone gives the name of God.[1]

In response, John Mackie accused Aquinas of begging the question:

> Unfortunately this argument is unsound. Although in a *finite* ordered series of causes the intermediate (or the earliest intermediate) is caused by the first item, this would not be so if there were an infinite series. In an infinite series, every item is caused by an earlier item. The way in which the first item is "removed" if we go from a finite to an infinite series does not entail the removal of the later items. In fact, Aquinas . . . has simply begged the question against an infinite regress of causes. . . .[2]

Explain and evaluate Mackie's objection. Does Aquinas beg the question? Why or why not?

SELF-SEALERS

It is characteristic of certain positions that no evidence can *possibly* refute them. This may seem to be a wonderful feature for a position to have. In fact, however, it *usually* makes the position useless. We can start with a silly example. A Perfect Sage claims to be able to predict the future in detail. The Perfect Sage's predictions take the following form:

> Two weeks from today at 4:37 you are going to be doing *exactly* what you will be doing.

Of course, whatever you are doing at that time will be exactly what you are doing, so this prediction cannot possibly be wrong. But this is only because it does not tell us anything in particular about the future. *Whatever* happens, the prediction is going to be true, and this is just what is wrong with it. The prediction is *empty* or *vacuous*.

People do not, of course, go around making predictions of this kind, but they do sometimes hold positions that are empty or vacuous in much the same way. A clairvoyant claims to be able to predict the future, but every time a prediction fails, she says that this just proves that someone set up bad vibrations that interfered with her visions. So, if the prediction turns out to be true, she claims that this shows her clairvoyance; if it turns out to be false, she cites this as evidence of interference. No matter what happens, then, the clairvoyant's claim to be clairvoyant cannot be refuted. Her claim to clairvoyance is as empty and vacuous as the Perfect Sage's prediction.

Positions that are set up in this way so that nothing can possibly refute them are called *self-sealers*. A self-sealing position is one that is so constructed that no evidence can possibly be brought against it no matter what happens. This shows its vacuity, and it is precisely for this reason that we reject it.

People do not usually hold self-sealing positions in a blatant way; they tend to back into them. A person who holds that the American economy is controlled by an international Jewish conspiracy will point out people of Jewish extraction (or with Jewish names) who occupy important positions in financial institutions. This at least counts as evidence, though very weak evidence. And there seems to be much stronger evidence on the other side: There are a great many people in these institutions who are not Jews. To counter this claim, the person now argues that many of these other people are secretly Jews or are tools of the Jewish conspiracy. The Jews have allowed some non-Jews to hold important positions in order to conceal their conspiracy. What evidence is there for this? Well, none really, but that only helps prove how sneaky the Jewish conspiracy is. At this point, the position has become self-sealing, for all evidence cited against the existence of the conspiracy will be converted into evidence for its cleverness.

Self-sealing arguments are hard to deal with, because people who use them will often shift their ground. A person will begin by holding a significant position that implies that facts are one way rather than another, but under the pressure of criticism will self-seal the position so that no evidence can possibly count against it. That is, the person will slide back and forth between two positions—one that is not self-sealed (and so is significant but subject to refutation) and another that is self-sealed (and so is not subject to criticism but is also not significant). The charge that is leveled against a theory that vacillates in this way is that it is either *vacuous* or *false*. It is vacuous if self-sealing, false if not.

One way of challenging a self-sealing position is to ask what possible fact could prove it wrong. This is a good question to ask, but it can be misunderstood and met with the triumphant reply: "Nothing can prove my position wrong, because it is right." A better way to show the insignificance of a self-sealing theory is to put the challenge in a different form: "If your position has any significance, it should tell us that certain things will occur whereas certain other things will not occur. If it cannot do this, it really tells us nothing at all; so please make some specific predictions, and we will see how they come out."

Ideologies and worldviews tend to be self-sealing. The Marxist ideology sometimes has this quality. If you fail to see the truth of the Marxist ideology, that just shows that your social consciousness has not been raised. The very fact that you reject the Marxist ideology shows that you are not yet capable of understanding it and that you are in need of re-education. This is perfect self-sealing. Sometimes psychoanalytic theory gets involved in this same kind of self-sealing. People who vigorously disagree with certain psychoanalytic claims can be accused of repressing these facts. If a boy denies that he wants to murder his father and sleep with his mother, this itself can be taken as evidence of the strength of these desires and of his unwillingness to acknowledge them. If this kind of reasoning gets out of hand, then psychoanalytic theory also becomes self-sealing and empty. Freud was aware of this danger and warned against it.

So far, we have seen two ways in which an argument can be self-sealing: (1) It can invent an ad hoc or arbitrary way of dismissing every possible criticism. The clairvoyant can always point to interfering conditions without going to the trouble of saying what they are. The anti-Semite can always cite Jewish cleverness to explain away counterevidence. We might call this self-sealing *by universal discounting*. (2) A theory can also counter criticism by attacking its critics. Critics of Marxism are charged with having a decadent bourgeois consciousness that blinds them to the facts of class conflict. The critic's response to psychoanalytic theory is analyzed (and then dismissed) as repression, a reaction formation, or something similar. Here self-sealing is achieved through an ad hominem fallacy. We might call this self-sealing *by going upstairs*, because the theorist is looking down on the critic.

Yet another form of self-sealing is this: (3) Words are used in such a way that a position becomes true *by definition*. For example, a person makes the strong claim that all human actions are selfish. This is an interesting remark, but it seems to be false, for it is easy to think of cases in which people have acted in self-sacrificing ways. To counter these obvious objections, the argument takes the following turn: When a person acts in a self-sacrificing way, what that person *wants* to do is help another even at her own expense. This is her desire or her motive, and that is what she acts to fulfill. So the action is selfish after all, because the person is acting to achieve what she wants. This is a self-sealing move, for it will not help to cite any behavior—even heroic self-destructive behavior—as counterevidence. If a person desires to do something even if it involves the sacrifice of her life, then she acts to fulfill her desire, and the act is again called selfish.

It is not hard to see what has happened in this case. The arguer has chosen to use the word "selfish" in a new and peculiar way: A person is said to act selfishly if she acts to do what she desires to do. This is not what we usually mean by this word. We ordinarily say that a person acts selfishly if she is too much concerned with her own interests at the expense of the interests of others. On this standard use of the word "selfish," there are any number of counterexamples to the claim that all human actions are selfish. But these counterexamples do not apply when the word "selfish" is used in a new way, where "acting selfishly" comes close to meaning just "acting." The point is that under this new meaning of "selfish," it becomes empty (or almost empty) to say that all human actions are selfish. We are thus back to a familiar situation. Under one interpretation (the ordinary interpretation), the claim that all human actions are selfish is interesting but false. Under another interpretation (an extraordinary interpretation), the claim is true but vacuous. The position gets all its *apparent* interest and plausibility from a rapid two-step back-and-forth between these positions.

Self-sealing arguments are not easy to handle, for they change their form under pressure. One good strategy is to begin by charging a person who uses such an argument with saying something trivial, vacuous, or boring. If, to meet this charge, he or she says something quite specific and important, then argument can proceed along normal lines. But it is not always easy to get down to brass tacks in this way. This becomes clear if you examine an argument between a Marxist and an anti-Marxist, between a psychoanalyst and a critic of psychoanalysis, or between individuals with different religious views. Their positions are often sealed against objections from each other, and then their arguments are almost always at cross-purposes.

Although we have emphasized how large-scale ideologies can become self-sealing, small-scale claims in everyday life are also often sealed against any possible refutation. In fact, a number of common words are used to this end. If someone says, "All true conservatives support school prayer," and a critic points out a conservative who opposes school prayer, then the original claim might be defended by saying, "He is not *truly* (or *really*) a conservative." If this response is trotted out in every case, it turns out that the original claim does not exclude anything. Similarly, the claim that "some students need to work harder than others, but if any student works hard enough, he or she will get good grades" can be protected simply by declaring that any student who works hard but does not get good grades does not work hard *enough*. Finally, someone who says, "If you think it over thoroughly, you will agree with me" can dismiss anyone who disagrees simply by denying that he thought it over *thoroughly*. Of course, these terms—"true," "real," "thorough(ly)," and "enough"—do not always make positions self-sealing. Nonetheless, these and other common terms are often used to seal positions against any possible criticism. When these terms are used in these ways, the resulting positions are empty and can be criticized in the same ways as self-sealing ideologies.

DISCUSSION QUESTIONS

1. Antony Flew famously wrote:

   Now it often seems to people who are not religious as if there was no conceivable event or series of events the occurrence of which would be admitted by sophisticated religious people to be a sufficient reason for conceding "There wasn't a God after all" or "God does not really love us then." Someone tells us that God loves us as a father loves his children. We are reassured. But then we see a child dying of inoperable cancer of the throat. His earthly father is driven frantic in his efforts to help, but his Heavenly Father shows no obvious sign of concern. Some qualification is made— God's love is "not merely human love" or it is "an inscrutable love," perhaps—and we realize that such offerings are quite compatible with the truth of the assertion that "God loves us as a father (but, of course . . .)." We are reassured again. But then perhaps we ask: what is this assurance of God's (appropriately qualified) love worth, what is this apparent guarantee really a guarantee against? Just what would have to happen not merely (morally and wrongly) to tempt us but also (logically and rightly) to entitle us to say "God does not love us" or even "God does not exist"?[3]

   How would you answer Flew's question? If the answer to Flew's question were that nothing could entitle us to say this, as Flew suggests, then would this show that religious positions like this are self-sealing? That they are empty? Why or why not?

2. During the nineteenth century, evidence mounted that apparently showed that the Earth had existed for millions, perhaps hundreds of millions, of years. This seemed to contradict the account given in Genesis that holds that the Earth was created less than 10,000 years ago. In response to this challenge, Philip Henry Gosse, an English theist, replied roughly as follows: In creating Adam and Eve, God would endow them with navels, and thus it would seem that they had been born in the normal way, and thus also seem that they had existed for a number of years before they were created by God. Beyond this, their hair, fingernails, bones, and so on would all show evidence of growth, again giving evidence of previous existence. The same would be true of the trees that surrounded them in the Garden of Eden, which would have rings. Furthermore, the sediment in the rivers should suggest that they had flowed for very many years in the past. In sum, although the Earth was created fairly recently, God would have created it in a way that would make it appear that it had existed for many more years, perhaps millions of years in the past. Thus, the actual creation of the Earth less than 10,000 years ago is compatible with scientific evidence that suggests that it is much older than this. Evaluate this line of reasoning.

3. Some creationist critics of Darwin's theory of natural selection argue as follows:

   Natural selection is a tautologous concept (circular reasoning) because it simply requires the fittest organisms to leave the most offspring and at the same time it identifies the fittest organisms as those that leave the most offspring. Thus natural selection seemingly does not provide a testable explanation of how mutation would produce more fit organisms.[4]

   (continued)

Does this argument show that Darwin's theory is self-sealing? How could defenders of natural selection best respond?

4. Christina Hoff Sommers wrote:

The women currently manning—womanning—the feminist ramparts do not take well to criticism. How could they? As they see it, they are dealing with a massive epidemic of male atrocity and a constituency of benighted women who have yet to comprehend the seriousness of their predicament. Hence, male critics must be "sexist" and "reactionary," and female critics "traitors," "collaborators," or "backlashers." This kind of reaction has had a powerful inhibiting effect. It has alienated and silenced women and men alike.[5]

Do you agree? Why or why not? If feminists are guilty of what Sommers claims, does this make their positions self-sealing? Does it make their positions empty?

NOTES

[1] *The Summa Theologica of St. Thomas Aquinas*, Part I, Question 2, Article 3, 2nd and rev. ed., 1920, trans. Fathers of the English Dominican Province. Online edition © 2002 by Kevin Knight, http://www.newadvent.org/summa/100203.htm. We replaced the phrase "take away" with the word "remove" to fit Mackie's objection.

[2] J. L. Mackie, "The Regress of Causes" in *The Miracle of Theism* (Oxford: Oxford University Press, 1982), 90.

[3] Antony Flew, "Theology and Falsification," in *New Essays in Philosophical Theology*, ed. A. Flew and A. MacIntyre (New York: Macmillan, 1955), 98–99.

[4] Duane T. Gish, Richard B. Bliss, and Wendell R. Bird, "Summary of Scientific Evidence for Creation," *Impact* 95–96 (May/June 1981).

[5] Christina Hoff Sommers, *Who Stole Feminism? How Women Have Betrayed Women* (New York: Simon & Schuster, 1994), 18.

17

REFUTATION

chapter 1 showed how arguments can be used for justification and for explanation, but arguments can also be used for another purpose: refutation. *This chapter will explain the nature of refutation and explore some of the main ways in which arguments can refute another argument or claim. These methods of refutation include counterexamples, reductio ad absurdum, and parallel reasoning. This last kind of refutation can reveal a large variety of fallacies in addition to those studied in previous chapters.*

WHAT IS REFUTATION?

In addition to justifying and explaining their conclusions, arguments are also sometimes used to refute other arguments. To *refute* an argument is to show that it is no good. Some writers, however, incorrectly use the term "refute" to mean something much weaker. They say such things as that Bill Clinton refuted the charges brought against him by those attempting to impeach him, meaning nothing more than that he rejected or replied to the charges. This, however, is not what the word "refute" means. To refute the charges brought against him, Clinton would have to *give reason to believe* that these charges were erroneous. Refuting a charge requires giving an adequate argument against it. This takes a lot more work than simply denying it.

On the other hand, it is also important to remember that we can refute an argument without proving that its conclusion is false. A refutation of an argument is sufficient if it raises objections that cannot be answered. Consequently, the patterns of successful refutations mirror the criteria for a good argument, because the point of a refutation is to show that one of these criteria has not been met. Refutations, then, take four main forms: (1) We can argue that some of the premises are dubious or even false. (2) We can argue that the conclusion of the argument leads to absurd results. (3) We can show that the conclusion does not follow from the premises (or, in the case of an inductive argument, that the premises do not provide strong enough support for the conclusion). (4) We can show that the argument begs the question. This last charge was discussed in Chapter 16, so here we will focus on the first three methods of refutation.

Is refuting an argument the same as justifying a belief that its conclusion is false? Is it the same as justifying a belief that the argument is invalid or weak? Why or why not?

COUNTEREXAMPLES

The first main way to attack an argument is to challenge one of its premises. We can argue that there is no good reason to accept a particular premise as true, asking, for example, "How do you know that?" If the premise is not justified, then the argument fails to justify its conclusion. More strongly, we can argue that the premise is actually false. In this second case, we refute an argument by refuting one of its premises.

One common way to refute a premise by showing that it is false is by producing a counterexample. Counterexamples are typically aimed at universal claims. This is true because a *single* contrary instance will show that a universal claim is false. If someone claims that *all* snakes lay eggs, then pointing out that rattlesnakes bear their young alive is sufficient to refute this universal claim. If the person retreats to the weaker claim that *most* snakes lay eggs, the guarding term makes it much harder to refute the claim. A single example of a snake that bears its young alive is not enough to refute this claim; we would have to show that a majority of snakes do not lay eggs. Here, instead of trying to refute the statement, we may ask the person to produce his *argument* on behalf of it. We can then attack this argument. Finally, if the person retreats to the very weak claim that at least *some* snakes lay eggs, then this statement becomes very difficult to refute. Even if it were false (which it is not), to show this we would have to check every single snake and establish that it does not lay eggs. So, as a rough-and-ready rule, we can say that the stronger a statement is, the more subject it is to refutation; the weaker it is, the less subject it is to refutation.

When a universal claim is refuted by a single case, that case is a *counterexample* to the universal claim. The pattern of reasoning is perfectly simple: To refute a claim that *everything* of a certain kind has a certain feature, we need find only *one* thing of that kind lacking that feature. In response to a counterexample, many people just repeat the misleading saying, "That's the exception that proves the rule." What most people do not realize is that "proves" originally meant "tests," so all this saying means is that an apparent exception can be used to test a rule or a universal claim. When the exception is a true counterexample, the universal claim fails the test.

There are only two ways to defend a universal claim against a purported counterexample. Because the universal claim says that all things of a certain kind have a certain feature, (1) one can deny that the apparent counterexample really is a thing of that kind, or (2) one can deny that the supposed counterexample really lacks that feature. For example, a defender of the claim that all snakes lay eggs might deny (1) that rattlesnakes are snakes, or (2) that rattlesnakes bear their young alive. Neither of these responses is plausible in this case. That is what makes this counterexample *decisive*.

Other counterexamples are not decisive. Indeed, some purported counterexamples miss their targets entirely. If a person claims that all snakes except rattlesnakes lay eggs, someone might respond with another counterexample: male snakes. This counterexample does not really refute the intended claim, since that claim was meant to be about the methods by which female snakes of various species give birth when they do give birth.

When a counterexample can be answered with a simple clarification or modification that does not affect the basic force of the original claim, it is a *shallow* counterexample. A *deep* counterexample is one that requires the original claim to be modified in more important or interesting ways. Shallow counterexamples can sometimes be fun as jokes, but they are usually not much help in refuting arguments, since basically the same argument can be resurrected in a slightly different form. Indeed, people who give too many shallow counterexamples can be annoying. If you really want to understand a subject matter, you should look for counterexamples that are deep.

Deep and decisive counterexamples are not always easy to think up, but Socrates was a genius in this respect. In one dialogue by Plato, Theaetetus and Socrates are trying to define "knowledge." They notice an important difference between knowledge and mere belief: It is possible for someone to *believe* something that is false, but it is not possible for someone to *know* something that is false. This leads Theaetetus to suggest a simple definition of knowledge: Knowledge equals true belief. This proposed definition is refuted in the following exchange:

SOCRATES: [There is] a whole profession to prove that true belief is not knowledge.

THEAETETUS: How so? What profession?

SOCRATES: The profession of those paragons of intellect known as orators and lawyers. There you have men who use their skill to produce conviction, not by instruction, but by making people believe whatever they want them to believe. You can hardly imagine teachers so clever as to be able, in the short time allowed by the clock, to instruct their hearers thoroughly in the true facts of a case of robbery or other violence which those hearers had not witnessed.

THEAETETUS: No, I cannot imagine that; but they can convince them.

SOCRATES: And by convincing you mean making them believe something.

THEAETETUS: Of course.

SOCRATES: And when a jury is rightly convinced of facts which can be known only by an eye-witness, then, judging by hearsay and accepting a true belief, they are judging without knowledge, although, if they find the right verdict, their conviction is correct?

THEAETETUS: Certainly.

SOCRATES: But if true belief and knowledge were the same thing, the best of jurymen could never have a correct belief without knowledge. It now appears that they must be different things.[1]

One thing to notice about this discussion is that Theaetetus does not dig in his heels and insist that the ignorant members of the jury do know that the person is innocent provided only that they believe it and it is true. Faced with the counterexample, he retreats at once. Why is this? Why not stay with the definition and reject the counterexample as false? The answer is that for many concepts, there is general agreement about their application to particular cases, even if there is no general agreement about a correct definition. To take an extreme example, everyone agrees that Hitler was a dictator (even Hitler), and no one supposes that Thomas Jefferson was a dictator (even his enemies). So any definition of "dictator" must be wrong if it implies that Hitler was not a dictator or that Thomas Jefferson was a dictator. Of course, people do disagree about borderline cases, so there might be no perfectly exact definition of "dictator." Nonetheless, any definition that does not square with the clear cases can be refuted by citing one of these clear cases as a counterexample.

Ethics is an area where arguments often turn on counterexamples. Consider the traditional moral precept "Do unto others as you would have them do unto you." This principle captures an important moral insight, but, if taken quite literally, it is also subject to counterexamples. Jones, a sadomasochist, enjoys beating other people. When asked whether he would like to be treated in that way, he replies, "Yes." It is obvious that the Golden Rule was not intended to approve of Jones's behavior. The task, then, is to reformulate this rule to avoid this counterexample. That is not as easy as it might seem.

No discussion of counterexamples is complete without a mention of the Morgenbesser retort. Though the exact story is now shrouded in the mists of time, it has come down to us from the 1950s in the following form: In a lecture, a British philosopher remarked that he knew of many languages in which a double negative means an affirmative, but not one language in which a double affirmative means a negative. From the back of the room came Morgenbesser's retort: "Yeah, yeah."

EXERCISE I

Find a counterexample to each of the following claims, if possible.

Example: *Claim:* "Sugar" is the only word in which an *s* is pronounced *sh*.
Counterexample: Oh, sure.

1. No prime number is even.
2. Three points always determine a plane.

3. Balloons that are filled with helium always rise in the air.

4. All mammals bear their young live.

5. You can never get too much of a good thing.

6. What you don't know can't hurt you.

7. You can't be too careful.

8. You should never look a gift horse in the mouth.

9. It is always wrong to tell a lie.

10. You should never ask someone else to do something that you are not willing to do yourself.

11. If lots of people do something, then it must not be wrong for me to do it.

12. If it would be horrible for everyone to do something, then it would be morally wrong for anyone to do it.

13. If it would not be horrible for everyone to do something, then it would not be morally wrong for anyone to do it.

14. Wherever you use the word "nearly," you could use the word "almost" instead, without affecting the truth or the good sense of what you have said.

EXERCISE II

There cannot possibly be any counterexamples to the following claims. Explain why.

1. There is life on the moon.

2. Killing is usually wrong.

3. Any short person is a person.

4. Every horse is an animal.

5. $2 + 2 = 4$.

6. Everything with a size has a shape.

7. Everything that is green has a shape.

8. There's no way to turn a right-hand glove around to get a left-hand glove.

DISCUSSION QUESTIONS

1. How can the Golden Rule best be reformulated to avoid the above counterexample of the sadomasochist? Can you think of any counterexamples to this reformulation of the Golden Rule?

2. Is the Morgenbesser retort a shallow counterexample or a deep counterexample? Why?

(continued)

3. When theologians claim that God can do anything, atheists sometimes respond that God cannot make a stone that is so large that God cannot lift it, or that God cannot make a circle with four sides. Are these really counterexamples to the theologians' claim? Why or why not?

4. Suppose there are only two balls in a bag, and someone claims, "Most of the balls in the bag are red." Does a single black ball in the bag refute this claim? Is it a counterexample to this claim? Is it also a counterexample to the claim that no counterexamples can refute any claim that is not universal?

5. When people today respond to counterexamples by saying, "That's the exception that proves the rule," they usually do not mean, "That's the exception that tests the rule," which was its original meaning. What do they mean?

REDUCTIO AD ABSURDUM

Particular counterexamples can normally be used to refute claims only if those claims are universal, so how can we refute claims that are not universal? One method is to show that the claim to be refuted implies something that is ridiculous or absurd in ways that are independent of any particular counterexample. This mode of refutation is called a *reductio ad absurdum*, which means a reduction to absurdity. Reductios, as they are called for short, can refute many different kinds of propositions. They are sometimes directed at a premise in an argument, but they can also be used to refute a conclusion. This method of refutation will not show exactly *what* is wrong with the argument for that conclusion, but it will show that *something* is wrong with the argument, because it cannot be sound if its conclusion is false. That might be enough in some situations.

For example, suppose someone argues that because there is a tallest mountain and a heaviest human, there must also be a largest integer. We might respond by arguing as follows: Suppose there is a largest integer. Call it N. Since N is an integer, $N + 1$ is also an integer. Moreover, $N + 1$ is larger than N. But it is absurd to think that any integer is larger than the largest integer. Therefore, our supposition—that there is a largest integer—must be false.

In this mathematical example a contradiction is derived, but absurdity also comes in other forms. Suppose a neighbor tells a parent, "The local public schools are so bad that you ought to send your kids to private school," and the parent responds, "Do you think I'm rich?" The point of this rhetorical question is that it is absurd to think that the parent is rich, presumably because of her lifestyle or house, which the neighbor can easily see. Without being rich, the parent cannot afford a private school, so the neighbor's advice is useless.

Often the absurdity is derived indirectly. A wonderful example occurred in the English parliamentary debate on capital punishment. One member of

Parliament was defending the death penalty on the grounds that the alternative—life in prison—was much more cruel than death. This claim was met with the following reply: On this view, those found guilty of first-degree murder ought to be given life in prison, and the death penalty should be given to those who commit some lesser offense. The first speaker could respond in several ways, because this reductio depends on background assumptions that the first speaker could question. First, he might deny that the most severe crime should receive the most severe penalty possible. If the first speaker sees life in prison as too cruel to be inflicted on anyone, then he might call for the abolition of life imprisonment and keep the death penalty as the most severe punishment. Alternatively, the first speaker could claim that, even though the death penalty is less severe than life in prison, it is still fitting in some other way for the most severe crime, first-degree murder. Finally, of course, the first speaker could simply *accept* the supposedly absurd result and apply life imprisonment to first-degree murder, while using the death penalty for lesser crimes. In fact, however, the first speaker was unwilling to accept any of these alternatives. He simply tried a rhetorical trick and got caught.

These reductios are fairly good, but other reductios fail for a variety of reasons. To succeed in refuting a claim, a reductio ad absurdum argument must meet two main requirements. First, the result must really be *absurd*. Often opponents try to reduce a view to absurdity but really only draw out implications of the view that are not absurd at all. For example, in a famous debate in which Thomas Huxley defended a theory of evolution, Bishop Wilberforce asked Huxley whether he had descended from apes on his mother's side or on his father's side of the family. This question was intended to draw laughter from the crowd, and it did, partly because they and Wilberforce thought that any answer to the question would be absurd. Nonetheless, Huxley could respond that he had descended from apes on both sides of his family. Because that response was not really absurd—regardless of how absurd it seemed to Wilberforce—the bishop's attempt did not really refute Huxley's claim.

In other cases, one cannot deny that a certain result really would be absurd, but the reductio still fails because the claim to be refuted does not really *imply* that absurdity. For example, opponents sometimes say that the theory of evolution implies that animals are constantly evolving, so they cannot be divided into separate species. This would be absurd, because it is easy to observe distinct species. The theory of evolution, however, does not really imply this absurdity, so this reductio fails to refute that theory. It fails to meet the second requirement for successful reductios, which is that the claim to be refuted must actually imply the absurdity.

Finally, it is important to notice that reductios can be deep or shallow in much the same way as counterexamples. Sometimes a claim really does imply a result that is absurd, but it can be modified in some minor way so as to avoid the absurd result. For example, if a fan says, "Tiger Woods is better than any golfer ever," someone might respond that Woods is himself a golfer, so this claim implies that Woods is better than himself, which is absurd.

Of course, the fan meant to say, "Woods is better than any *other* golfer ever," so this reductio is shallow. The reductio does refute the original form of the claim, but the main force of the claim is restored by the minor modification. A reductio ad absurdum is deep only if it reveals that a claim implies an absurd result that cannot be avoided without modifying the claim in essential respects or giving it up entirely.

In sum, then, a reductio ad absurdum argument tries to show that one claim, *X*, is false because it implies another claim, *Y*, that is absurd. To evaluate such an argument, the following questions should be asked:

1. Is *Y* really absurd?
2. Does *X* really imply *Y*?
3. Can *X* be modified in some minor way so that it no longer implies *Y*?

If either of the first two questions is answered in the negative, then the reductio fails; if the third question receives an affirmative answer, then the reductio is shallow. Otherwise, the reductio ad absurdum argument is both successful and deep.

EXERCISE III

Evaluate the following reductio ad absurdum arguments by asking the above three questions.

1. CLAIM TO BE REFUTED: Even the worst of enemies can become friends.

   REDUCTIO: If people are enemies, then they are not friends. If they do become friends, then they are not enemies. So it's absurd to think that enemies can be friends.

2. CLAIM TO BE REFUTED: This ball is both red all over and green all over.

   REDUCTIO: If it is red, it reflects light within a certain range of wavelengths. If it is green, it reflects light within a different range of wavelengths. These ranges do not overlap, so it is absurd to think that anything can reflect both kinds of light. Thus, a ball cannot be both red and green all over.

3. CLAIM TO BE REFUTED: Most children in Lake Wobegon are above average (in intelligence).

   REDUCTIO: If so, the average (intelligence) would really be higher than it is; and then it would not be true that most children in Lake Wobegon are above the real average (intelligence).

4. ARGUMENT TO BE REFUTED: Your brain is mostly empty space, because the subatomic particles in it are very far apart.

   REDUCTIO: That's absurd, because my brain is solid, and it works pretty well.

5. CLAIM TO BE REFUTED: Some things are inconceivable.

   REDUCTIO: Consider something that is inconceivable. Since you are considering it, you are conceiving it. But then it is conceivable as well as inconceivable. That is absurd. So nothing is inconceivable.

Spell out a reductio ad absurdum argument to refute each of the following claims. If no such reductio is possible, explain why.

1. Some sisters are nephews.
2. Some fathers were never children.
3. Most students scored better than the median grade on the last test.
4. Almost everyone in this class is exceptional.
5. There is an exception to every universal claim.
6. I know that I do not know anything.
7. Some morally wrong actions are morally permitted.
8. God exists outside of time, and we will meet Him someday.
9. There is a male barber in this town who shaves all and only the men in this town who do not shave themselves. (Hint: Does he shave himself?)
10. Most of the sentences in this exercise are true.

1. Marc Antony's funeral oration, quoted in a Discussion Question in Chapter 2, uses several reductio ad absurdum arguments to refute Brutus's claim that Caesar was ambitious. Are these reductios deep or shallow? How could Brutus respond?

2. The legal case of *Plessy v. Ferguson*, 163 U.S. 537 (1896), questioned the constitutionality of a law requiring racial segregation in railroad cars. Opponents of the law gave the following reductio argument. How could defenders of segregation respond to this argument? Is their response adequate? Is any response adequate? Why or why not?

   The same argument that will justify the state legislature in requiring railways to provide separate accommodations for the two races will also authorize them to require separate cars to be provided for people whose hair is of a certain color, or who are aliens, or who belong to certain nationalities, or to enact laws requiring colored people to walk upon one side of the street, and white people upon the other, or requiring white men's houses to be painted white, and colored men's black, or their vehicles or business signs to be of different colors, upon the theory that one side of the street is as good as the other, or that a house or vehicle of one color is as good as one of another color.

3. Many atheists try to refute belief in God with the following reductio ad absurdum argument: God is defined to be all-good and all-powerful (as well as all-knowing). If God is all-good, then God prevents as much evil as He can. If God is all-powerful (and all-knowing), then God can prevent all evil. Thus, if a traditional God did exist, there would be no evil in the world. But that's absurd. There is obviously lots of evil in the world. Therefore, God does not exist. (Compare Chapter 21 in Part V on Religious Reasoning.) Evaluate this reductio argument. How could religious believers best respond?

STRAW MEN AND FALSE DICHOTOMIES

Very often when trying to refute either by counterexample or by reductio, people move too quickly. The general rule is this: Before trying to refute someone's claim, it is important to make sure that you understand his or her position. If you misunderstand what your opponent is claiming, but you go ahead and attack a specific claim anyway, then the claim you attack will not be the claim that your opponent made. You might even fail to refute any position that anyone ever really held. This is called the fallacy of *attacking a straw man.*

Sometimes people attack a straw man intentionally. They mischaracterize their opponents' position on purpose in order to make their opponents look silly by associating their opponents with a position that really is silly. One example comes from the 2004 presidential election, when John Kerry suggested that the United States should have conferred more with its allies, including the French, before attacking Iraq. In response, at the Republican National Convention Senator Zell Miller said that Kerry would "let Paris decide when America needs defending." Surely Miller knew that this mischaracterization of Kerry's position was unfair, but it achieved the desired reaction from the crowd.

The fallacy of attacking a straw man can also arise from an honest mistake. Some people get so wrapped up in their own arguments that they forget the view against which they are arguing. The opponent can also be partly to blame. If someone states her position obscurely, it might not be clear whether the speaker would go so far as to make a certain claim. Then someone might attack that further claim, honestly believing that the speaker had adopted it. Alternatively, a critic might refute that further claim simply to make the speaker clarify her position by explicitly saying that that is not what she meant to say. In such ways, it might be useful to refute a position that the speaker does not really hold, even though, of course, doing so does not refute any position that the speaker actually does hold.

In more insidious cases, straw men are often set up by means of a related fallacy—*false dichotomy.* With regard to the Iraq war, President Bush often said something like this: "I had a choice to make: Either take the word of a madman [Saddam Hussein] or defend America. Given that choice, I will defend America every time." The crucial phrase, of course, is "given that choice." If those were the only options, then Bush's critics would also defend America every time. The problem lies in Bush's suggestion that his opponents do not want to defend America and would instead "take the word of a madman." That insinuation sets up a straw man.

Political rhetoric is filled with such false dichotomies that set up straw men. A cable news host is reported to have said, "Sure, it's not great having the government collect our telephone records, but it is better than having them collect our body parts." Let's hope there is a third option! Opponents of the government collecting phone records, of course, think that there is another way to avoid having to collect body parts. But then they sometimes add, "Either you are opposed to the government collecting phone records or you don't care about civil rights." This is just a false dichotomy on the other side.

Those who favor the government collecting phone records do care about civil rights, even though they favor some intrusions (which they see as minor intrusions) on those rights in order to fight terrorism.

False dichotomies like these are parodied by Stephen Colbert when he says, "Either you are with us or you are with the terrorists," "Either you're for the war [in Iraq] or you hate America," and his best, "George W. Bush: great president or the greatest president?" The trick here is obviously to give you some choice, so that you end up committed to the option that you choose, but your choices are limited to ones that Colbert gives you.

After listing his dichotomy, Colbert usually adds, "It's that simple!" The best response is to recognize that these issues are usually not simple at all. These tricks work partly because many people long for simple choices or they fail to notice any third option. Whenever someone tells you that you have only two alternatives, you should look carefully for other possibilities. And whenever your choice among the options seems obvious, you should ask whether the rejected options have been set up as straw men rather than characterized fairly.

EXERCISE V

Do the following arguments attack straw men? Why or why not?

1. Anyone who thinks that the United States should not have sent troops to Iraq must think that the suffering Saddam Hussein inflicted on his own citizens doesn't matter much.

2. Anyone who thinks that the United States should have sent troops to Iraq must think that they will only be there for a short time.

3. Humans could not have been created in the image of God, because God is not a physical being, and only physical beings can have images.

4. Atheists think that God does not exist, so everything is permitted. But even atheists must admit that I would not be permitted to kill them! So atheism is nonsense.

5. The theory of evolution says that humans are no different from apes, but humans are clearly smarter than apes, so the theory of evolution must be wrong.

6. Stephen Colbert again: "Evolutionists' main claim is that one day we decided to stop being monkeys and turned ourselves into humans. Well, if that's true, why aren't more monkeys escaping from zoos? Think about it. They could turn into humans, then disguise themselves as janitors and walk out of their cages. But I guess evolution doesn't have an answer for that one."[2]

DISCUSSION QUESTION

Find five more examples of attacking straw men in your local newspaper, in a talk show on television, or in a college course.

REFUTATION BY PARALLEL REASONING

Even if its premises and conclusion cannot be refuted by any counterexample or reductio, a deductive argument can also be refuted by showing that it is invalid. We know that an argument is not valid if it starts from true premises and leads to a false conclusion. Often, however, we cannot point this out to refute an argument, because the truth or falsity of the conclusion is the very thing at issue. When this problem arises, a typical device is to point out that by arguing in the same way, or a similar way, we can reach a conclusion that is unsatisfactory.

Here is a simple example:

> CARY: Most of the people in this class are college students. Most college students study hard. Therefore, most of the people in this class study hard.
>
> DAVID: That's just like arguing that most whales live in the sea, and most animals that live in the sea are fish, so most whales are fish.

At first sight, it might not be clear how the second argument could show anything about the first argument. What do whales have to do with students? The point, however, is simply that the two arguments share a basic form. Thus, if the second argument is not valid by virtue of that form, then the first is also not valid by virtue of that same form. The second argument is obviously not valid, since its premises are true but its conclusion is false. This shows that the first argument is not valid, at least by virtue of this shared form. Even though the first argument still might be valid on some other basis, its defenders at least owe an alternative account of its validity. Often there will be none.

Refuting an argument by showing that it is *just like* another argument that is obviously no good is a common device in everyday discussions. Here's another example:

> MATTHEW: If I had a higher salary, I could buy more things; so, if everyone had higher salaries, everyone could buy more things.
>
> KIRSTY: That's just like arguing that, if one person stands up at a ball game, he will get a better view; so, if everyone stands up, everyone will get a better view.

At first sight, it may not be obvious whether Matthew's style of reasoning is valid or not. Kirsty's response shows that Matthew's argument is invalid by providing an instance in which the same style of reasoning takes us from something true to something that is obviously false, because, if everyone stands up at a ball game, only the tallest people will be able to see better. Kirsty's response also shows *why* Matthew's argument is invalid: Just as one person's ability to see can be affected by other people standing up, because this raises the height that is necessary to see, so one person's ability to buy can be affected by other people having more money, if this raises prices and thereby raises the amount of money that is necessary to buy things.

This fallacy is often called a *fallacy of composition*, because it rests on the mistaken assumption that what is true of the parts is also true of the whole that is composed out of those parts. Each person in a class has a mother, but the whole class does not have a mother. The earth might be heating up on average in the long run even if some locations on earth have a cool summer one year. These obvious mistakes can be cited to show that and why potentially misleading arguments with the same form are no better. Lots of new fallacies can be revealed in this way by deploying this method of refutation by parallel reasoning.

Of course, not every refutation of this kind is so simple or so successful. To understand the criteria that must be met for such a refutation to work, it will be useful to consider a more complex example that reveals some of the ways to respond to a charge of "That's just like arguing. . . ." The example concerns proposed legal restrictions on gun ownership. The National Rifle Association (NRA) feared that these restrictions would lead to a total ban on guns, which they opposed, so they widely distributed a bumper sticker that read:

(1) If guns are outlawed, only outlaws will have guns.

The point, presumably, was that most people would add the suppressed premise:

(2) It would be bad if only outlaws had guns,

and then reach the conclusion:

(3) Therefore, guns should not be outlawed.

This argument is not completely clear, partly because it is not clear who counts as an "outlaw." Some critics poke fun at this bumper sticker because (1) seems true by definition if outlaws include anyone who breaks any law, because anyone with a gun breaks a law if guns are outlawed. But what the NRA probably means by "outlaws" are people who commit violent crimes, such as robbery and murder. It is not strictly true that these will be the only people with guns if guns are outlawed, since police and some present gun owners would keep their guns. Nonetheless, these exceptions do not touch the NRA's main claim, which is that law-abiding people who would give up their guns if guns were outlawed would then not have guns to defend themselves against violent criminals.

How can an opponent try to refute this argument? There are several possibilities, but what defenders of gun control in fact did was distribute other bumper stickers. One of them read:

(1*) If gum is outlawed, only outlaws will have gum.

The main point might be just to parody the NRA bumper sticker, but, if we take it more seriously, (1*) also suggests an application of the method of refutation by parallel reasoning. The parallel argument would continue like this:

(2*) It would be bad if only outlaws had gum.

∴(3*) Therefore, gum should not be outlawed.

This conclusion, however, is not obviously false. Indeed, it seems true: People should be allowed to chew gum. Moreover, (2*) seems false, because nothing particularly bad would happen if only outlaws chewed gum. For these reasons, this bumper sticker cannot really refute the original argument. This failure illustrates two general tests: A refutation by parallel reasoning works only if the conclusion of the parallel argument really is unacceptable and only if the premises of the parallel argument really are true.

But opponents of the NRA did not stop there. They distributed a third bumper sticker:

(1**) If guns are outlawed, only outlaws will shoot their children by mistake.

The argument behind this new bumper sticker is again not clear. If it is a straightforward instance of refutation by parallel reasoning, then the parallel argument would add, "It would be bad if only outlaws shot their children by mistake" and conclude, "Guns should not be outlawed." But that is the very conclusion the NRA wants to reach; so this newest argument could not refute the original one. Nonetheless, a different argument might lie behind this third bumper sticker. The point seems to be that gun owners sometimes shoot their children by mistake, and we can minimize such tragedies by reducing the number of gun owners through laws against guns. The argument then runs something like this:

(1**) If guns are outlawed, only outlaws will shoot their children by mistake.

(2**) It would be good if outlaws were the only ones who shot their children by mistake.

∴(3**) Therefore, guns should be outlawed.

This conclusion would seem false to the NRA, and this argument might also seem to suggest that the same form of reasoning could lead to opposite conclusions: (3) and (3**). Moreover, (2**) seems true. This premise does not say that it is good for outlaws to shoot their children by mistake. Instead, it says that it would be good if nobody else shot their children by mistake. So far, so good. Notice, however, that this latest argument, (1**)–(3**), does not have the same form as the original argument, (1)–(3), because (2**) and (3**) are about what is good and what ought to be law, whereas (2) and (3) are about what is bad and what ought not to be law.

The next question is whether this disanalogy is *important*. If not, the latest bumper sticker still might refute the original one. The NRA, however, might argue that this difference *is* important. The fact that a law has bad effects overall *does* show that the law should not be passed, whereas the fact that a law would have good effects overall is *not* enough to show that the law should be passed, since the law still might violate individual rights that cannot be overridden by good effects on others. This claim is controversial, but, if it can be defended, then this parallel argument, (1**)–(3**), fails to show that the original argument, (1)–(3), is invalid. More generally, then, a refutation by parallel reasoning works only if the two arguments really do have relevantly similar structures—that is, only if one argument really is *just like* the other in relevant respects.

In sum, the method of refutation by parallel reasoning can be used to show that an argument is invalid by presenting another argument with essentially the same form in which the inference takes us from obvious truths to an obvious falsehood. In response to such an attack, a defender of the original argument has three main options. The defender might

1. deny that the conclusion of the parallel argument is false,

2. deny that the premises of the parallel argument are true, or

3. deny that the supposedly parallel argument really has essentially the same form.

If any of these responses is justified, then the attempt to refute the original argument by parallel reasoning fails.

This procedure is admittedly imprecise. There will sometimes be disputes about whether the premises of the parallel argument really are true, or clearly true, and whether the conclusion of the parallel argument really is false, or clearly false. Moreover, we have given no general explanation of the notion that two arguments have the *same basic form*. Some forms of argument were discussed in previous chapters, but they are only part of the story. We have not discussed and cannot discuss all possible forms of argument. Yet it remains a fact that people can often see that two arguments have the same essential form and, through seeing this, decide that an argument presented to them is invalid. This ability is the basis of sound logical judgment. It is also the basis of wit. It is at best mildly funny to say that if God had wanted us to fly, He would have given us wings. You have to be fairly clever to reply at once, "If God had wanted us to stay on the ground, He would have given us roots."

EXERCISE VI

In each of the following examples, does the parallel argument succeed in refuting the original argument? Why or why not? Consider the three possible responses listed above. If the original argument is refuted, is there some simple way to fix it so that it cannot be refuted by this parallel reasoning? If so, how? (You might try to add a premise whose analogue would be false in the parallel argument.)

(continued)

1. **Chris:** The United States is wealthy, so its citizens are wealthy as well.

   Pat: That's just like arguing that a building is expensive, so the nails in its walls are expensive as well.

2. **Chauvinist:** Since women are the only people who can bear children, they should bear children.

   Feminist: That's like arguing that, if I am the only person who can wiggle my own ears, then I should wiggle my ears.

3. **Newt:** Orphanages are fine places, as the movie *Boys Town* shows.

   Critic: That's just like saying that Oz is a fine place, as *The Wizard of Oz* shows.

4. **A Young Child at 6:00 am:** It's morning. Morning is the time to wake up. So it's time to wake up.

   The Child's Sleepy Parent: That's just like arguing that it's daytime, and daytime is the time to eat lunch, so it's time to eat lunch.

5. **Mark:** You shouldn't walk on that grass, because if everybody did that, the grass would die.

   Bob: That's just like arguing that I shouldn't go to this movie right now, because if everybody did that, the theater would be packed like a can of sardines.

6. **Thomas:** Everything in the world has a cause, so the world itself must have a cause.

   Tony: That's just like arguing that every leg in the relay race was run by a single runner, so the entire race itself must have been run by a single runner.

7. **Hawk:** Nuclear deterrence must work, because we have never had a nuclear exchange as long as we have maintained nuclear deterrence.

   Dove: That's just like arguing that hanging garlic by the front door must keep thieves away, because I put garlic there and my house has never been robbed.

8. **Liberal:** We ought to provide condoms for high school students, because they are going to have sex anyway.

   Conservative: That's just like arguing that we should provide high school students with guns, because they are going to use guns anyway.

9. **Scientist:** My initial steps toward human cloning, no matter how controversial, are important because they bring the debate out into the public.

   Opponent: That's just like arguing that we should start a fire in a house in order to bring the debate about getting a new fire engine out into the public. (paraphrased from an actual interview on National Public Radio)

10. **King:** "In your statement you asserted that our actions, even though peaceful, must be condemned because they precipitate violence. But can this assertion be logically made? Isn't this like condemning the robbed man because his possession of money precipitated the evil act of robbery?" (from Martin Luther King's "Letter from Birmingham Jail")

11. **A:** He owns a red car, so he owns a car.

   B: That's just like arguing that he owns a toy duck, so he owns a duck.

12. **A:** He is holding a baby girl, so he is holding a baby.

   B: That's just like arguing that he is driving a fire truck, so he is driving a fire.

Exercise VII

For each of the following arguments, find another argument with the same basic form in which the premise or premises are clearly true and the conclusion is clearly false.

1. If tea is dangerous, so is coffee. Tea isn't dangerous. So coffee isn't either.

2. If it were about to rain, it would be cloudy. It is cloudy. So it's about to rain.

3. Fred had either ice cream or cake for dessert. He had cake. So he must not have had ice cream.

4. You cannot pass laws against dangerous drugs, because there is no way to draw a sharp line between dangerous and nondangerous drugs.

5. If you have never written a novel, then you are in no position to make judgments about novels. So don't presume to criticize mine.

6. Since I have written several novels, I am in a position to know which novels are good. So you ought to trust me when I say that this one is great.

7. There's nothing wrong with smoking, since the longer you smoke, the longer you live.

8. If one has nothing to hide, one should not be afraid of being investigated. So no one should object to being investigated.

9. Radicals should not be granted freedom of speech, because they deny this freedom to others.

10. In nature, a species is more likely to survive when its weak members die out, so we should let the weak in our society die out.

11. Buses use more gas than cars, so the city cannot reduce gas consumption by providing more buses.

12. Boxing can't be very bad, since so many people like it.

13. This war is just, for to say otherwise in public would be to aid our enemies.

14. If you don't buy the most expensive shoes, you buy cheap ones. You don't want cheap shoes. So you should buy the most expensive shoes.

15. I'd rather be smart than strong, so I am going to quit exercising and spend all day in the library.

16. You don't want to be this murderer's next victim, so you had better convict her and send her to prison where she can't hurt you.

17. If it weren't for America, these refugees would have nowhere to go; so they should adopt the American way of life and give up their old culture.

18. You can't be right, because, if the answer were that obvious, someone would have thought of it before.

```
DISCUSSION QUESTIONS
```

1. In Chapter 22 below, Searle tries to refute Turing by means of parallel reasoning about a Chinese room. Using the standards discussed above, assess Searle's attempted refutation.

2. In *St. Anselm's Proslogion with a Reply on Behalf of the Fool by Gaunilo and the Author's Reply to Gaunilo*, trans. M. J. Charlesworth (Oxford: Clarendon Press, 1965), St. Anselm gives an ontological argument (in the form of a reductio ad absurdum) for the existence of God and then Gaunilo replies with a refutation by parallel reasoning. Reconstruct and assess both of their arguments, using the standards discussed above.

GOD TRULY EXISTS
—————————■—————————
by St. Anselm

Well then, Lord, You who give understanding to faith, grant me that I may understand, as much as You see fit, that You exist as we believe You to exist, and that You are what we believe You to be. Now we believe that You are something than which nothing greater can be thought. Or can it be that a thing of such a nature does not exist, since "the Fool has said in his heart, there is no God" [Ps. xiii. I, lii. I]? But surely, when this same Fool hears what I am speaking about, namely, "something-than-which-nothing-greater-can-be-thought," he understands what he hears, and what he understands is in his mind, even if he does not understand that it actually exists. For it is one thing for an object to exist in the mind, and another thing to understand that an object actually exists. Thus, when a painter plans beforehand what he is going to execute, he has [the picture] in his mind, but he does not yet think that it actually exists because he has not yet executed it. However, when he has actually painted it, then he both has it in his mind and understands that it exists because he has now made it. Even the Fool, then, is forced to agree that something-than-which-nothing-greater-can-be-thought exists in the mind, since he understands this when he hears it, and whatever is understood is in the mind. And surely that-than-which-a-greater-cannot-be-thought cannot exist in the mind alone. For if it exists solely in the mind even, it can be thought to exist in reality also, which is greater. If then that-than-which-a-greater-cannot-be-thought exists in the mind alone, this same that-than-which-a-greater-*cannot*-be-thought is that-than-which-a-greater-*can*-be-thought. But this is obviously impossible. Therefore, there is absolutely no doubt that something-than-which-a-greater-cannot-be-thought exists both in the mind and in reality.

A REPLY TO THE FOREGOING BY A CERTAIN WRITER ON BEHALF OF THE FOOL

by Gaunilo

. . . they say that there is in the ocean somewhere an island which, because of the difficulty (or rather the impossibility) of finding that which does not exist, some have called the "Lost Island." And the story goes that it is blessed with all manner of priceless riches and delights in abundance, much more even than the Happy Isles, and, having no owner or inhabitant, it is superior everywhere in abundance of riches to all those other lands that men inhabit. Now, if anyone tell me that it is like this, I shall easily understand what is said, since nothing is difficult about it. But if he should then go on to say, as though it were a logical consequence of this: You cannot any more doubt that this island that is more excellent than all other lands truly exists somewhere in reality than you can doubt that it is in your mind; and since it is more excellent to exist not only in the mind alone but also in reality, therefore it must needs be that it exists. For if it did not exist, any other land existing in reality would be more excellent than it, and so this island, already conceived by you to be more excellent than others, will not be more excellent. If, I say, someone wishes thus to persuade me that this island really exists beyond all doubt, I should either think that he was joking, or I should find it hard to decide which of us I ought to judge the bigger fool—I, if I agreed with him, or he, if he thought that he had proved the existence of this island with any certainty, unless he had first convinced me that its very excellence exists in my mind precisely as a thing existing truly and indubitably and not just as something unreal or doubtfully real. . . .

NOTES

[1] Plato, *Theaetetus,* trans. Francis M. Cornford, in Cornford's *Plato's Theory of Knowledge* (New York: Liberal Arts Press, 1957), 141.

[2] Stephen Colbert, *I Am America (And So Can You!)* (New York: Grand Central Publishing, 2007), 198.

Note: Page numbers followed by letter n indicate footnotes.

n = footnote

n = footnote

n = footnote

n = footnote

n = footnote

n = footnote

n = footnote

n = footnote

n = footnote

n = footnote

n = footnote

n = footnote

n = footnote

n = footnote